To you from afar

DISTANZ

BASTA

REGLÉ

LAS PRIMERAS VACACIONES
DE CECILIA MARIA

IVO sur la Côte d'Azur

Photo
A LA MINUTE

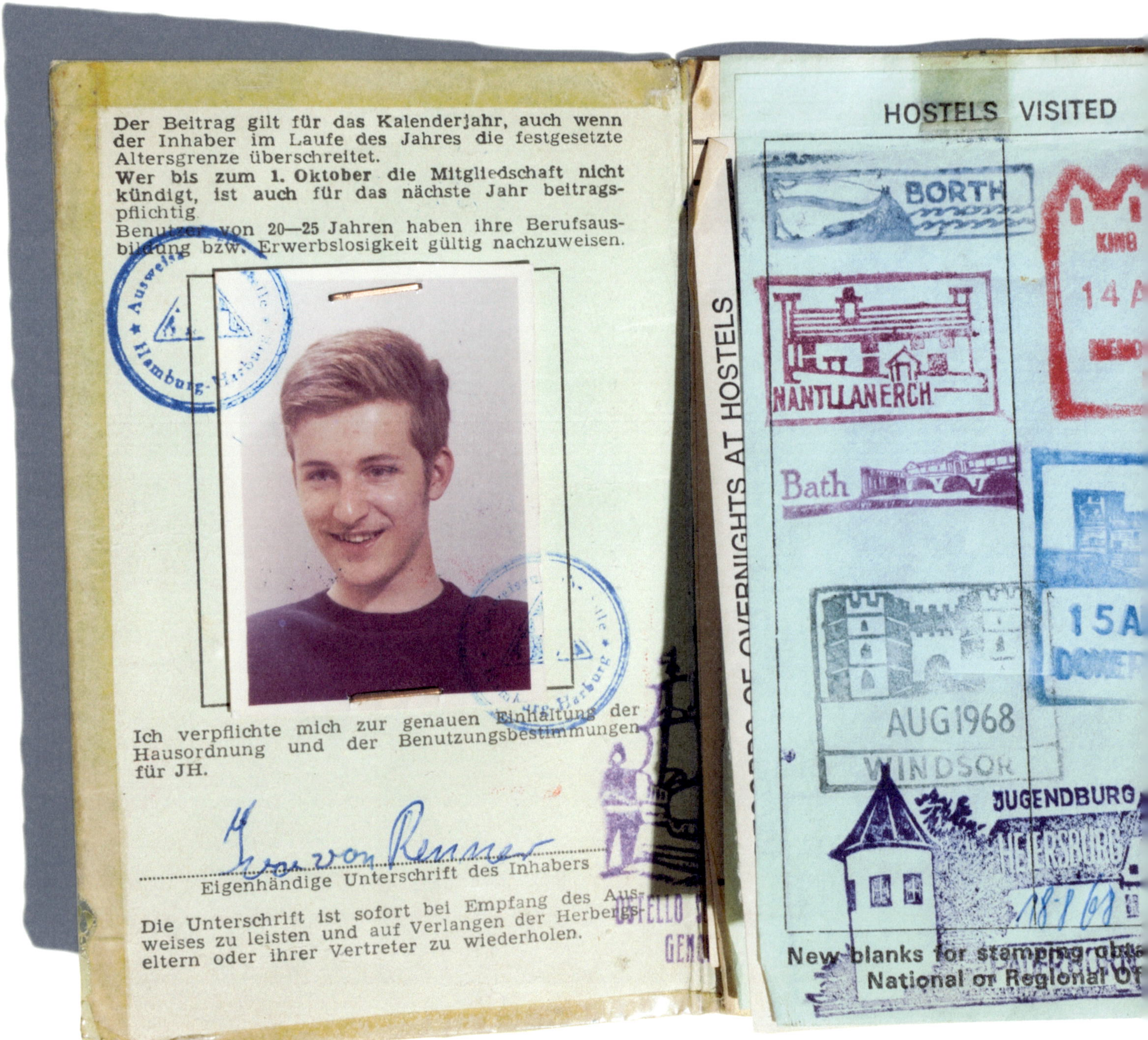
Der Beitrag gilt für das Kalenderjahr, auch wenn der Inhaber im Laufe des Jahres die festgesetzte Altersgrenze überschreitet.
Wer bis zum 1. Oktober die Mitgliedschaft nicht kündigt, ist auch für das nächste Jahr beitragspflichtig.
Benutzer von 20—25 Jahren haben ihre Berufsausbildung bzw. Erwerbslosigkeit gültig nachzuweisen.
Hamburg-Harburg
Ich verpflichte mich zur genauen Einhaltung der Hausordnung und der Benutzungsbestimmungen für JH.
Eigenhändige Unterschrift des Inhabers
Die Unterschrift ist sofort bei Empfang des Ausweises zu leisten und auf Verlangen der Herbergseltern oder ihrer Vertreter zu wiederholen.
RECORDS OF OVERNIGHTS AT HOSTELS
HOSTELS VISITED
BORTH
NANTLLANERCH
Bath
AUG 1968
WINDSOR
JUGENDBURG
15 A
14 A
New blanks for stamping obta
National or Regional Of

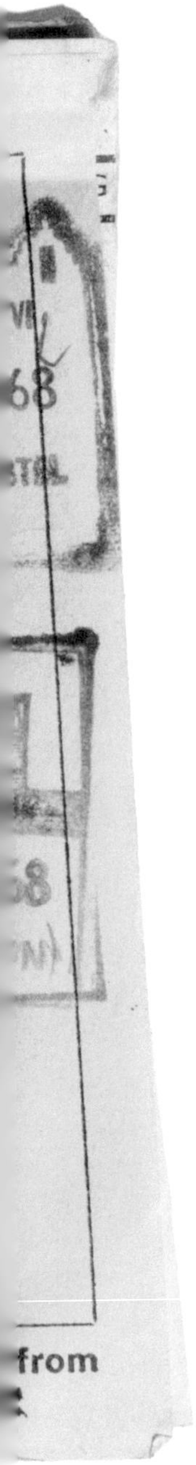

My first fascination with rubber stamps can be traced back to a bike tour I took to England, Scotland, Ireland and back. Every stamp was a souvenir and a piece of evidence that I had been somewhere, and reached another goal. I, coming from the Continent (as the British liked to call it), was not familiar with such lovingly designed stamp motifs. My children would never believe I had gone on these bike trips, if I didn't have the stamps to prove it: 4,785 km in five and a half weeks. Sounds like a lot, but it felt pretty refreshing.

Ivo von Renner

To you from afar

For Dagmar, Cecil and Antony

… and all those, that had to wait for me at breakfast or wherever else.

VORWORT

The photographer, Ivo von Renner, invites us to see the world through his eyes. Just as he saw or wanted to see it as he pressed the shutter of his camera. Thus, he shares a moment with us that has passed, and exists further only in form of a picture, evidence or "icon". The photographer makes us an accomplice of his intimacy, his astonishment, his pain, his passion, illusion or his truth. Helmut Newton, for example, celebrated a kind of elitist frivolity in his pictures, which he allowed the viewer to see as through a keyhole. This view could be more or less shocking, depending on your social status. Bettina Rheims, on the other hand, uses her pictures to share "injured" or "vulnerable" beauties with our empathy, all the while prohibiting voyeurism. In Horst P. Horst's work, silence reigns as in a gallery of antique statues. The ancient sensual game of watching people undress and dress is what gives nude and fashion photographers their daily bread and appreciation.

I don't take photos, I draw. Fictional figures. Almost daily. When drawing portraits of real people, however, the lines on the paper occasionally burn themselves into my consciousness as tattoos do onto skin. This is how I collect images of people. And these images communicate with my subconscious. I best communicate through pictures I create using the means placed at my disposal. We live in a world of images – of slogans, too – less so in a world of poetry and prose. I only save few of the pictures I produce. Without making a direct selection. The past, with its images and impressions, is growing too fast. Disproportionately to the future, which is still available. The man of today hardly produces new imagery, but instead tries to optimise his private collection on a daily basis. A sort of amateurish marketing strategy, aiming to match or adjust either to an elite or to the mainstream. "Fake" is indistinguishable from "real". (Who cares?)

Now there is an amazingly genuine, emotive photo album in front of me. A puzzle of memories. Designed in a strangely private and calm manner. You might ask the book: “What do you want from me? What have you got to tell me?” It’s like a bouquet of wild flowers, picked somewhere at some time – then dried and kept to be passed on. To who? To those, to whom the so-called modernity appears spent. Used and emotionally inoperative. I know this exact feeling from the end of the 60s. When the “Youthquake” faded away, the utopia of the era shifting to dystopia. When the desire for eccentricity, the elite, the private, the patinated gave way to prescribed egalitarianism. The appointment made with pictures of the mainstream of the time was denounced by a guild of bohemians, connected by one word: “Nostalgia”. The romantic search for a lost time began in the late 60s and culminated in the 70s. In figures that Fassbinder and Bertolucci brought to life in their films, figures whose pathos was melancholy. Fashion knows when a period has passed, one that was dedicated to it in everything that was possible during the time. To do, to ask, to live and to see. Could the pursuit of happiness, which can be successful in consciousness and sensuality, be the non-plus-ultra of an avant-garde of the new millennium? When everything is public, there is a great demand for privacy. Time can be precious, if you make it precious. And what is precious is easily lost.

This book tells of the value of a happily lived life. Quietly.
To you from afar.

Wolfgang Joop

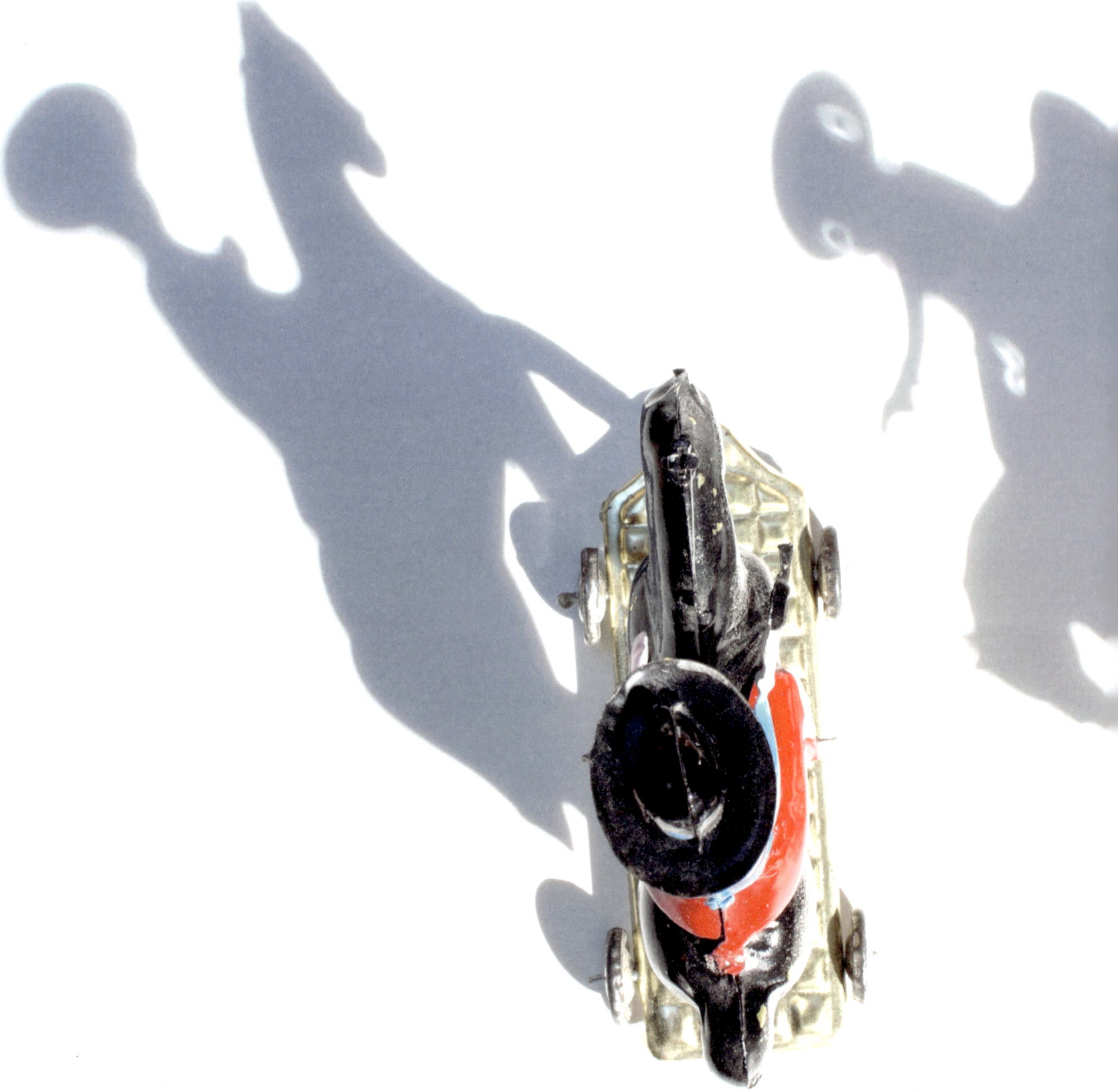

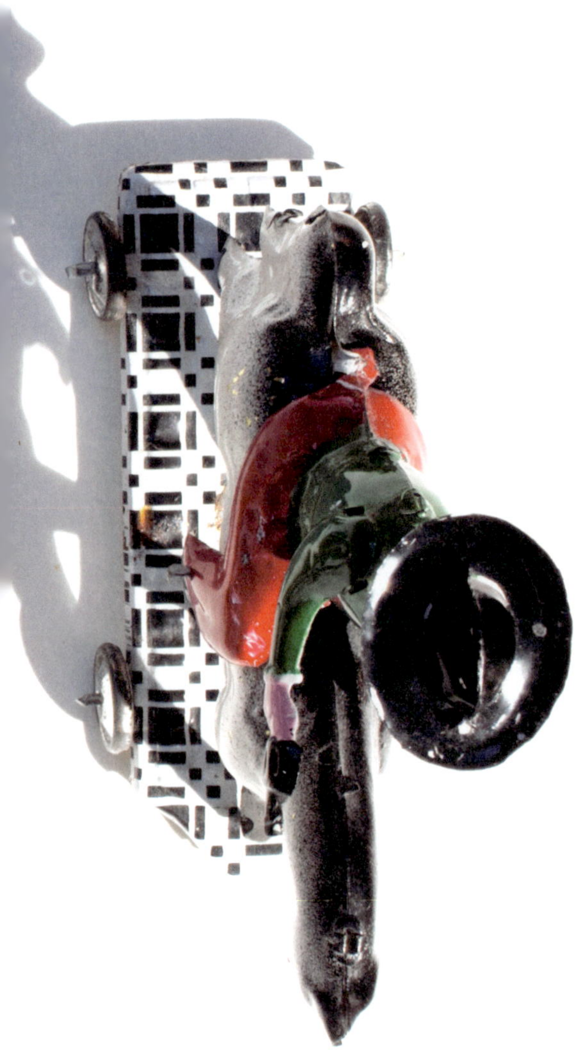

Contents

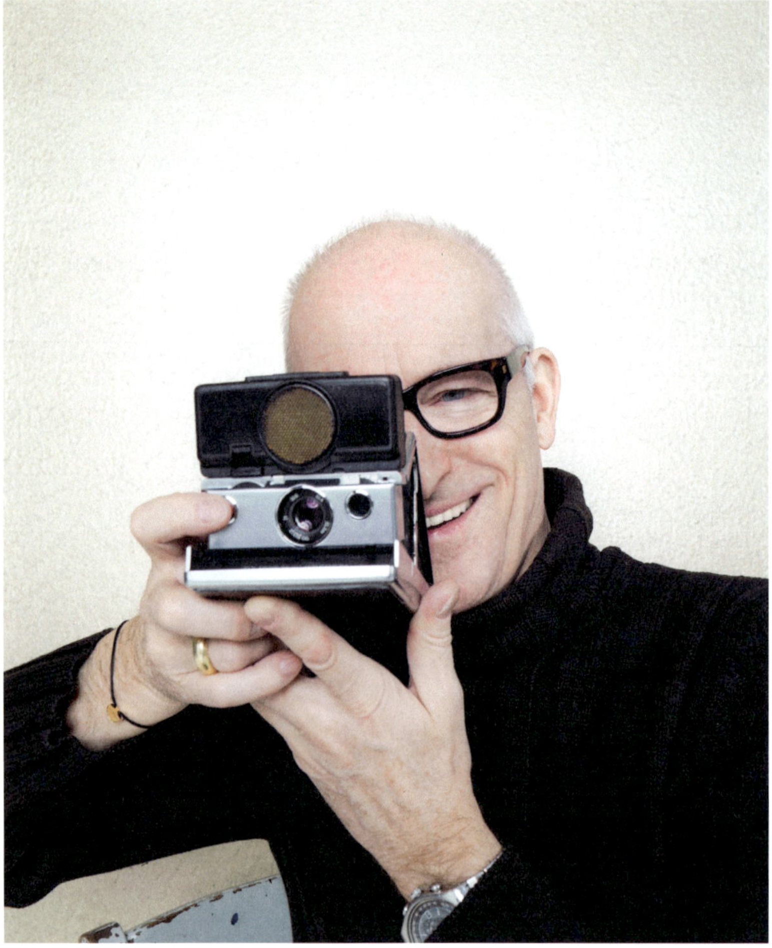

»
Travelling is the longing for an unknown world, an escape from the repetition of everyday life, and an opportunity to see people, to discover them or to learn to love them. The pain created by the distance mutates to an unknown and new bond with the familiar. I started each journey euphorically. Sometimes I travelled a hundred kilometres, sometimes thousands. The longest distance does not always leave the deepest impression. The question remains: What does "home" mean, does it have anything to do with this life, is it replaceable? Jean-Paul Sartre once wrote: If, as a child, you grew up on the tenth floor, you will never be able to live on the ground floor. I've moved houses eight times since I was a child. Almost always, the floor remained the same: a little above ground level, with a light view of the world.
«

Originally I wanted to be an actor …

I studied painting and illustration, and graduated as a graphic designer of magazines. Originally, I wanted to be an actor, then a fashion designer. My parents successfully talked me out of it. I've compensated this in my photo-crew group shots for the past 30 years. So I had finished studying, and there was only one thing on my mind: Taking photos and telling stories. I began with editorial articles for the "ZEITmagazin", as well as other magazines. I seemed to fit in well, and my career quickly flourished. I was asked "Are you available for …" I wanted to see and do everything, especially because my ice cream at the petrol station during location scouting was paid by the client. I wasn't born with a silver spoon in my mouth. My childhood was fulfilling, and of course there were several friends who had less than us. Now, life was nice and colourful, and this freedom was what caused my passion for writing postcards and taking group photographs. I often started during the hotel breakfasts. Sometimes, this lead to our delayed arrival on set. I spent many nights next to the hotel TV in Nice, which showed James Bond's "The Man with the Golden Gun" on a weekly basis, drawing letter by letter onto envelopes. Preparation days were around nine hours long, photo days between 10–16, depending on the length of the drive. And, now and then, it rained. Despite the delayed start of our journey, we still had 14 days of rain in Nice, in the legendary snowy winter in January of 1986. The art director called the Hamburg agency every three days, to check if we should stay. The client was Lada (the Russian car), and they wanted us to persevere. I had a leather bag made for me by the now-famous designer Volker Lang, which gave me easy access to my Polaroid SX70, as well as holding my coloured pencils, sharpener, eraser and the stamps. I drove around 300,000 km by car at the Côte d'Azur. After three days of non-stop rain, you start considering alternative ways of life, and I drove to other regions, other museums or little restaurants.

Many of my cards and letters were meant for later years, as the texts only make sense to grown ups. Cecil was just 5 weeks old, and Antony hadn't started speaking when he received his first postcard. But they were lovingly explained to them by their mother; and we all know how the power of speech and its melody anchors itself into our hearts at an early age. "Look at the tower – crooked like yours!" would only be funny when our sons have children of their own. The fact that daddy is flying in a helicopter, however, is already exciting at an early age.

Cecil, our firstborn, used to pull me towards him holding onto my ears, and bite into my nose, until he got his second tooth. For a long time, Antony's vocabulary consisted of "a-a", which meant no, and "da", which was meant as a passionate affirmation, given that the "a" was emphasized in a certain way. When you come home from a long and exhausting journey and your children savage you like lions, everything else is forgotten. Recently, I reread the postcards which my father sent to the youth hostels that I stayed in during my bicycle tour through England and Ireland. He wrote them on his typewriter for spacial reasons. He wrote about my mother making strawberry jam, and told me that the plums were ripe. Only today do I understand the bond that was created through this, and how, naturally, I would seek out the post shelf as soon as I arrived at the youth hostels.

The use of the images and work of other artists displayed on the stamps and postcards has been handled with much love and gratitude to them. Carrying around entire sheets of matching stamps with me at all times, they would find their way onto my mail in different restaurants, cafés, and hotels around the world.

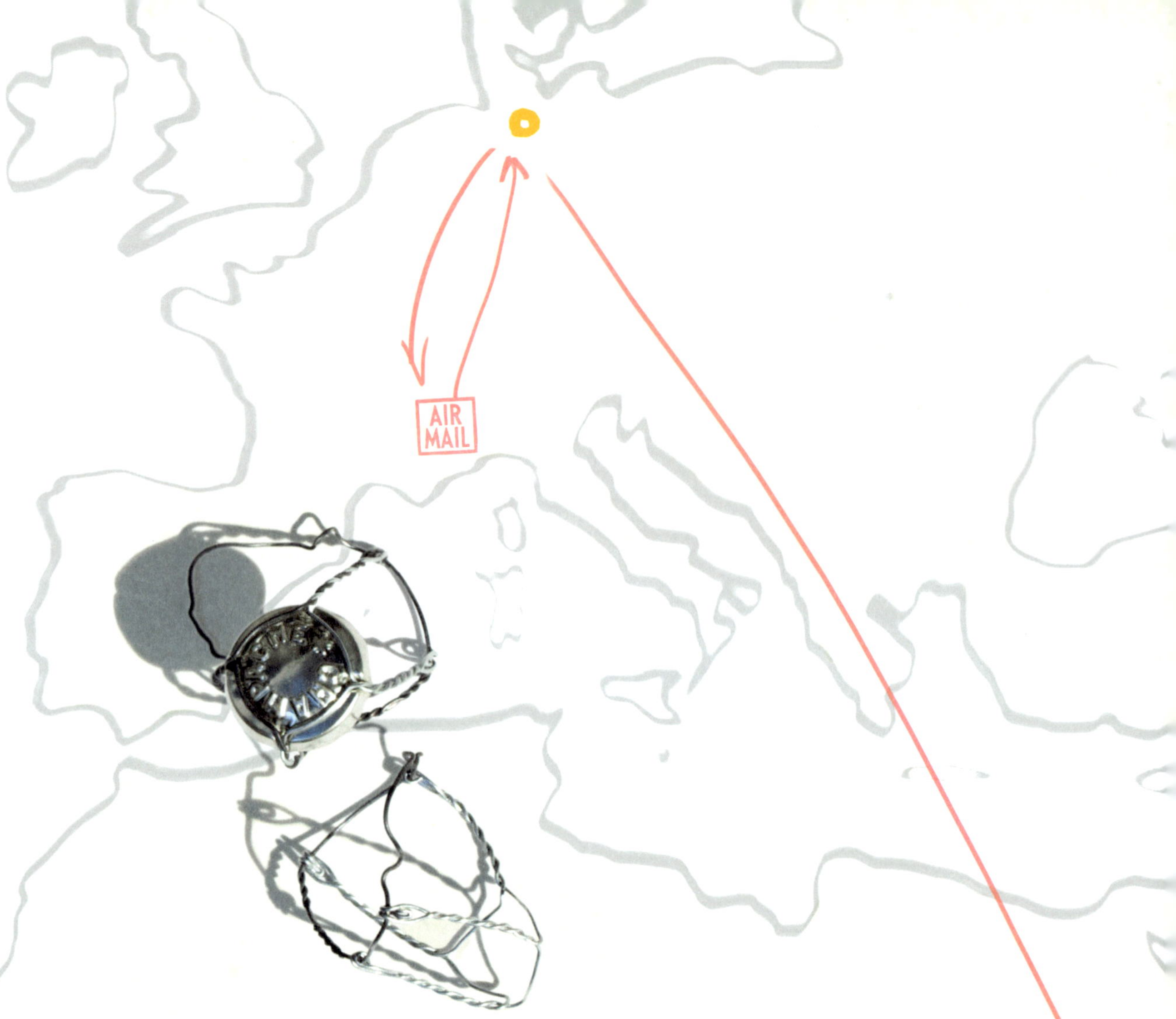

1983–1986
France
Kenya

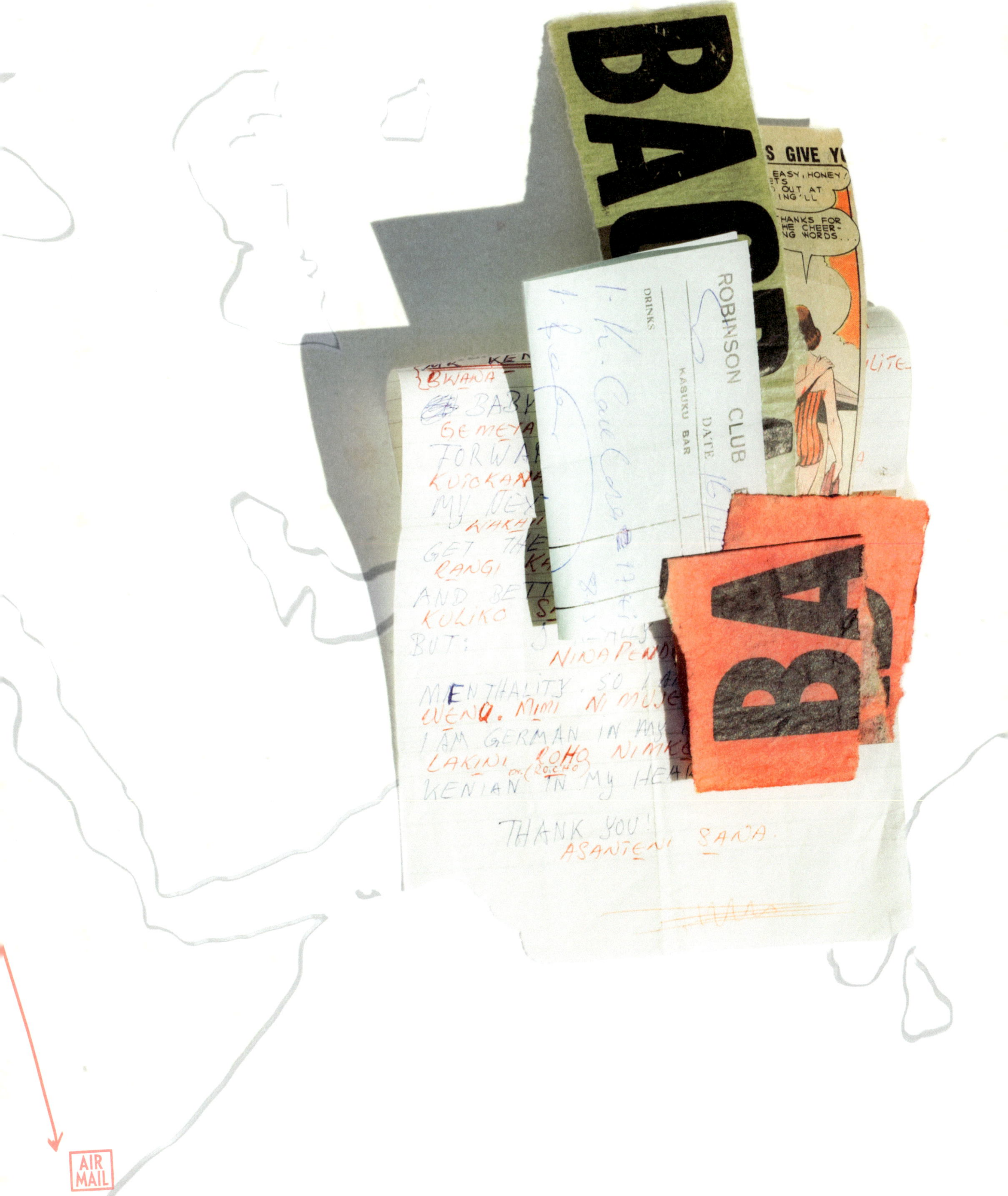
BA
S GIVE YO
THANKS FOR THE CHEER-ING WORDS.
ROBINSON CLUB
KASUKU BAR
DRINKS
DATE
BWANA
BABY
MENTHALITY. SO
WENQ. MIMI NI MUJE
I AM GERMAN IN MY
LAKINI ROHO NIMK
KENIAN IN MY HEA
THANK YOU!
ASANTENI SANA.
BA
AIR MAIL

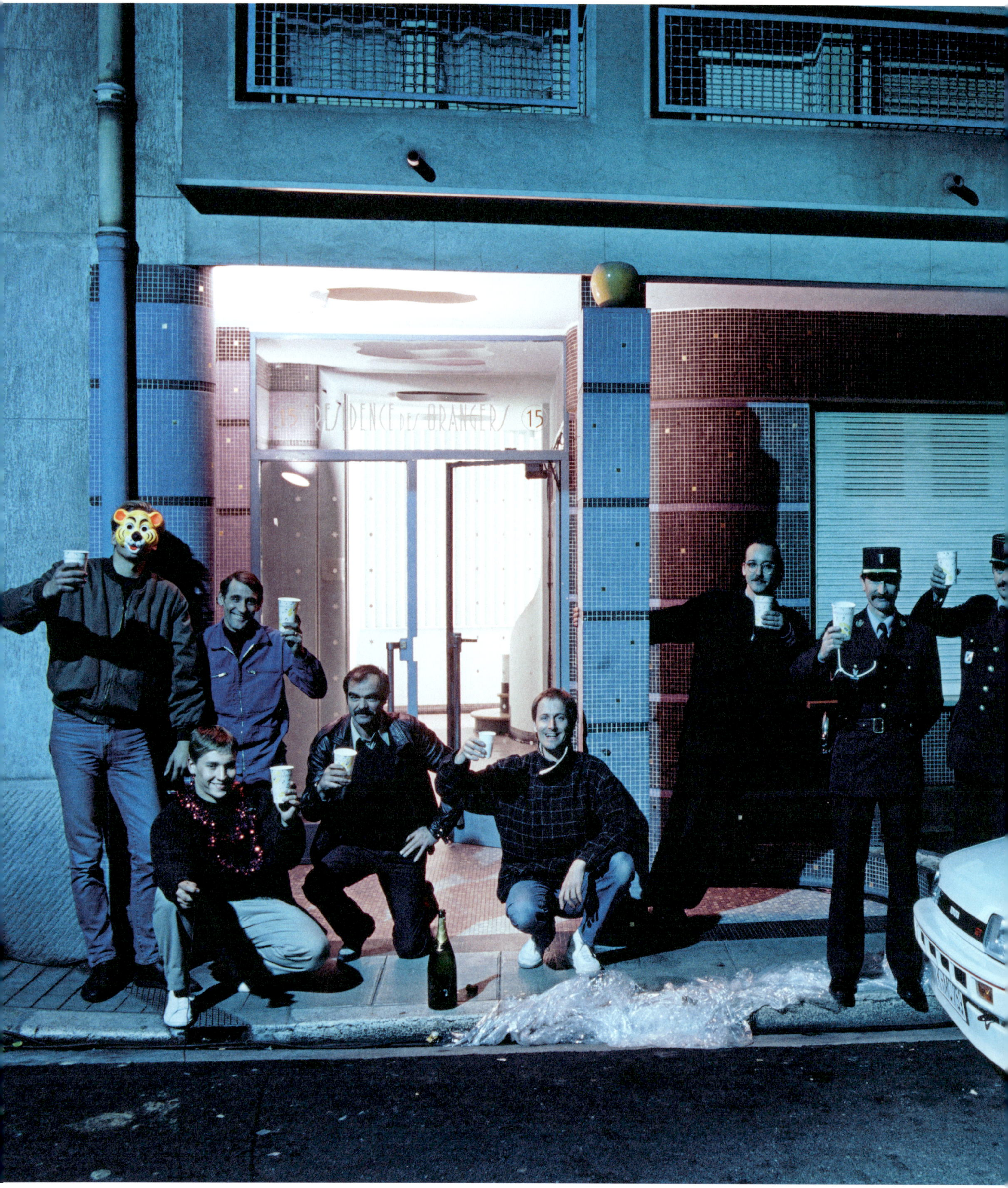
15 RESIDENCE DES ORANGERS 15

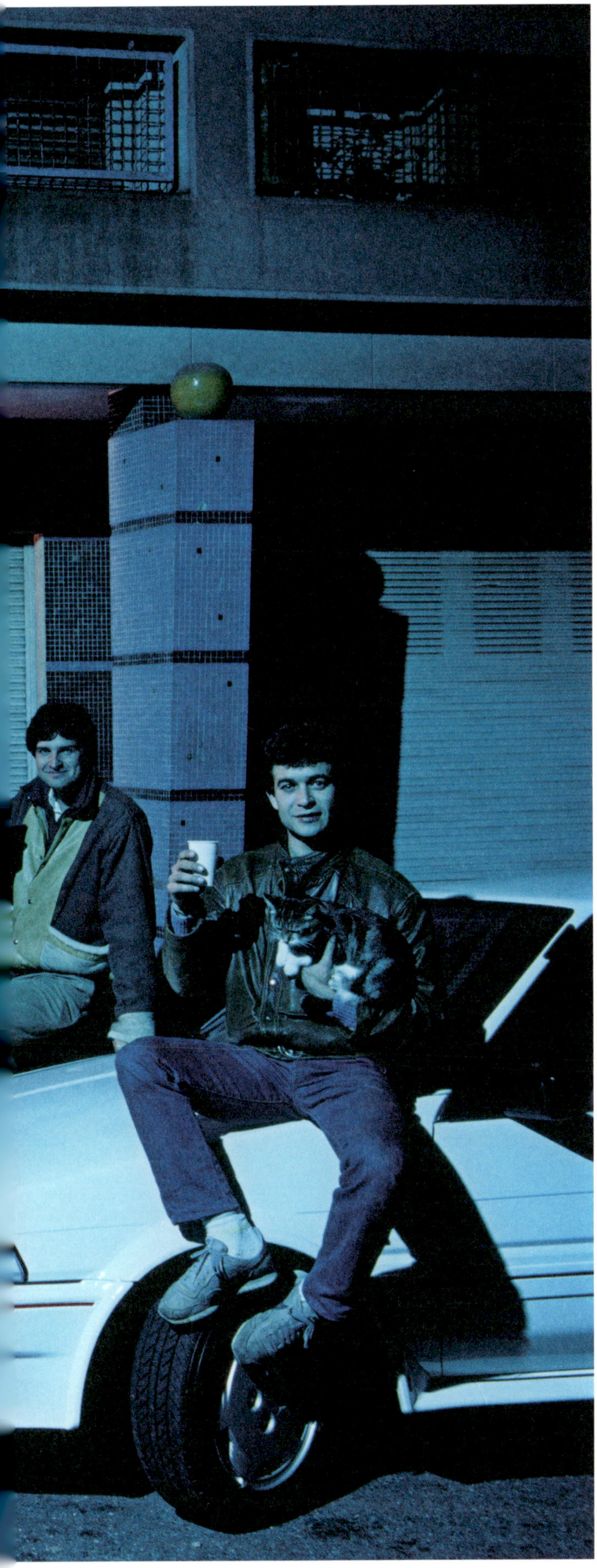

Nice 1983 — Toyota.

During this week, the chief constable of the Nice police department had already been photographed as a burglar, waiting in front of a bank in a Toyota. The advertisement had a little footnote saying "with the kind permission of the chief constable of Nice". In the south of Europe, the gendarmerie isn't only in charge of keeping things in order. They also live with the citizens.

Cheers!
Cheers!

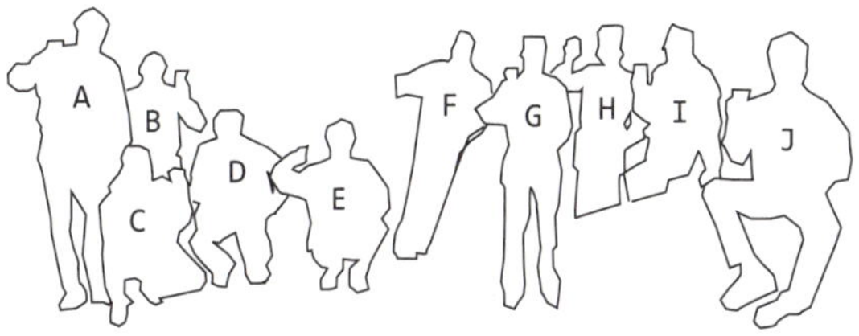

Group photo with the crew for a job in Nice

A Assistant
B The caretaker
C Phillip Radowitz, assistant
D I don't remember
E Me
F Michael Stockmann, creative director
G Policeman
H Policeman (not wearing a costume, obviously!)
I Francis Missana, productioneer
J The owner of the cat

Nice 1984 — Toyota.

»
It's the first year of a love with a long future. I'm still trying to present myself a little. My travel luggage contains at least two different-coloured ink pots, as well as the Polaroid SX70 as my closest companion.
«

No harm was ever done by a little warm air in November. Toyota was still building cars with doors that were always slightly thinner than those of the European companies, making them slightly cheaper as well. A trip like this usually took 3 weeks. Upon arrival, we began location scouting as well as casting. Once, the casting was even announced on the local radio, and 200 of the 300 by-now-familiar amateur models from the area came.

Next to wannabe dancers, musicians, office workers, students, heirs and pensioners, an ex-Nato general and his wife, the muse and once closest friend of Christian Dior, the future wife of my productioneer and friend Francis Missana, who studied medicine, the cashier of a bathing beach and our hotel's foyer-pianist, who folded his trouser legs 20 cm inwards at the seam, as was the fashion in the south of France at the time. There were days on which two people met, only to find out that they had both been booked for the same job with me the next morning. Our teams were small, in comparison to today. I brought an assistant from Germany, my stylist Marianne Wedekind and the make-up artist Renate Pfab.

The art director drove the car, shovelled sand or exchanged car tyres, if one of us wasn't doing so already. We washed and polished the cars ourselves, and then took the photos. The focus was laid more on the complete work of the story, than on the details of the hyper-sharp, idolised status symbol of the present time. Every comparison falls short; a completely different lifestyle dominated at the beginning of the 80s. When I photograph a group of people from a distance nowadays, I can see each person in all their detail, even when the picture is enlarged to 150 cm. This has a totally new quality to it.

NICE
November 30th, 1984
–
The moon sank,
Dior resurrected.
The sun suits me –
it does as well.
I love you.

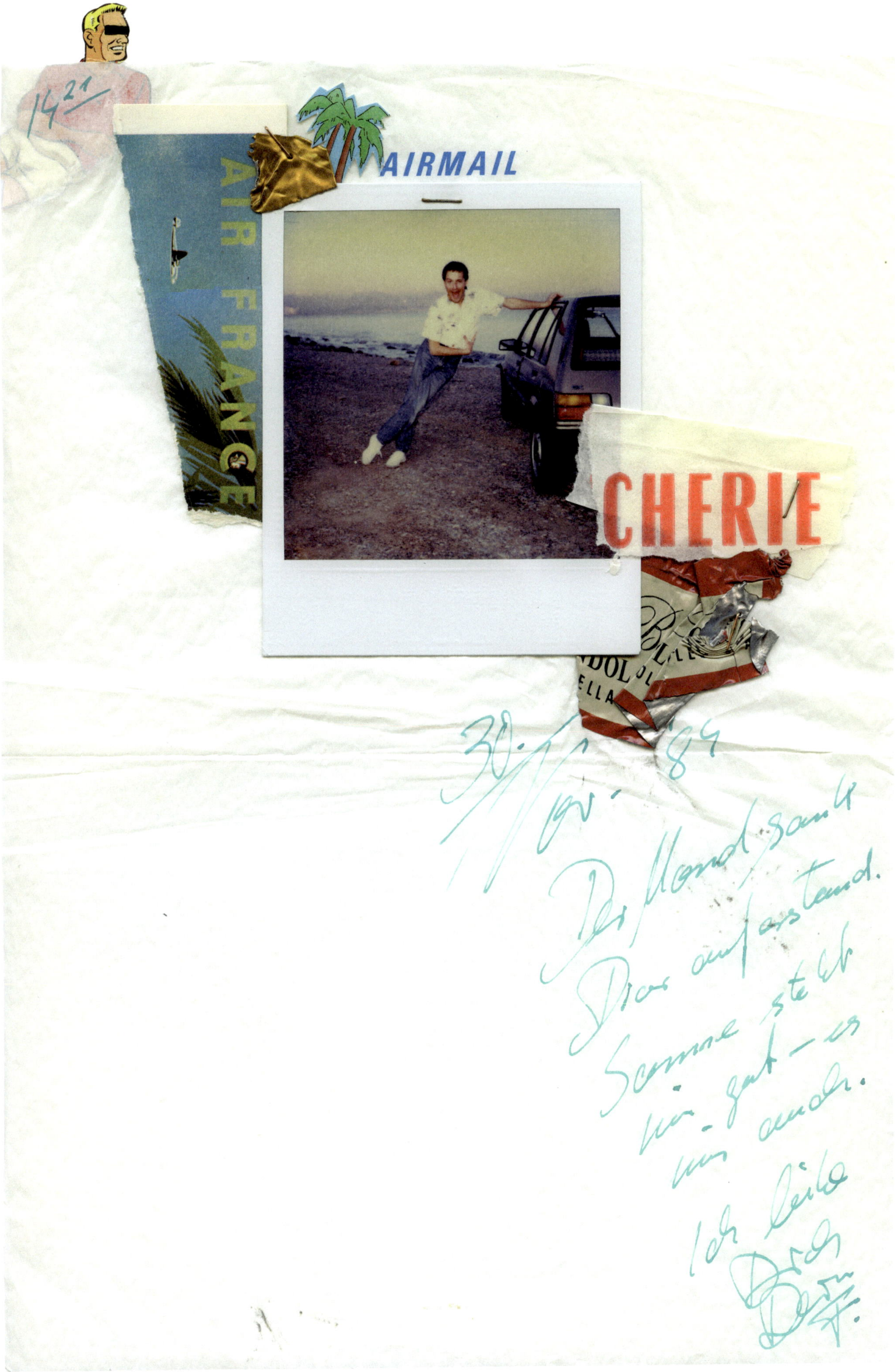
1421
AIRMAIL
AIR FRANCE
CHERIE
30. Nov. '84
Der Mond sank
Dir aufstand.
Sonne steht
hier gut – es
war anders.
Ich liebe
Dich

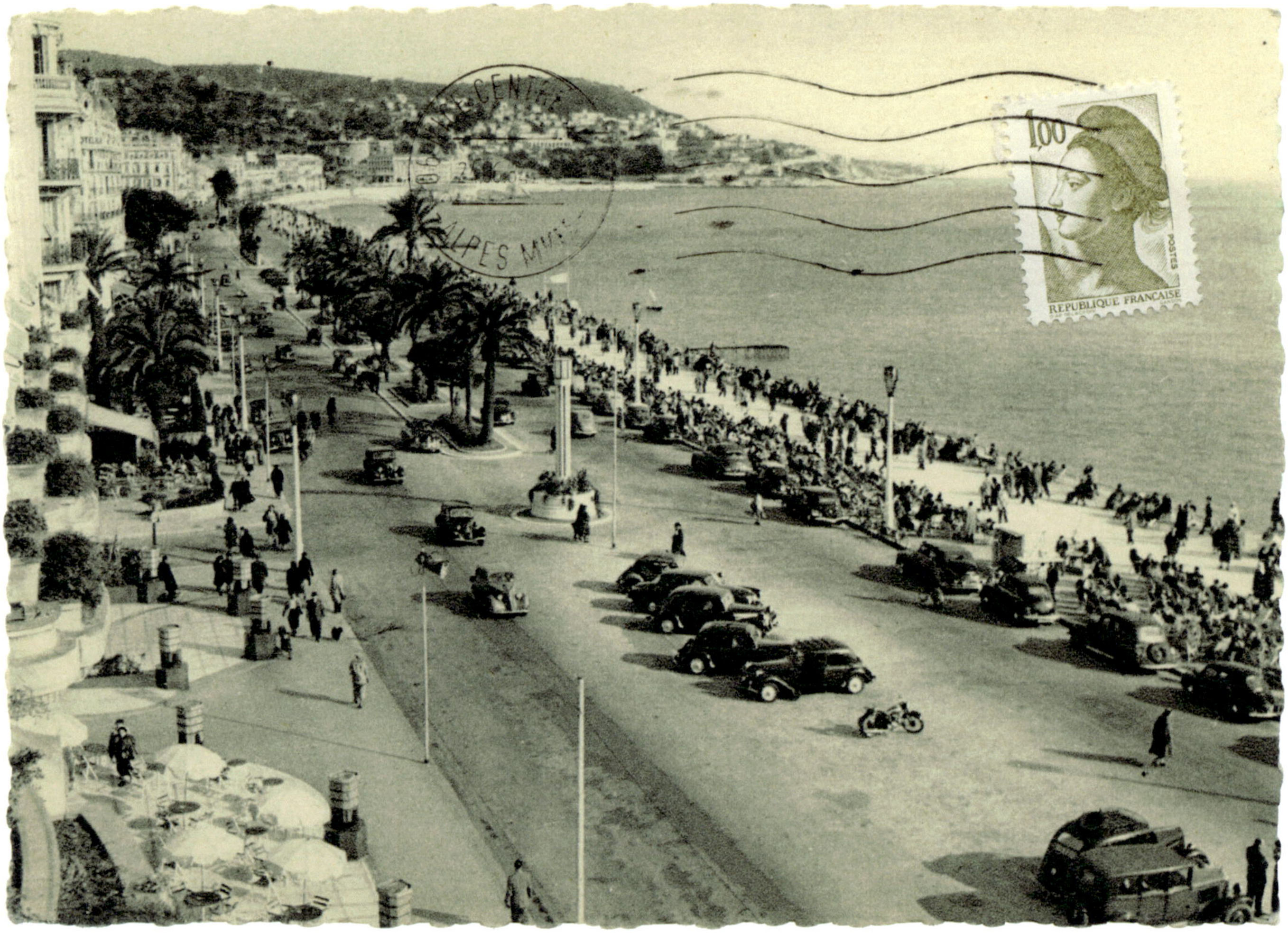

On this card, Nice's best time is yet to come: the 50s!

NICE

June 24th, 1984

–

In June of 1984.

Greeting you from Nice,

His Excellency

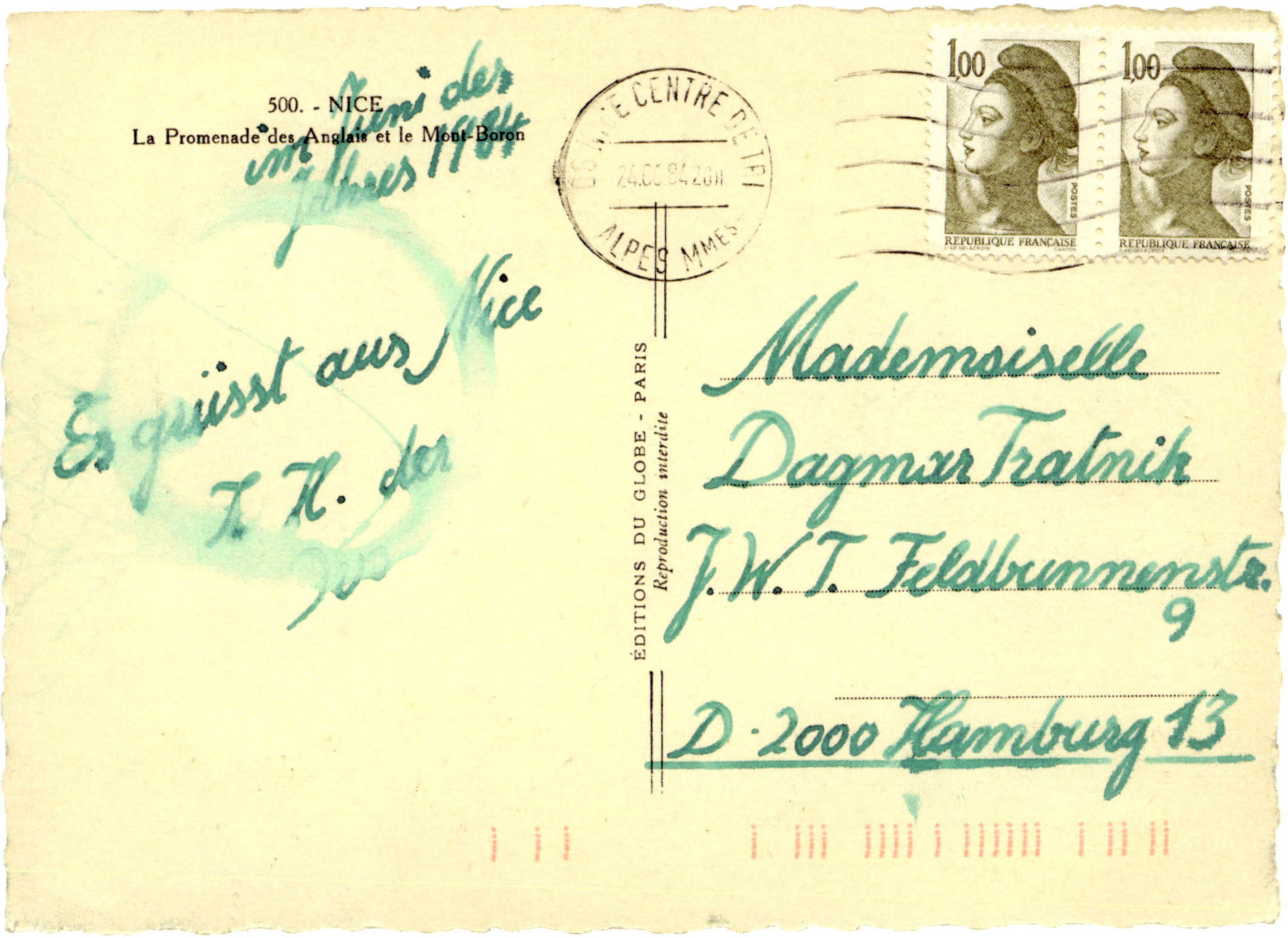

… this is an ironic reference to mail which is regularly sent to me by a vineyard that I worked for during my studies. The eighty-six-year-old secretary, who was still operating during the 70s, passed over the mailing list to a younger employee, who took over this relic from the past, not knowing any better. The mail arrived like this until the mid-90s.

Nice 1985 — Renault.

As the trips to the Côte d'Azur have started to become a regularity, I already prenumbered some cards from my collection by typewriter in Hamburg: la cinquième, le huitième ... Ivo

The learnt and recurring travel pace helps me to make preparations, in order to uphold my aimed quota of cards. These cards were printed in black and white, and then furnished with additional colours. Today, it looks a little like bad Photoshop. The appeal of old cards lies in their manufacturing and, often, their hand-colouring. The pale card and the motif, chosen with love, often showing empty streets, is transformed into a new little work of art. It shows a place I drive through, in which I take a coffee break with my crew or which I use as a location for my work.

NICE
February 12th,
1985
-
"la cinquième,
… Ivo."

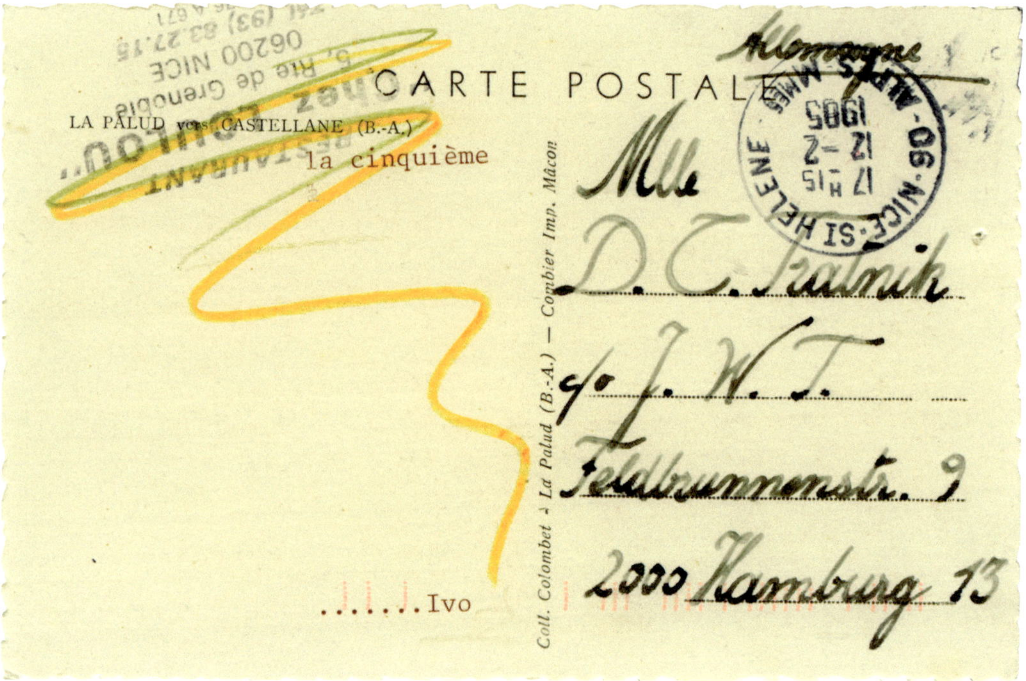

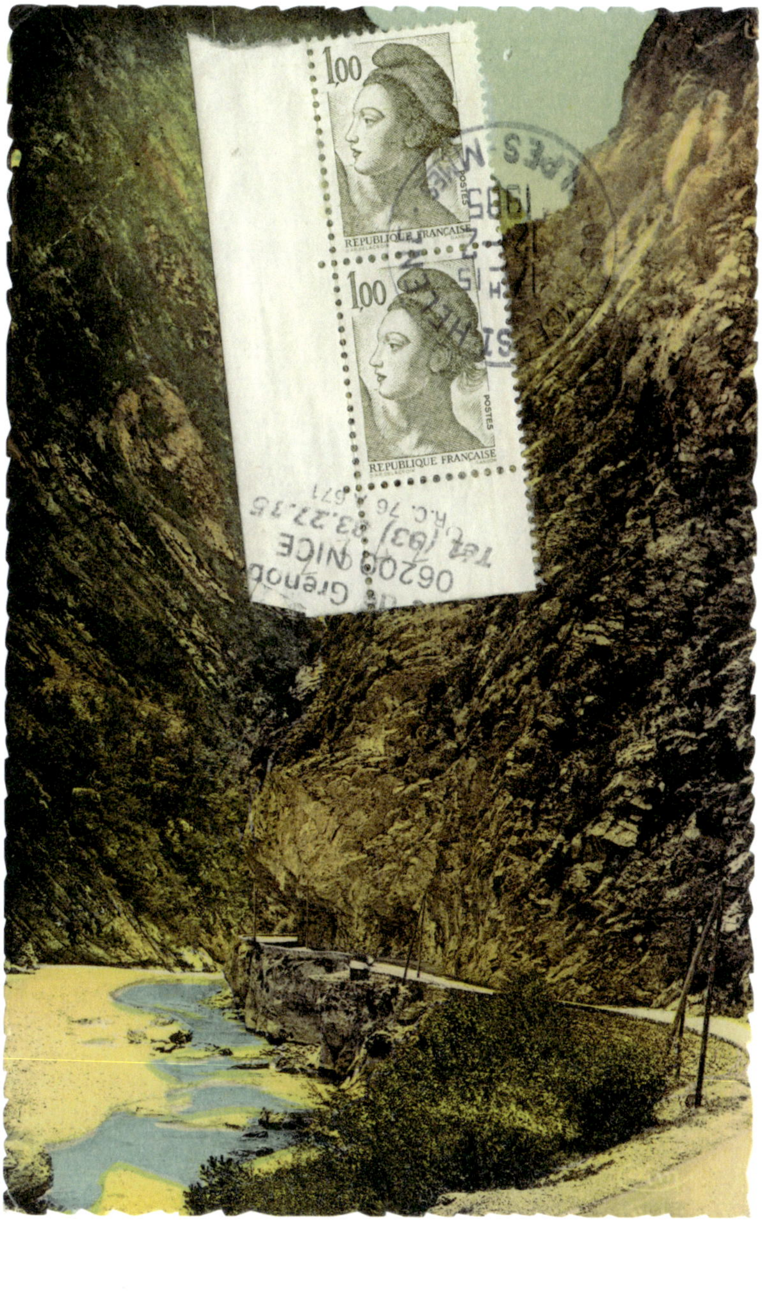
1,00
REPUBLIQUE FRANÇAISE
POSTES
1,00
REPUBLIQUE FRANÇAISE
POSTES

NICE
February 13th, 1985
–
“Mes amitiés du
troisième jour,
Ivo”

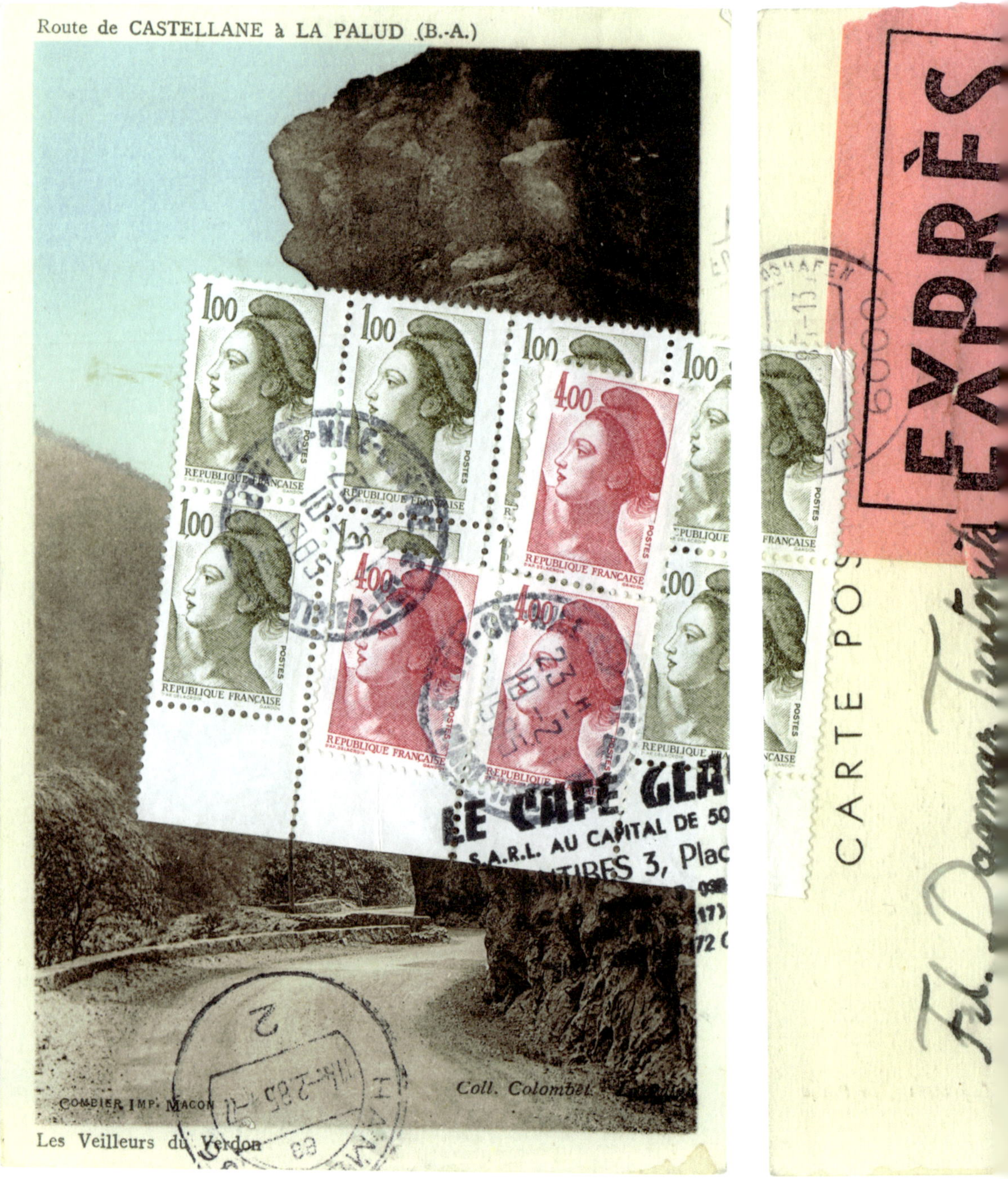

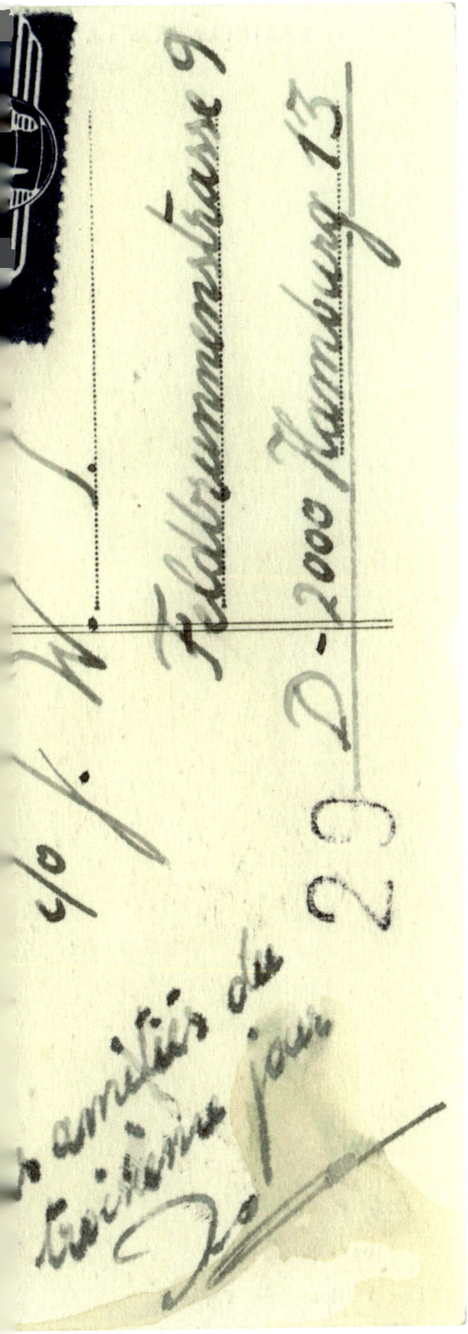

»

I drive on the street to the Gorges du Verdon at least 30 times in the Nice years. Nothing changes, except for the asphalt covering.

«

EXPRÈS helps to ensure that the tardily mailed cards and letters arrive before your own return home. It always costs a little extra, generates more attention and increases the feeling of greater importance.

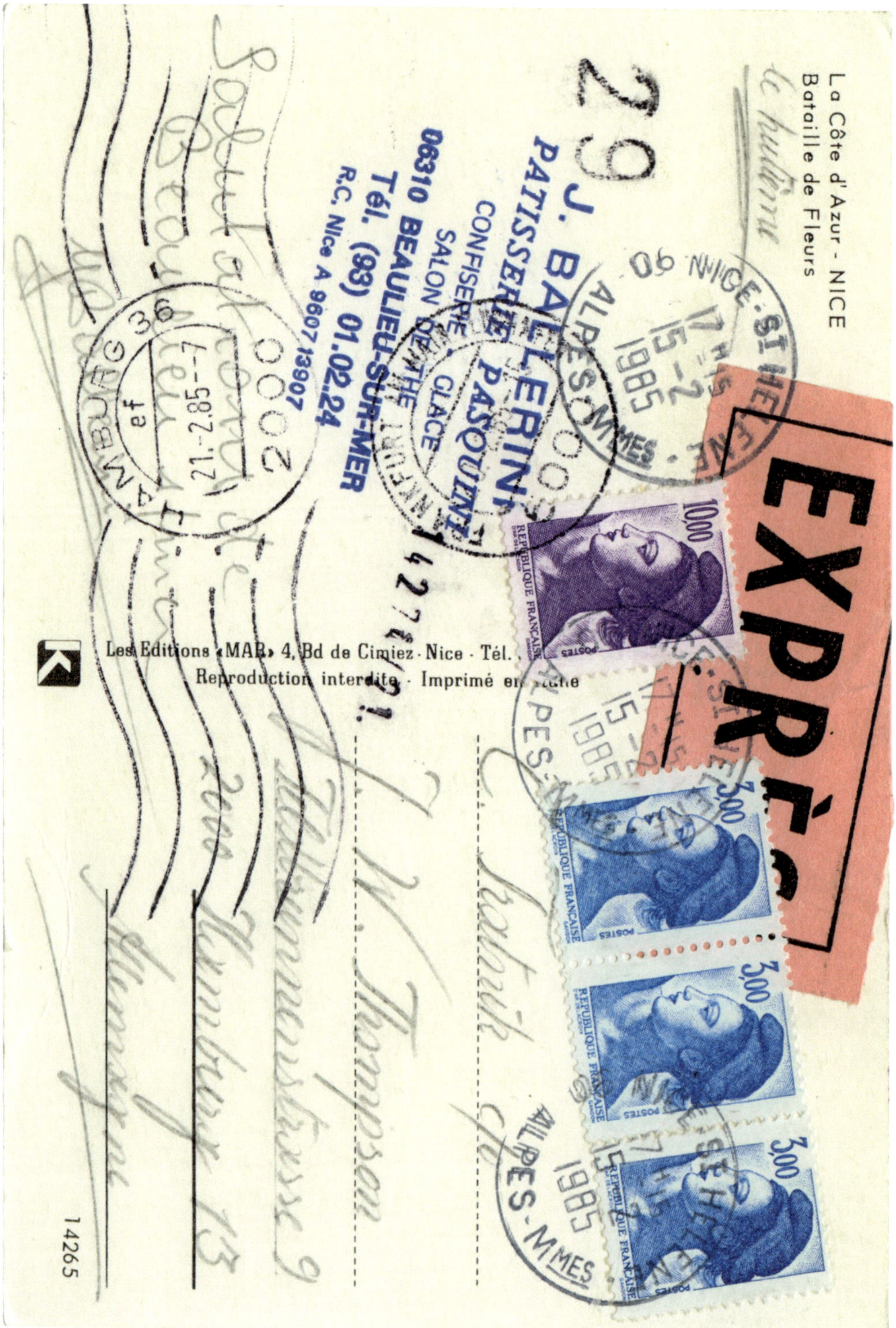
La Côte d'Azur - NICE
Bataille de Fleurs
EXPRÈS
Les Editions «MAR» 4, Bd de Cimiez - Nice - Tél.
Reproduction interdite - Imprimé en
14265

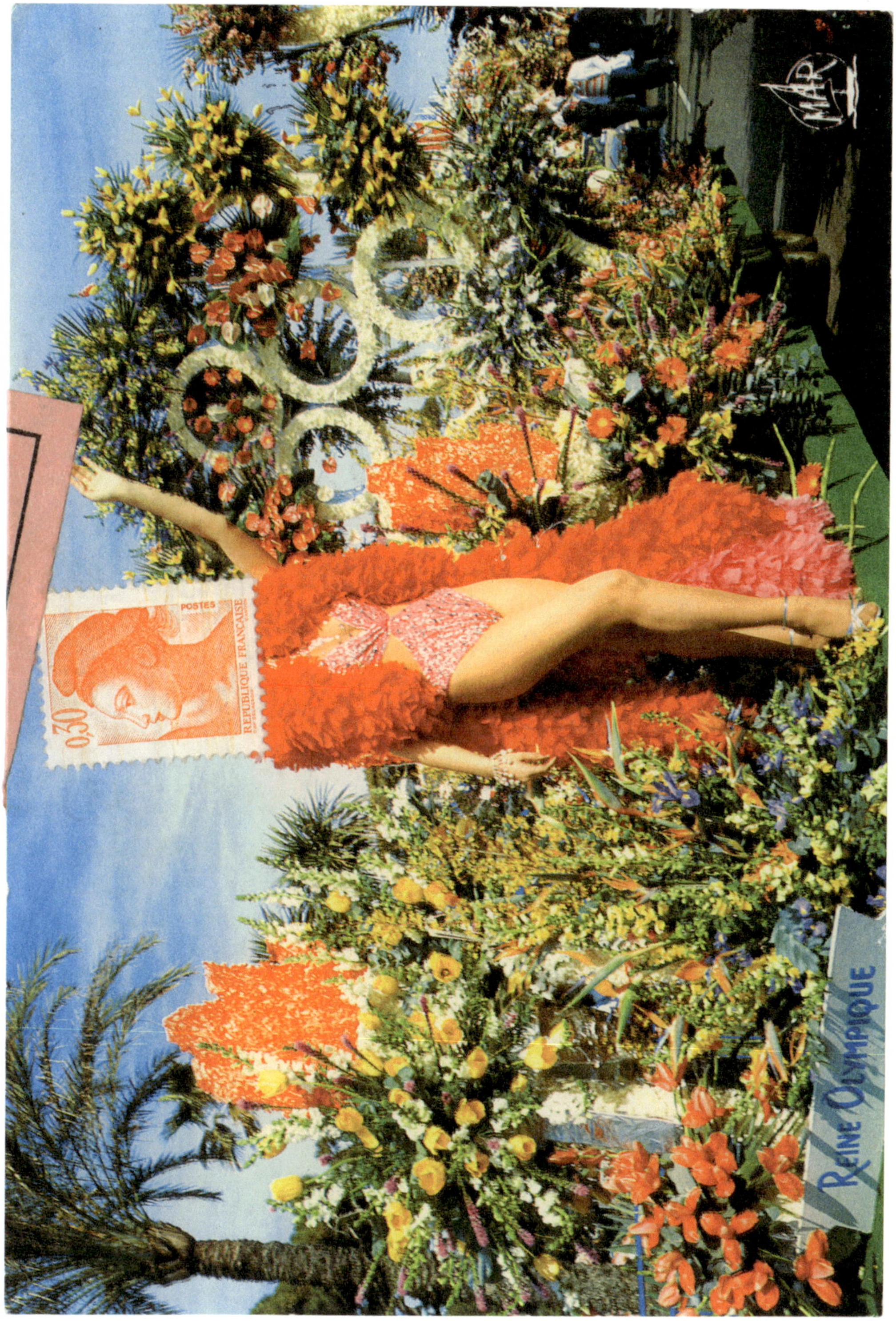

NICE

February 15th, 1985

–

“Le huitième”

Simple casting.

In late autumn we are travelling to Nice for the second time. Two Toyota Tercel are driven from Frankfurt to the Alps by us, in order to be photographed there. After casting the entire small town in the town church hall during bingo, we find our dream protagonist sitting 100 km away behind the steamed up window of a restaurant in Switzerland: an architect from Israel, who is working in Italy, currently on a skiing vacation in Switzerland and is now being photographed in the French Alps by a German team for a Japanese car as a mountain farmer.

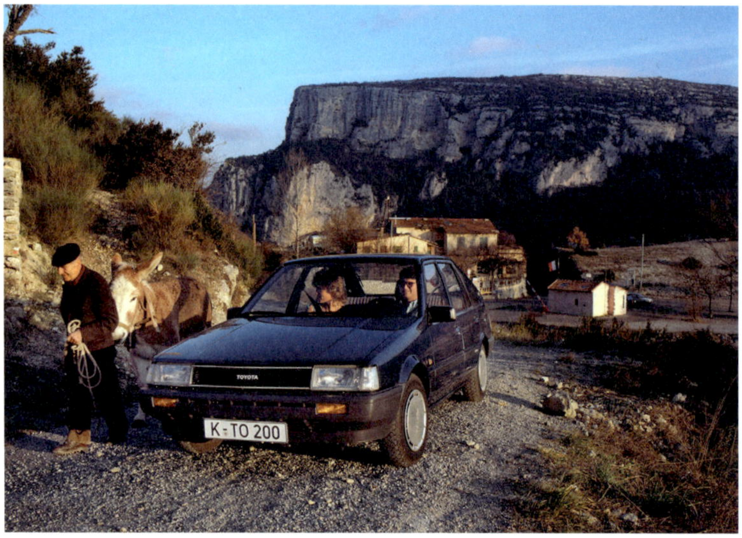

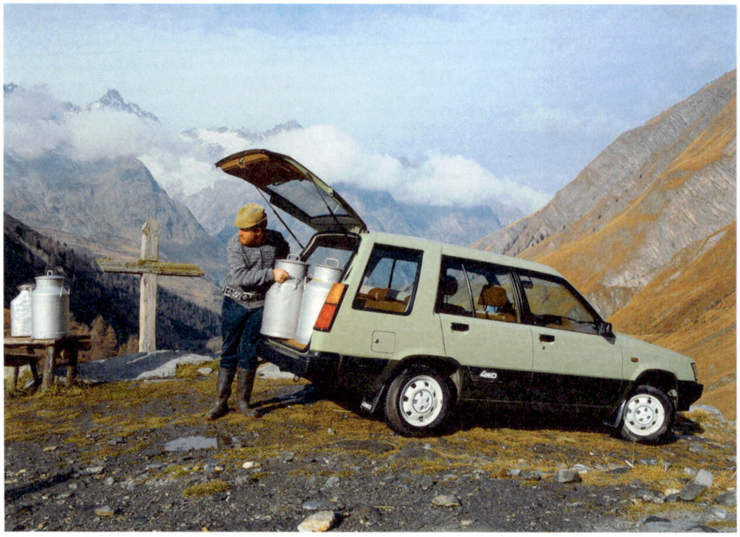

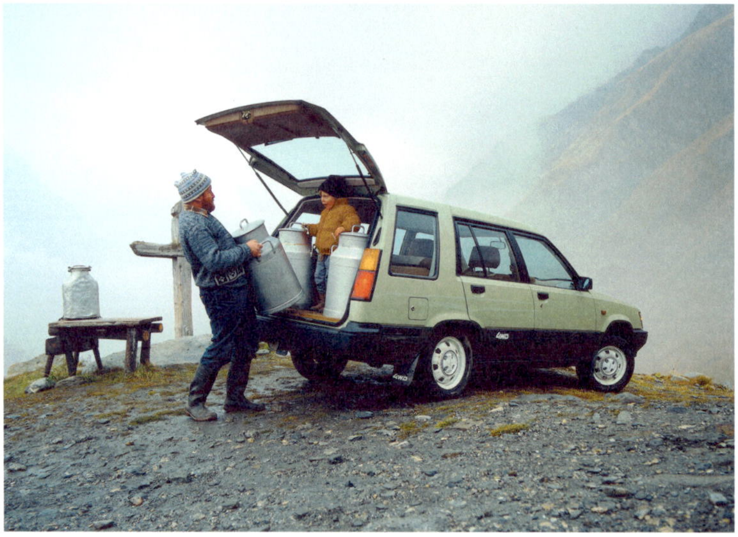

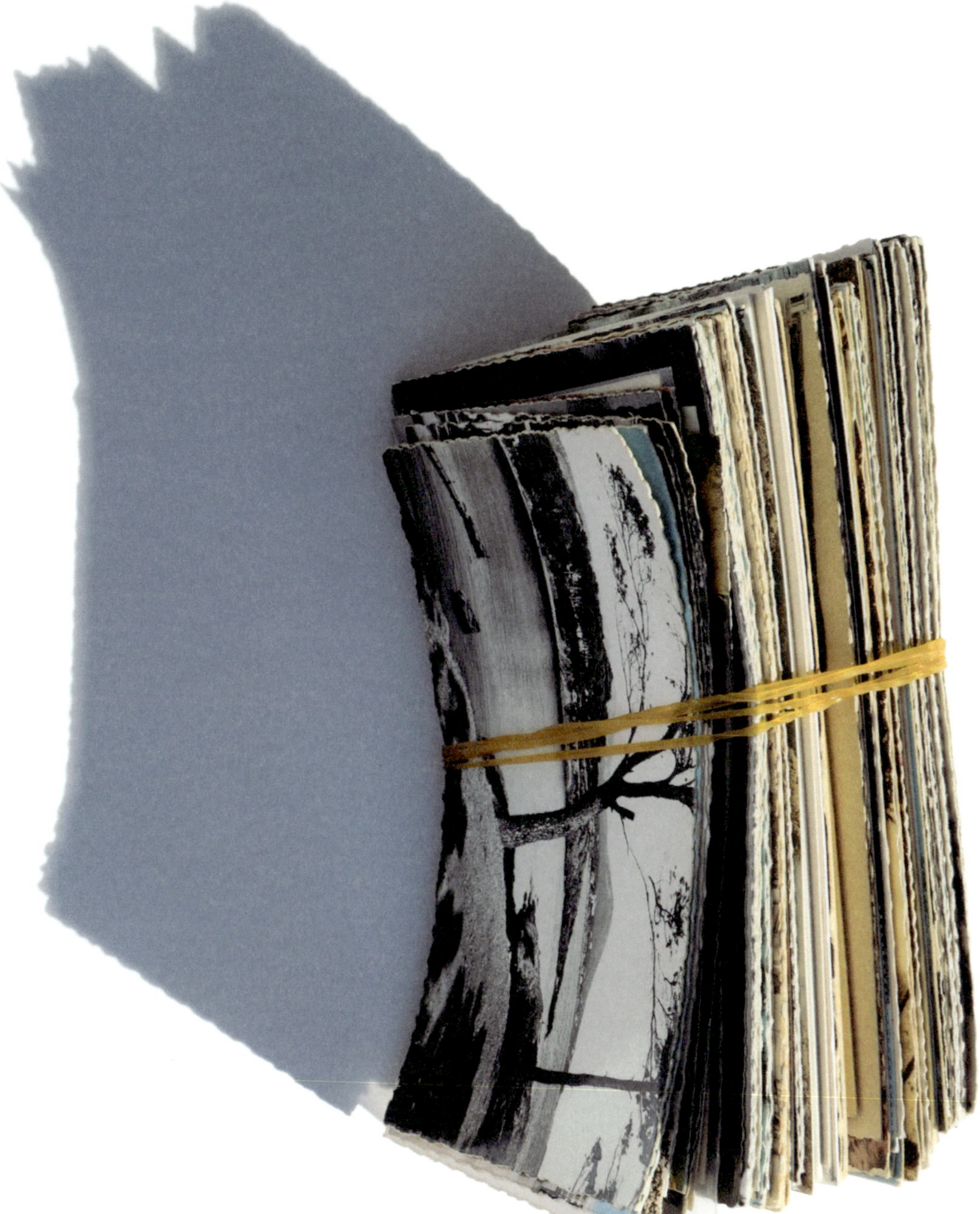

Friends who last.

The Gorges du Verdon is one of my favourite landscapes in the South of France. It takes around three and a half hours to get there from Nice. We are here for the second time, and photograph two brothers, who are 185 years old together, and are both shorter than 1.50 m. They own a colonial goods store, with endless postcards from the time between the two "world wars". This is soon to be my number one source for my postcard archive „South of France".

Years later, when I asked the only remaining brother for more postcards, he told me that a German man had been there, who had bought almost all of them. He didn't recognise me. I begin having restaurateurs sign and stamp my cards.

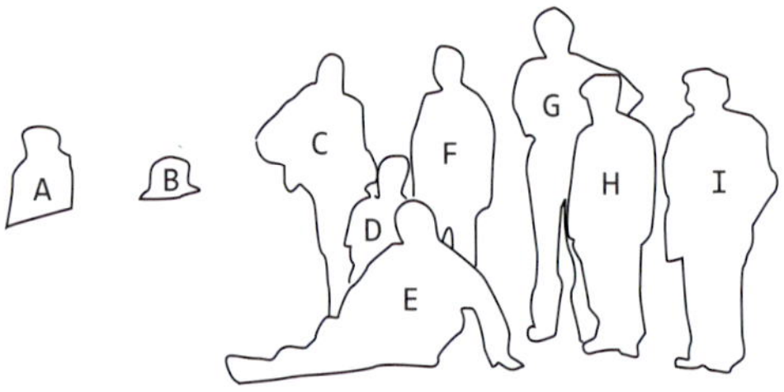

Group photo with the crew

A Woman from the village
B Female passenger
C Michael Stockmann, creative director
D Francis Missana, productioner
E Lukas Linder, assistant
F Francis' cousin, set designer
G Me
H Owner of ground and store, his brother

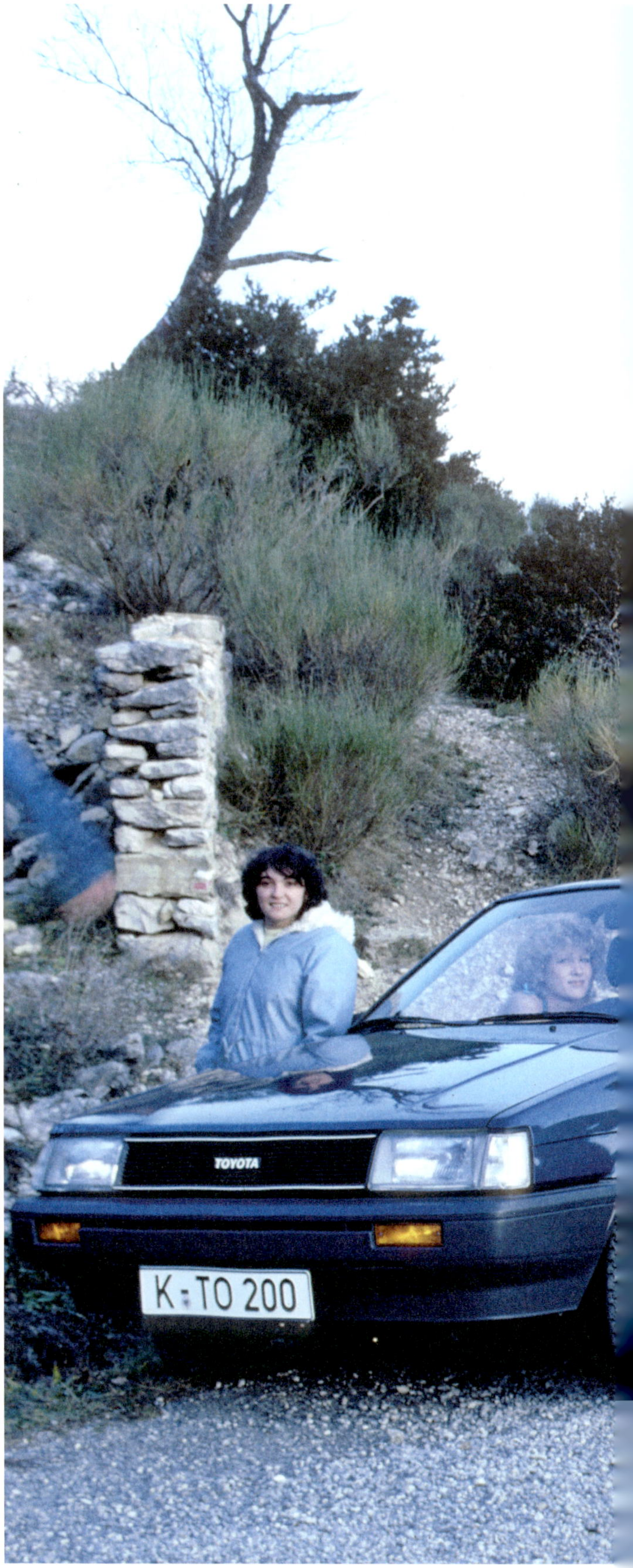

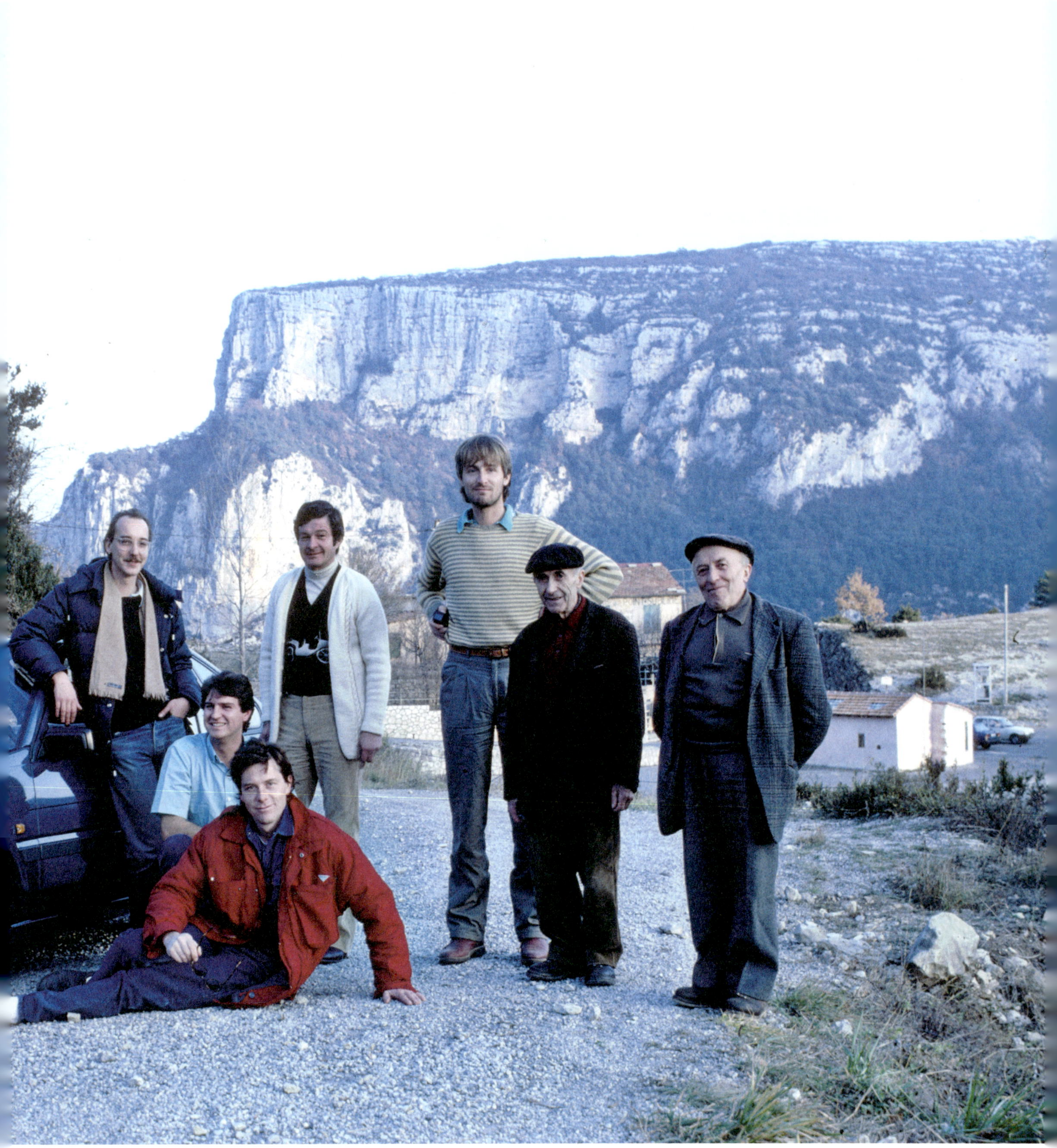

Africa – home at last.

I fly to Kenya with the Lufthansa subsidiary Condor to photograph a former Kenyan student for the German Federation of Pharmaceutical Industry, returning home from Germany, where his scholarship enabled him to become a doctor. Our drinks are taken from us half an hour before crossing the equator, due to turbulences. The steward counts down the seconds until we arrive at the equator, and the pilot gives the passengers and the plane a good shaking. The equator isn't visible, due to the clouds. It almost takes two minutes for the passengers to remove their curious noses from the windows, laughing. "Home at last" is meant ironically, as I am forced to repeat this journey at my own expenses a couple of days later, as my films were incorrectly exposed.

My letters are now sent to Dagmar's work address. At the time, she is working as a customer consultant at J. Walter Thompson in Hamburg.

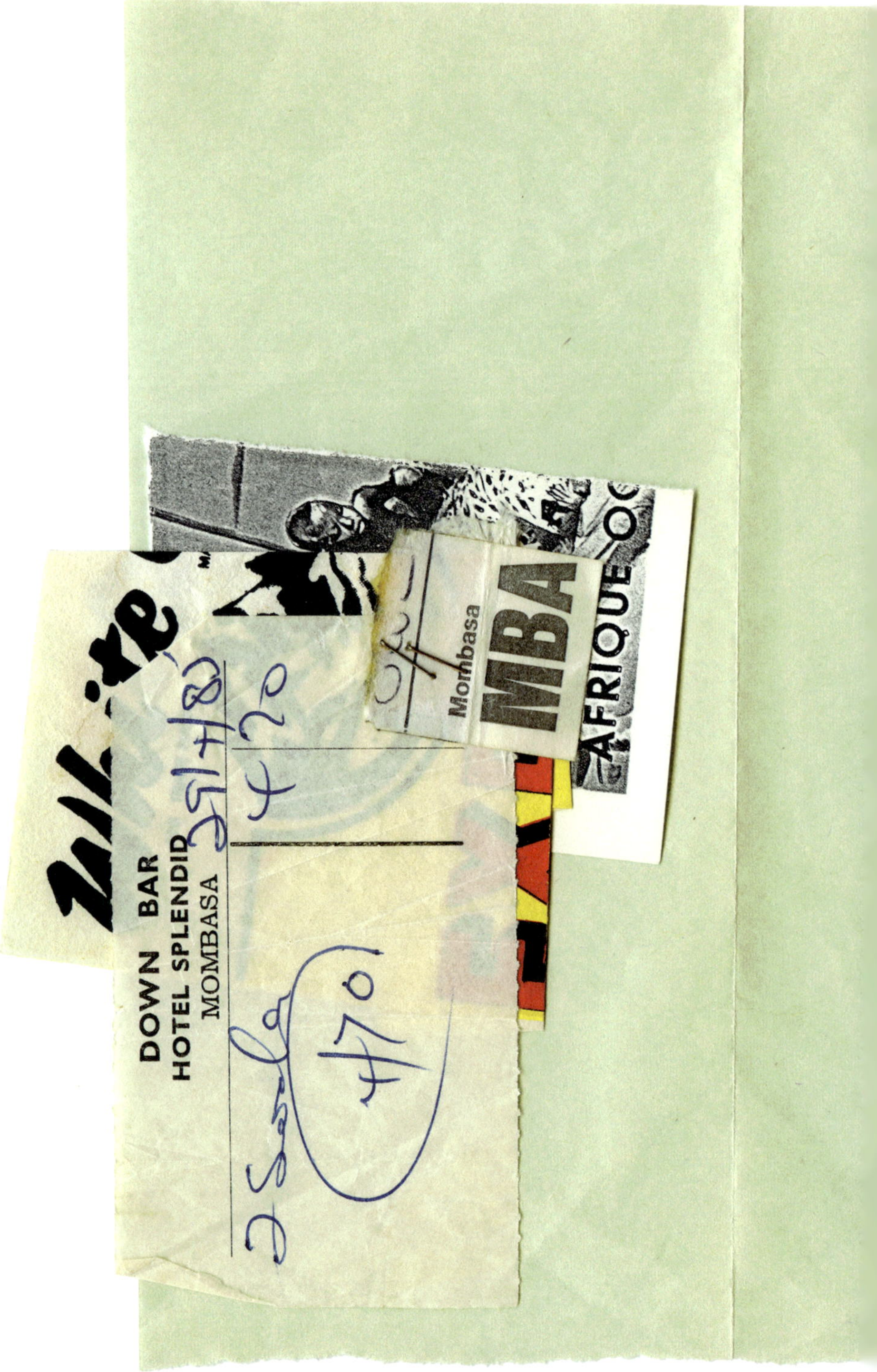

MOMBASA, UKUNDA
May 5th, 1985
–
The shirt sticks.
I'm chewing on a
fingernail. Why are
you so far?
Ivo

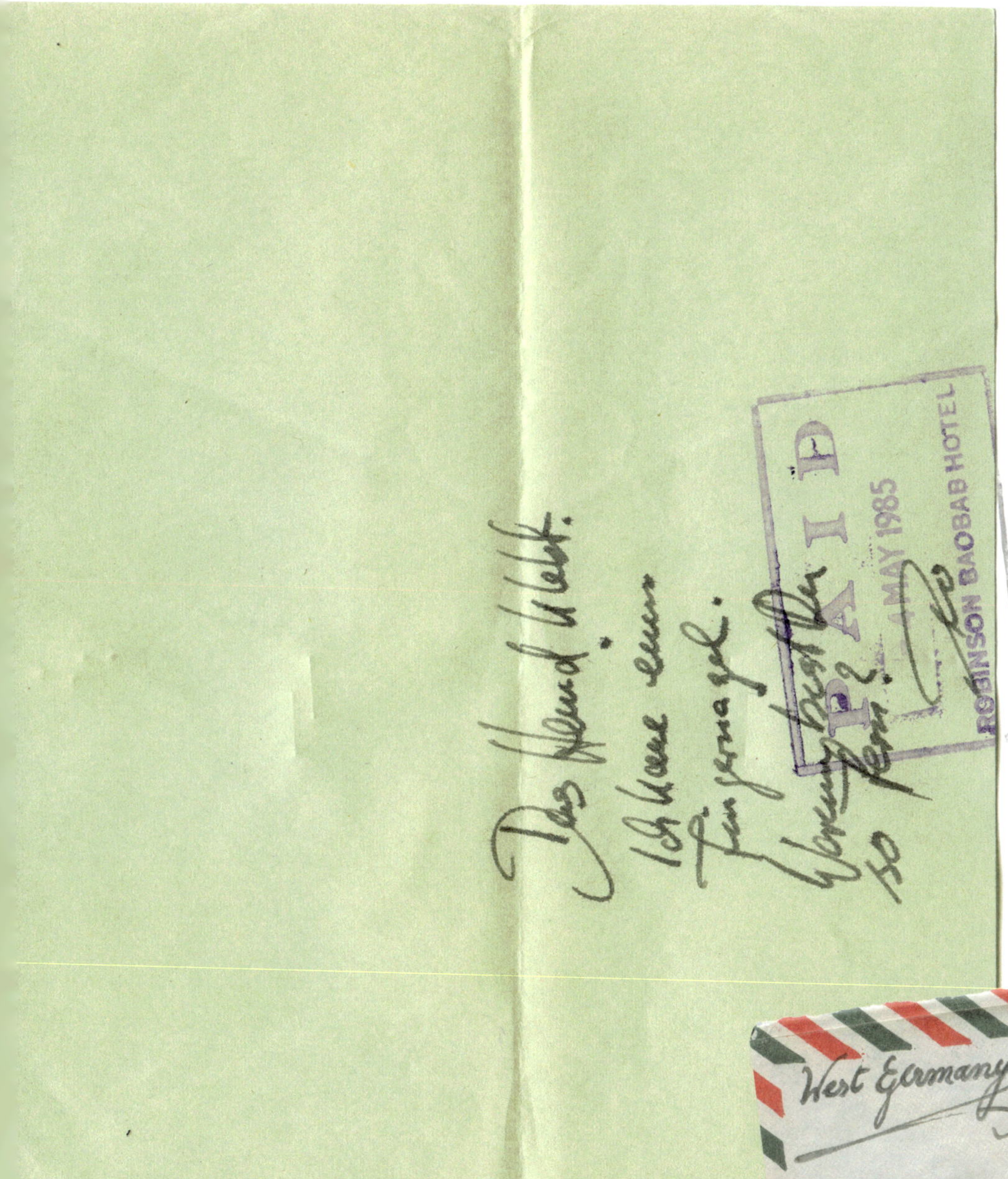

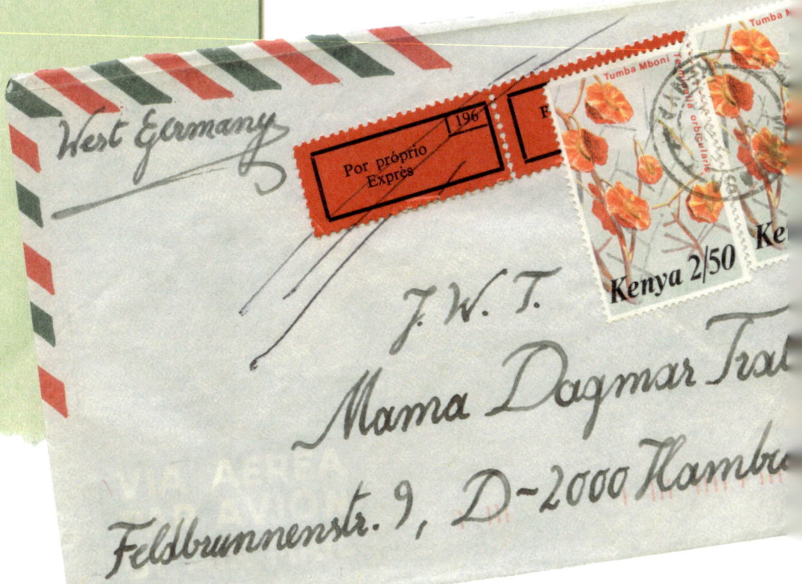

This is Dagmar's and my second year together. I get to fly to Kenya as, due to a photograph I had taken four years earlier in Somalia, I was said to "know my way" around Africa. I would never put a python around my neck again today. But I completely lost my fear of dogs a few years after this journey.

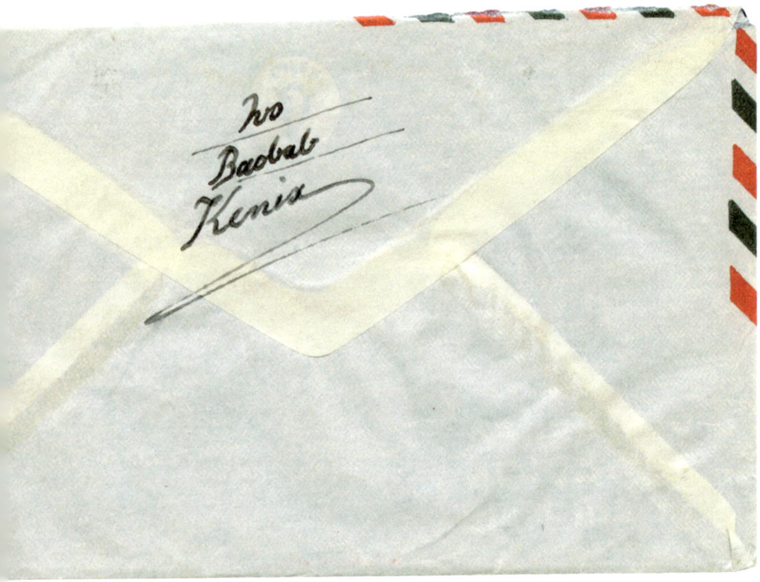

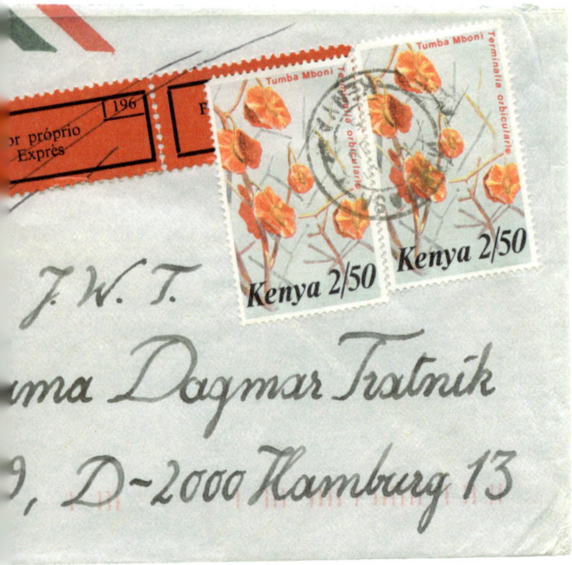

MOMBASA, UKUNDA
June 13th, 1985
-
For Mama long
and thin
and a fast
tongue

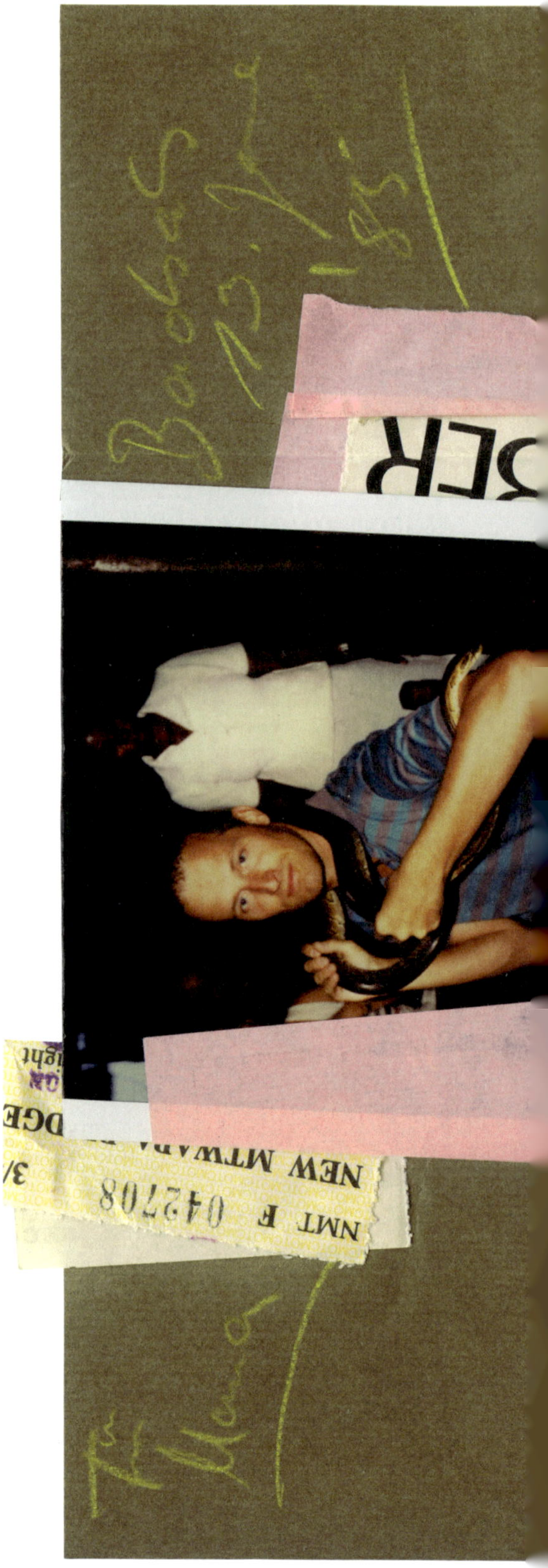

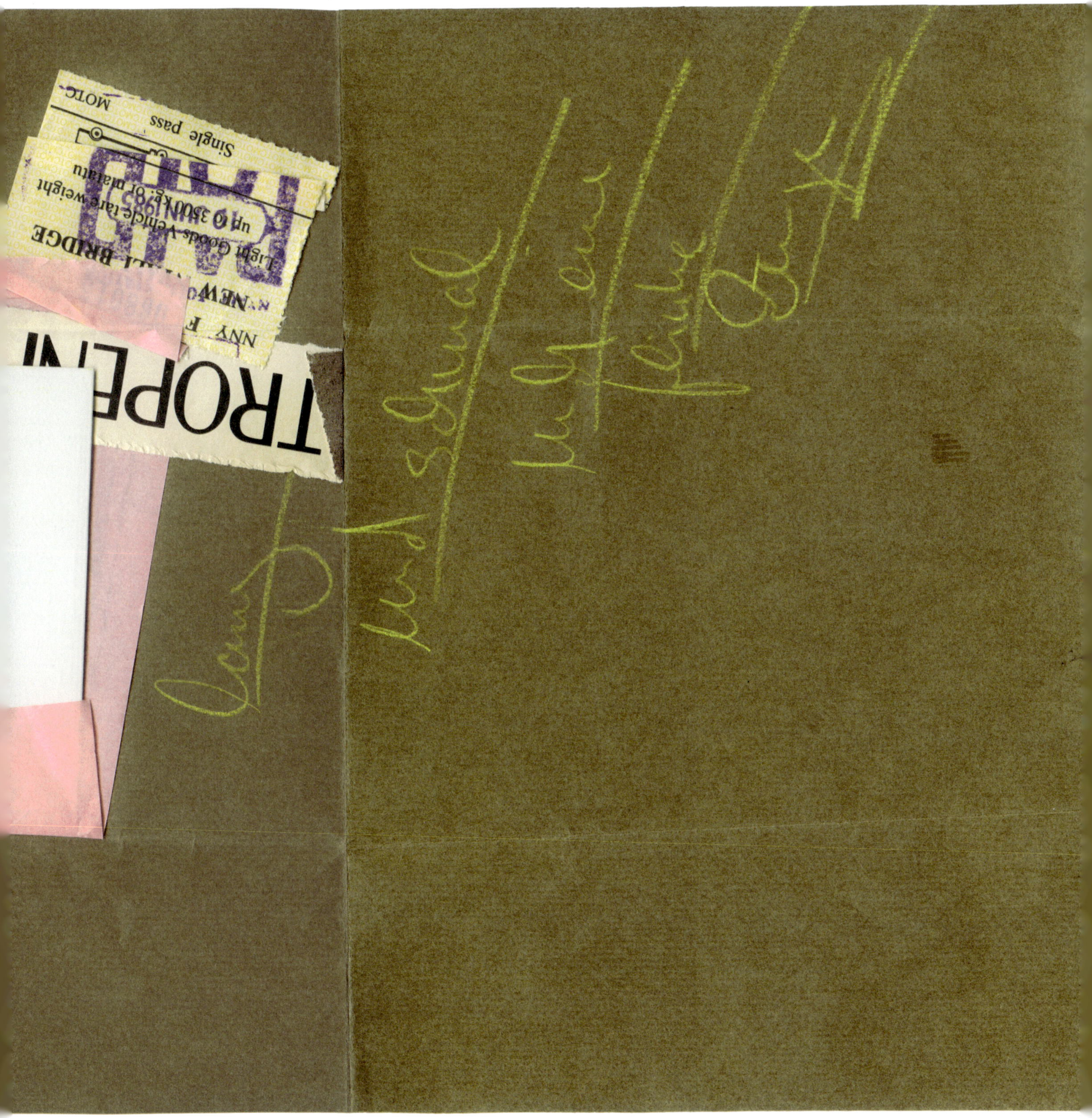
Single pass
Light Goods Vehicle tare weight
TROPEN

The professed self-evidence of travelling.

This night, "The Man with the Golden Gun" with Roger Moore is on TV again at the hotel. It's the free night programme, which is repeated once a week. I've been married for half a year. The tiny little restaurant in Saint-Paul, which seats a maximum of 12 guests and is always cold and draughty in the winter, becomes my favourite place of pilgrimage. A friendly old lady summons her even older Italian kitchen help to the vegetable box behind the restaurant, and then brings us ancient and expired champagne in 0.5 L bottles. Marianne is always freezing here, and sticks her cold feet into the leg of my trousers.

NICE
October 23rd, 1985
-
"Le deuxième jour,
Ivo"

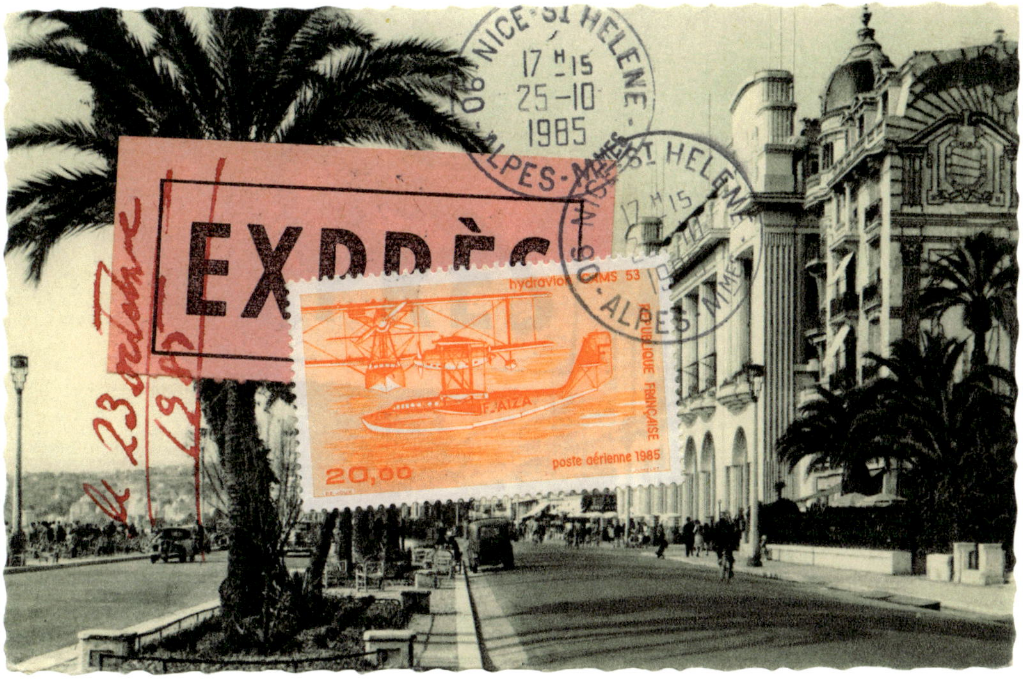
NICE-ST HELENE
17 H 15
25-10
1985
ALPES-MMES
EXPRÈS
hydravion CAMS 53
RÉPUBLIQUE FRANÇAISE
F-AIZA
poste aérienne 1985
20,00

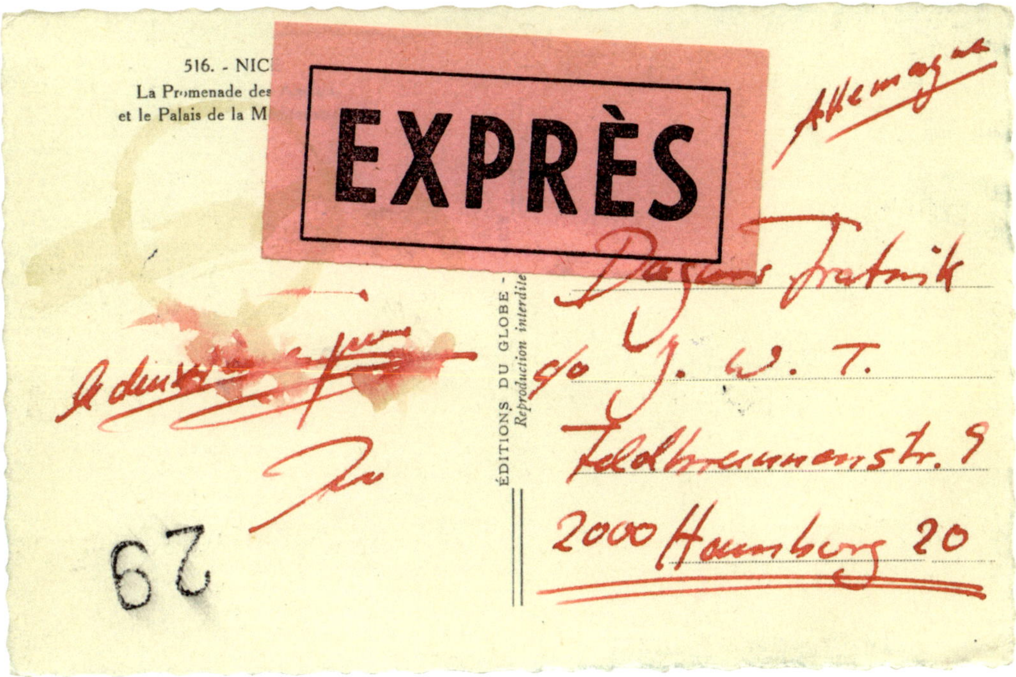
516. - NIC
La Promenade des
et le Palais de la M
EXPRÈS
ÉDITIONS DU GLOBE - Reproduction interdite
Allemagne
c/o J. W. T.
2000 Hamburg 20
29

The Hippodrome is a horse racing track by Cagnes-sur-Mer, between Nice and Antibes. The site hasn't undergone a single change for over 50 years. I'm planning to create a series of double-polaroids, following the Nissan campaign, for which I conduct a casting call in Hamburg. Ten days before the departure and after having carefully selected the props, the young lady cancels, as she prefers to be photographed by Helmut Newton. He, however, has no interest in her. However, he will have one of my erotic photos hanging in his kitchen in Paris a couple of years later, but that's irrelevant right now. A different series develops, with a different model. The Hippodrome is refurbished horribly a couple of years later. And my female first choice will regret her decision twenty years later. Those who say no to art, consequently sit in front of empty walls later on.

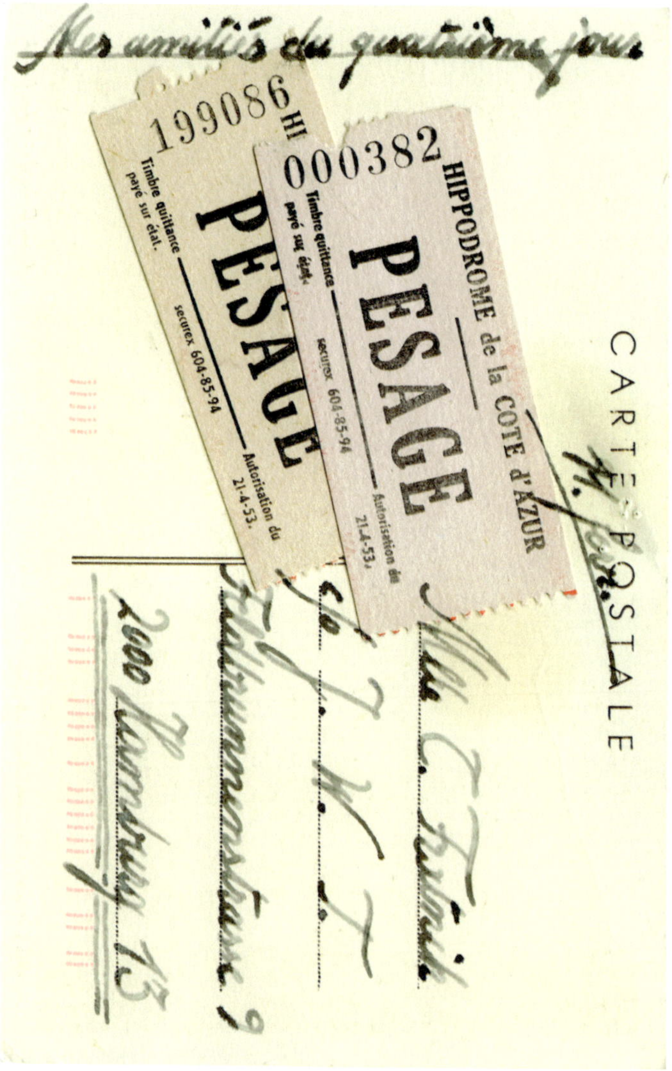

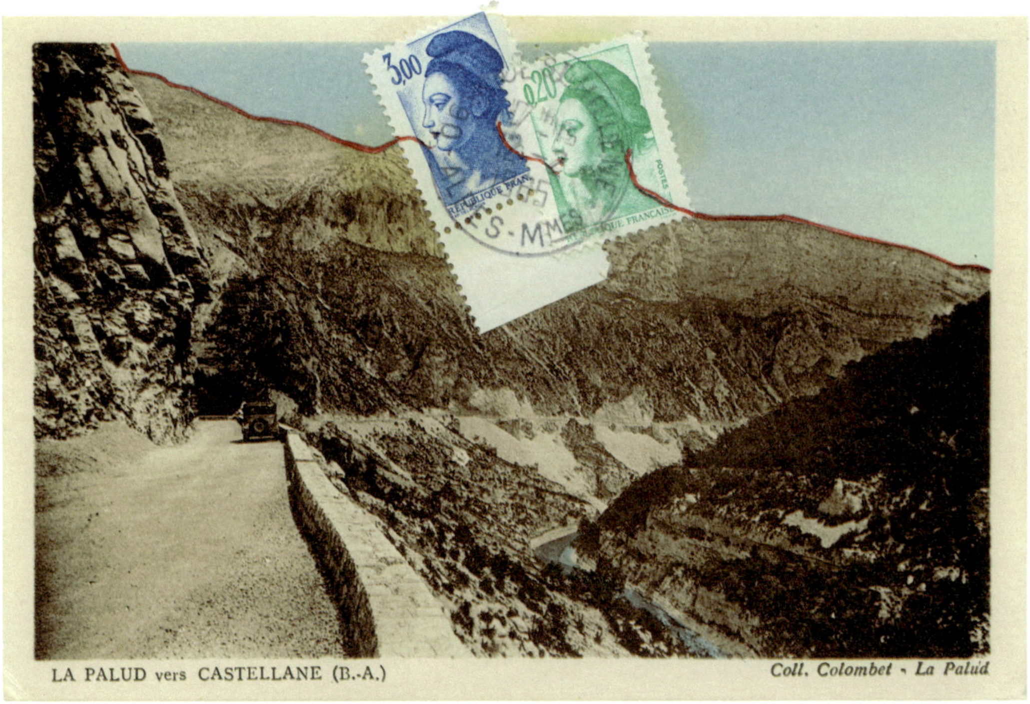

NICE
February 12th,
1985
–
"Mes amitiés du quatrième jour"

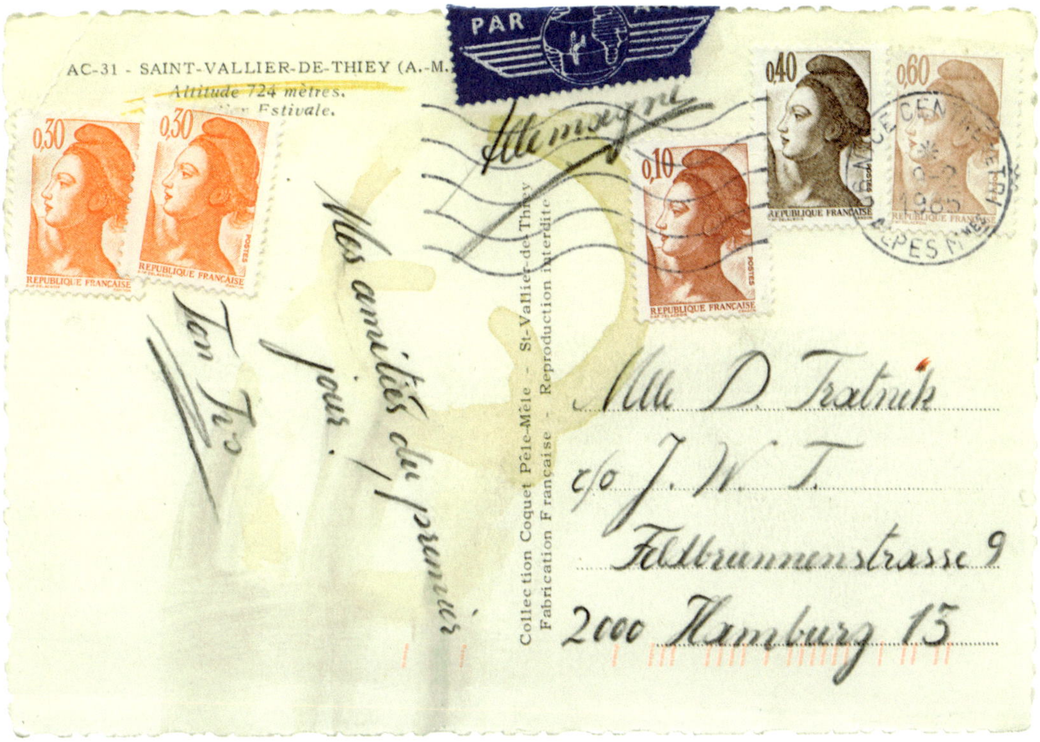

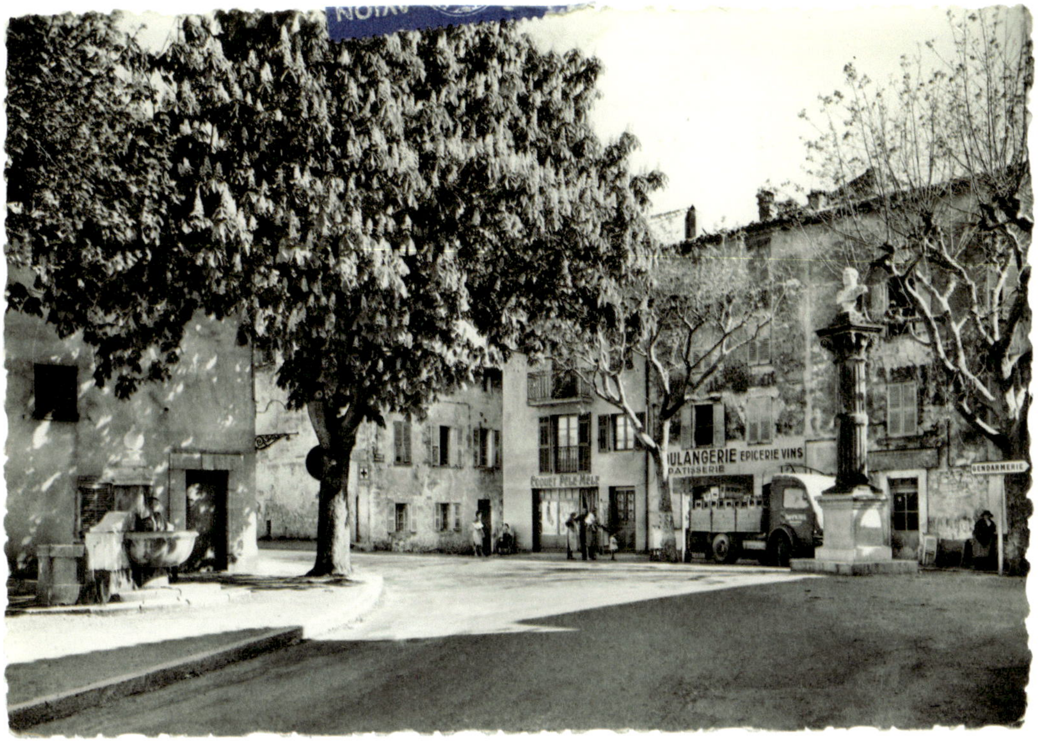

NICE
February 9th,
1985
–
“Mes amitiés du
premier jour,
Ton Ivo”

A reason to party.

On the 13th of February 1985, my assistant Philip Radowitz receives a telex (a news machine, which turns signals into strips of holes) announcing that he has been exempted from military service. I am happy to spend some celebratory money. We order a bottle of Pommery in the lobby, while the mediocre pianist plays the same songs as always. Always. Every day. He is short, and wears enormous glasses with tinted gradient lenses in a reddish brown, right below his toupet, high heels, and trousers that are folded 20 cm inwards at the seam. It's a historic day.

»
I always saw Jeanne d'Arc as a symbol for my freedom to work and live like this in France. I respected it, but at the same time it was reliable evidence, for my right to exist. I graphically integrated my heroine into the postcards with awe, in this case based on her shoulder line.
«

We are now taking pictures for Lada on the Côte d'Azur. The cars are stuck in the Rhone delta due to the snow catastrophe, and our trip has already been delayed by 14 days. We have four Russian cars. The first Lada Niva has a cable fire in the engine compartment on the motorway and is on fire for half an hour. The second surprises us with a rusty rear axle, which was caused by the long transport. A Toyota axle is installed. This does the car good. More surprises follow, but we take beautiful pictures.

NICE
February 13th, 1985
–
la 6ième

"signateurs:
Francis,
Elisabeth,
Philip (le chauffeur),
Marianne,
Burkhard,
Torsten, (Wascheur
le car?)"

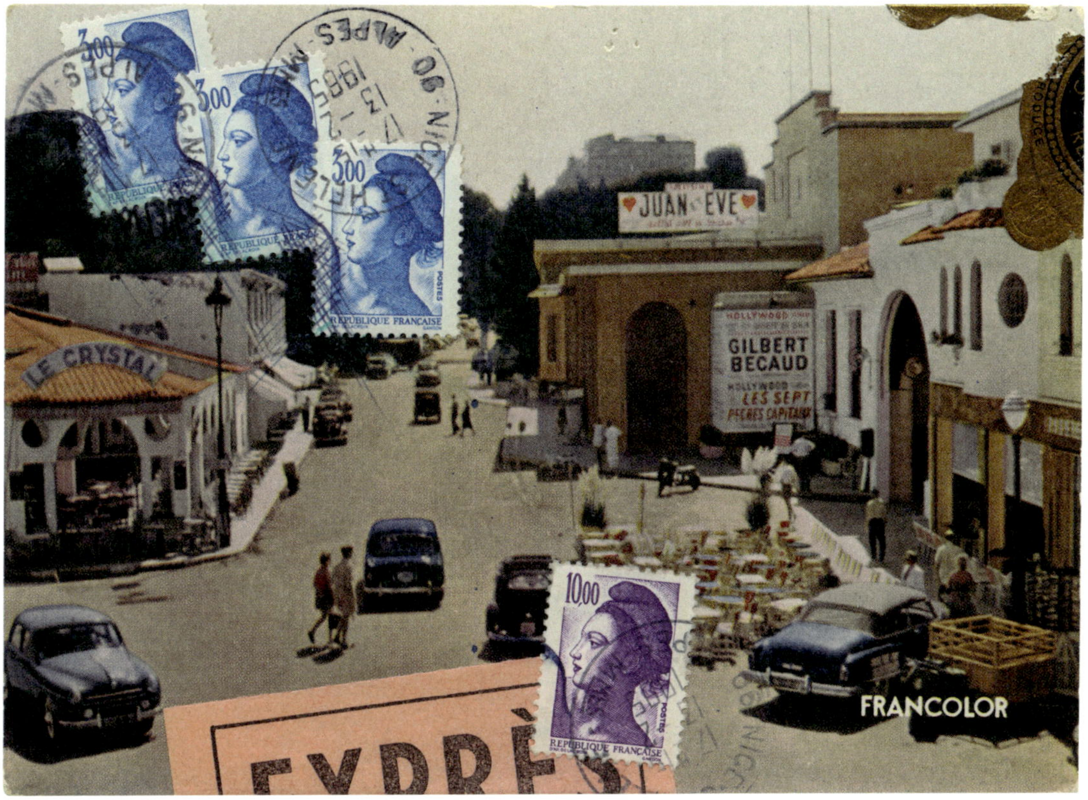
JUAN & EVE
LE CRYSTAL
GILBERT BECAUD
LES SEPT PÉCHÉS CAPITAUX
RÉPUBLIQUE FRANÇAISE
FRANCOLOR
EXPRÈS

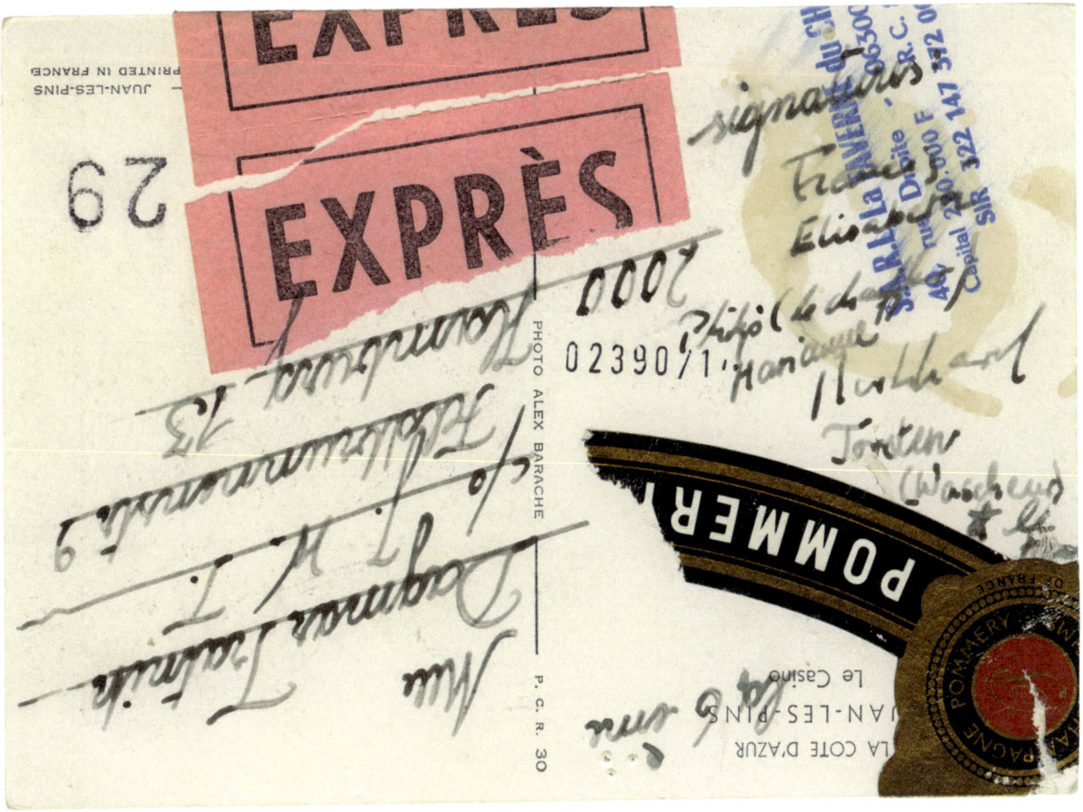
EXPRÈS
EXPRÈS
29
PRINTED IN FRANCE
JUAN-LES-PINS
PHOTO ALEX BARACHE
02390/1
POMMERY
LA COTE D'AZUR
JUAN-LES-PINS
Le Casino
P. C. R. 30

We cover the distance to the Gorges du Verdon over and over again. This time only to show my stylist Marianne the area on a rainy day. The world of the old postcards arouses the wish for fewer mobile homes, whose ugly appearances don't exactly improve the landscapes.

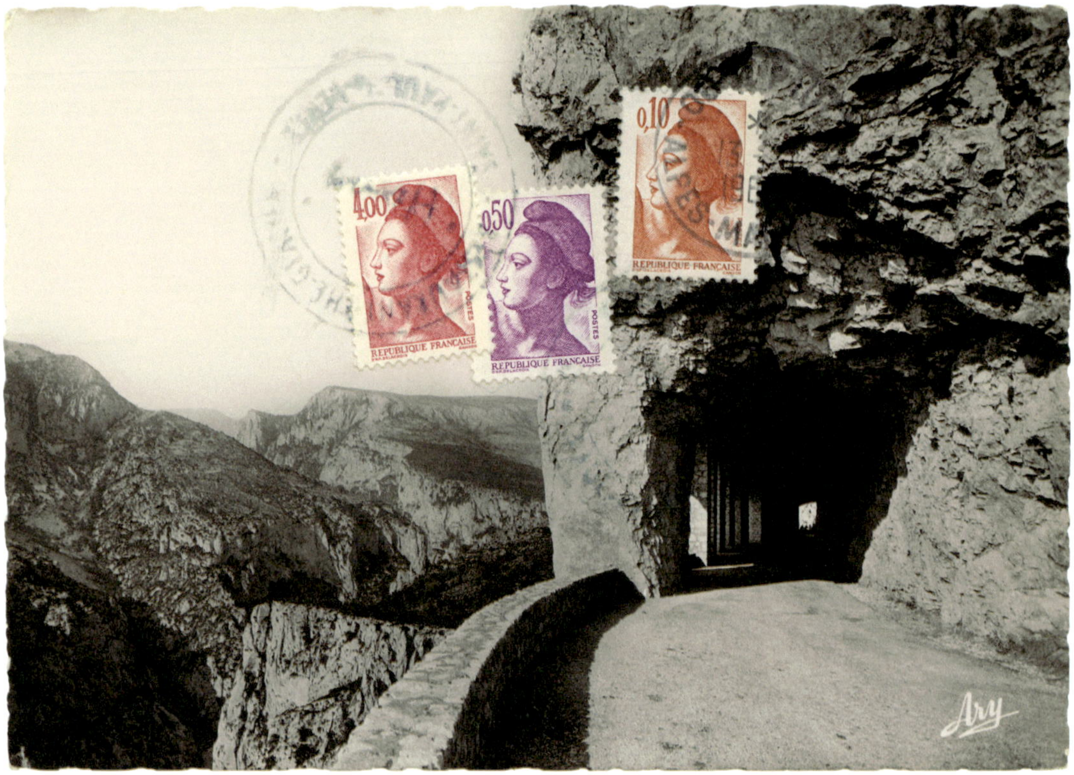

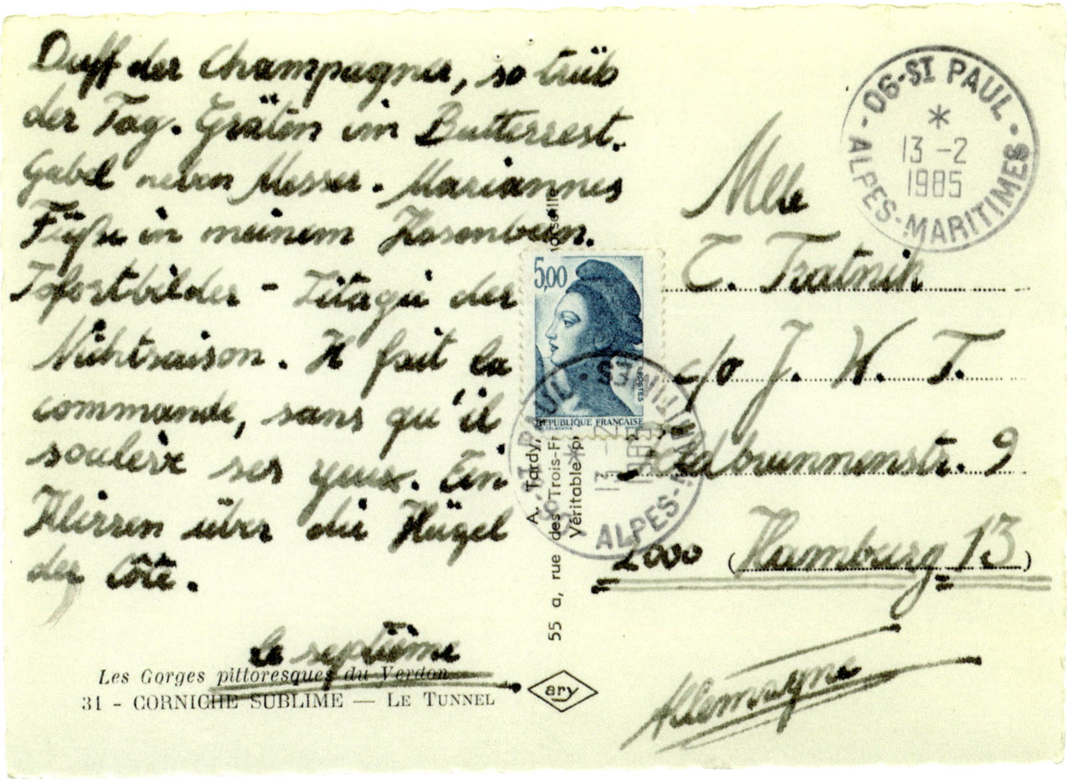

NICE

February 13th, 1985

–

Flat the champagne, as dull as the day. Fishbones in the butter scraps. Fork next to knife. Mariannes feet in my trouser leg. Instant photos – apathy of the off-season. Il fait la commande, sans qu'il soulève ses yeux, a clangour above the hills of the Côte.

la septième.

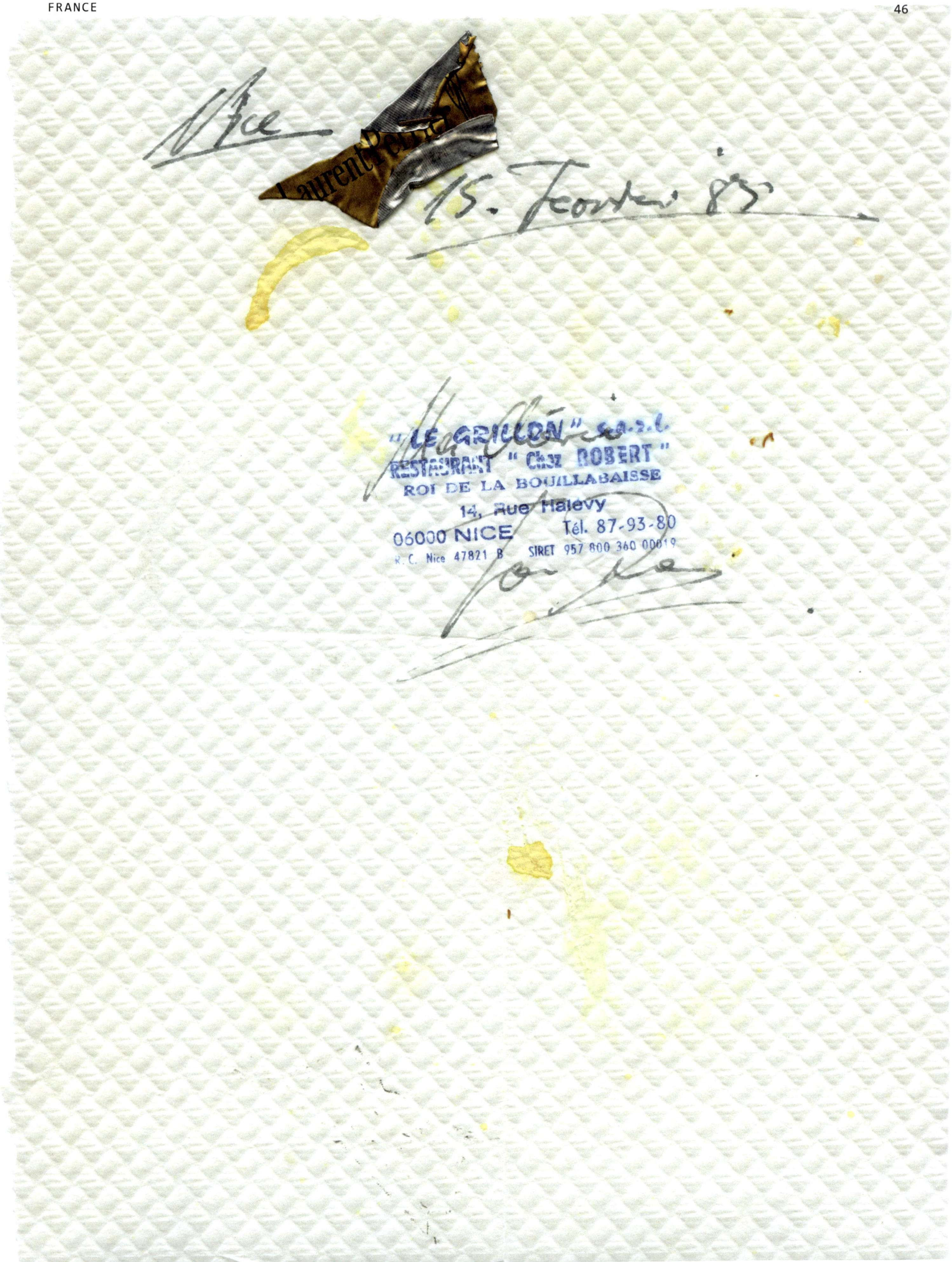
Nice
Laurent Perrier
15. Février 85
"LE GRILLON" s.a.r.l.
RESTAURANT "Chez ROBERT"
ROI DE LA BOUILLABAISSE
14, Rue Halevy
06000 NICE Tél. 87-93-80
R.C. Nice 47821 B SIRET 957 800 360 00019

NICE
February 2nd,
1985

The glamorous.

I think this text comes from the German Vogue. The French issue currently costs 36,00 DM in Germany. We either buy one upon arrival in Nice, or two before our departure. I design the lettering in Hamburg using Letraset, the rub-off letters of the 70s, and copy it onto envelopes using a Canon copier. The duty of titles. This begins with the first glance into the hotel bathroom mirror in the morning. That's what the client pays us for. One of my favourite performers of old men is Monsieur Boideff, a Romanian exile and ex-Nato general, who lives in seclusion to avoid being murdered for his nationality by communists operating abroad. And this wonderful elderly gentleman from a royal family is married to Tatiana, Princess Kropitkinie Boideff. She was Richard Avedon's first model. Richard is said to have been very excited during the photo shoot; Tatiana, on the other hand, was already very much in demand at the time. And she was Christian Dior's muse.

One day, the Boideffs invite us to their home. They serve lobster bisque and champagne in a tiny apartment. They are both way over 70, and sleep in a 120 cm wide French bed. "We have always slept in it. It's never going to change." And then she squeezes into five or six Dior dresses still hanging in her wardrobe, tucks in her tummy, and cuts a figure that women today should take as an example: grace, dignity, and a healthy amount of self-confidence. In the light of such stories, we feel honoured and glamorous, as good feelings can last, and the next trip to Nice is never far off.

Many of the beautiful, old postcards from antiquarian shops had already been written on. I stuck the yellow paper of our writing pads onto them. This was the trip for the relaunch of the Opel Vectra. During location scouting, we crossed the mountains on our drive to Nice from Geneva. My French-speaking assistant was no longer present, and my French was in need of corrections.

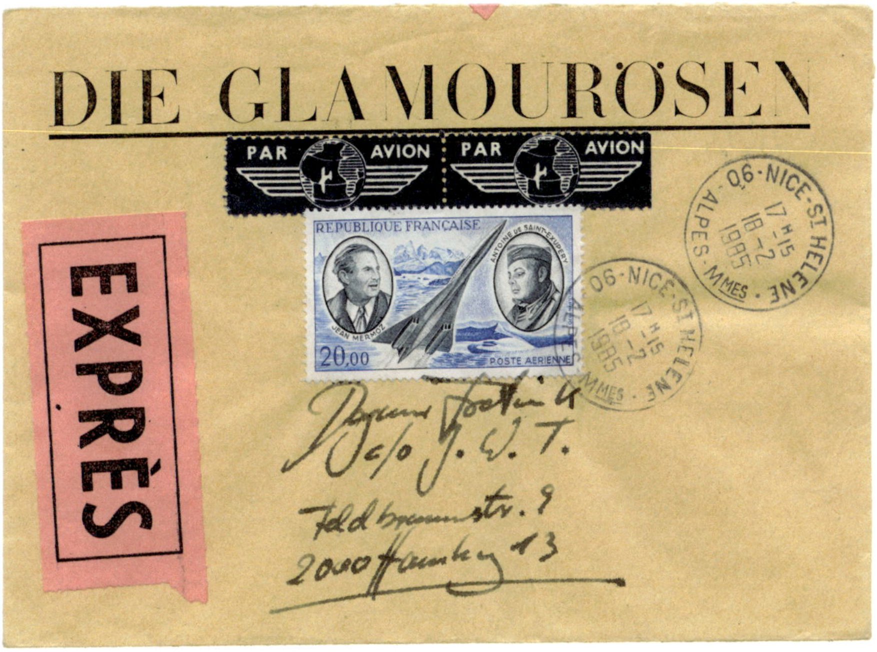

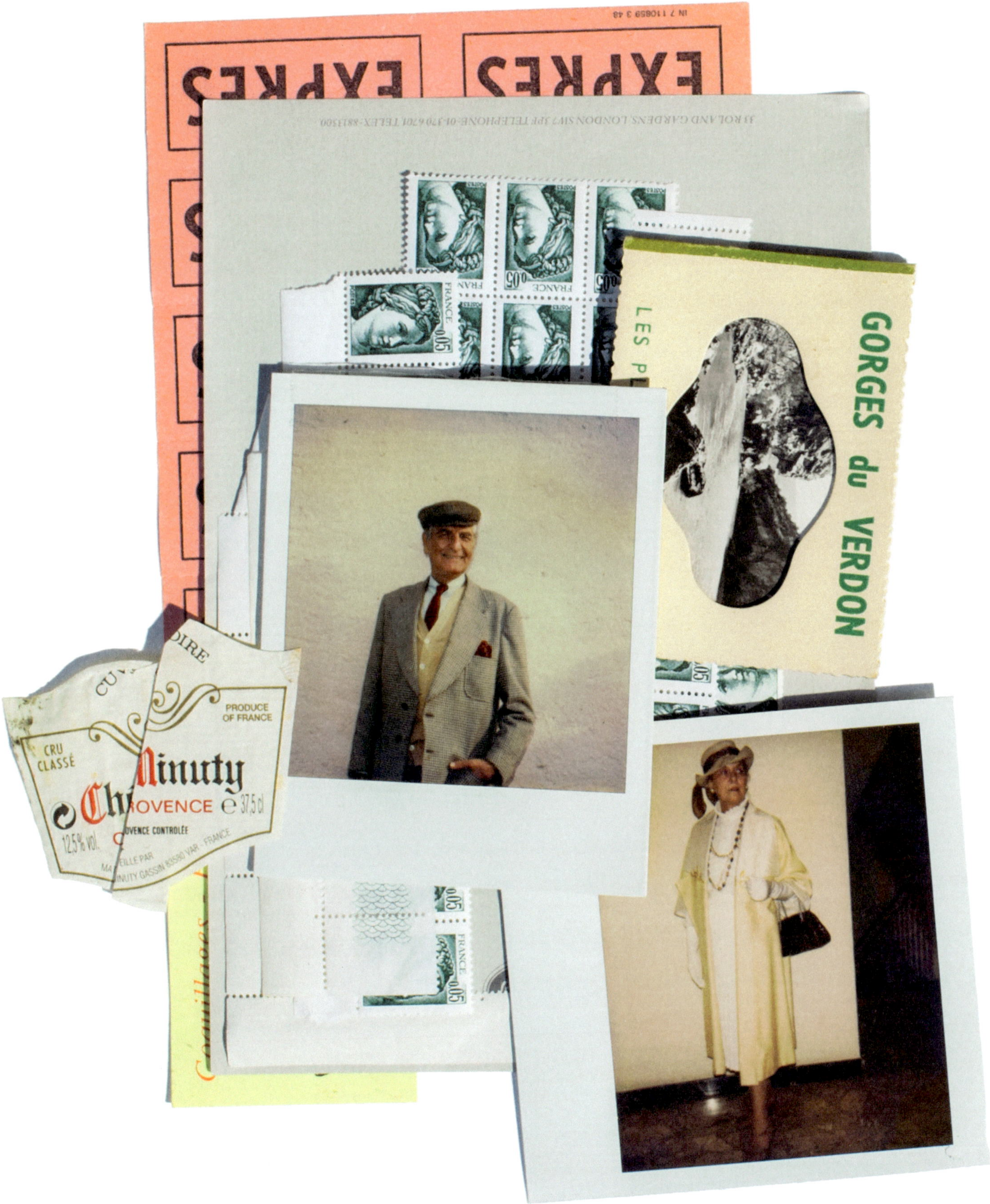
GORGES du VERDON
LES P
CRU CLASSÉ
PRODUCE OF FRANCE
Minuty
ROVENCE
37,5 cl
12,5% vol.
OVENCE CONTROLÉE
FRANCE
0,05

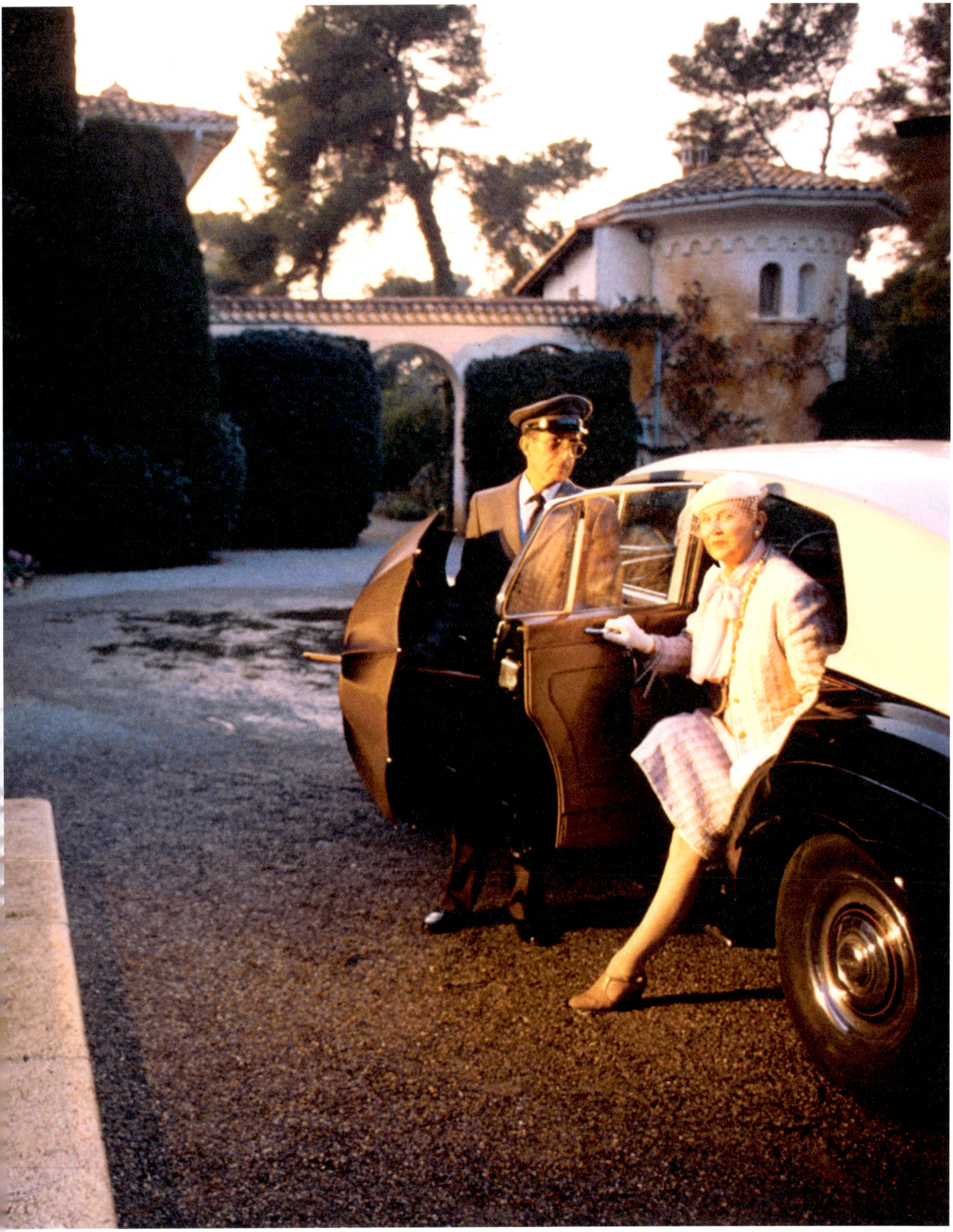

Manifestation of the moment.

My first rubber stamp is created. My productioneer, Francis Missana, introduces me to a company that still produces stamps by lead typesetting. The rubber stamps "Photo A LA MINUTE" for my Polaroids, "IVO sur la Côte d'Azur" (including a circle to add the date), as well as "L'ART APRÈS" are made using french type.

I bought the Aki Kudora card from 1983 in the Galerie Maeght in Saint-Paul-de-Vence. I pasted an official URGENT sticker across the front to mark the priority, and the Adenauer/de Gaulle stamp for the reconciliation of Germany and France. With this, Kudoras work is altered, and gains my signature as well as the "L'ART APRÈS" stamp: the subsequent art. Irony lies in my involuntary acquisition, as does respect.

Written above the address array: "timbre de l'autre côté" - stamp on the other side. All my mail arrives, except for a reworked Matisse series consisting of four postcards, sent from Nice to Antibes for the passing of Francis' father.

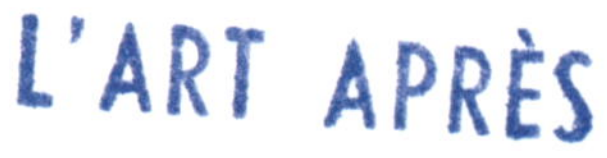

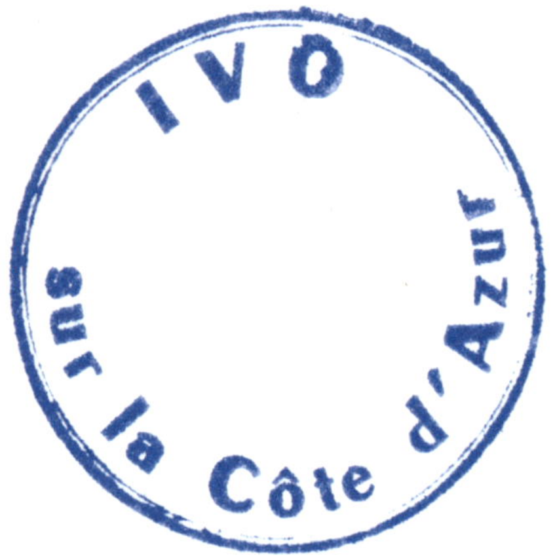

NICE
February 3rd, 1985
-
"2/2
Ivo von Renner, Nice"

"timbre de
l'autre côté"

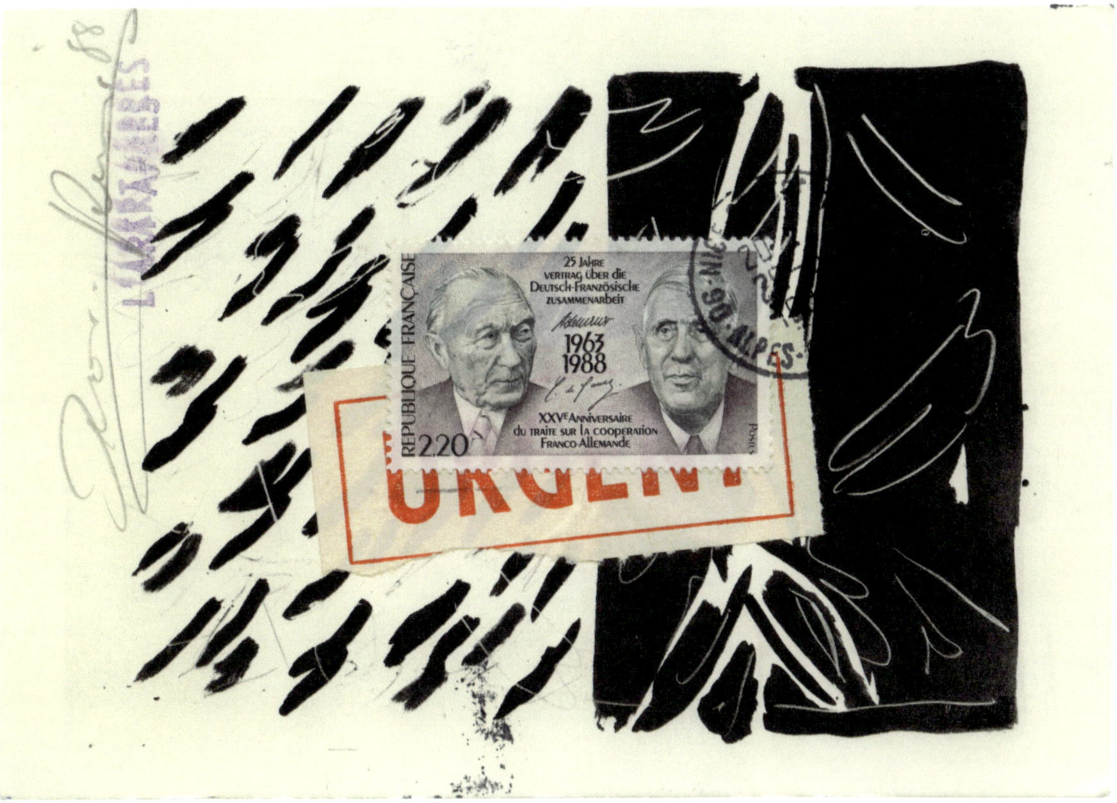
L'ARRABESQUES
25 JAHRE
VERTRAG ÜBER DIE
DEUTSCH-FRANZÖSISCHE
ZUSAMMENARBEIT
1963
1988
REPUBLIQUE FRANÇAISE
2,20
XXVe ANNIVERSAIRE
DU TRAITÉ SUR LA COOPÉRATION
FRANCO-ALLEMANDE
POSTES
URGENT
06-NICE
ALPES-

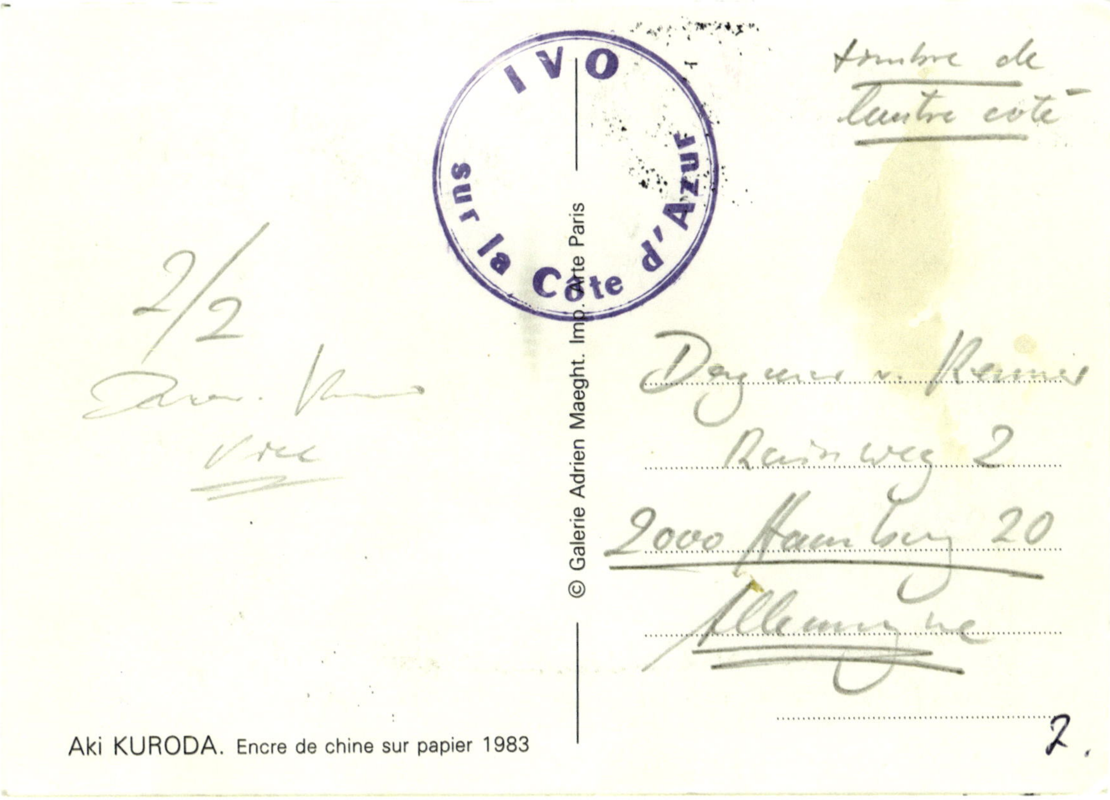
IVO
sur la Côte d'Azur
© Galerie Adrien Maeght. Imp. Arte Paris
timbre de l'autre côté
2/2
2000 Hamburg 20
Allemagne
2.
Aki KURODA. Encre de chine sur papier 1983

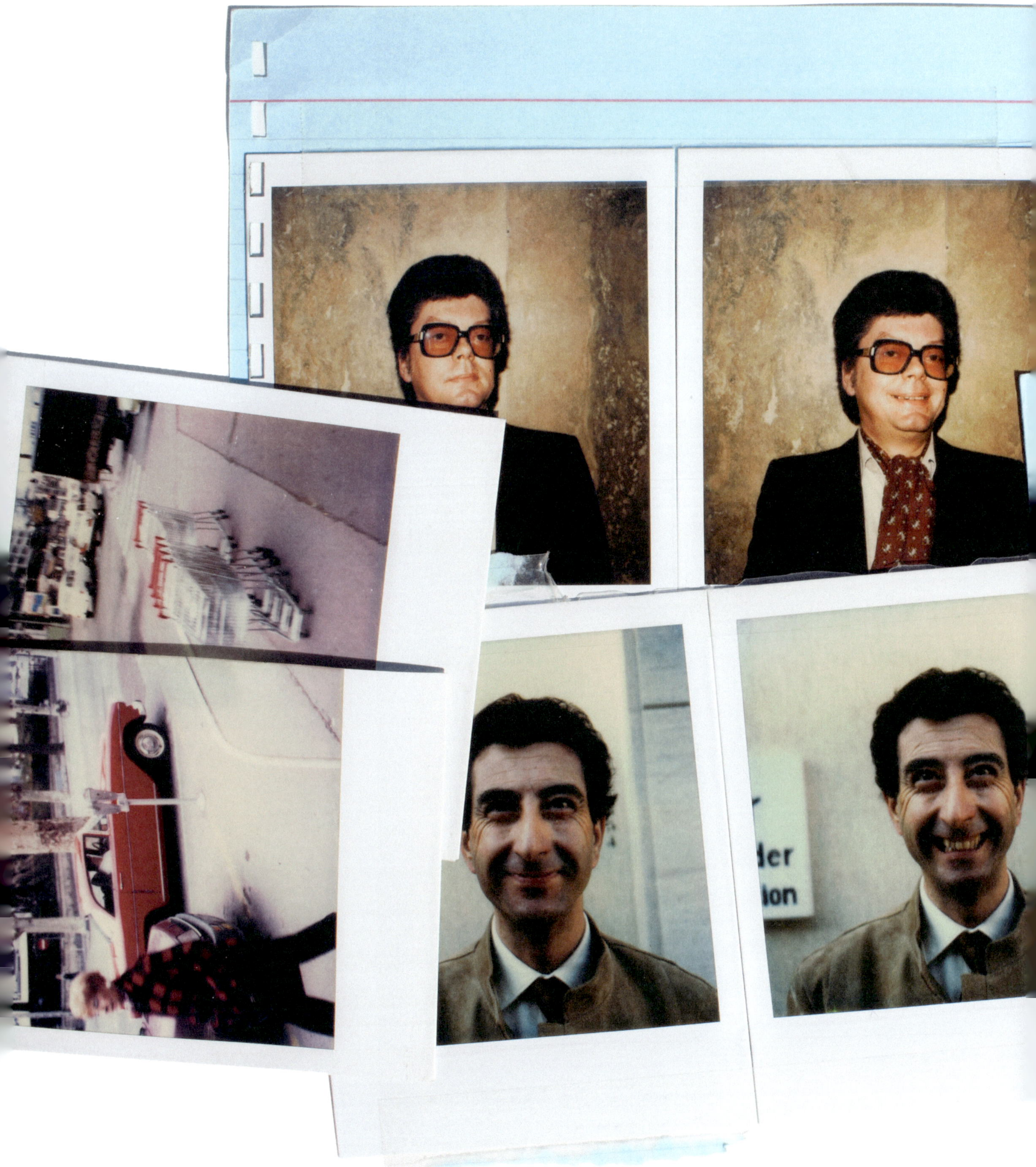

The hotel pianist (above) and Marco Martinozzi, my favourite model.

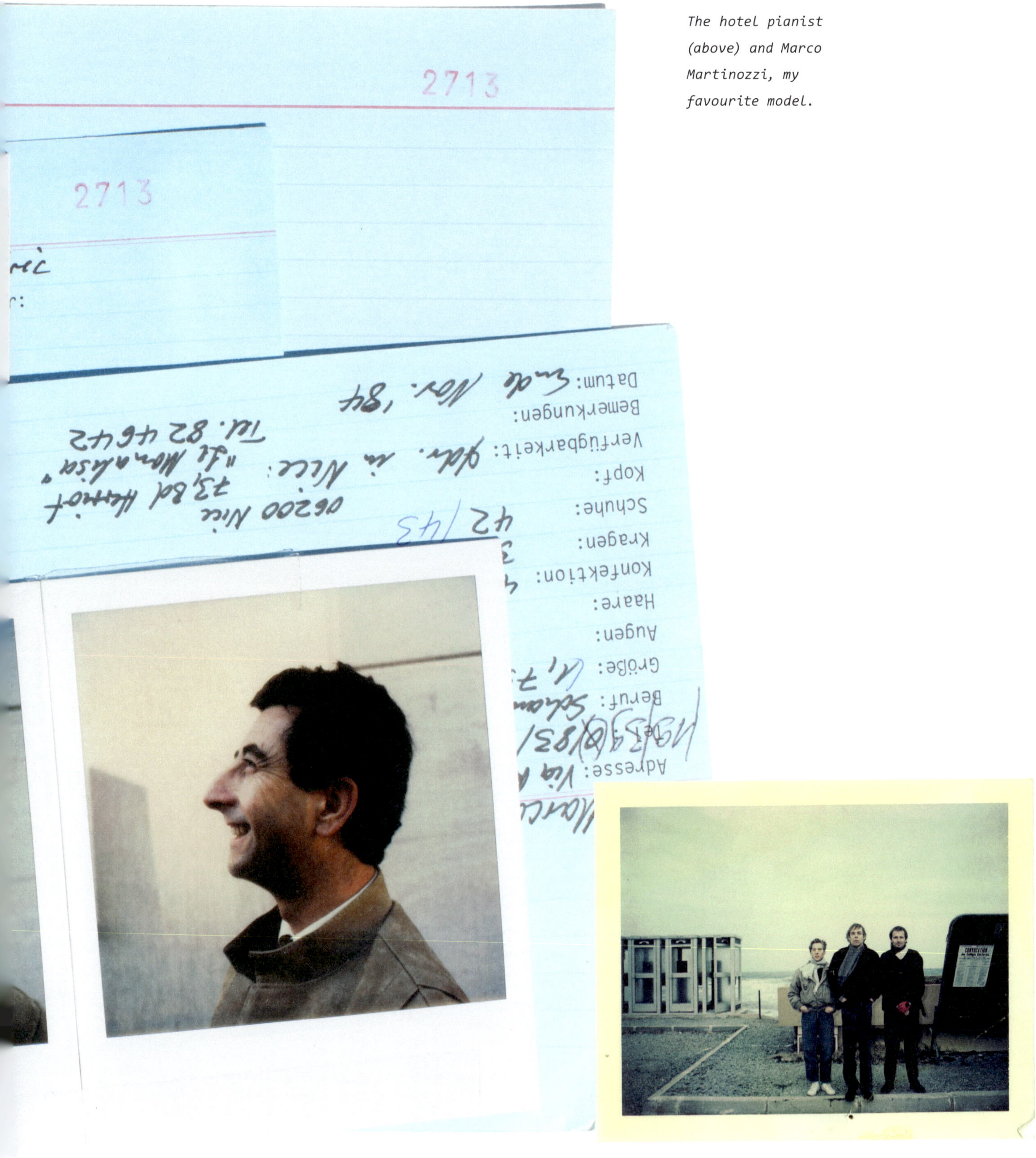

14 days of rain: Philip Radowitz, Burkhard Blum and I.

The Toyota and Renault family grows: Lada and Nissan.

Renault sends an enquiry about a campaign called "The little friend". And this car speaks to the driver, the well and the meadow. Due to the fact that no well exists, we have one built, and decorated with fresh tendrils. This requires only a small amount of effort. As our team is still small, my assistant even brushes the male model's hair. Catering is still meagre: two baguettes, one salami, a cutting board, maybe one piece of cheese, one bottle of water each, one bottle of red wine which we don't drink and coffee which is only lukewarm upon arrival. And delight.

The aim of the photoshoot is to drive an SUV through a ford, to show its suitability for offroad tracks. We all build the dam together. It takes us eight hours. Picnic as usual: No butter with the bread, but a bottle of red wine.

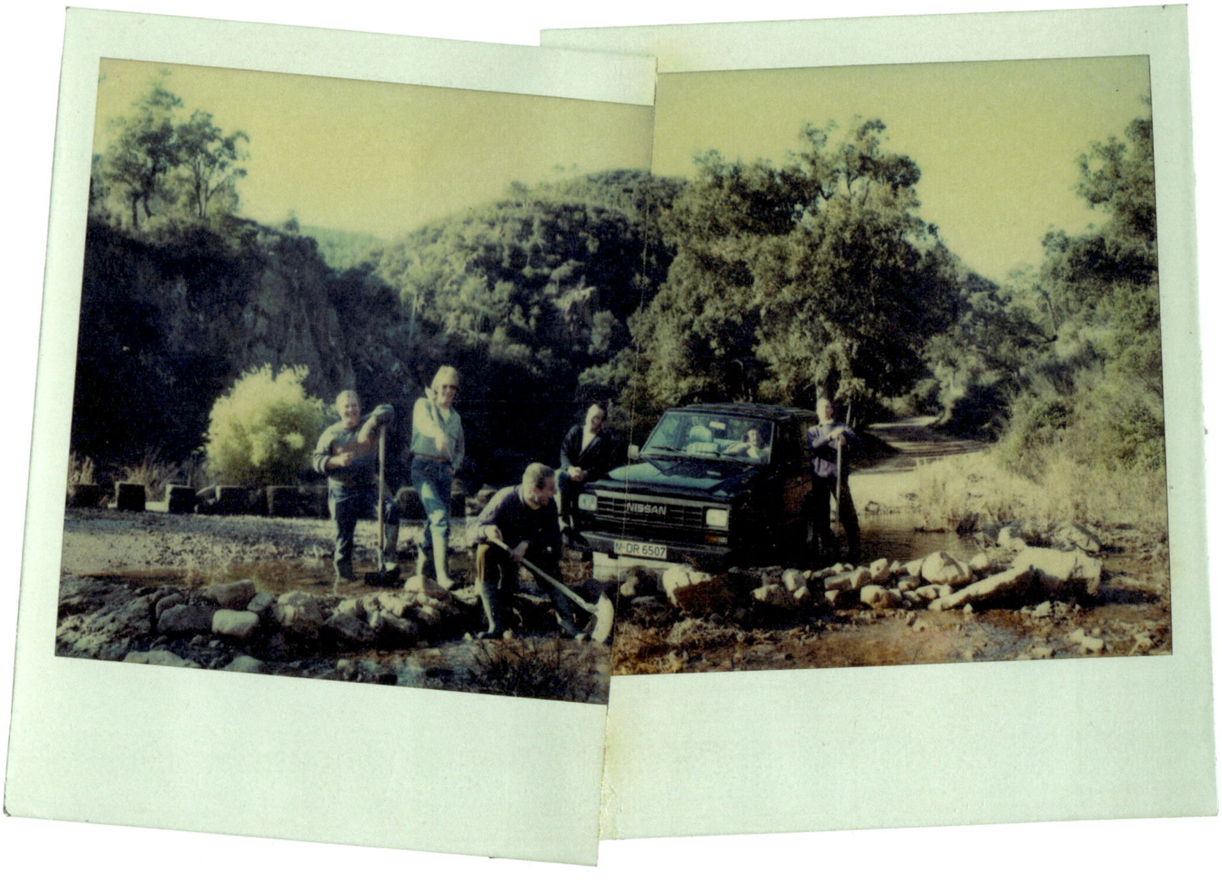

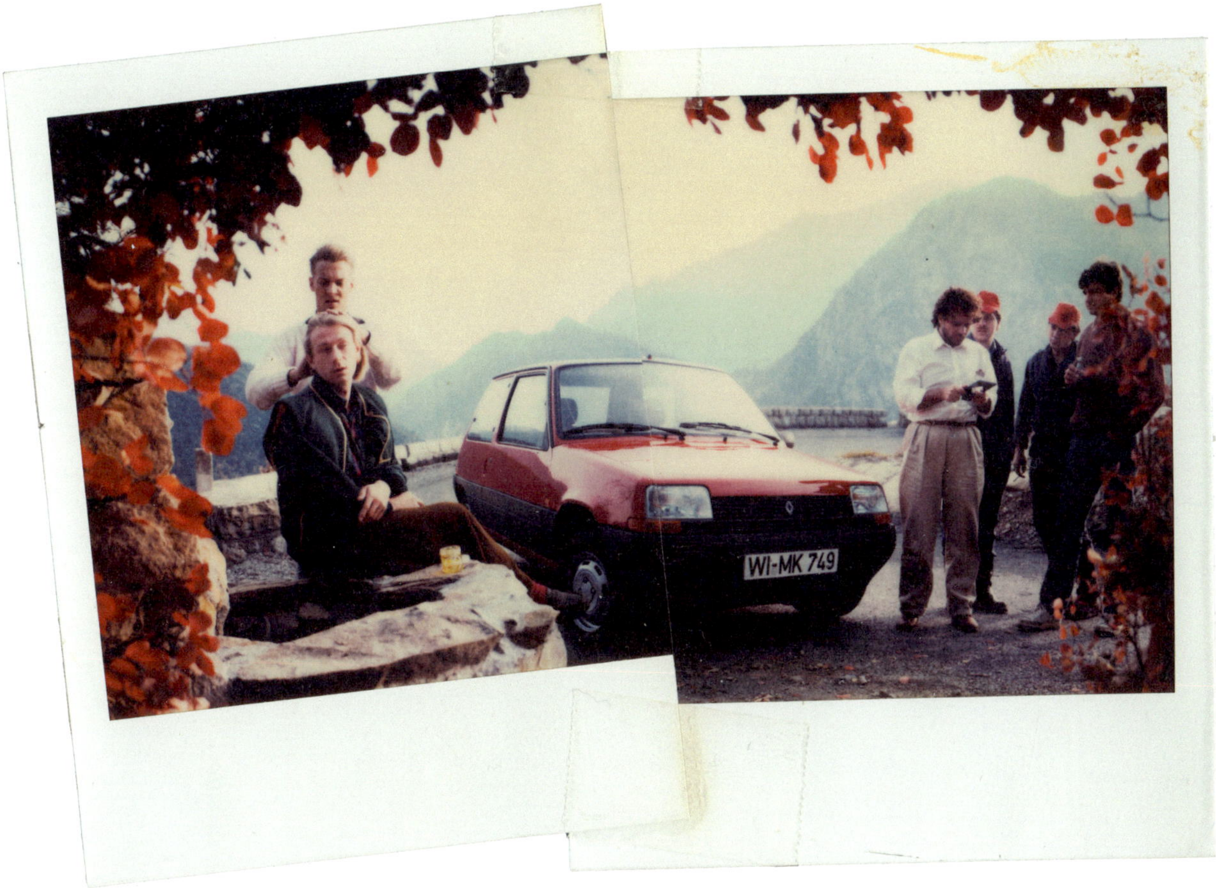

»

The Côte d'Azur promises reasonable weather during the winter months and doesn't have its name for no reason.

«

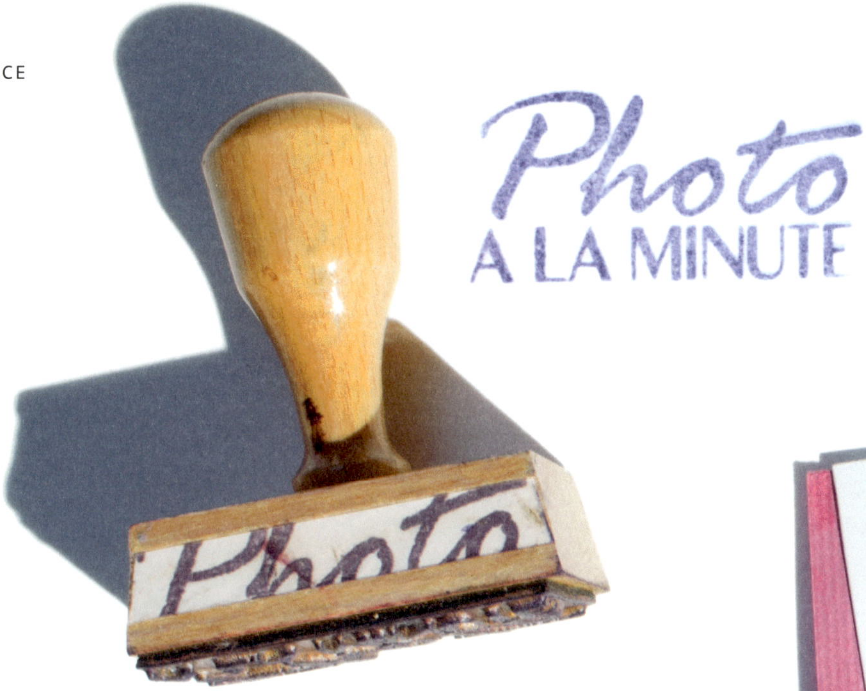

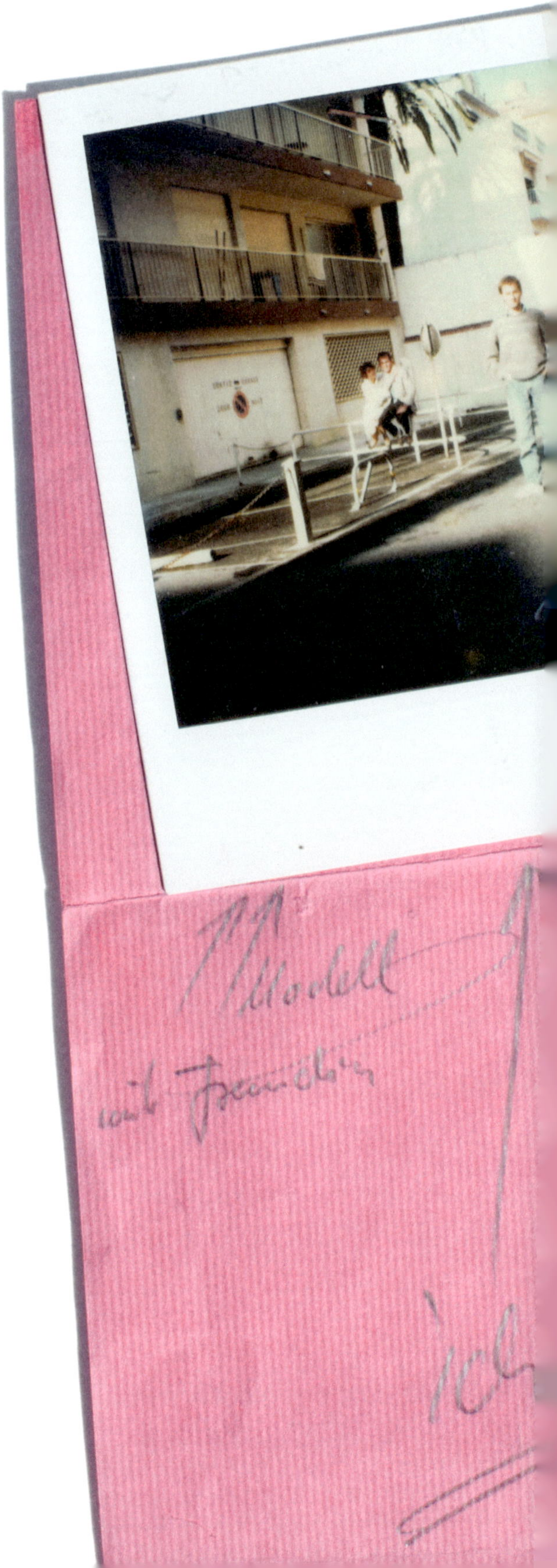

This is a letter to my mother, to show her how many people work on one picture.

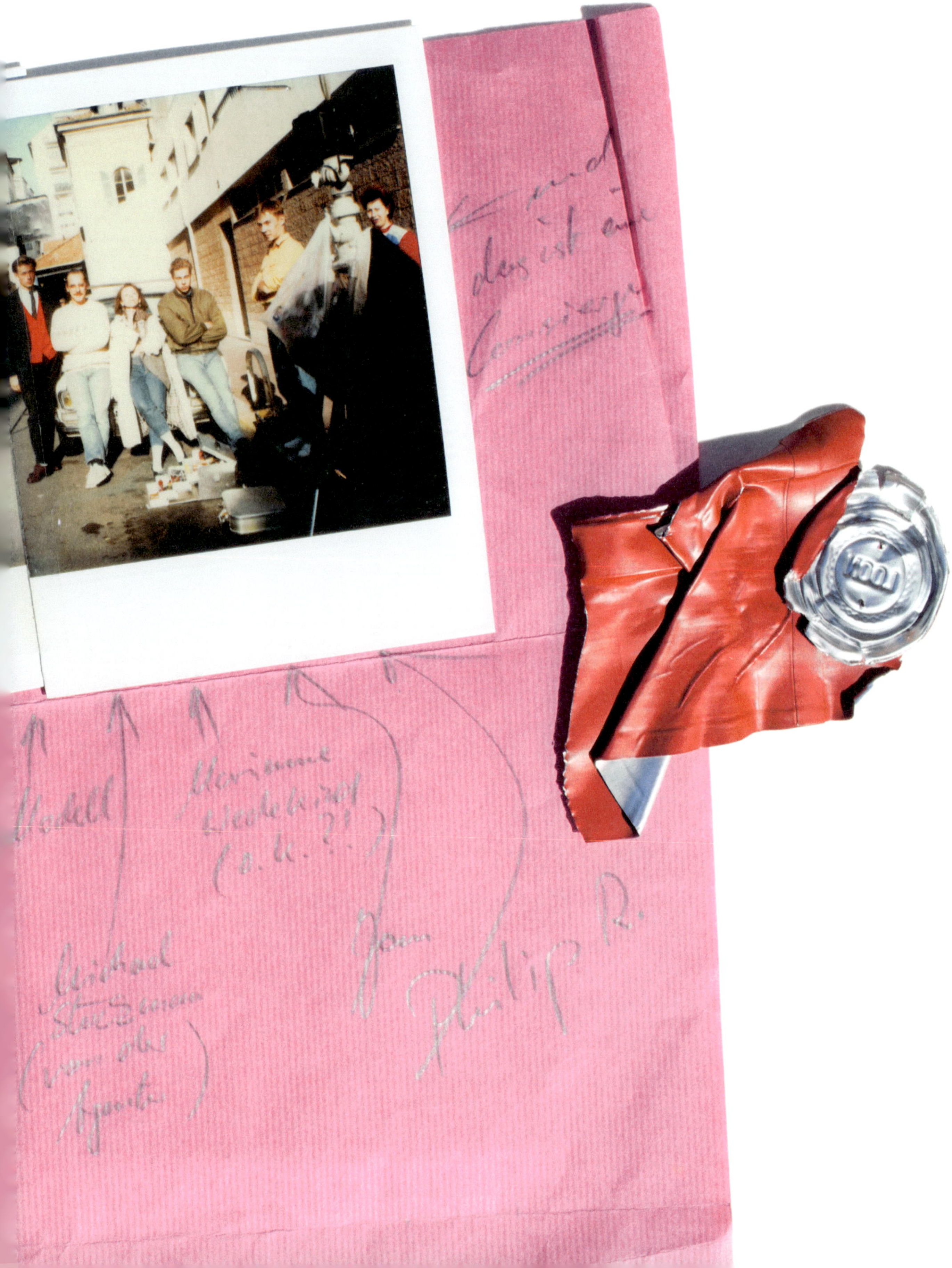
das ist eine
Philip R.

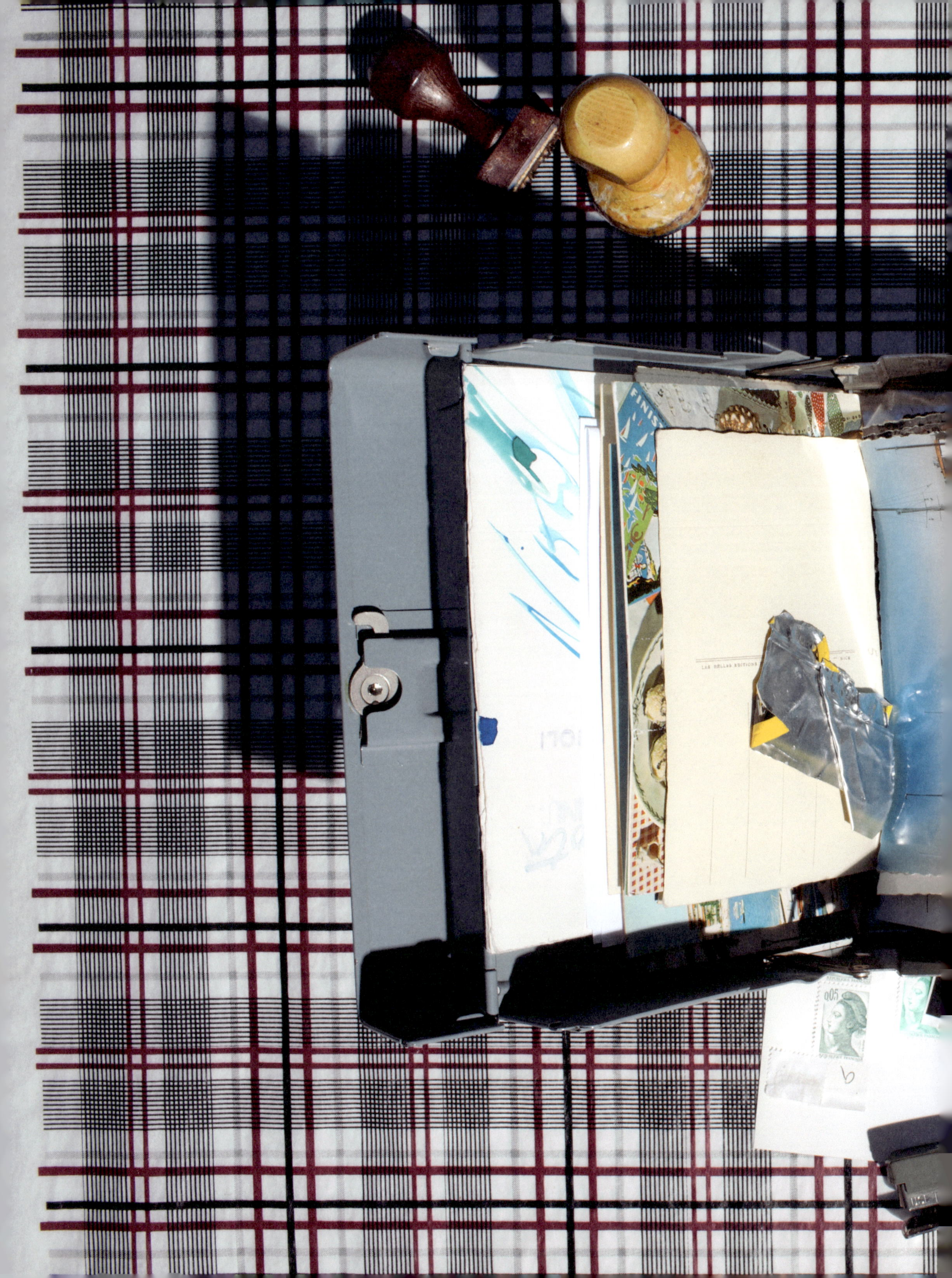

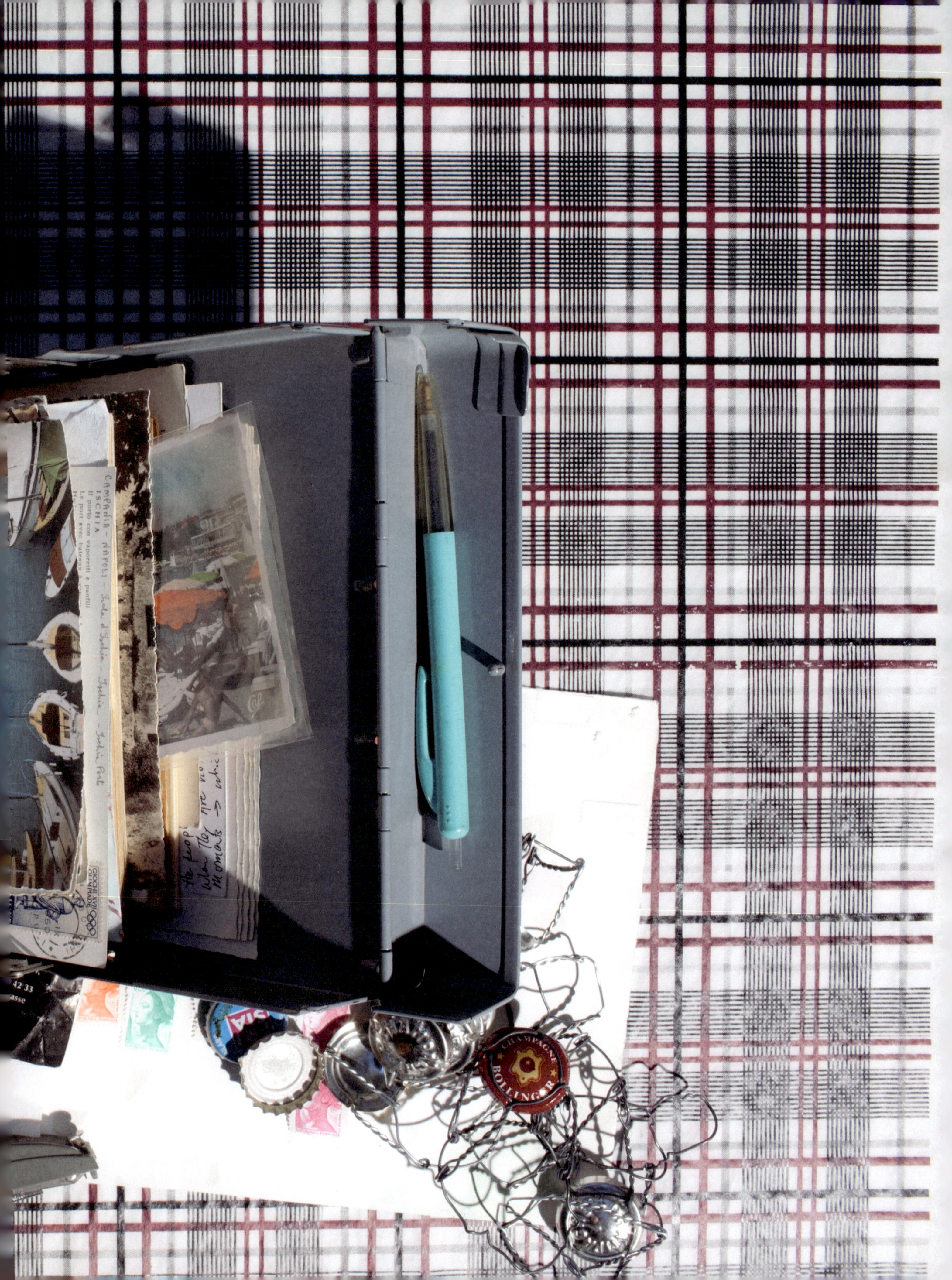
CAMPANIA - NAPOLI
ISCHIA
Il porto con vaporetti e panfili
CHAMPAGNE
BOLLINGER

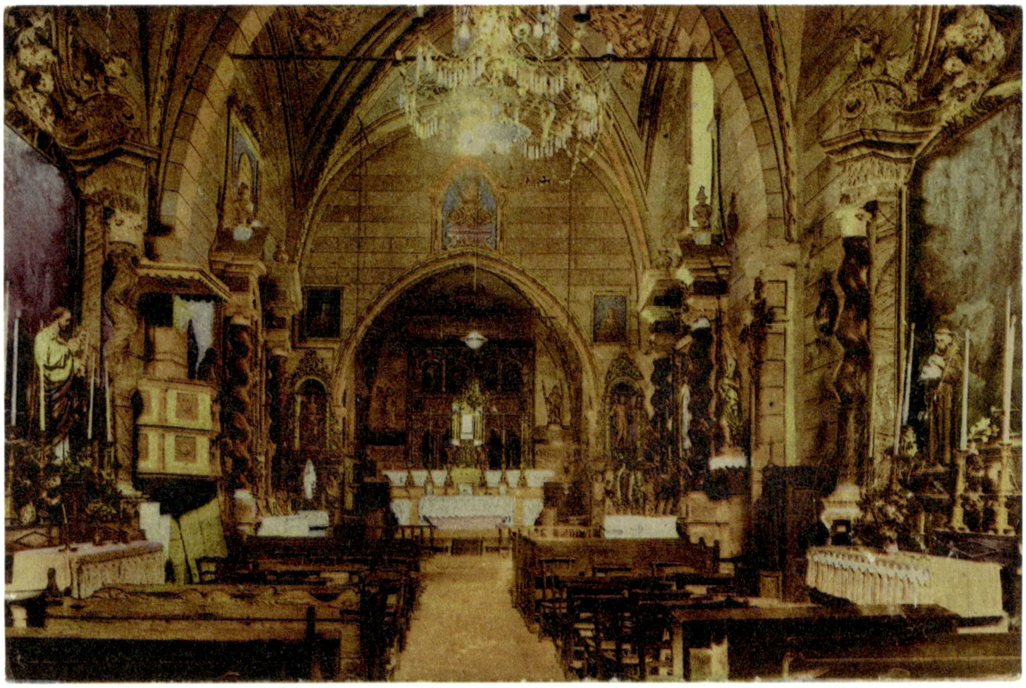

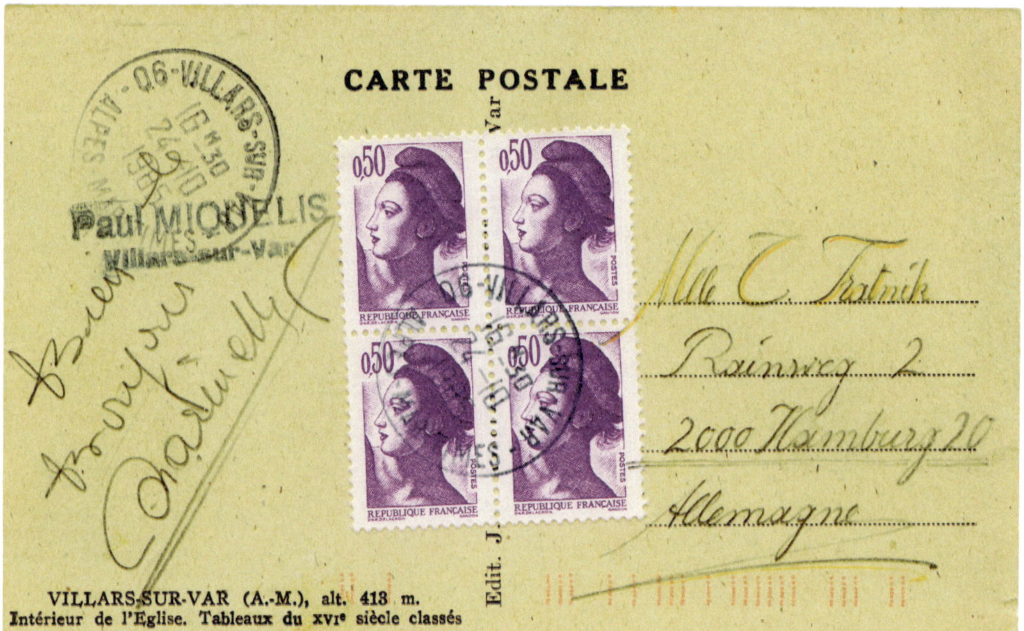

NICE
October 24th,
1985

The URGENT sticker is from Sri Lanka in 1980. The shop assistant told me that it was from the time of the English. When placed on the card, it boosted the importance of my intentions. In regards to the placement of the stamp, the post office obviously took marriage proposals very seriously.

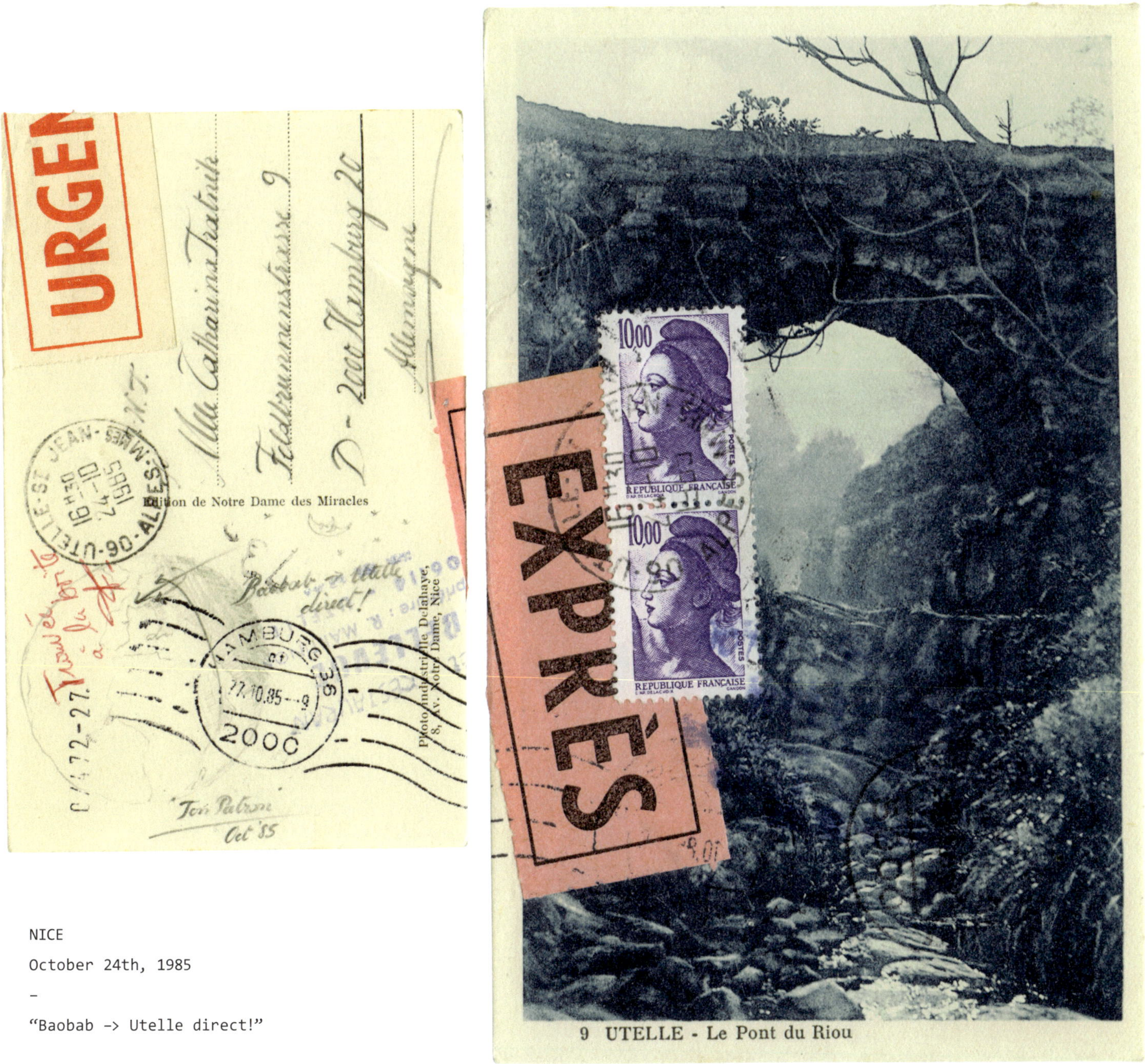

NICE
October 24th, 1985
–
“Baobab -> Utelle direct!”

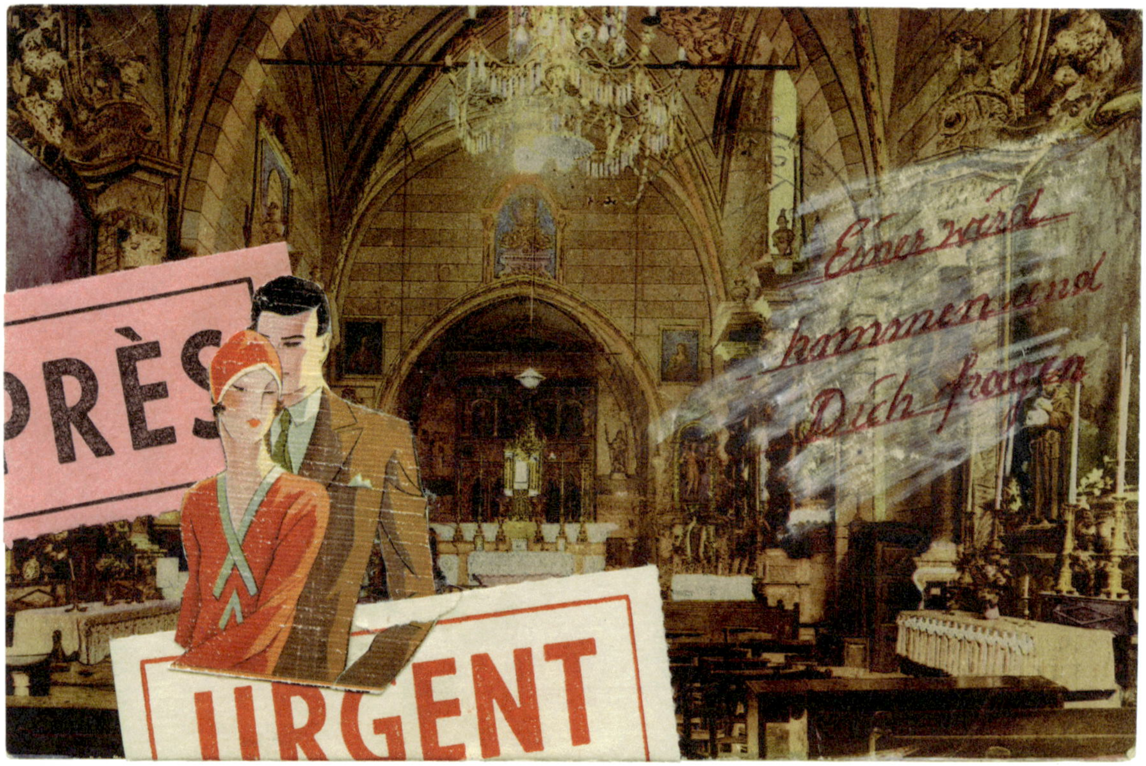

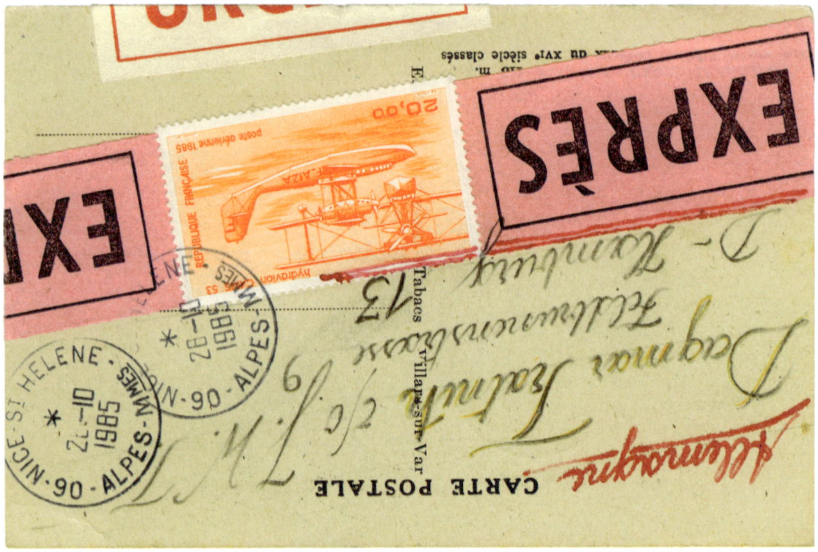

In order to communicate my feelings quicker and more directly, I always send my cards via express. The mail is delivered by car messenger as soon as it arrives at its destination. If, like now, I am to send a marriage proposal, special attention will be generated through its delivery, and I am additionally assured that the mail will reach Dagmars workplace by noon. Mobile phones don't exist yet, and calling from the local phone booth requires a great amount of change, which disappears into the machine at such a speed that makes it difficult to concentrate on anything other than constantly inserting more coins. I get married on the first of April 1986. This is cause for Dagmar's name to change from Tratnik to von Renner.

NICE
October 28th, 1985
–
"Someone will come and ask you" is a hidden marriage proposal.

A few days before Christmas, the "Little Friend's" journey continues to St. Moritz. The art director and copywriter insist on scouting the locations by themselves in advance. They go skiing for two days. With no results. The result of the photoshoot isn't noteworthy, but a beautiful postcard is created instead. We commence on the return journey at dawn of the 24th of December. Philip Radowitz drives home to his family in Paris from Hamburg in the same night. Arrival: 25th of December, 4 am.

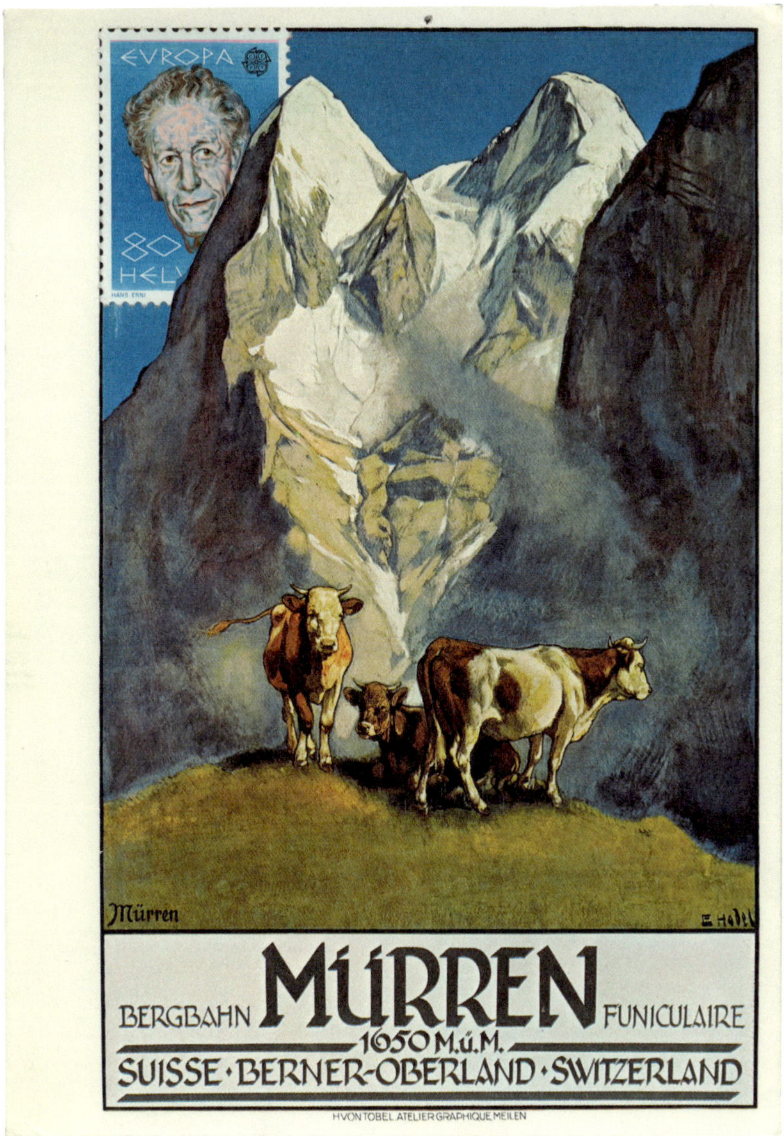

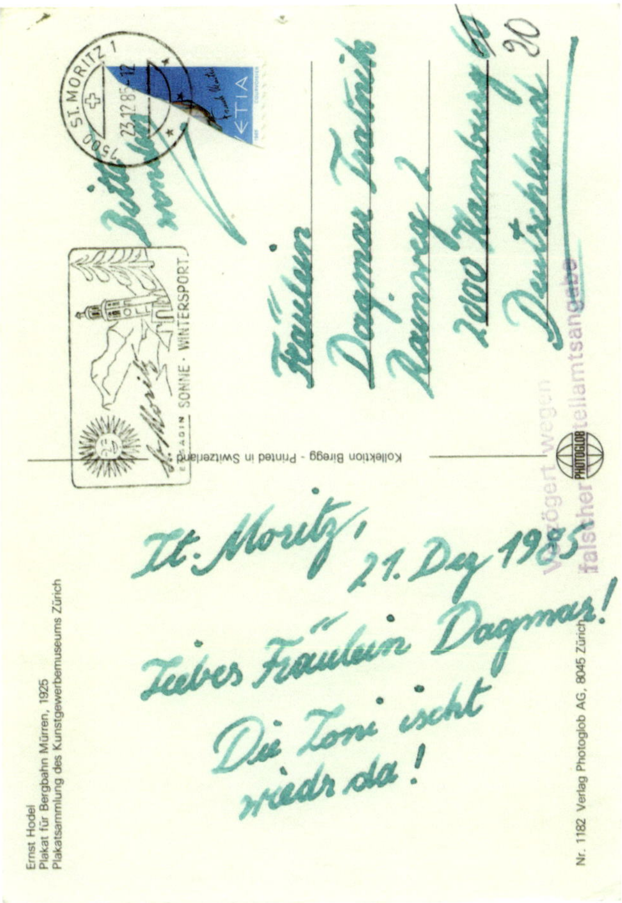

In her childhood in the Sauerland, Dagmar had her own cow named Loni. Of course, the term Fräulein was no longer in use at this time.

ST. MORITZ
December 21st, 1985
–
Dear Fräulein Dagmar
Loni has returned!

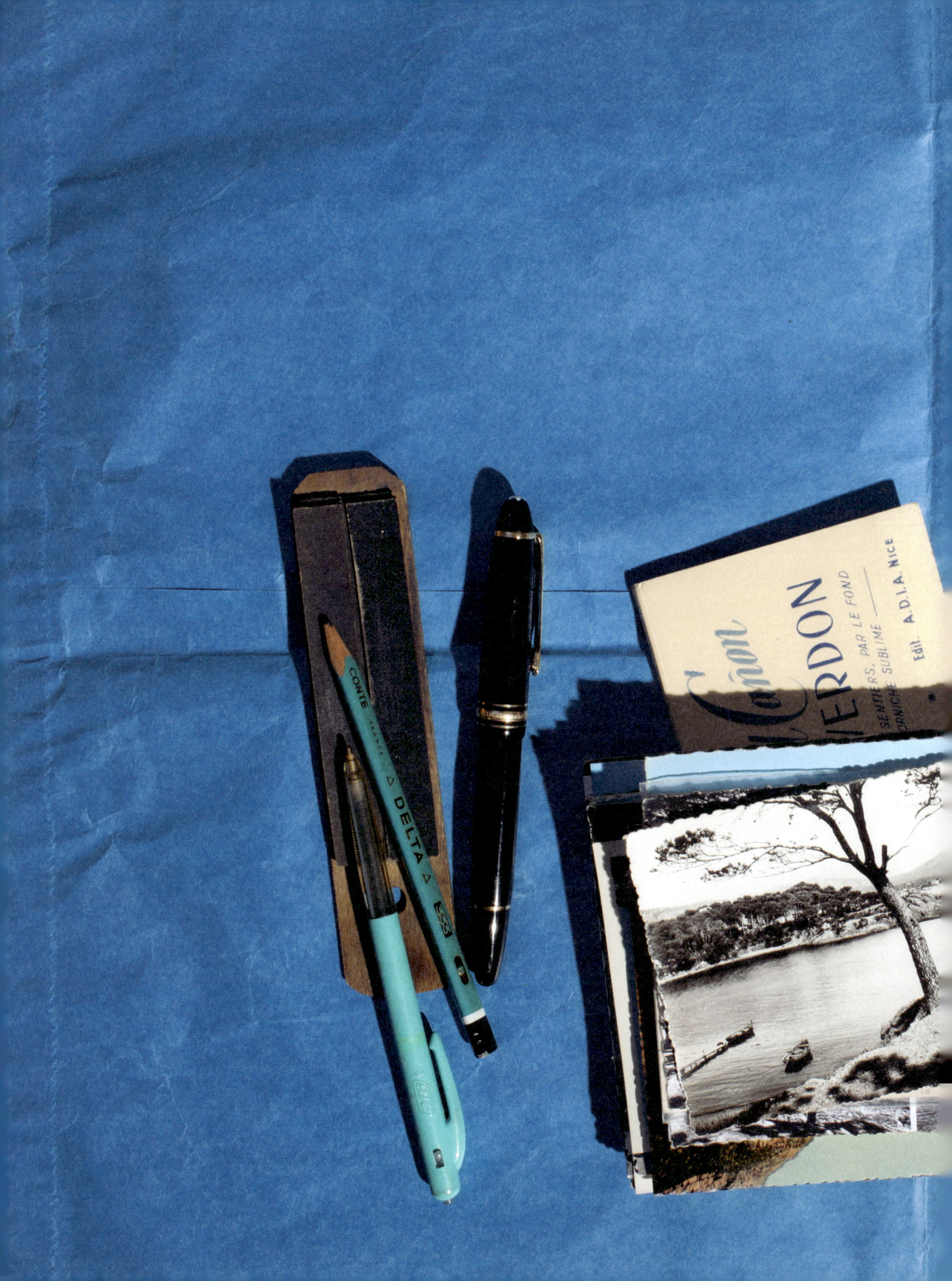
CONTE
DELTA
ERDON
SENTIERS. PAR LE FOND
ORNICHE SUBLIME
Edit. A.D.I.A. NICE

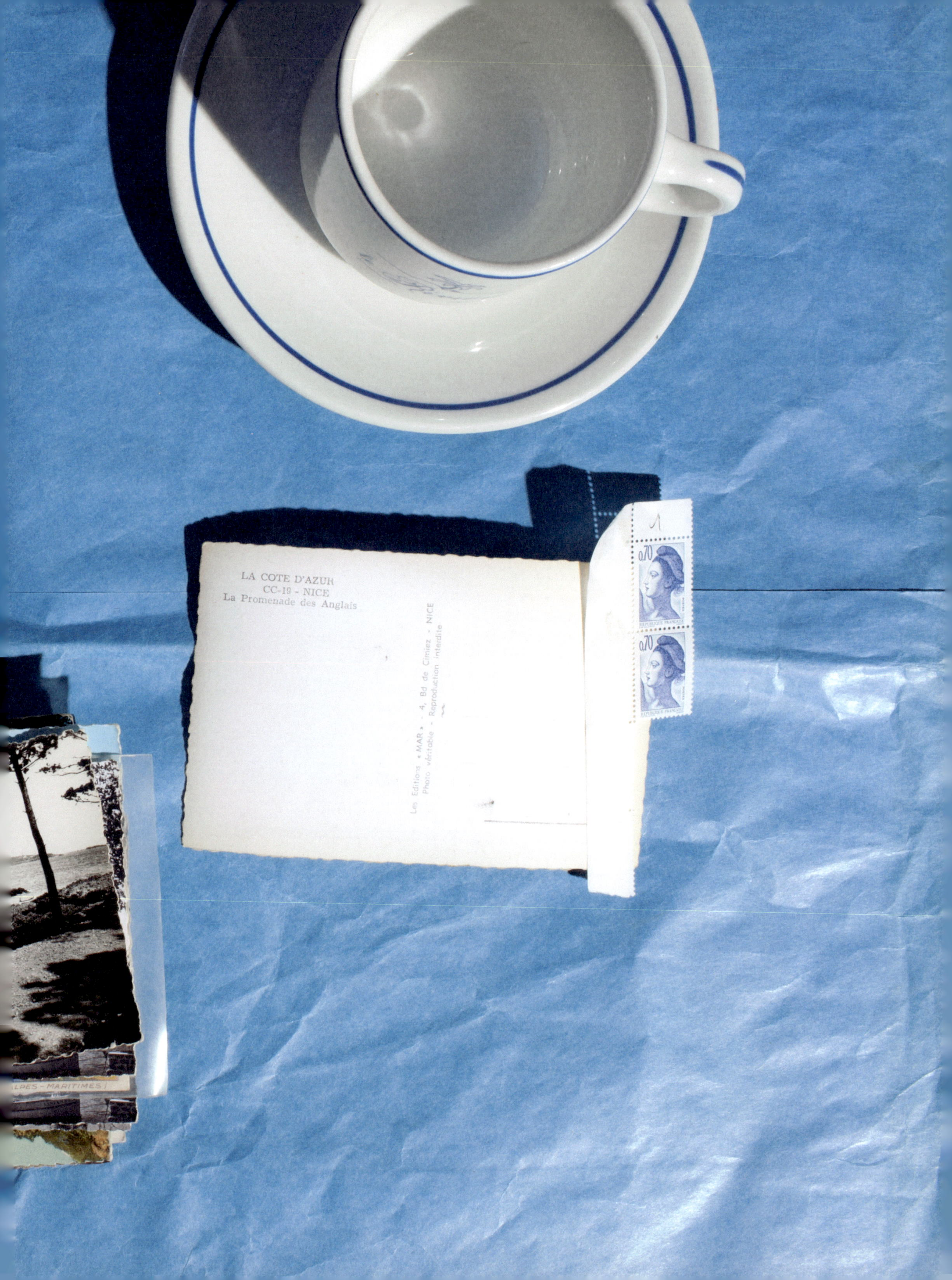
LA COTE D'AZUR
CC-19 - NICE
La Promenade des Anglais
Les Editions « MAR » - 4, Bd de Cimiez - NICE
Photo véritable - Reproduction interdite
0,70
0,70

Who even knows the orginals?

At the beginning of our trip for Pirelli, I find these cards at a random kiosk, showing classic press photos of internationally known actors (now known as celebrities), who had come to the Côte d'Azur for the film festival or their holidays. I immediately come up with the idea of turning them into fake autographs, because the pictures have such an appeal to them. After I've sent them all, we're sitting in Saint-Paul-de-Vence, where the singer and actor Yves Montand owns a café. I find a portrait of him at the bar, which completes my postcard series. He walks in while I'm in the middle of forging his signature. My art director is delighted, and prompts me to get an original autograph. He doesn't get my absurd interest in forgery.

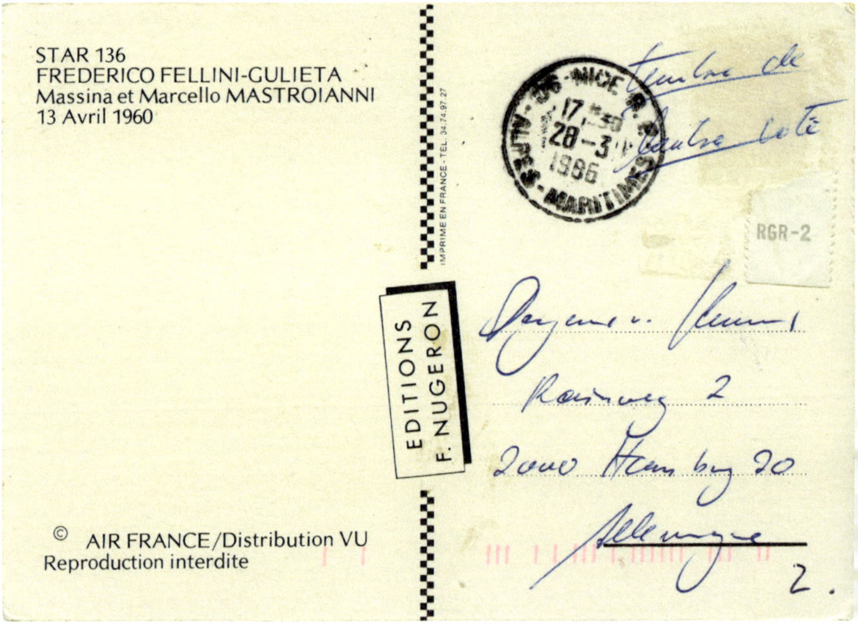

NICE
March 28th, 1986

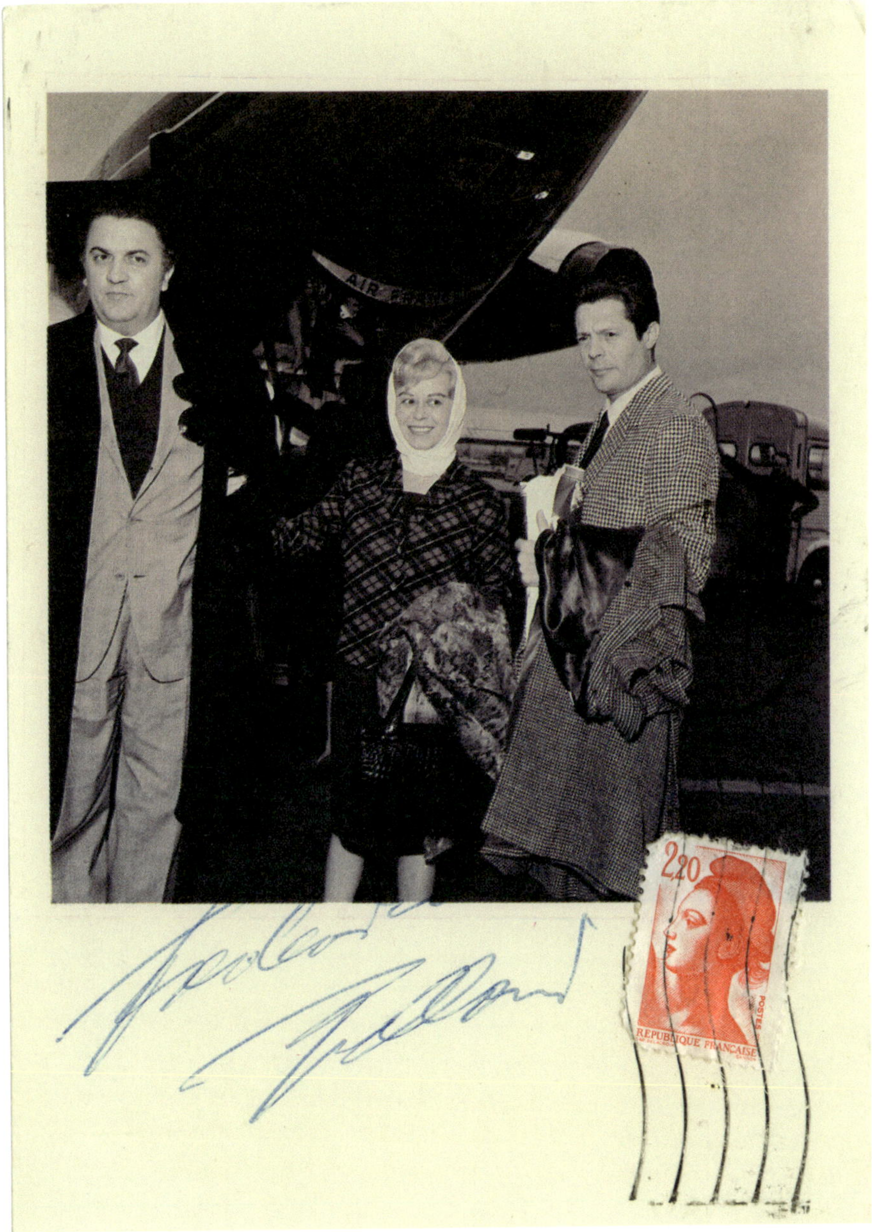

Federico Fellini, Giulietta Masina,
Marcello Mastroianni

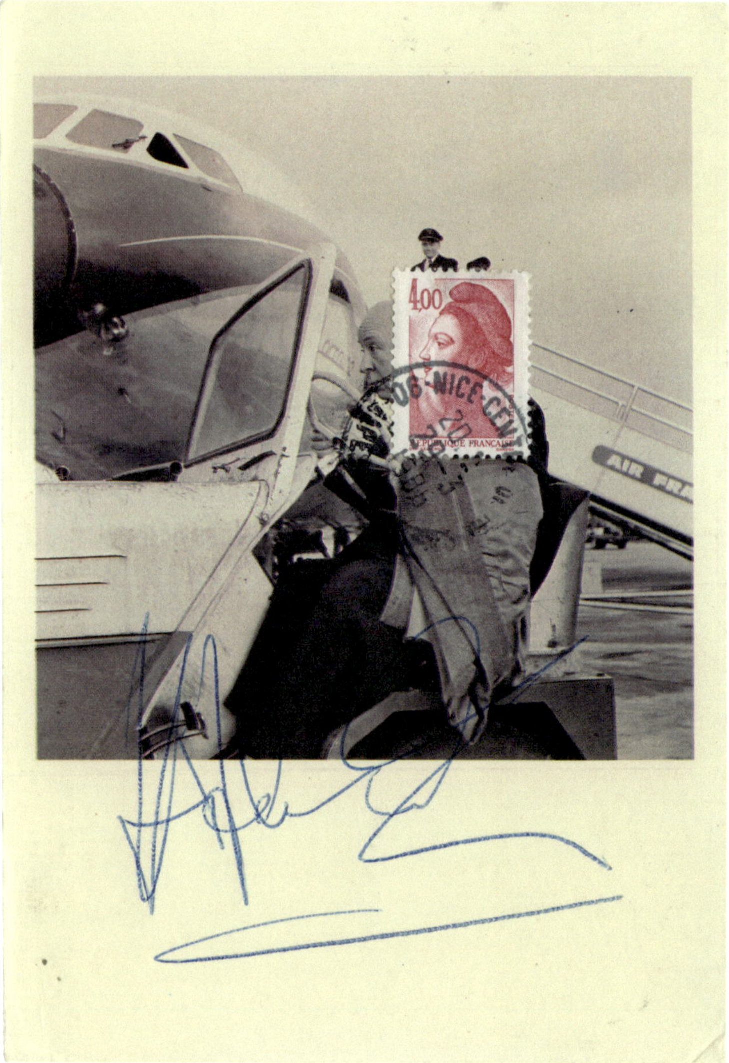

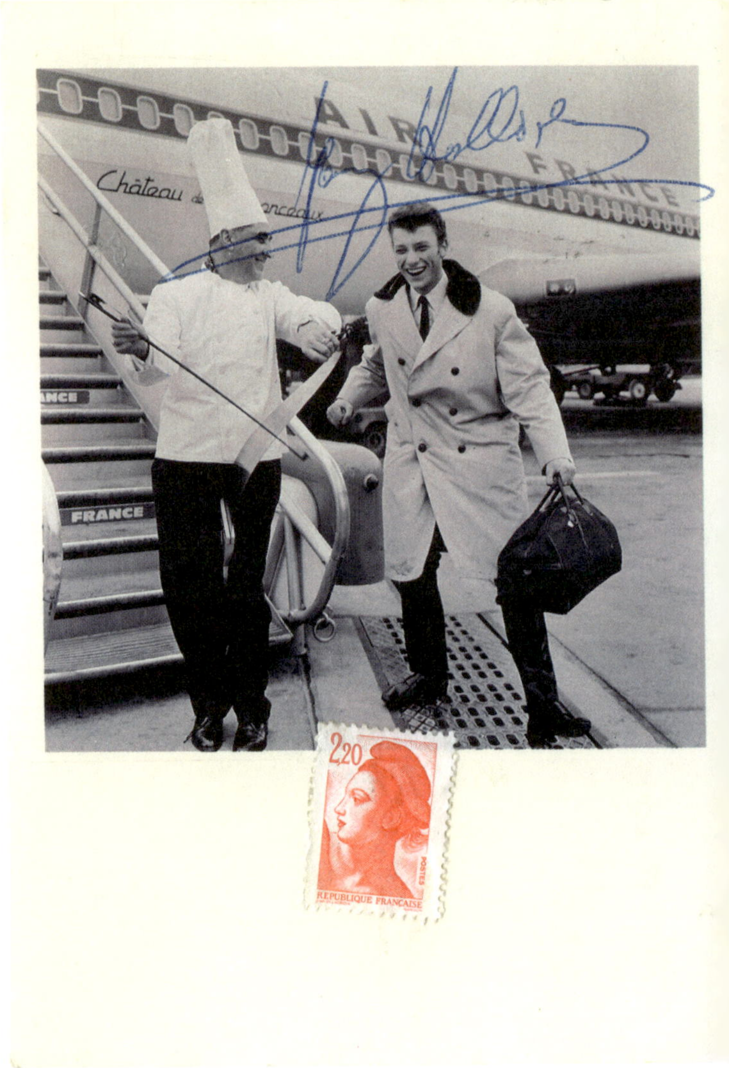

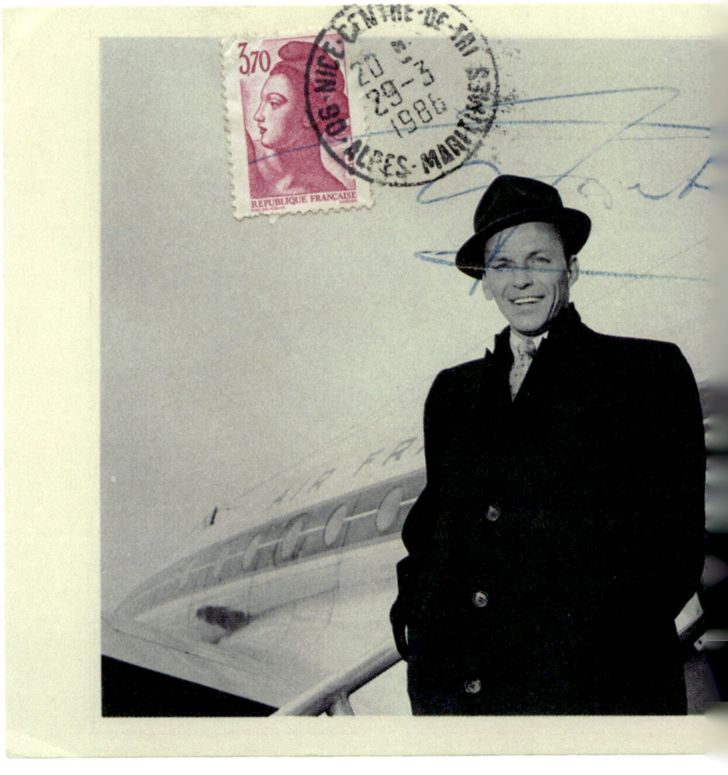

NICE

September 28th, 1986

-

From left to right

Alfred Hitchcock

Johnny Halliday

Duke Ellington

Frank Sinatra

Audrey Hepburn

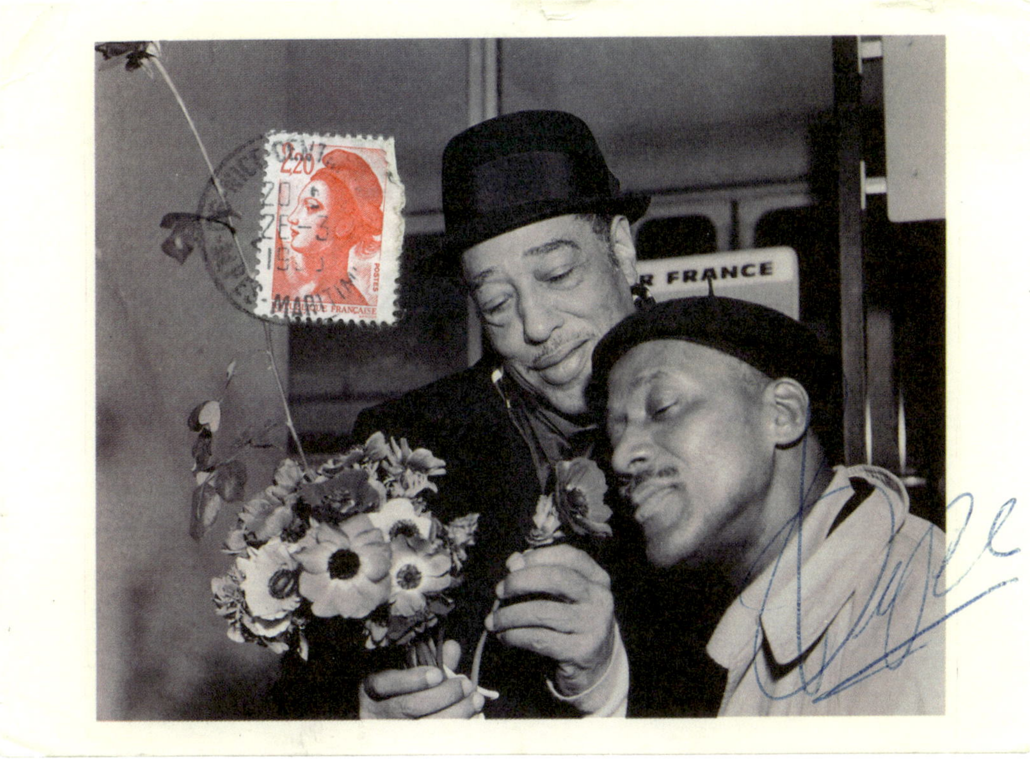

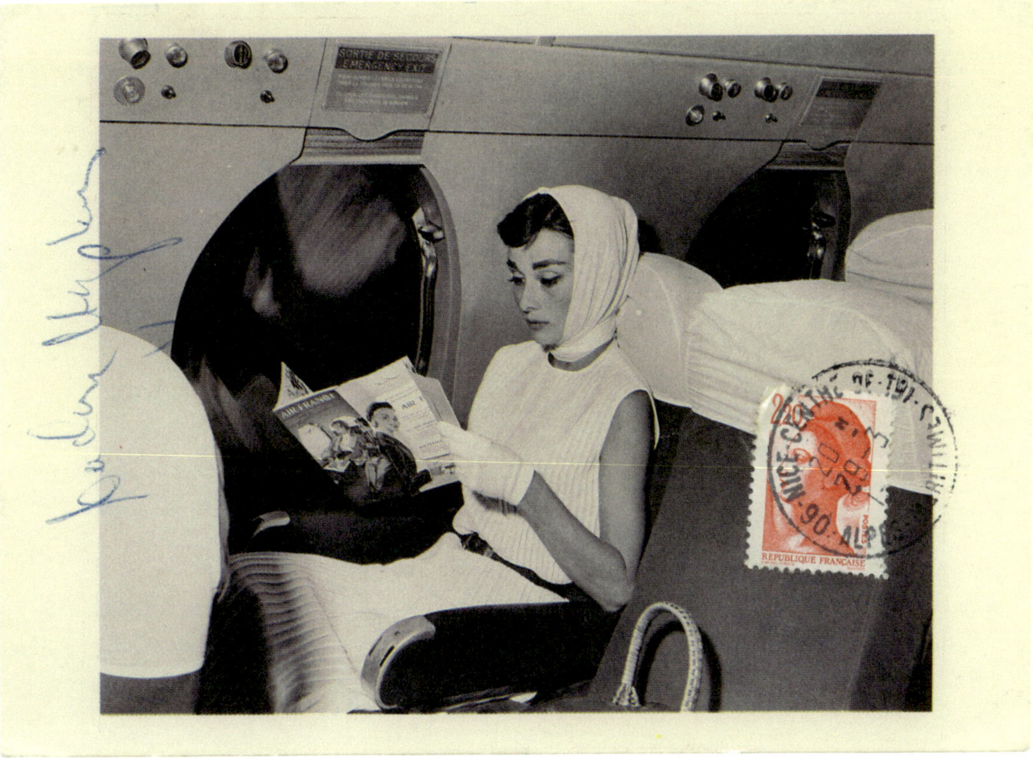

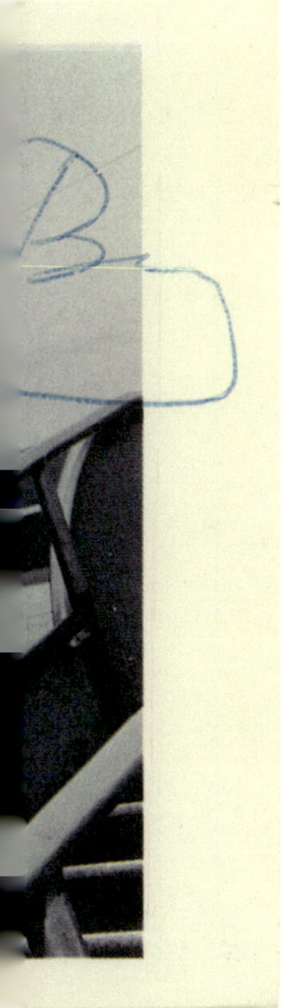

All signatures are purely fictitious.
But how many people know the real ones anyway?

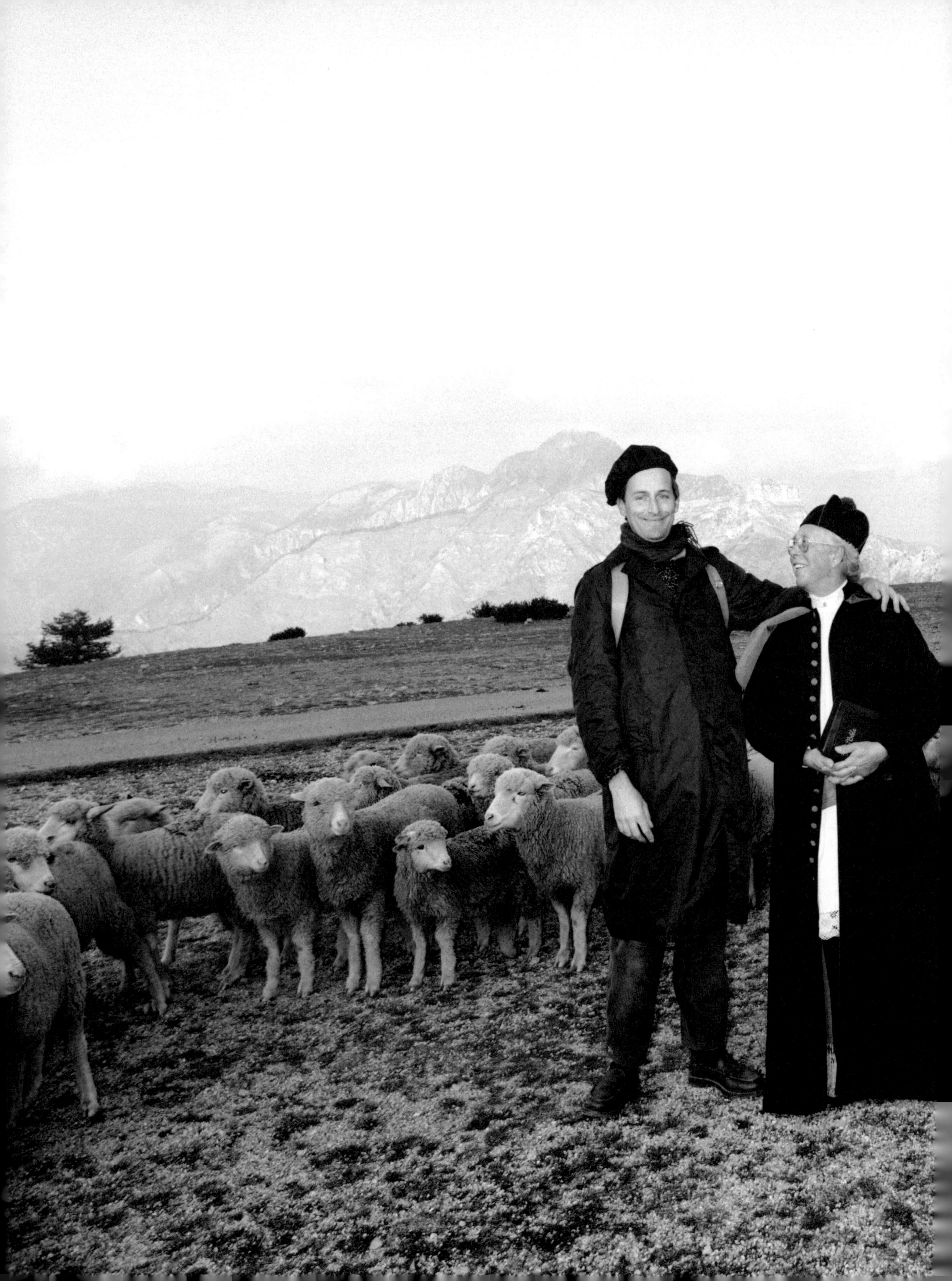

We start shooting the legendary Pirelli campaign here in 1986. One motif shows a priest walking past 200 sheep, with a church in the background, on a spinning tyre. The headline reads: "Sunday morning. Faster than the devil. On Pirelli." The priest is Mr. Schmitz, restaurateur from around the corner from our office in Hamburg. Most protagonists are so-called amateur models that we cast ourselves.

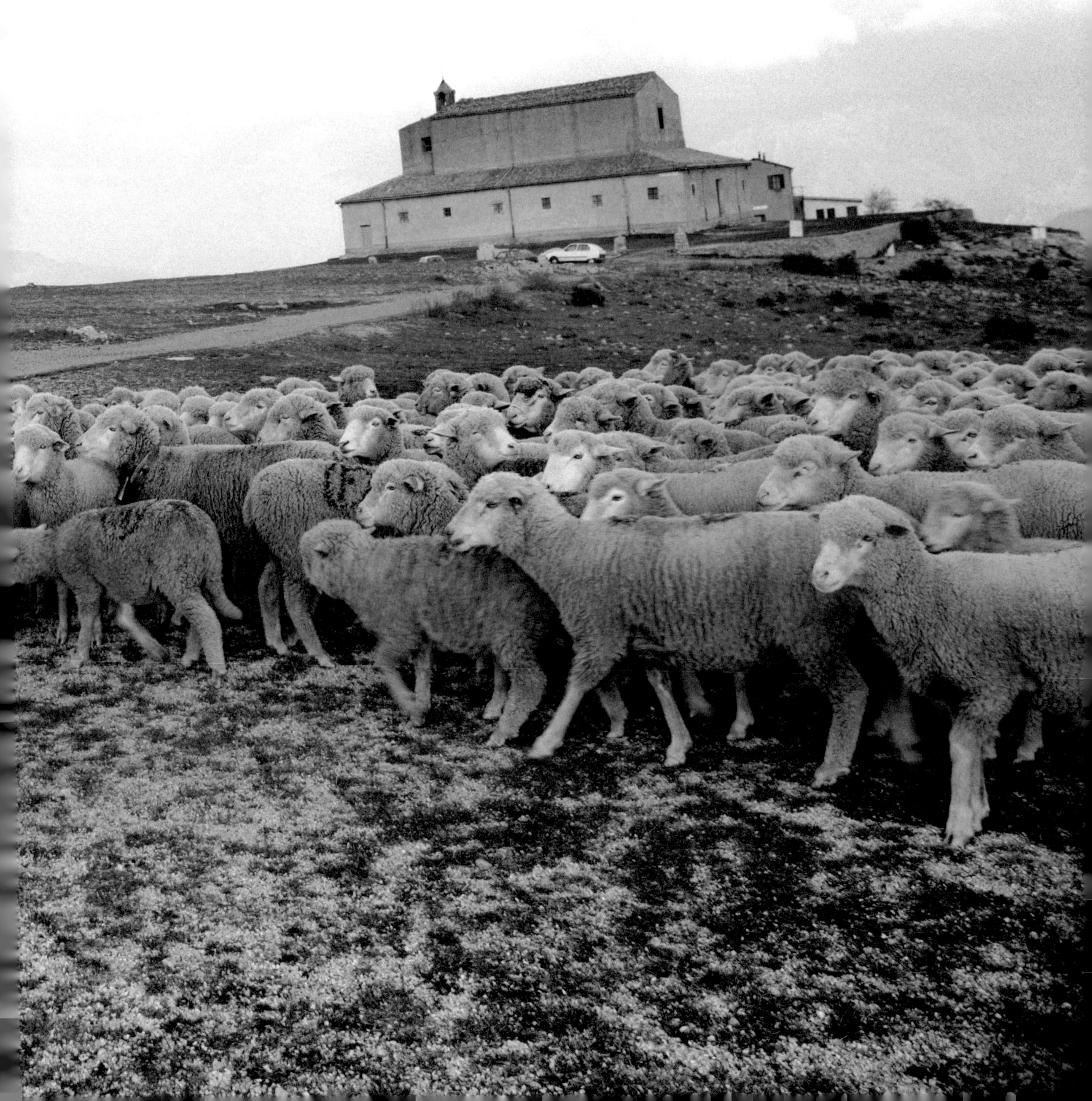

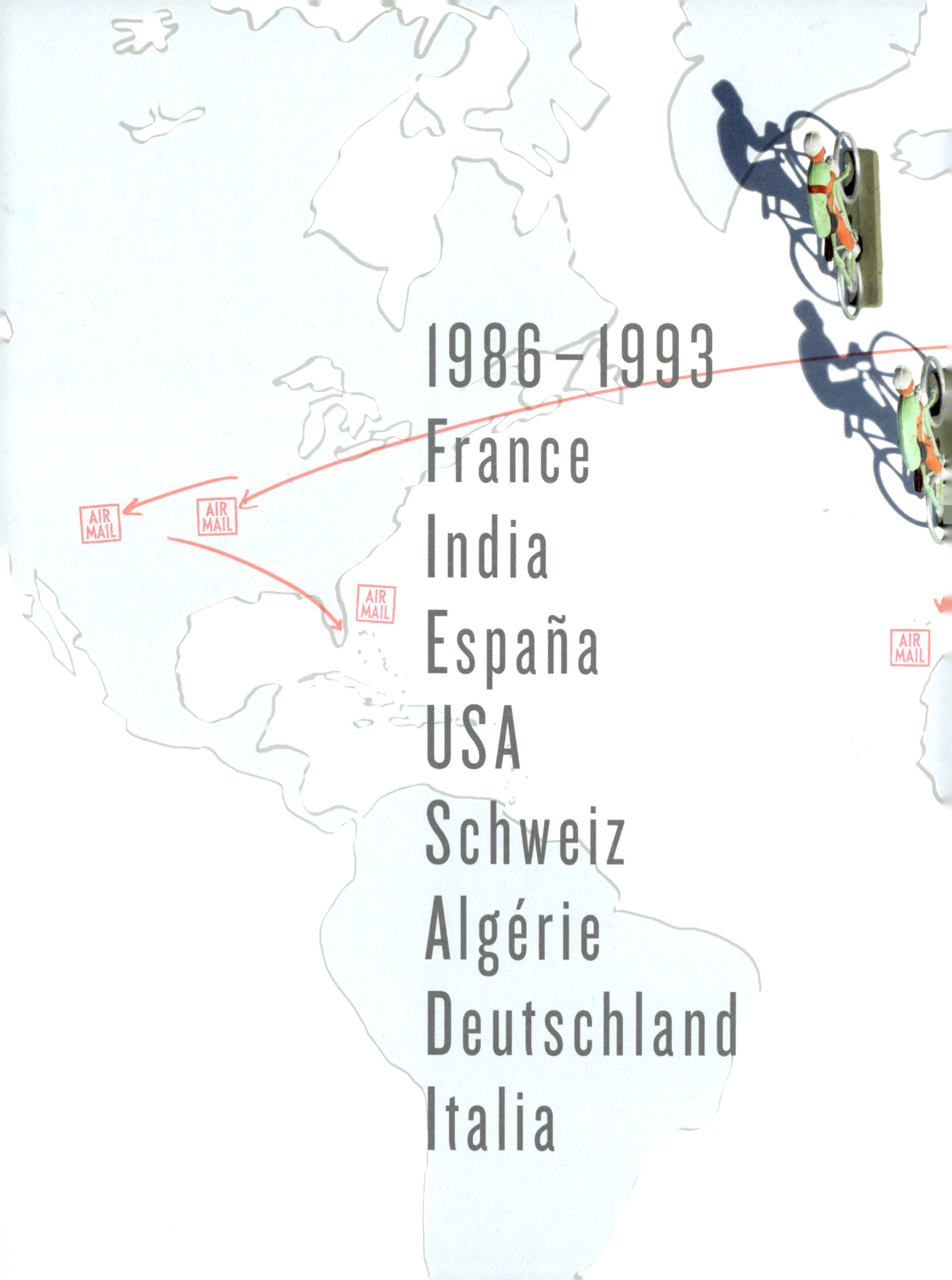

1986–1993

France
India
España
USA
Schweiz
Algérie
Deutschland
Italia

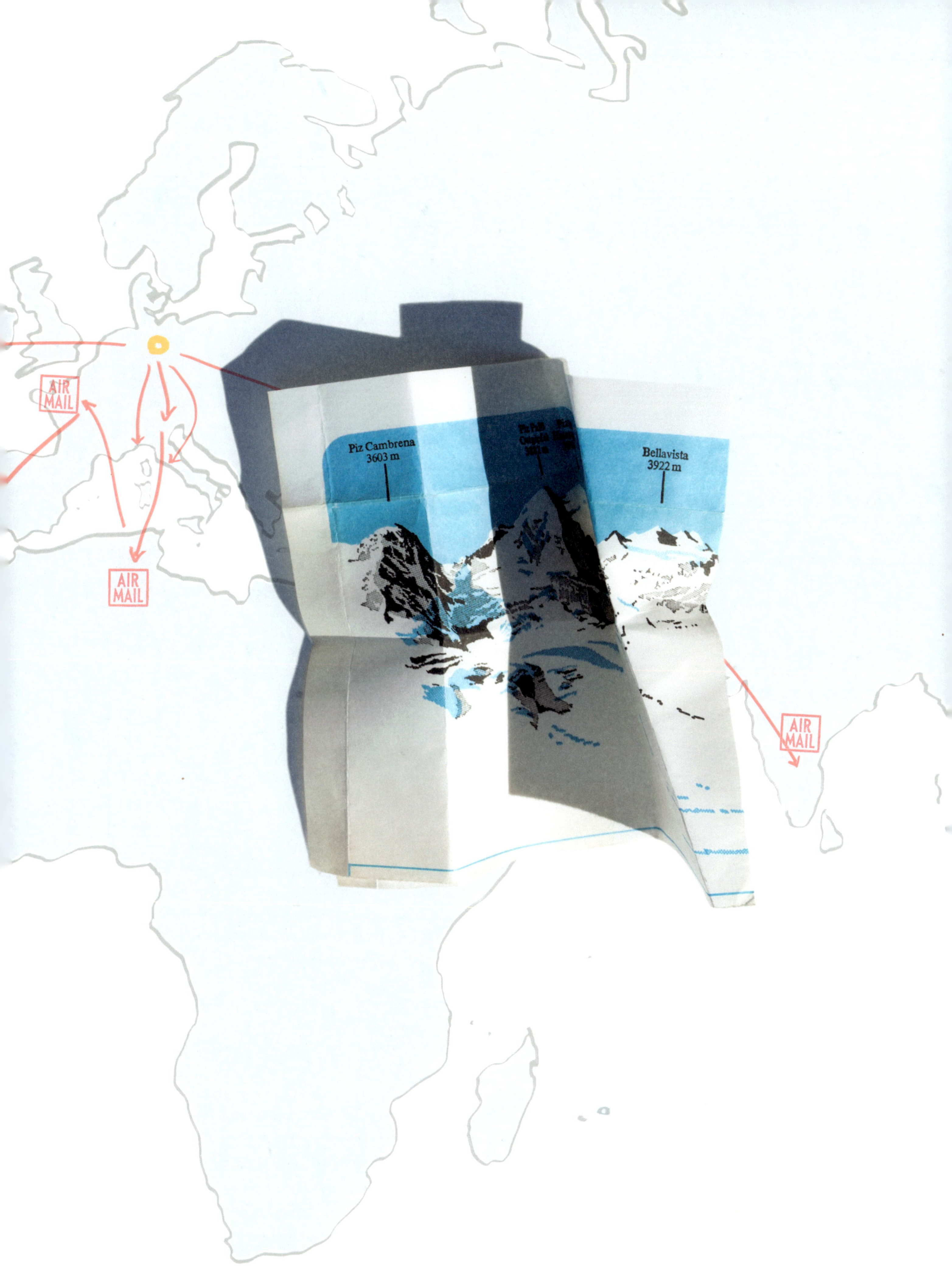
AIR MAIL
AIR MAIL
Piz Cambrena
3603 m
Bellavista
3922 m
AIR MAIL

That night "The Man with the Golden Gun" is running on the hotel TV again. I have now been married for half a year.

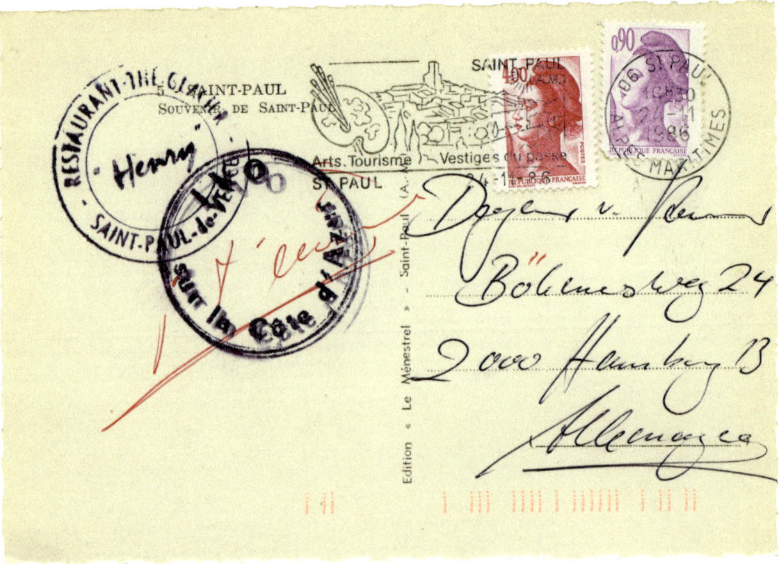

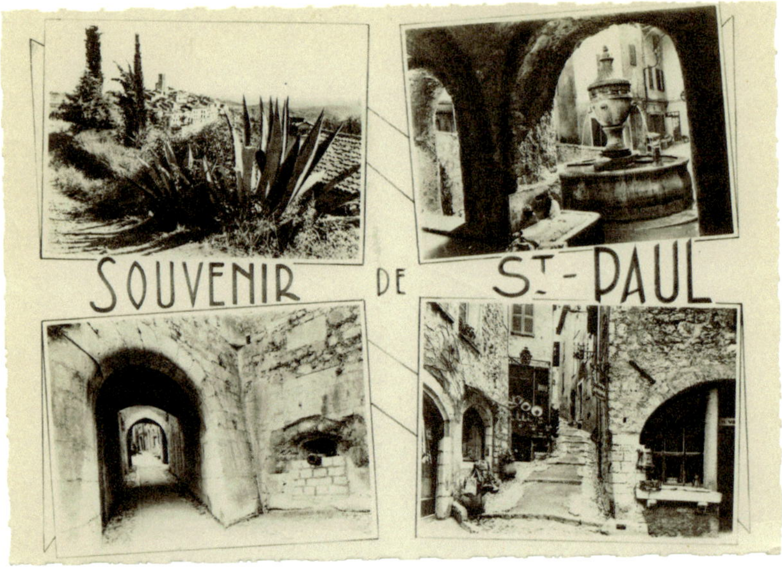

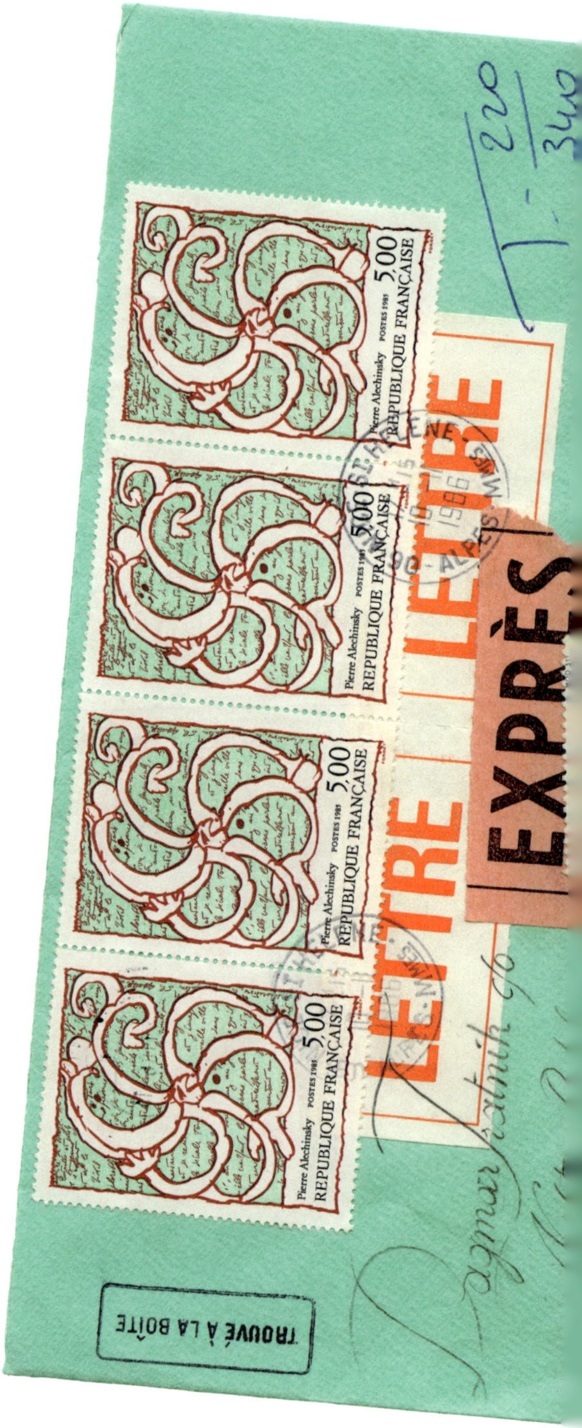

SAINT-PAUL
November 24th, 1984
–
"Je t'aime"

Next to a declaration of love, the card is additionally furnished with the stamp of our little restaurant in Saint-Paul.

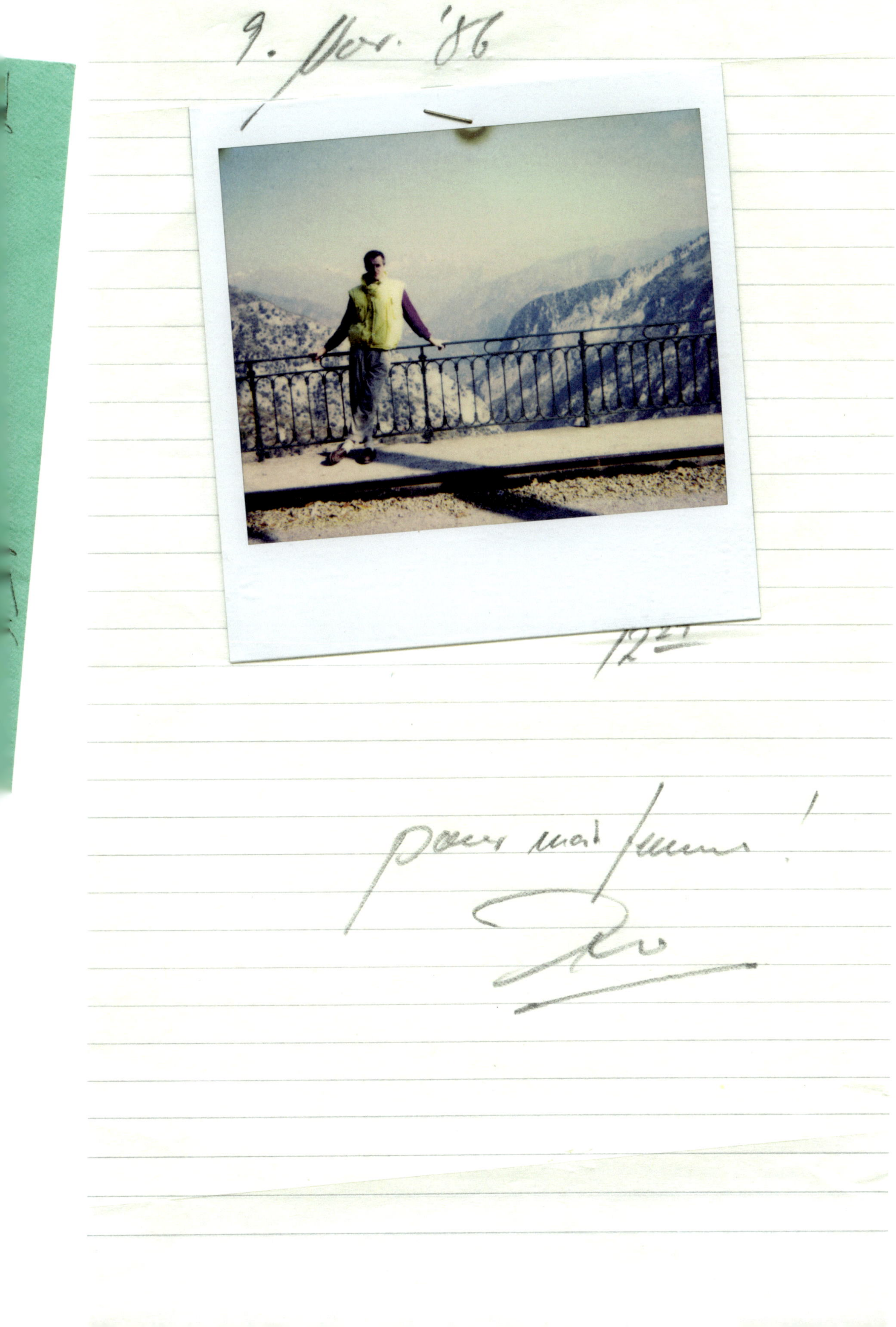
9. Nov. '86

A short smoking break.

A cigarette company brings us back to Nice in the spring. Due to the bad weather conditions, we have coffee in a secluded café/bar in the mountains. A classic time to spread out all my design tools across a table in an unfrequented place. They sell Gorges-du-Loup cards here. One card is three francs. The shown booklet is 10 F. I shop generously, and ask for a receipt. When we return the next day, the cards cost 20 F. When I finally decide to buy a book of postcards on the day of the photo shoot, the price has been raised to 100 F. I doubt that any tourist will buy a card there.

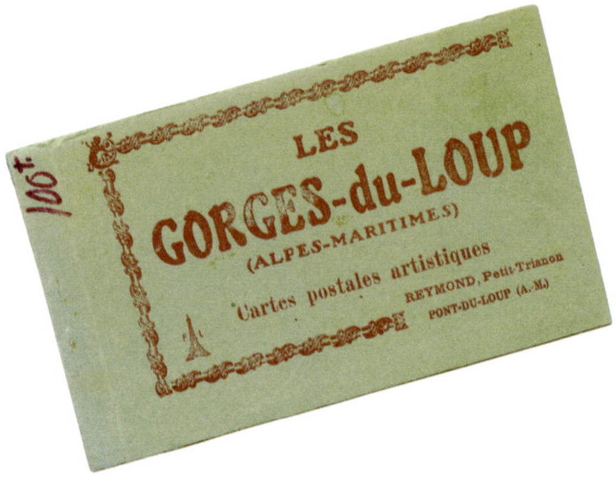

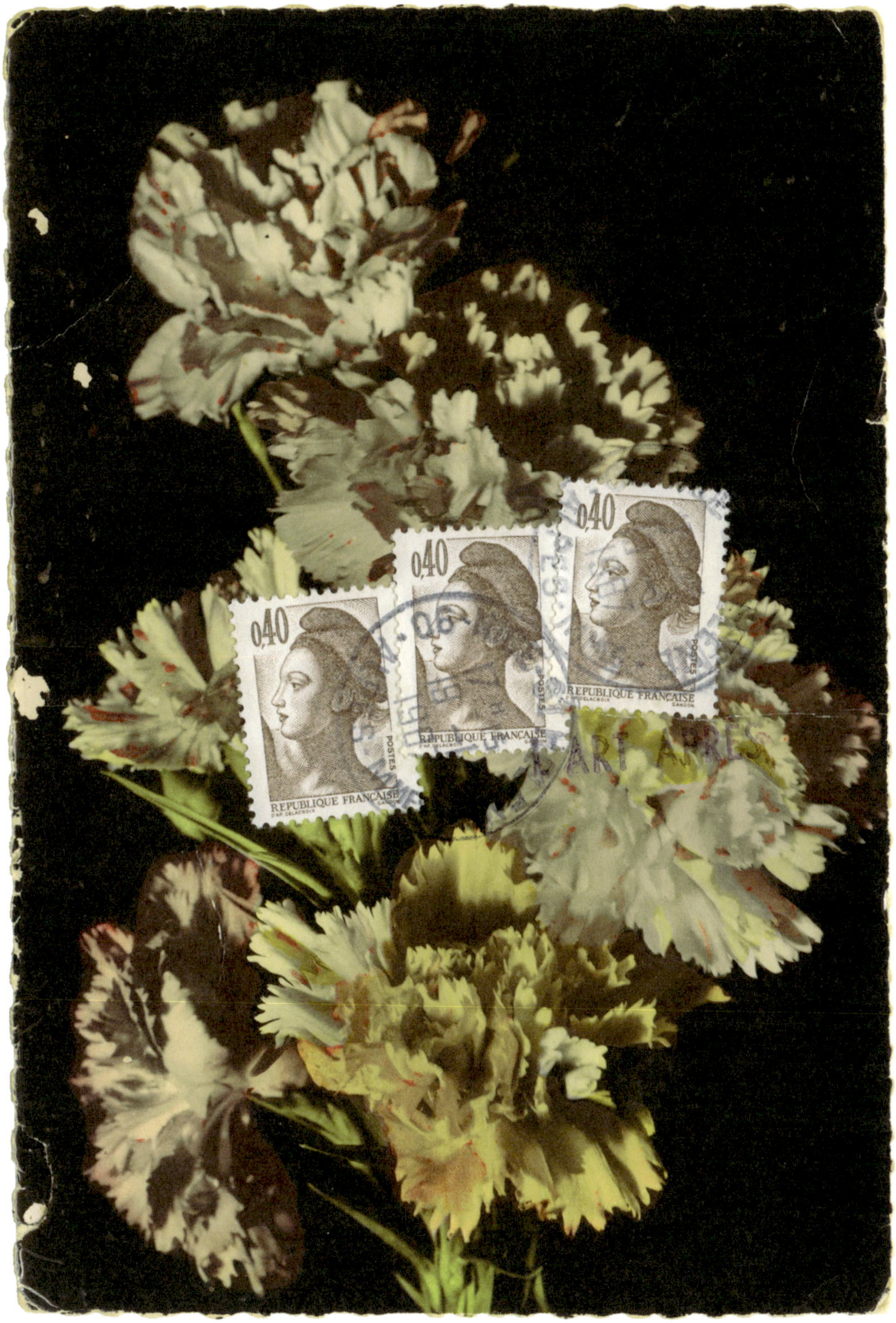

NICE
January 19th,
1987

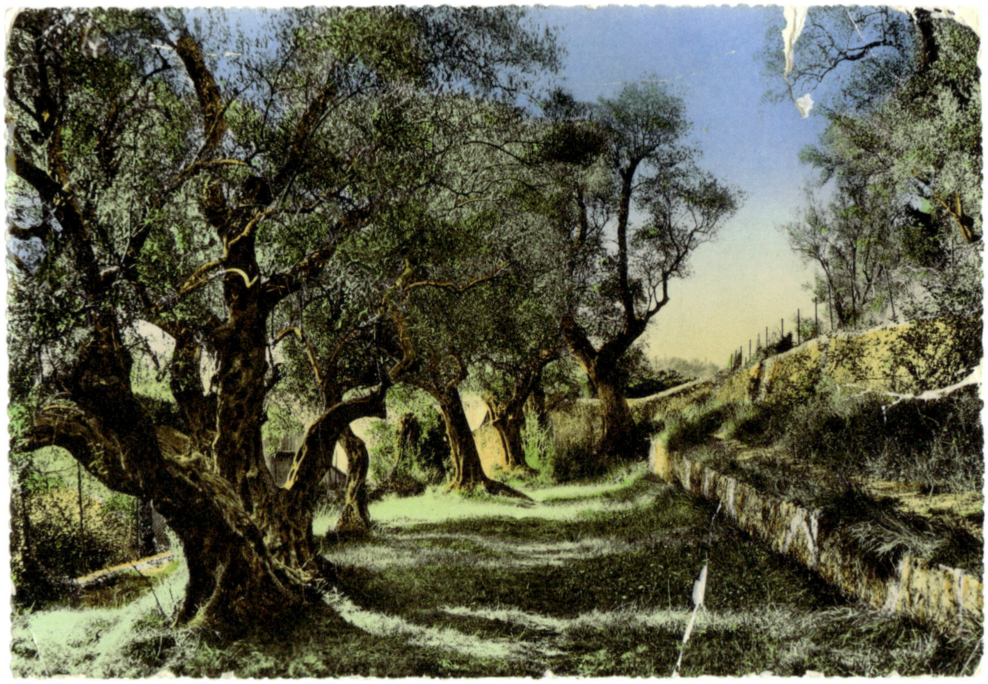

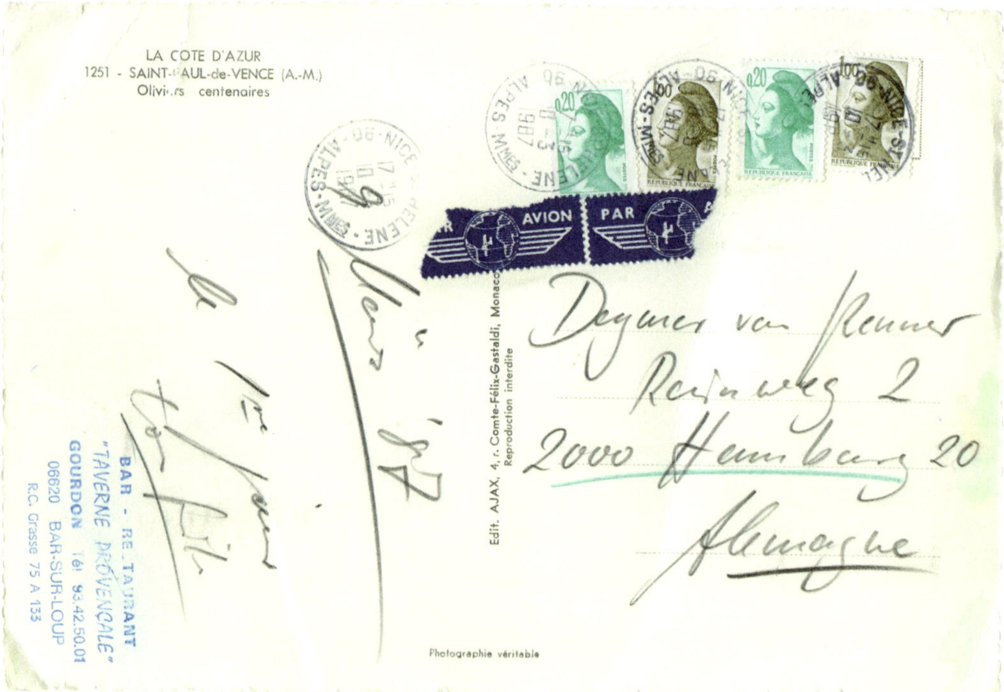

NICE

March 9th, 1987

–

“le 1er jour, ton fils”

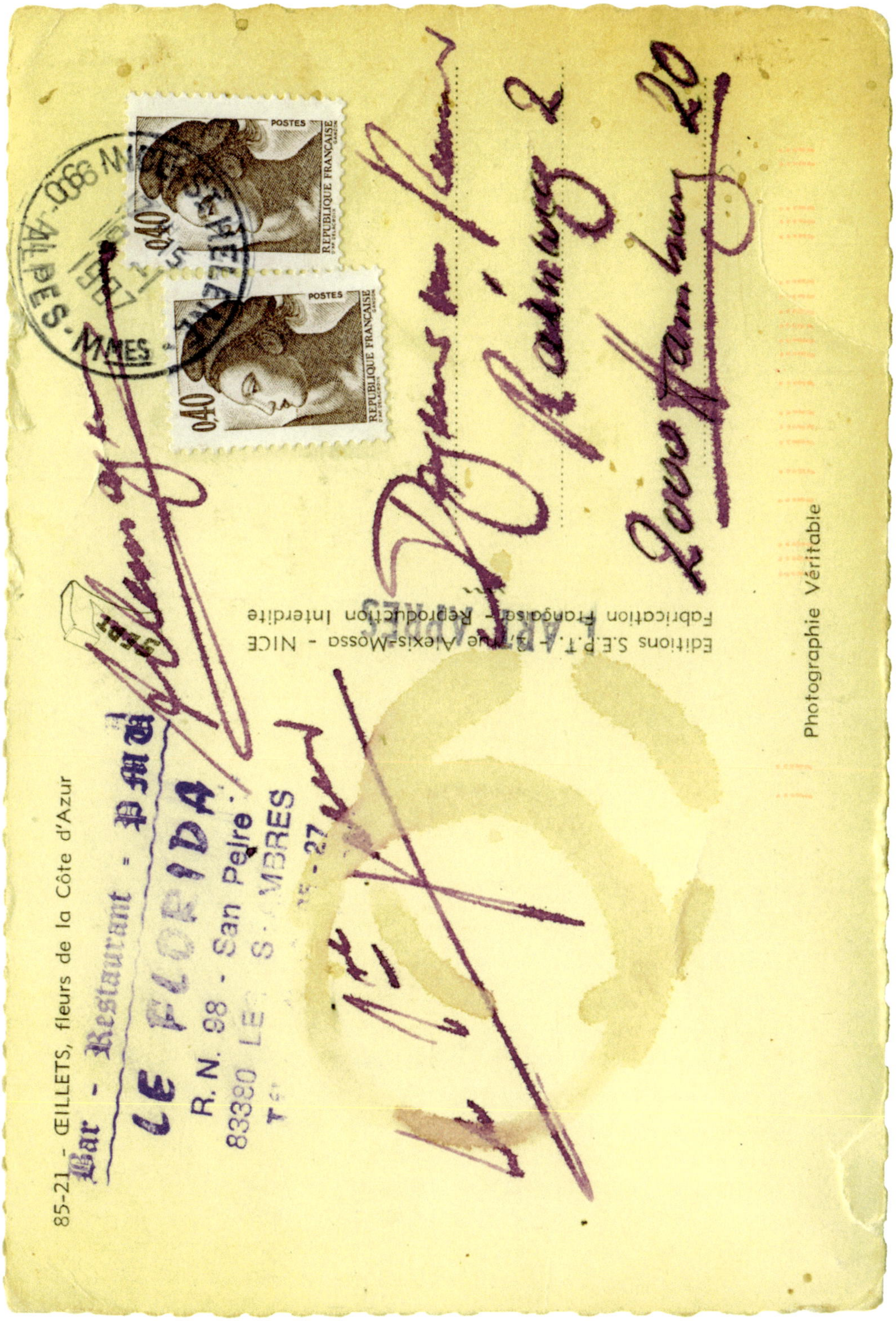

NICE

January 19th, 1987

–

“Le 1er jour”

Yes Madam, Sir!

In the coffee shop of the four star hotel we are staying at in New Delhi, which has not been renovated since the withdrawal of the English, neither in the bathrooms nor the sleeping area, we order freshly squeezed orange juice for breakfast. I am constantly addressed as "Madam, sorry sir", and after repeating my request three times, as well as taking written note, the young waiter leaves our table saying „Yes, madam". After ordering at the bar, he walks to a neighbouring restaurant and returns around 15 minutes later, carrying oranges. Another 15 minutes pass before the fresh juice is brought to the table. "Your orange juice, sir – madam – sir". We had ordered two juices. But there is only one. – "Two orange juice, madam – sir? Yes sir" – He leaves, taking the orange juice with him. After a discussion at the bar, the juice is poured back into the carafe and the glass is washed by hand. After around 50 minutes, we finally have two juices. We are the only guests here, except for four Czech railway engineers, wearing baggy grey suits and unbuttoned whitish shirts.

»
We return to Nice in February of 1987, then continue to New Delhi in India, and then back to Nice, where a long campaign for Nissan lets the sun shine on my face.
«

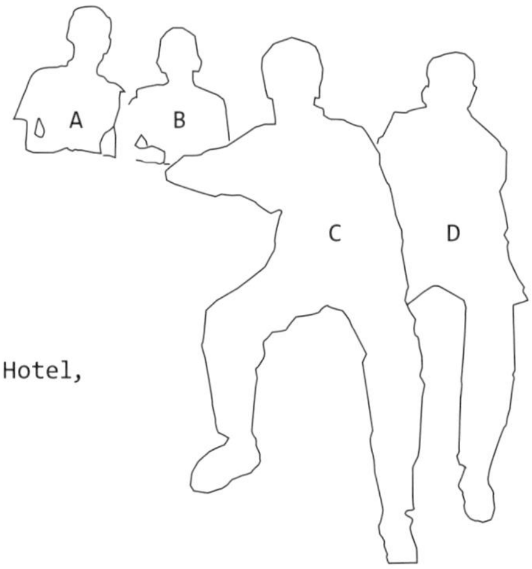

NEW DELHI
Bar of the Imperial Hotel,
February 1987

A Waiter 1
B Waiter 2
C Me
D Assistant Thomas Lemker

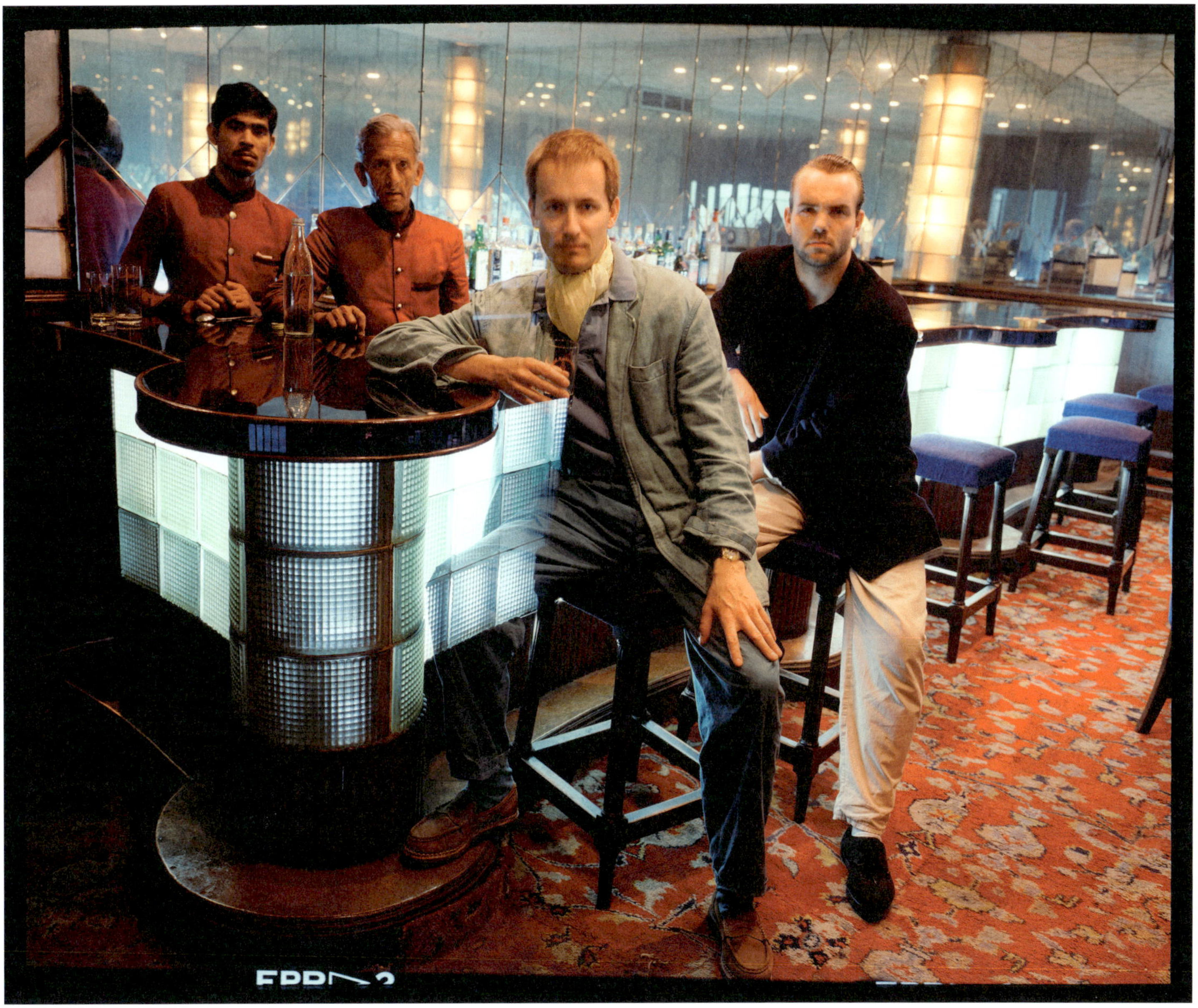

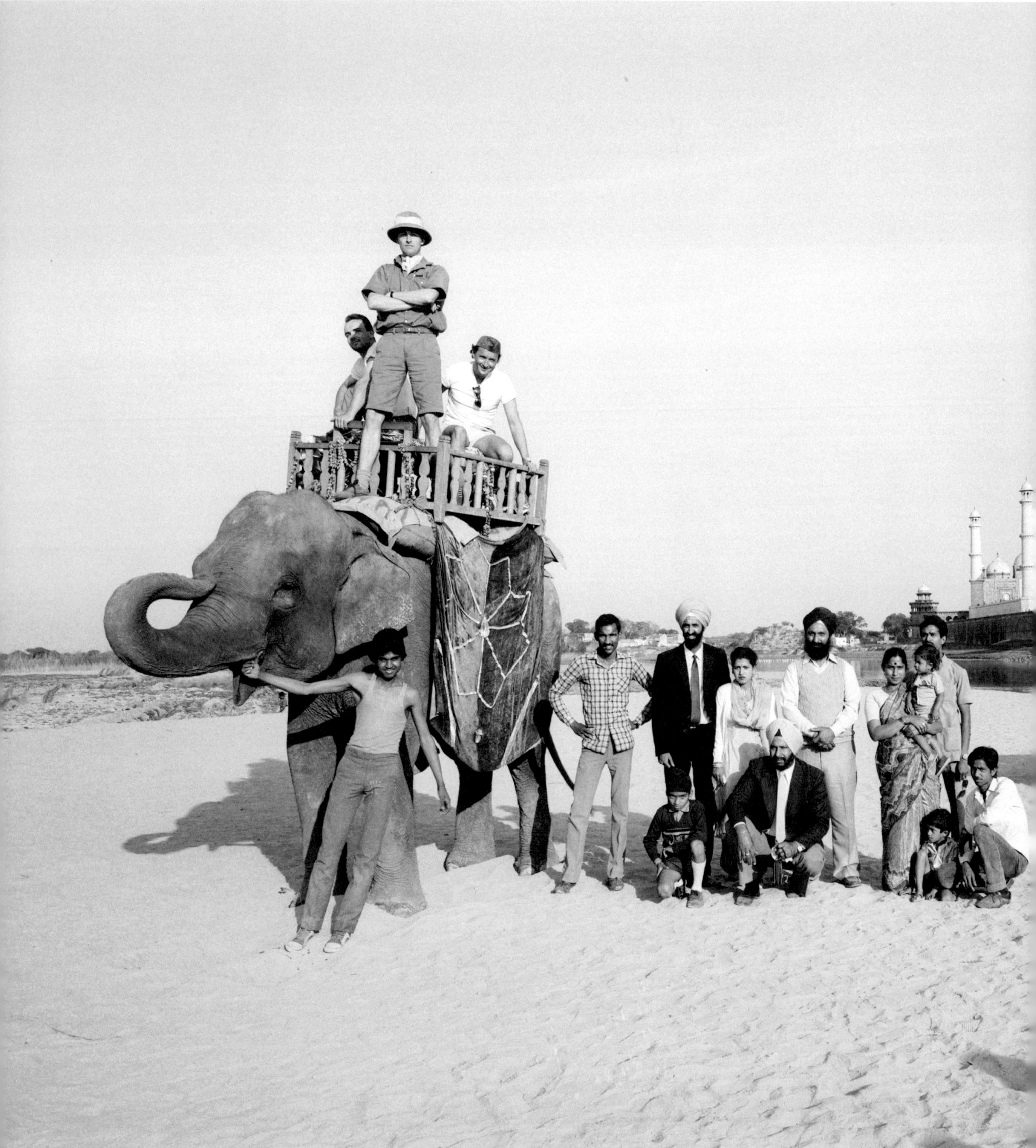

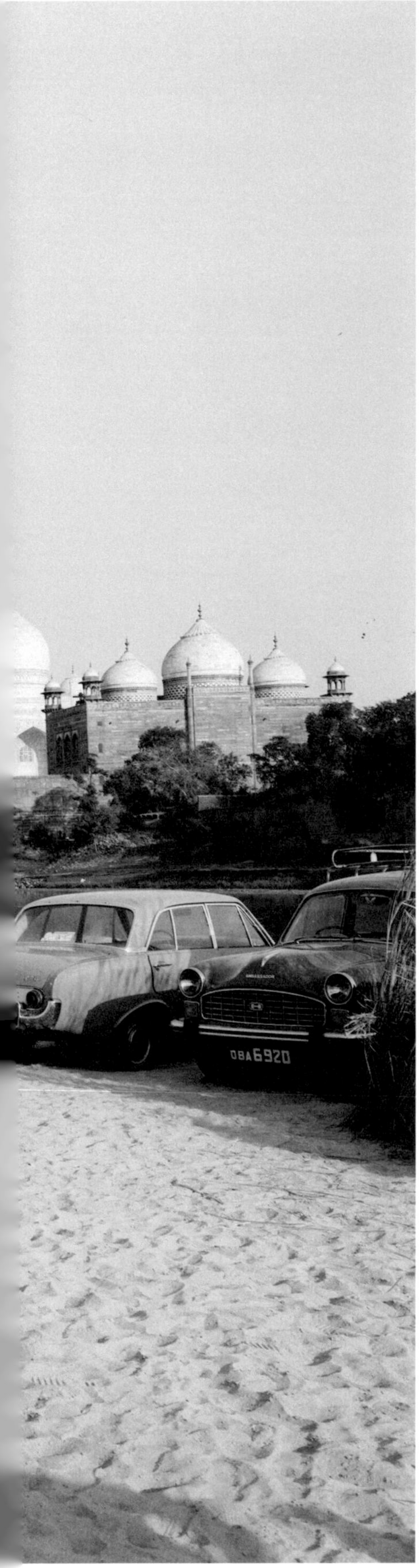

By the way, you do not stand very firmly on the back of an elephant.

We drive from New Delhi to Agra for Ford, to portray a German family that has driven to India by car. While the tourists take pictures of the Taj Mahal, an Indian family photographs the new Ford. We start talking to the owner of the light blue Taunus 17M after dinner at our hotel in New Delhi. He agrees to drive 235 km to Agra and back to take the picture for a very fair price. He is the man squatting at the front. We are on the road for 11 days for this picture. One whole day was wasted due to the elephant refusing to ford a river.

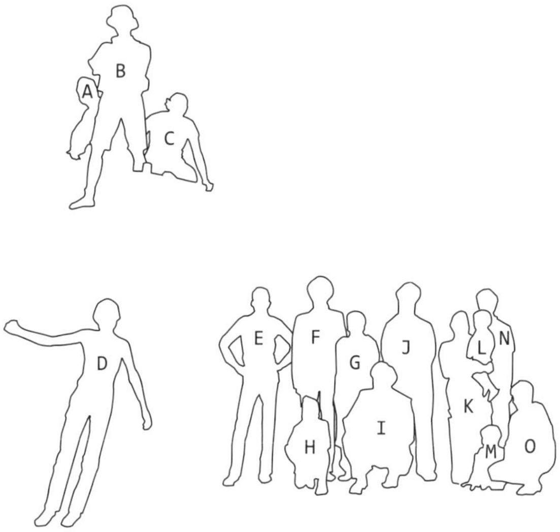

AGRA
Taj Mahal, Uttar Pradesh,
February 1987

A Thomas Lemker, assistant
B Me
C László Koroszy
D Elephant boy
E Our driver
F G H Indian family
I The owner of the Ford Taunus
J K L M N Indian family
O Our organiser

Switzerland, Algeria, Paris, Gran Canaria.

A manufacturer of weaving looms wants us to stretch red ropes across dramatic places of the world, over landscapes and canyons. We start with a meadow in Switzerland. We travel from there to Algeria, via Geneva, to continue into the desert. The lack of time prevents me from getting a carnet (a shipping document). Our equipment is confiscated in Algiers on a Thursday afternoon, and we are told to come back on Tuesday. Friday is a free day for customs, they are closed on Saturdays and Sundays, and Monday is a bank holiday. This makes us want to leave the country, as we hadn't even officially entered the country. It is clarified that the only way to leave the country is to enter it first. And moreover, they can't stand us Europeans anyway. We are confronted with swear words that would cause for severe penalties back in Germany. We stay in the spare room of a five star hotel's cellar, with no toilet or water, sleeping on cots and paying 280 DM per night. Our art director has a room with a shower. However, we are still forced to listen to accusations of all Europeans being rascist, and the hotel's bar staff refuses to serve us. The story goes on and on. After this emergency stay, we decide to drive to the dunes of Gran Canaria. Due to the fact that we didn't make a booking in advance, we spend 17 hours sitting on our suitcases or on the floor during our stopover in Paris. Here we decide to visit the Eiffel Tower, like tourists. This card of desperation is meant to remind me of springtime on the Côte d'Azur – I mail the old postcard of the crocuses from the Eiffel Tower. You can have your mail stamped on-site.

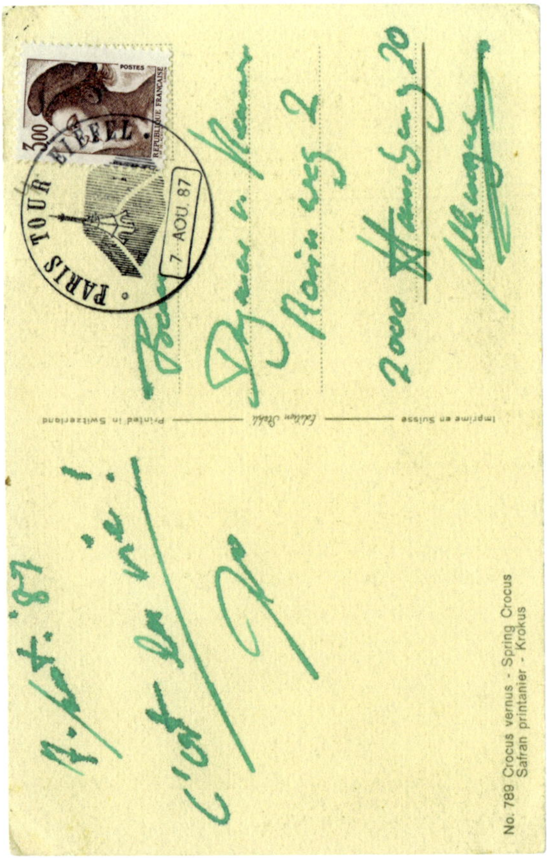

GRAN CANARIA
August 7th,
1987, Paris
–
"C'est la vie!
Ivo"

I send the old postcards with the crocuses from the Eiffel Tower. The mail can be stamped there on site.

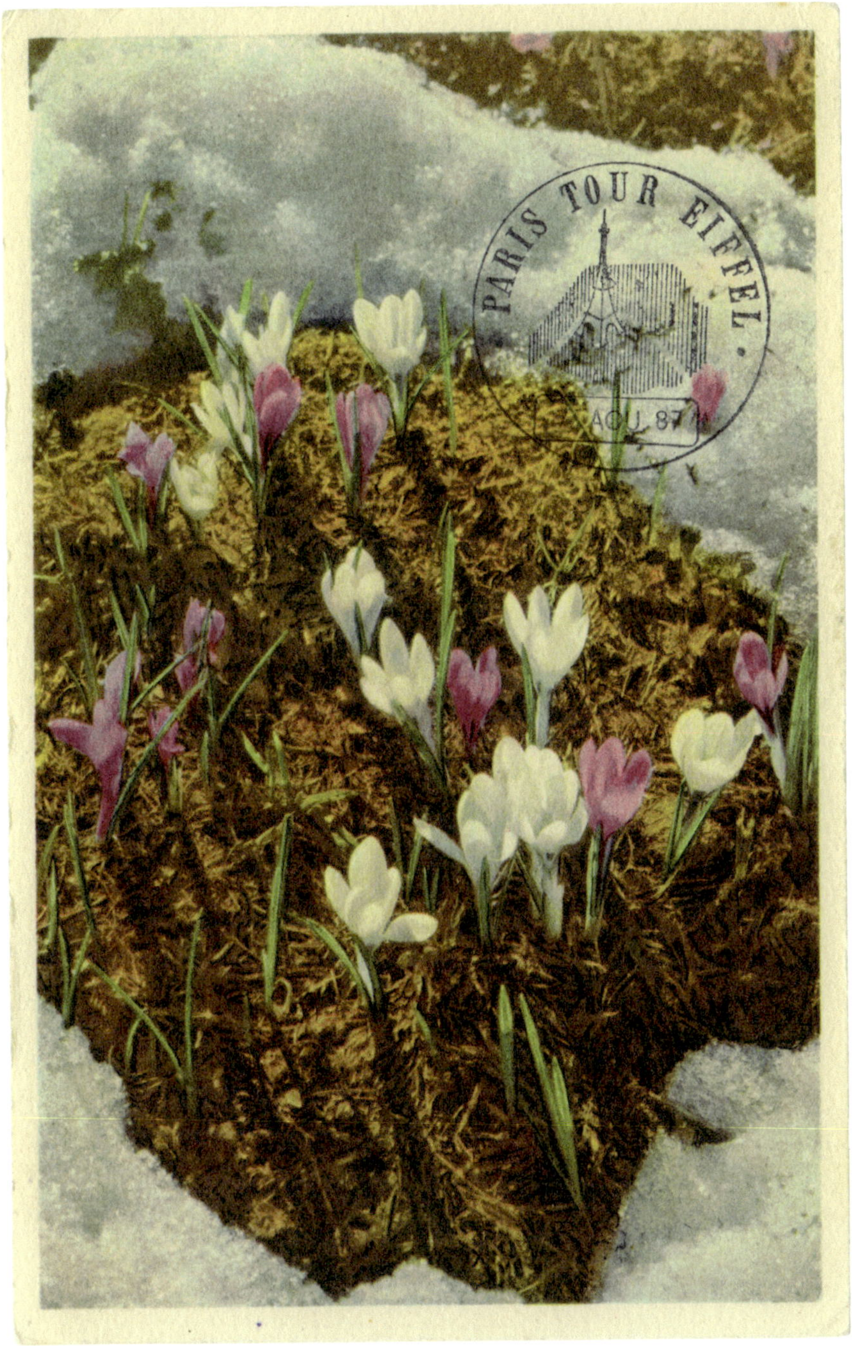

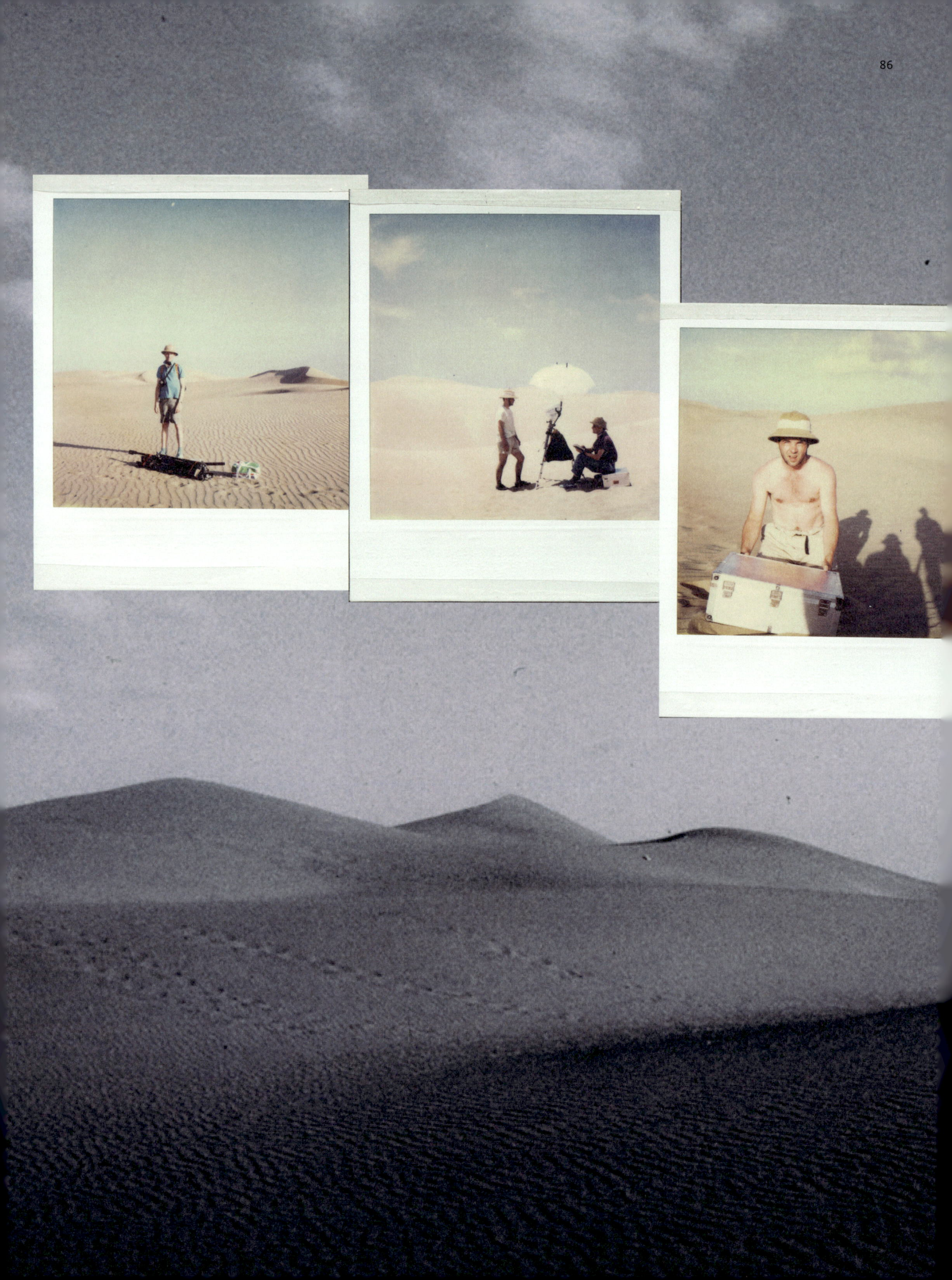

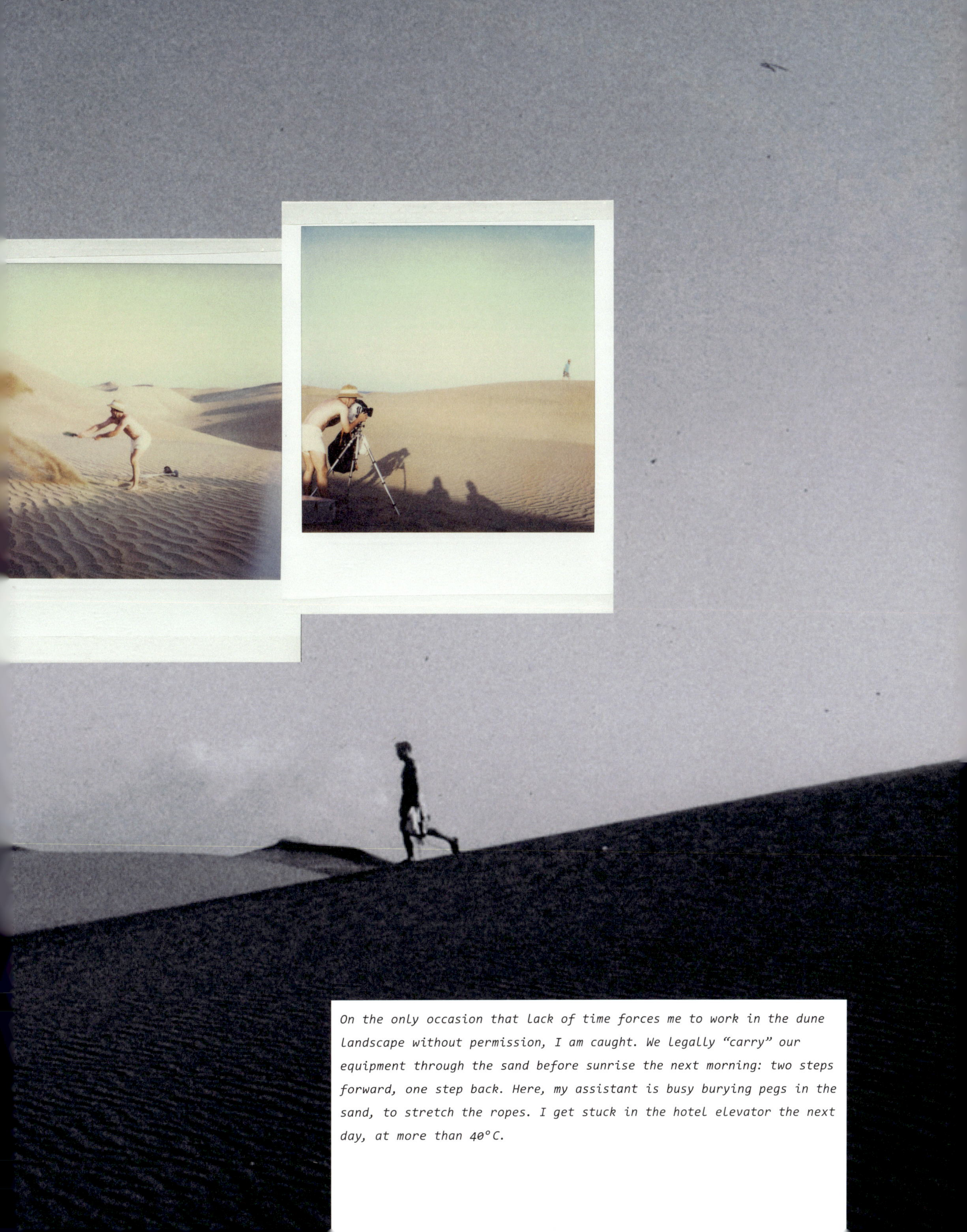

On the only occasion that lack of time forces me to work in the dune landscape without permission, I am caught. We legally "carry" our equipment through the sand before sunrise the next morning: two steps forward, one step back. Here, my assistant is busy burying pegs in the sand, to stretch the ropes. I get stuck in the hotel elevator the next day, at more than 40°C.

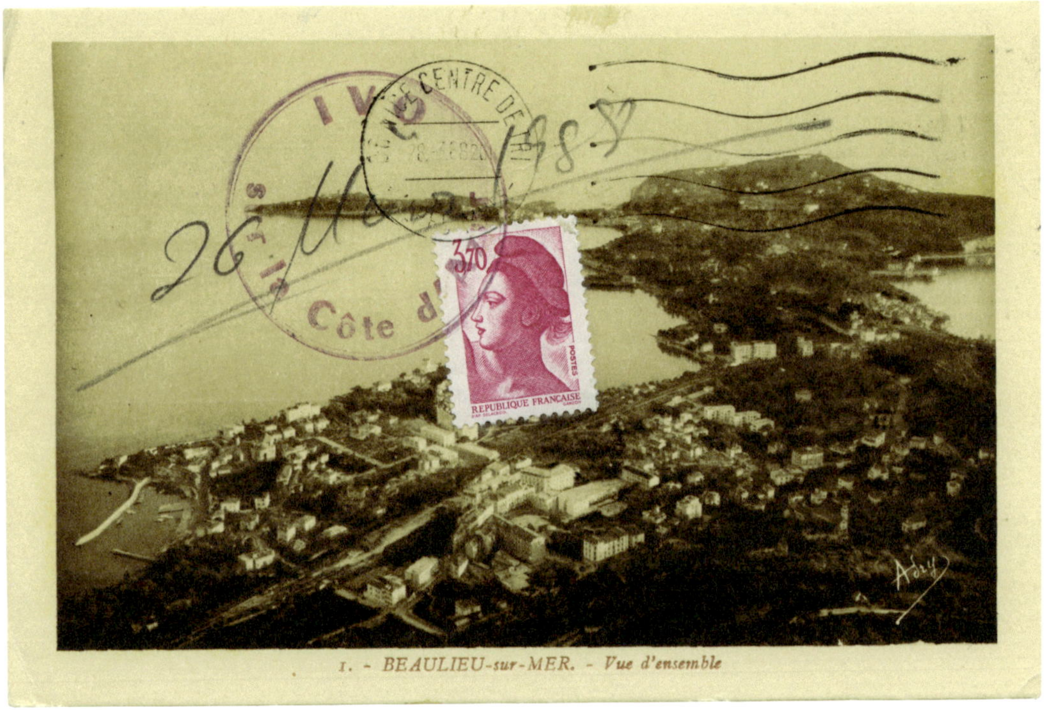

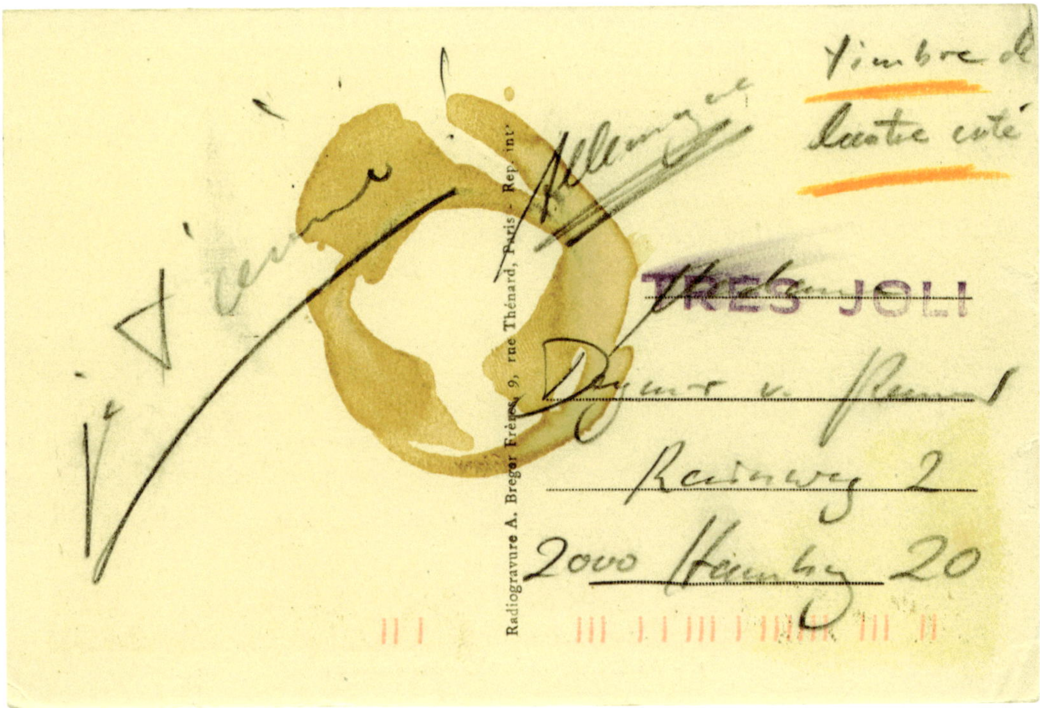

BEAULIEU-SUR-MER

March 26th, 1988

–

“je t’aime!”

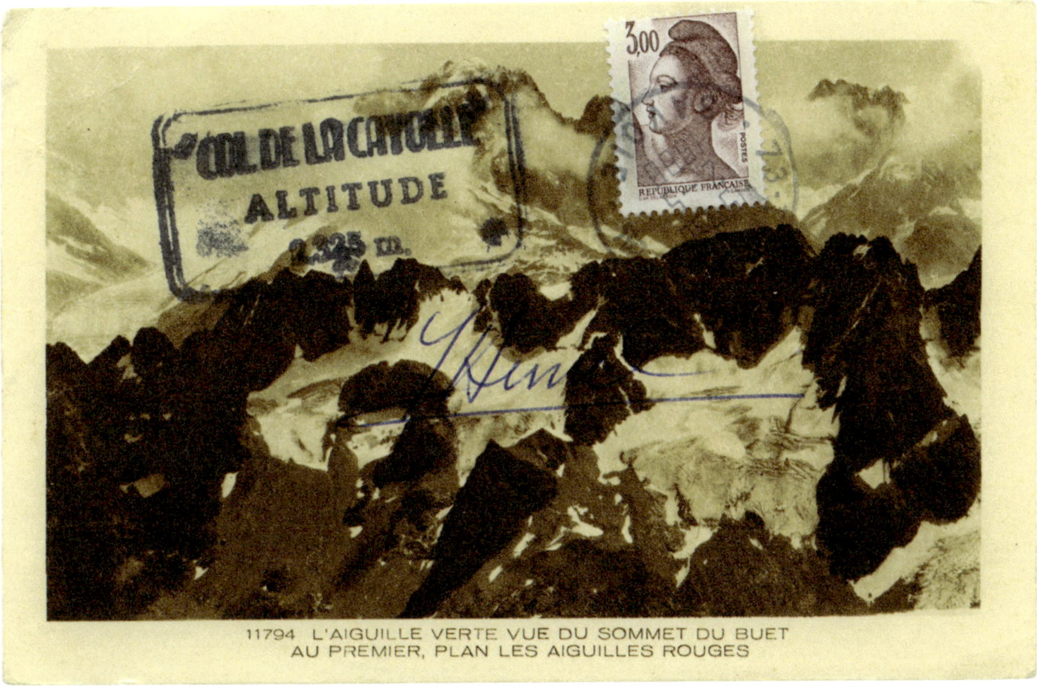

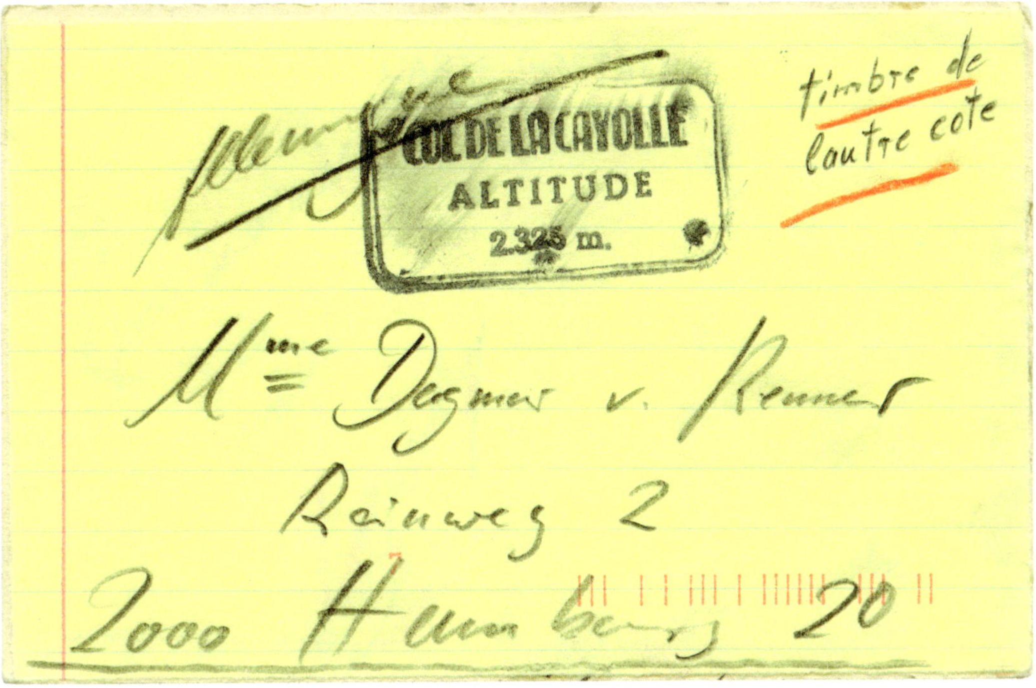

COL DE LA CAYOLLE
May 2nd, 1988

I start decorating cards and letters with wine and coffee residues as little culinary memories.

Five pictures and five weeks.

This was the relaunch of the Opel Vectra. Back then, pictures took more time, because retrofitting digitally was not yet an option. Although methods such as dye-transfer already existed, they were still very expensive. After neither we nor the scouts succeeded in finding a suitable water-side promenade between Marseille and Genoa for presenting the new Opel, we built one instead: 10 m wide and 50 m long. But then it started to rain. And we had built with wood on a rocky beach. We decided to take pictures in the Gorges du Verdon instead.

After escaping to the sunny mountains, away from the rain on the Côte d'Azur, the bad weather catches up with us. I send this little booklet of hand-coloured black and white photos with a gilded rim from the postcard collection that accompanies me.

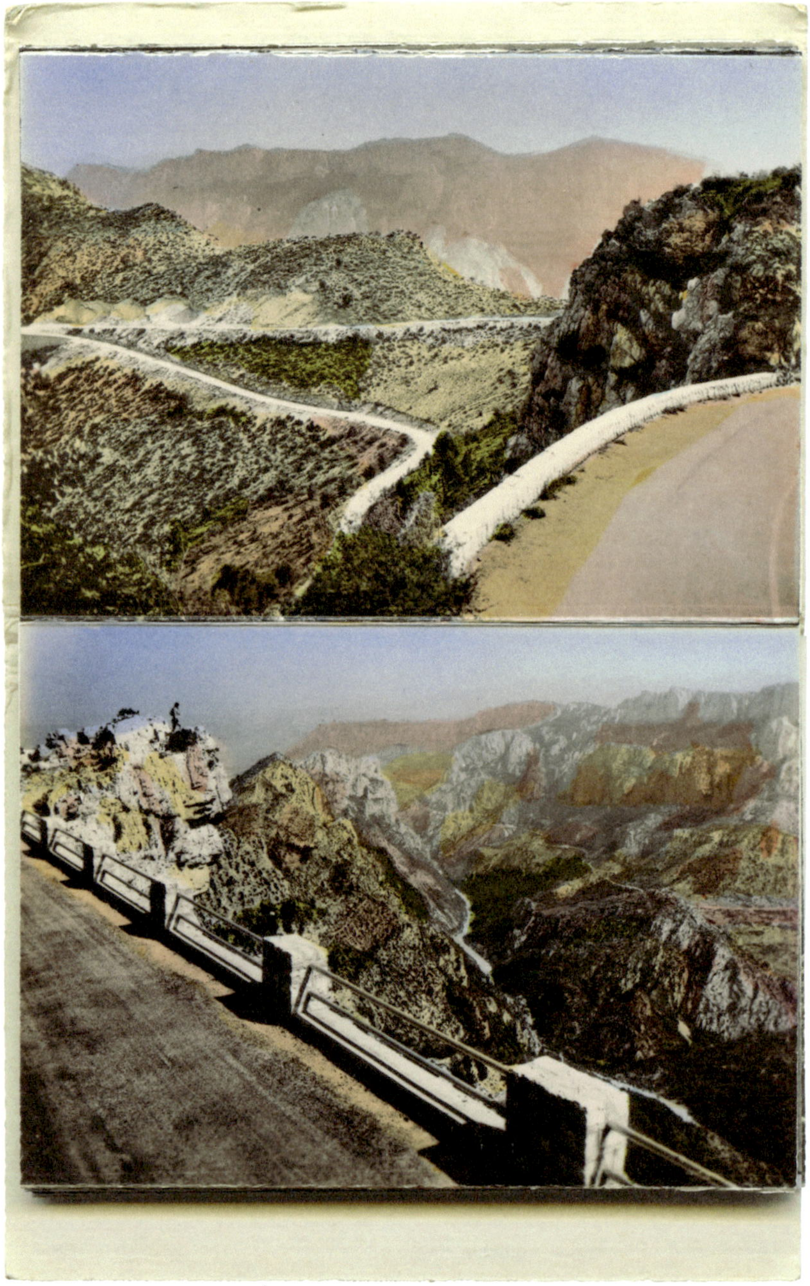

NICE
May 19th, 1988

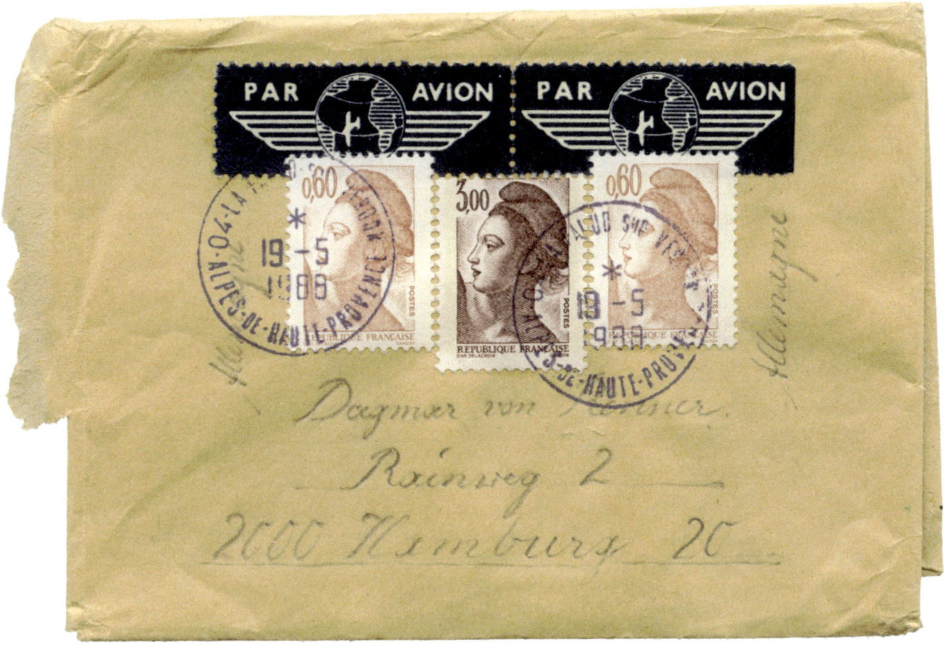
PAR AVION
PAR AVION
0,60
3,00
0,60
REPUBLIQUE FRANÇAISE
19-5
1988
ALPES-DE-HAUTE-PROVENCE
Rainweg 2
2000 Hamburg 20
Allemagne

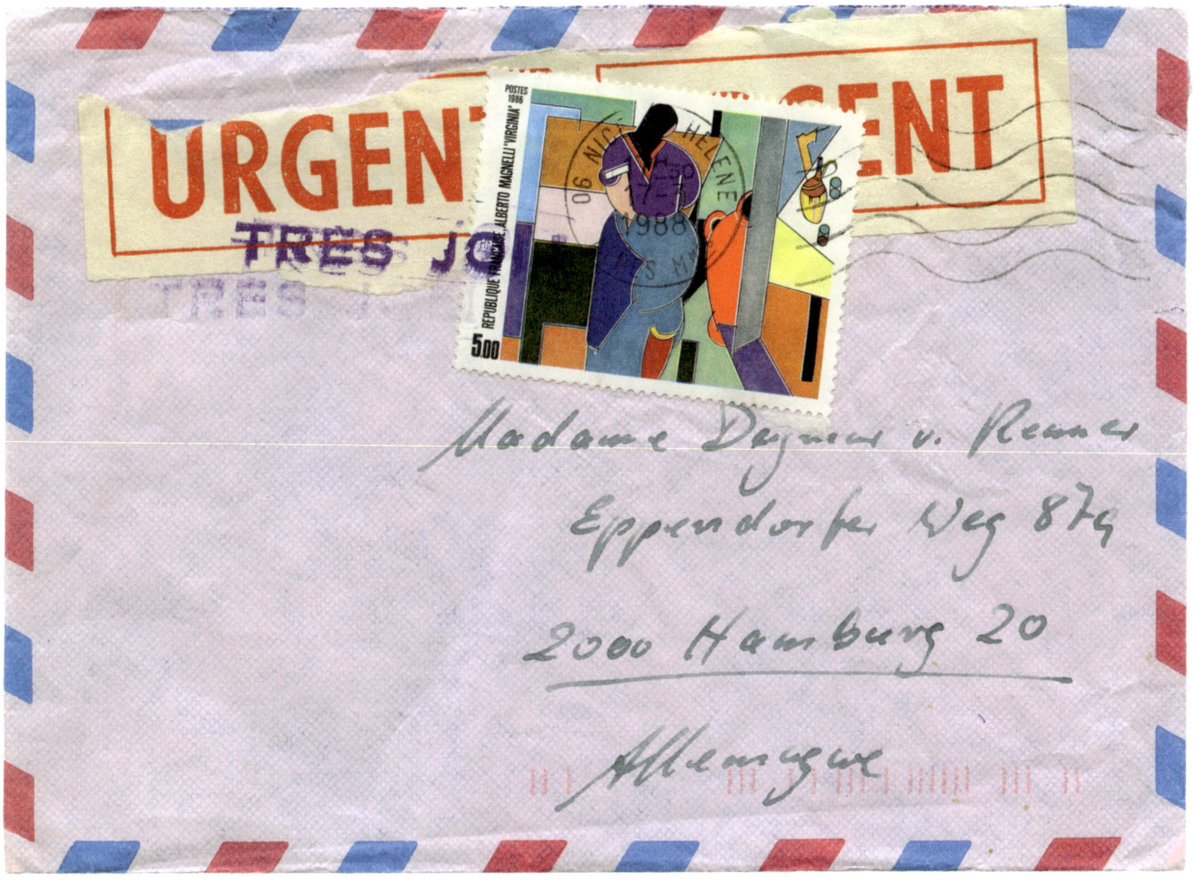
URGENT
TRES
POSTES
1986
REPUBLIQUE FRANÇAISE ALBERTO MAGNELLI "VIRGINIA"
5,00
Eppendorfer Weg 87a
2000 Hamburg 20
Allemagne

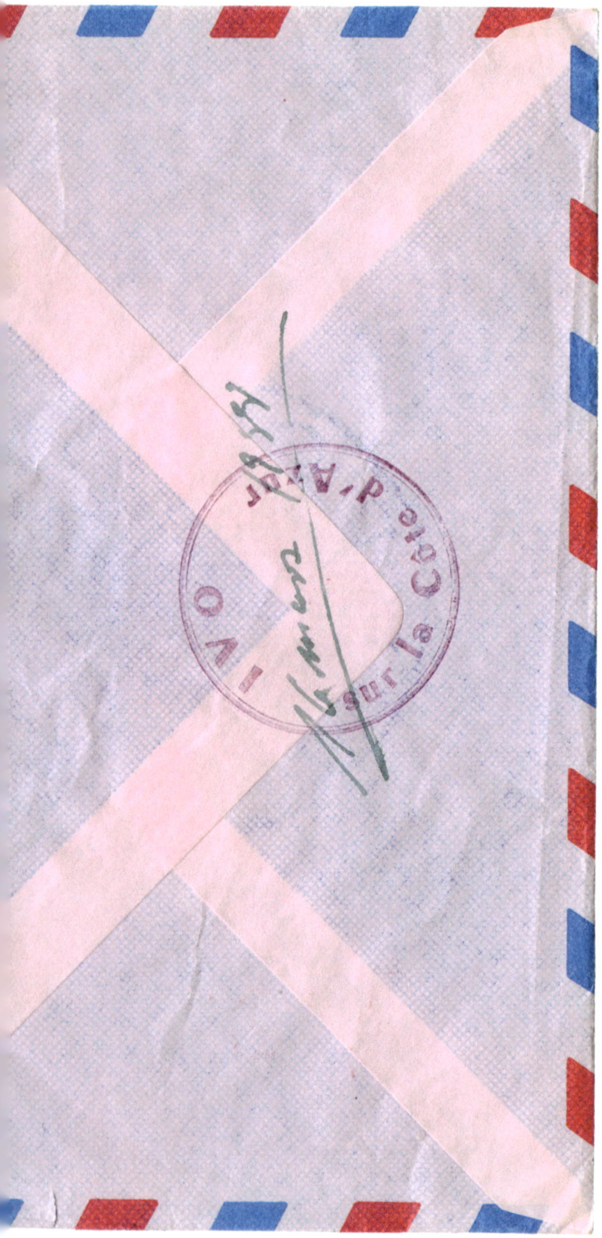

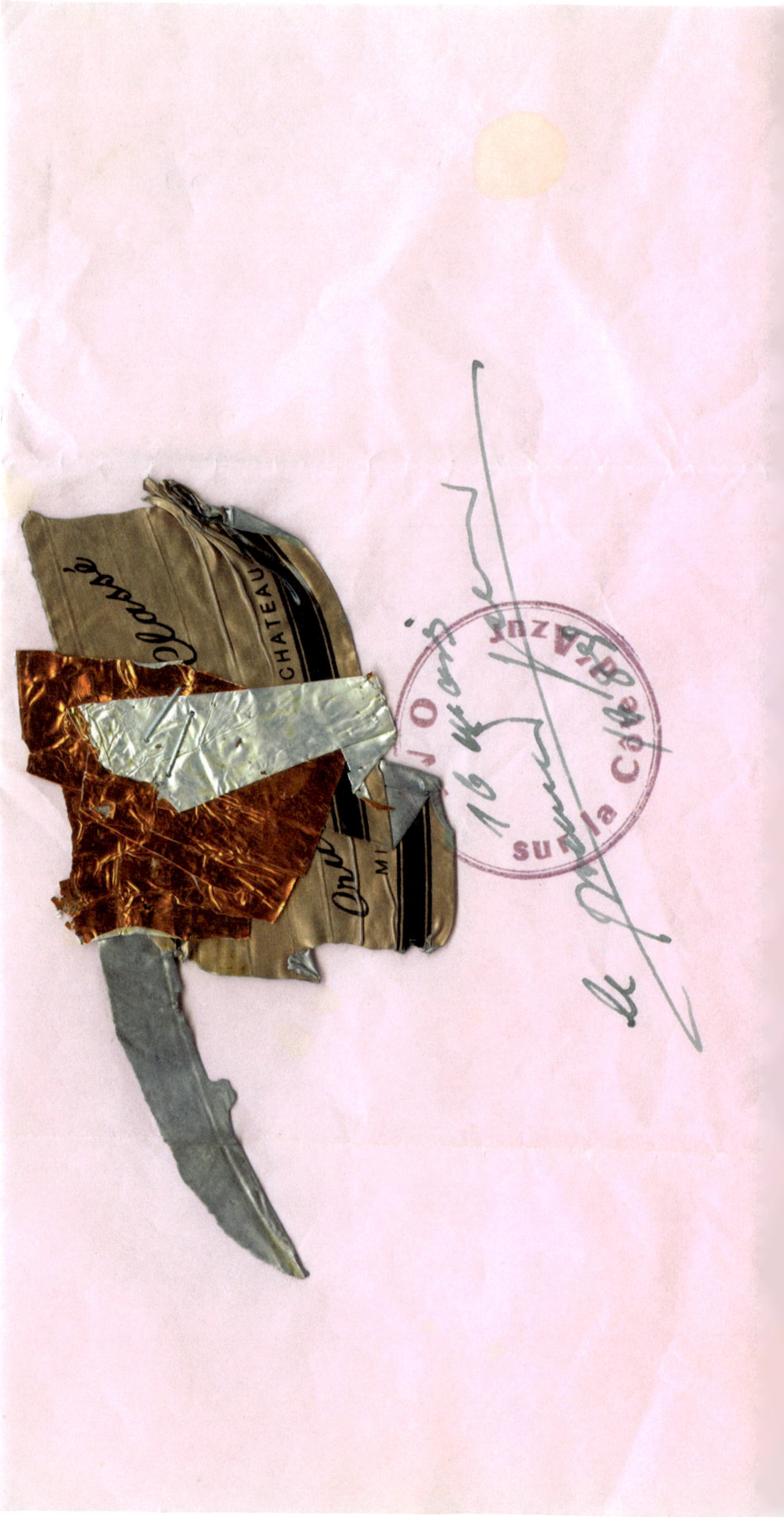

GORGES DU VERDON
March 18th, 1988
–
“Ton mari”

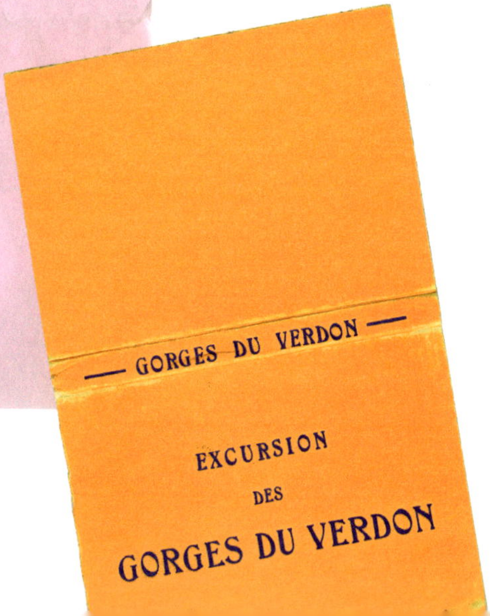
GORGES DU VERDON
EXCURSION
DES
GORGES DU VERDON

Photo
A LA MINUTE

30. Januar '87

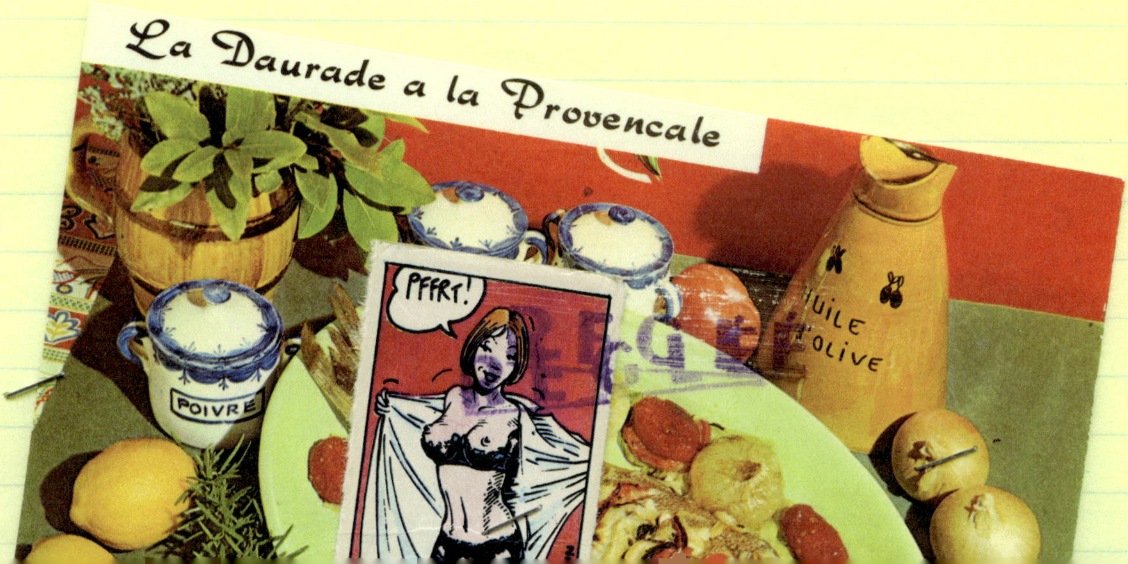

To give myself credit for my post-cards, the rubber stamp “L’ART APRÈS” is given a companion: “TRES JOLIE” (very pretty), for cards that turn out especially beautiful. As well as satisfying my ego, this is also meant ironically. But those who can’t applaud themselves, are also unable to doubt themselves later. Self-praise is part of my self-criticism.

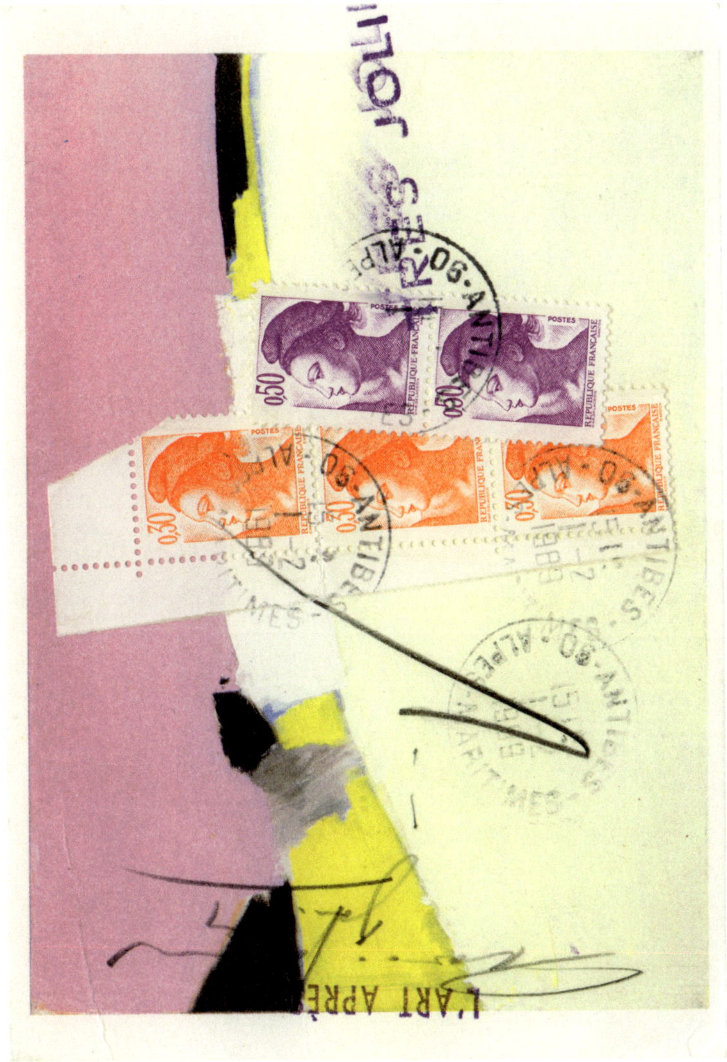

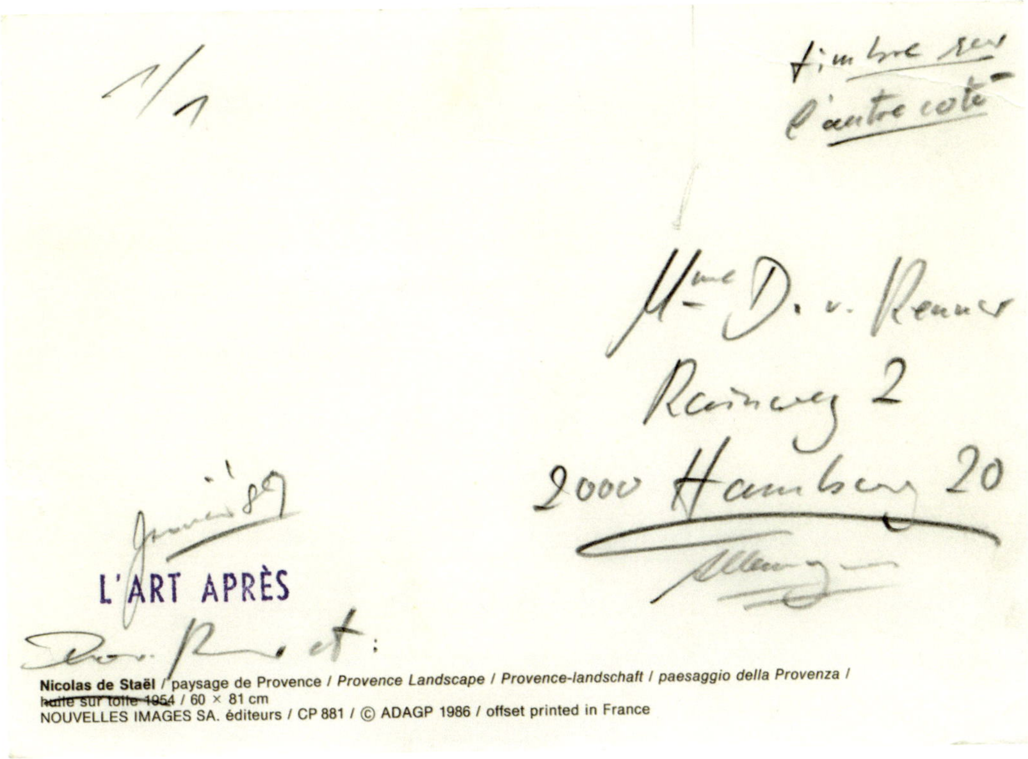

February 1st, 1989

Cecil is here!

Our first son is born in April of 1990. At the same time, an Italian photoagent sends a request for a job that he received from someone who would really like to work with me. The production is cancelled after several days of preparation and two days of bad weather. There will be no brochure in this season. I learn about the meaning of the word "Basta", and quickly have a rubber stamp made before our departure.

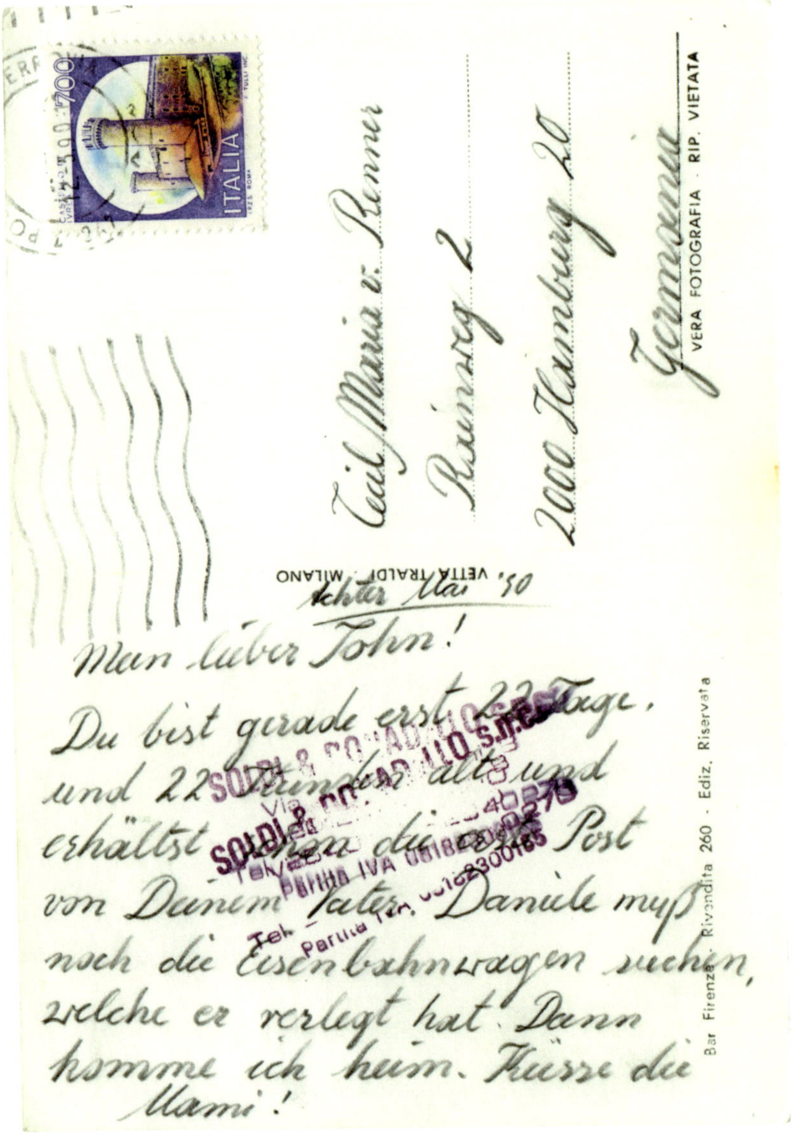

MILANO
May 1st, 1990
–
My dear son!
You are just 22 days and 22 hours old, and already receiving your dad's first mail. Daniele is still searching for the railroad car that he misplaced. Then I'll be home. Kisses to Mami!

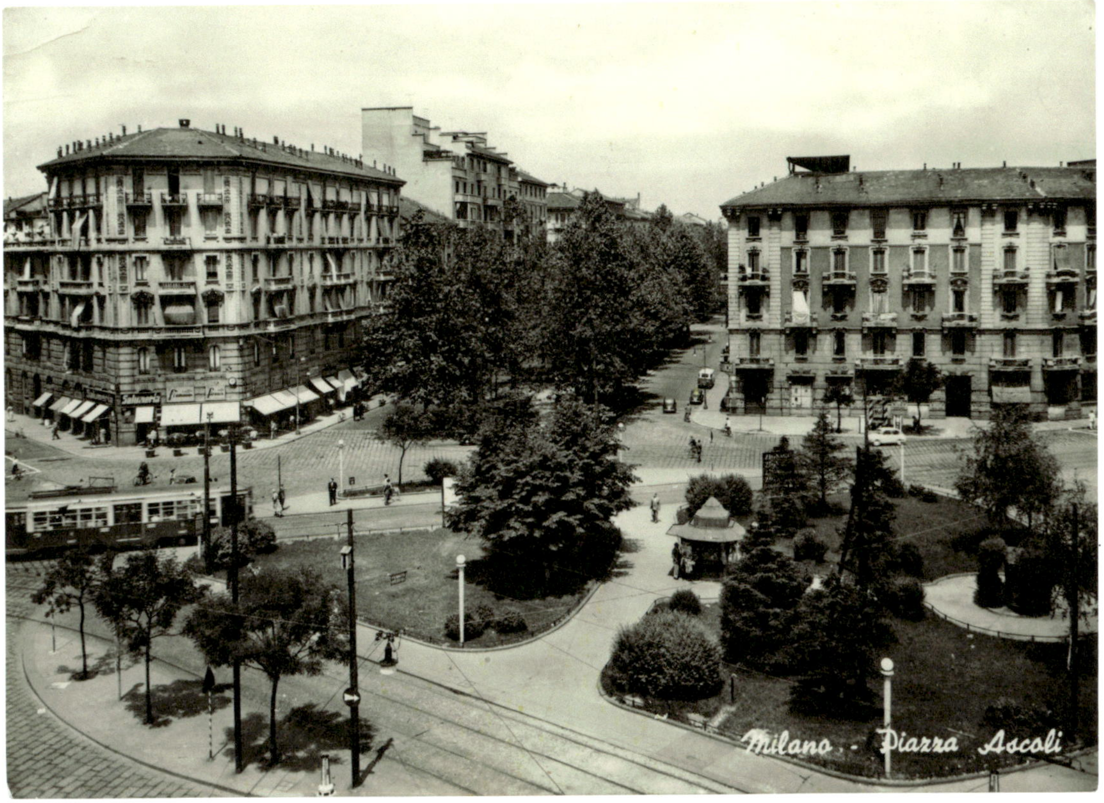

This is where my agent's office is. The card is sold on the street corner on the left.

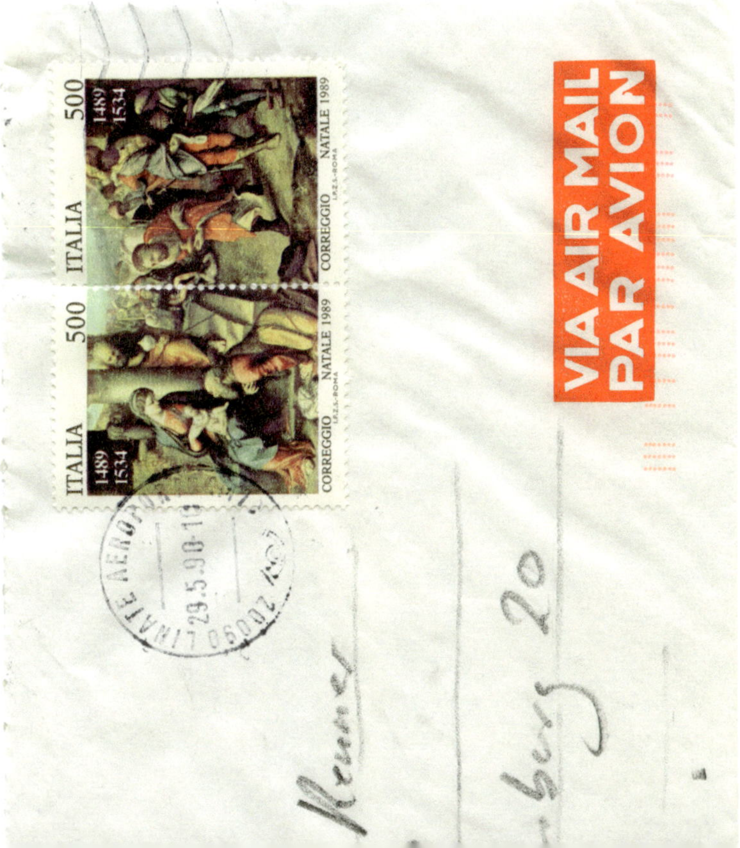

SHORTLY BEFORE BOLOGNA
May 1990

A journey into the relative (a train trip from Milano to Rimini), May '90.

Only when I'm travelling by myself, further - further away - and longer than expected. Two days turn into three - four turn into five. Chilled wine and poor lasagne imitations pass me by, factories, vines and landscapes - bit by bit - gleaming in the midday sun. I don't understand the language - the sounds are muted. And the clickediclack of the wheels leisurely sings: who are you, what do you do, what do you want, why? I travel. I am an important person; my ambition wants fame. My Keith Haring badge is mirrored by the window in the dining car. Oh yes! I've become a father - and am present for only 25 % of this new life. The waiter pushes the bill towards me: "tutto?". I find my suitcase. Italians have black hair. Yes - I have a wife and a child - clickediclack - clickediclack. I look into the pocket of my jacket: money - ticket - identity card - clickediclack, everything is real.

Where in the name of God is Rimini? The German legions of post-war tourism are said to have conquered it at a single stroke. But I don't even know an Italian whose mother-in-law could ever have been there. Rimini! Magic formula for fashion photography or tonight's horror?

In Bologna, a telephone call for 6.30 DM and the timetable information is false.

I have a single seat again; I am hot and my hands burn from the constant up and down of the stairs while changing trains.

Clickediclack - clickediclack - what is German taste? Maybe all that doesn't look like VOGUE, ELLE and marie claire, including the models? "I take pictures for the wall - art for books." - And now with an Italian accent: "But they don't want to see it" clickediclack - clickediclack - everything is so far - and relative.

Maybe I should make films instead.

Wife and child.

Clickediclack.

Rimini is approaching.

I should go home soon!

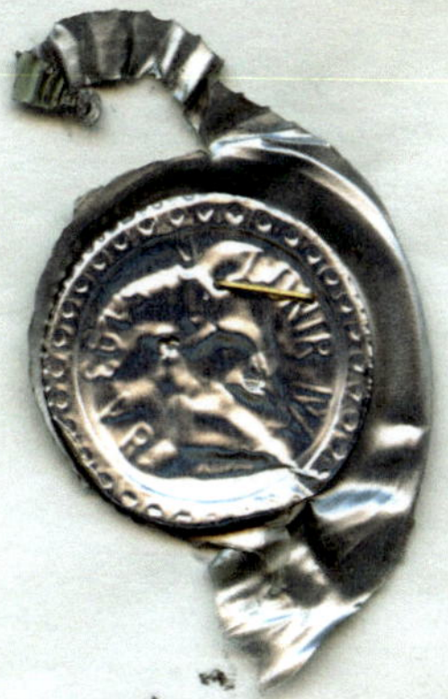

Die Reise war schön – doch komme zurück!

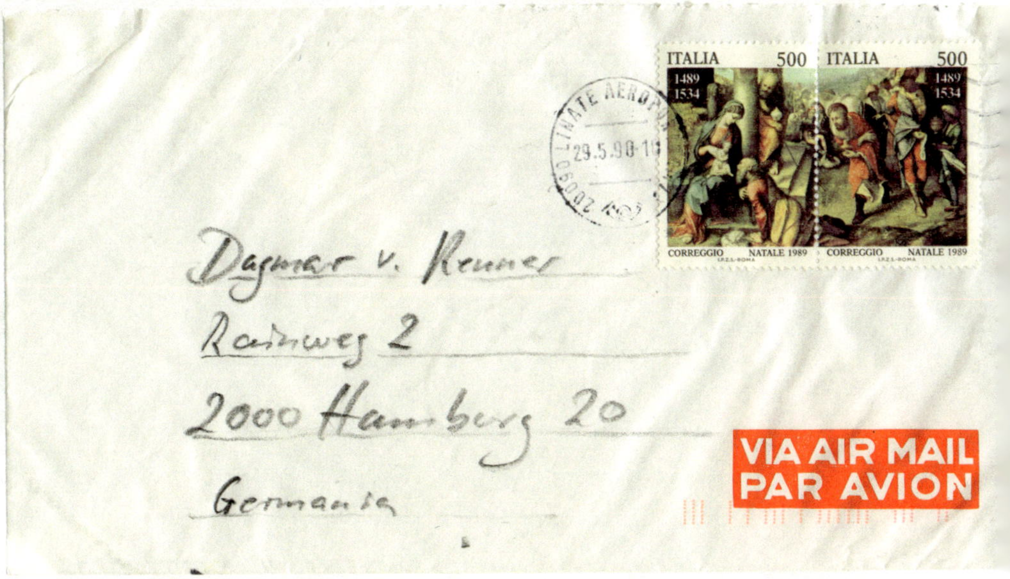

24. Mai '90

BASTA

Mod. 2
ESPRESSO
(EXPRÈS)

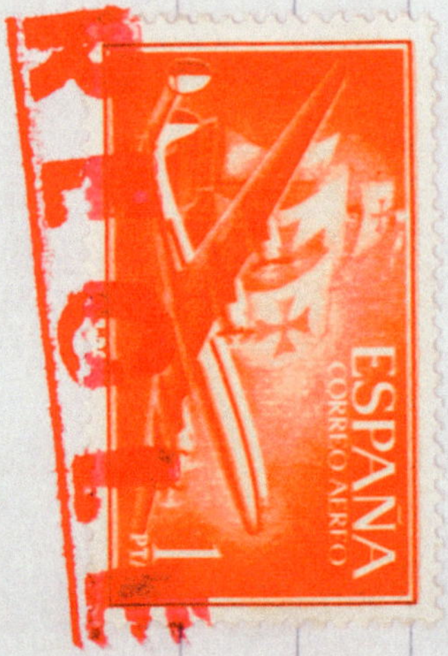

Cecil flies from Hamburg to Mallorca with us when he is six weeks old.
He manages to divert the stewardess's attention from me to himself, which will never change. I have a stamp made for this journey saying "LAS PRIMERAS VACACIONES DE CECIL MARIA". Cecil Maria's first journey.

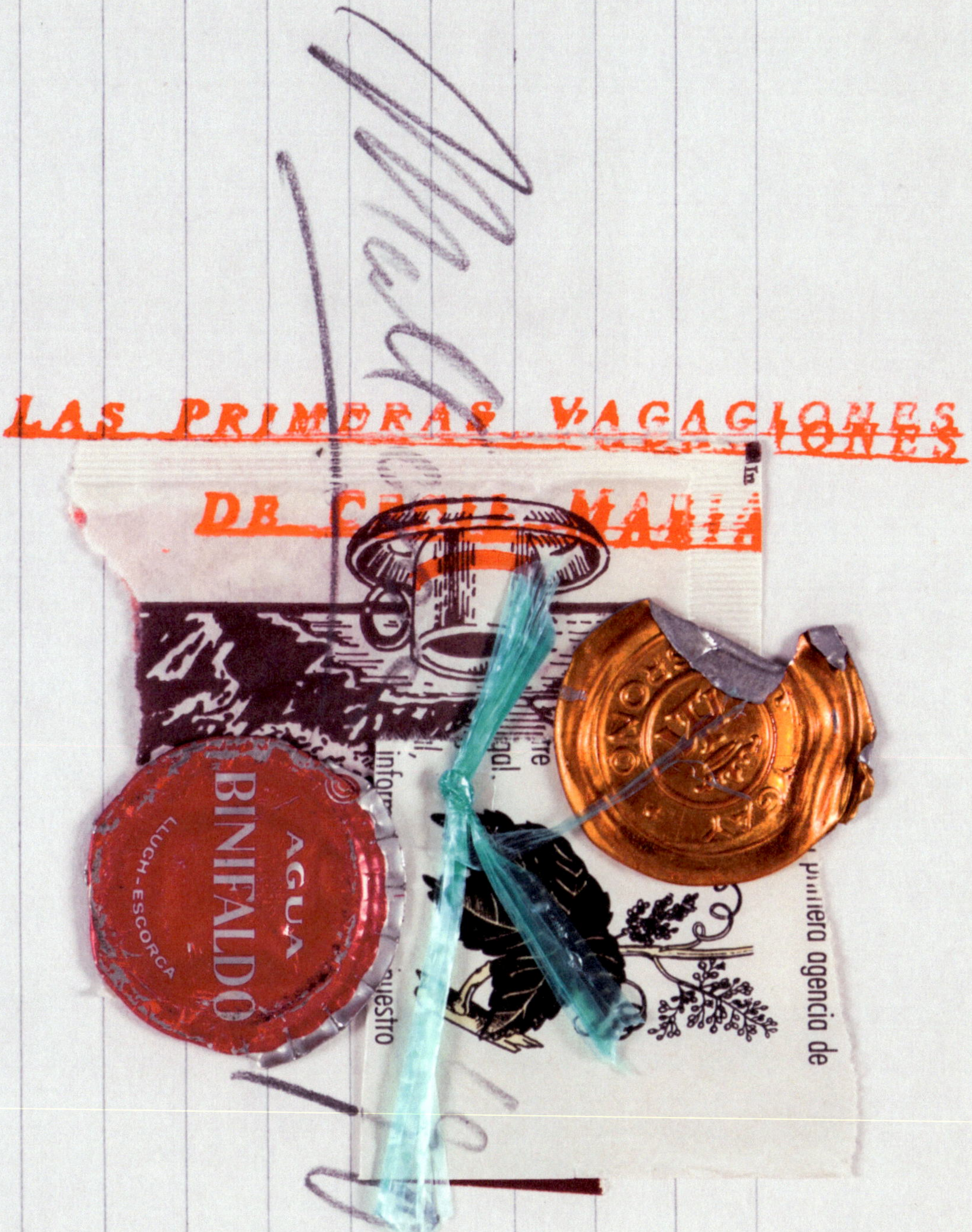
LAS PRIMERAS VACACIONES
AGUA
BINIFALDO
LLUCH-ESCORCA
primera agencia de

My dreams.

We receive a big job for Volvo in 1990. A single page is followed by a fold-out double page, which turns into a four-page advertisement. The subject is a doctor on a sabbatical, who crosses the continents in his Volvo. While crossing unstable terrain, I am standing on the flat wagon of a steam locomotive on a 34m bridge in the Colorado mountains. We, the crew, are the protagonists. I see my dream car at the petrol station the next morning, a Ford Thunderbird 1959, original colour, completely intact. The owner tells me that he only drives cars like this. He recently bought it for $4000, and offers it to me for the same amount. Cash. Today or tomorrow. I owned the matchbox version of this model as a child. I've carried my dream car in my heart ever since. But I refuse to use 30 litres of petrol in the city just after becoming father to a son.

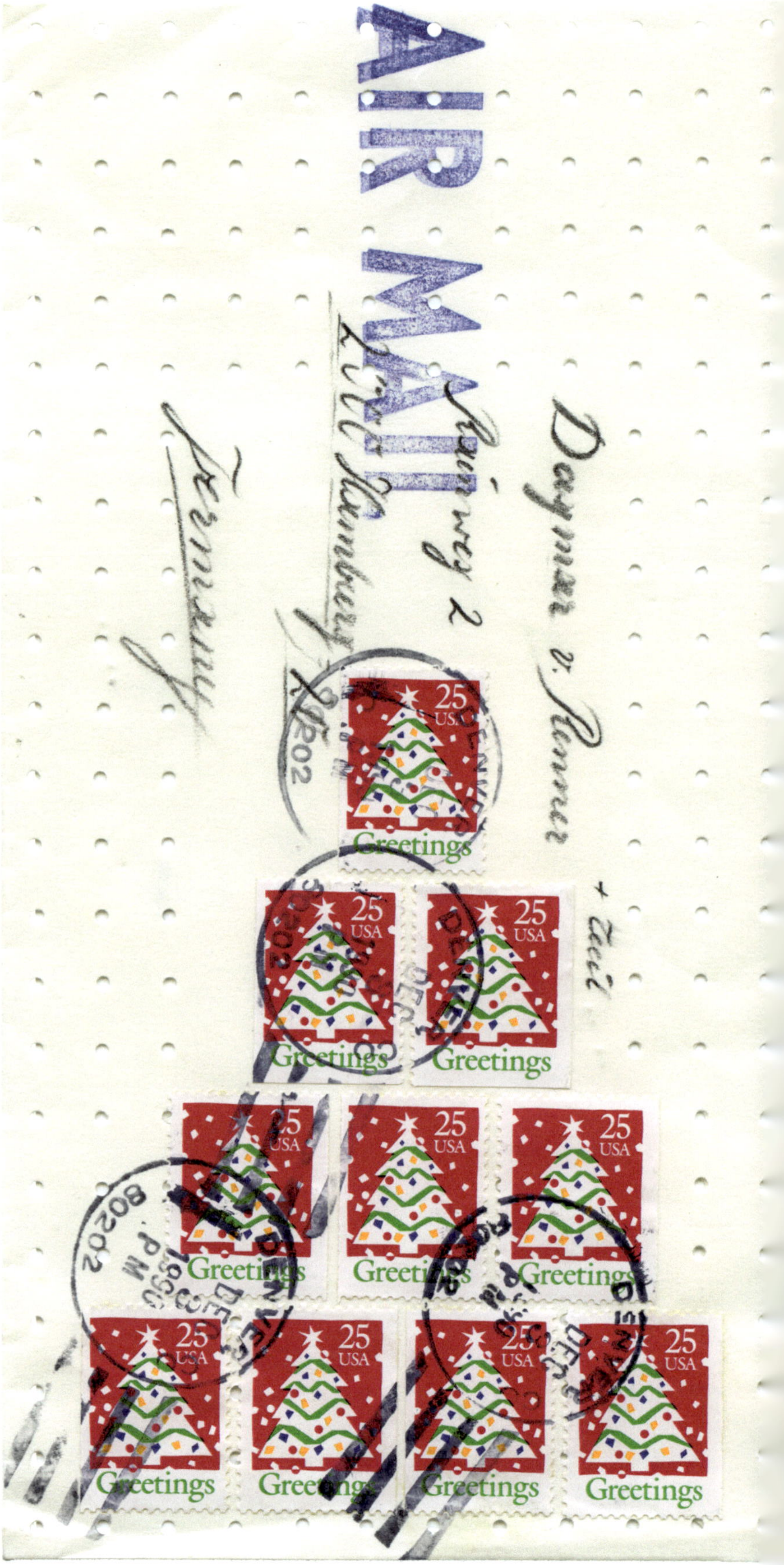

DENVER
December 12th, 1990

The Polaroid of the Ford Thunderbird is glued onto the receipt from one of the world's largest model railway stores. I spend my time waiting 5 3/4 hours for the Volvo, which is not yet available, in front of shelves holding hand-built models, as well as display copies of all books that have ever been published on the American market about this subject. I leave four thousand and twenty eight dollars in this paradise.

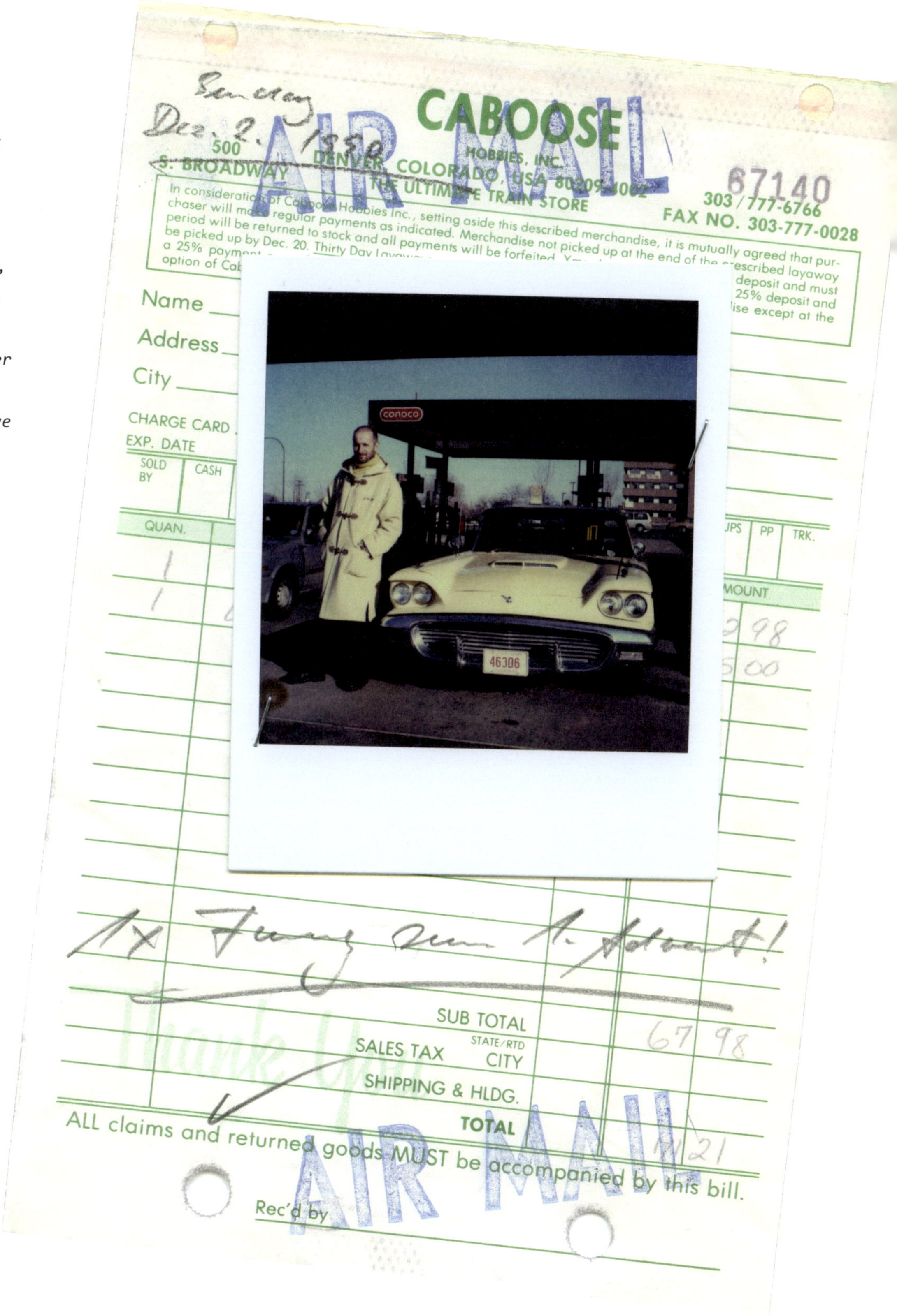

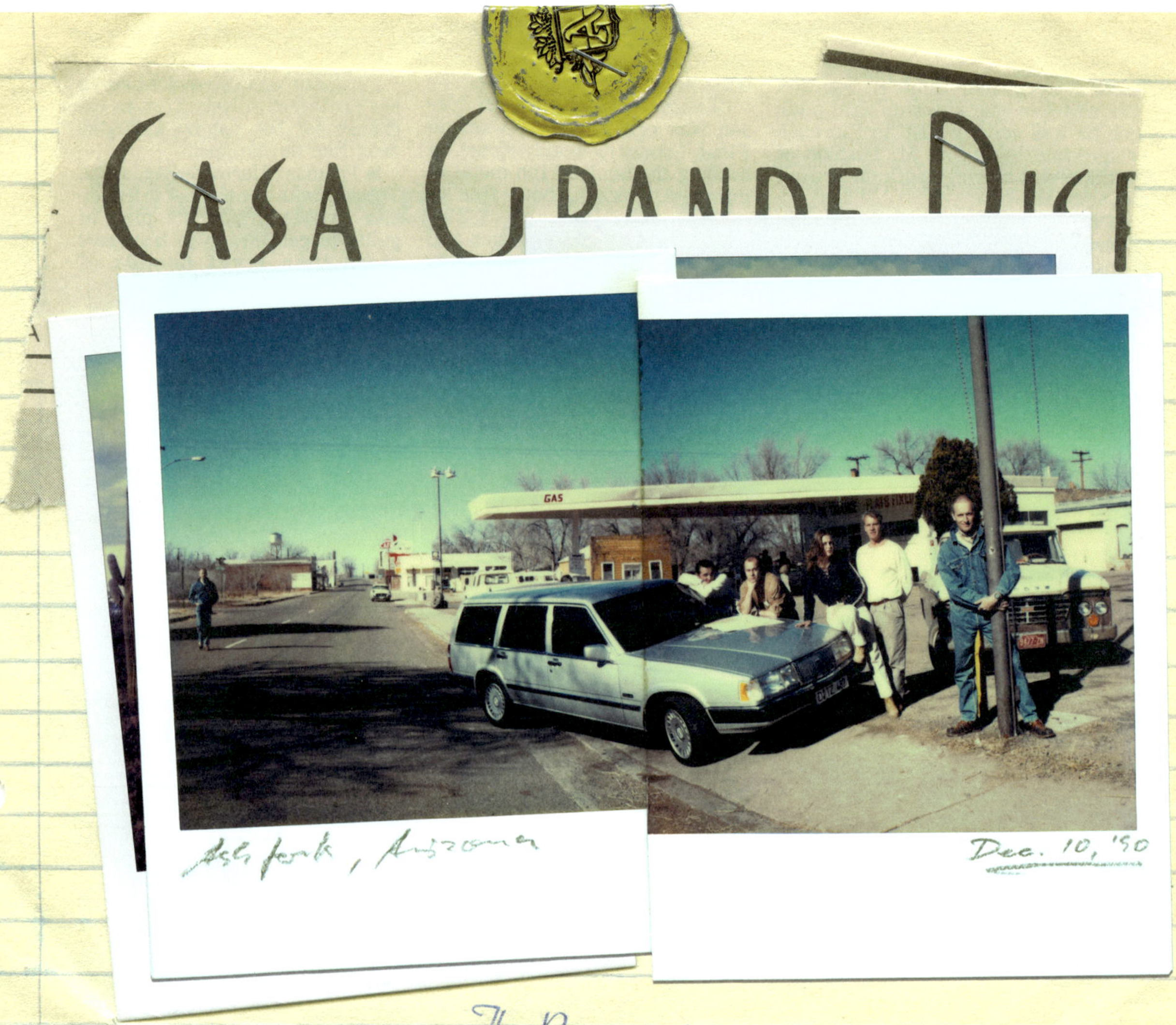

The Pioneers of the 760th

COLORADO • ARIZONA • UTAH • FLORIDA

Falk von der Brueggen
Kenneth J. Bruns
Antonina Gern
Carsten Greiner
Ivo von Renner
Peter Wendling
Hanno Wismar

“The Pioneers of the 760th” stamp (should really be called 760s) quotes the Volvo journey from Denver, Colorado via Arizona and Utah to Florida.

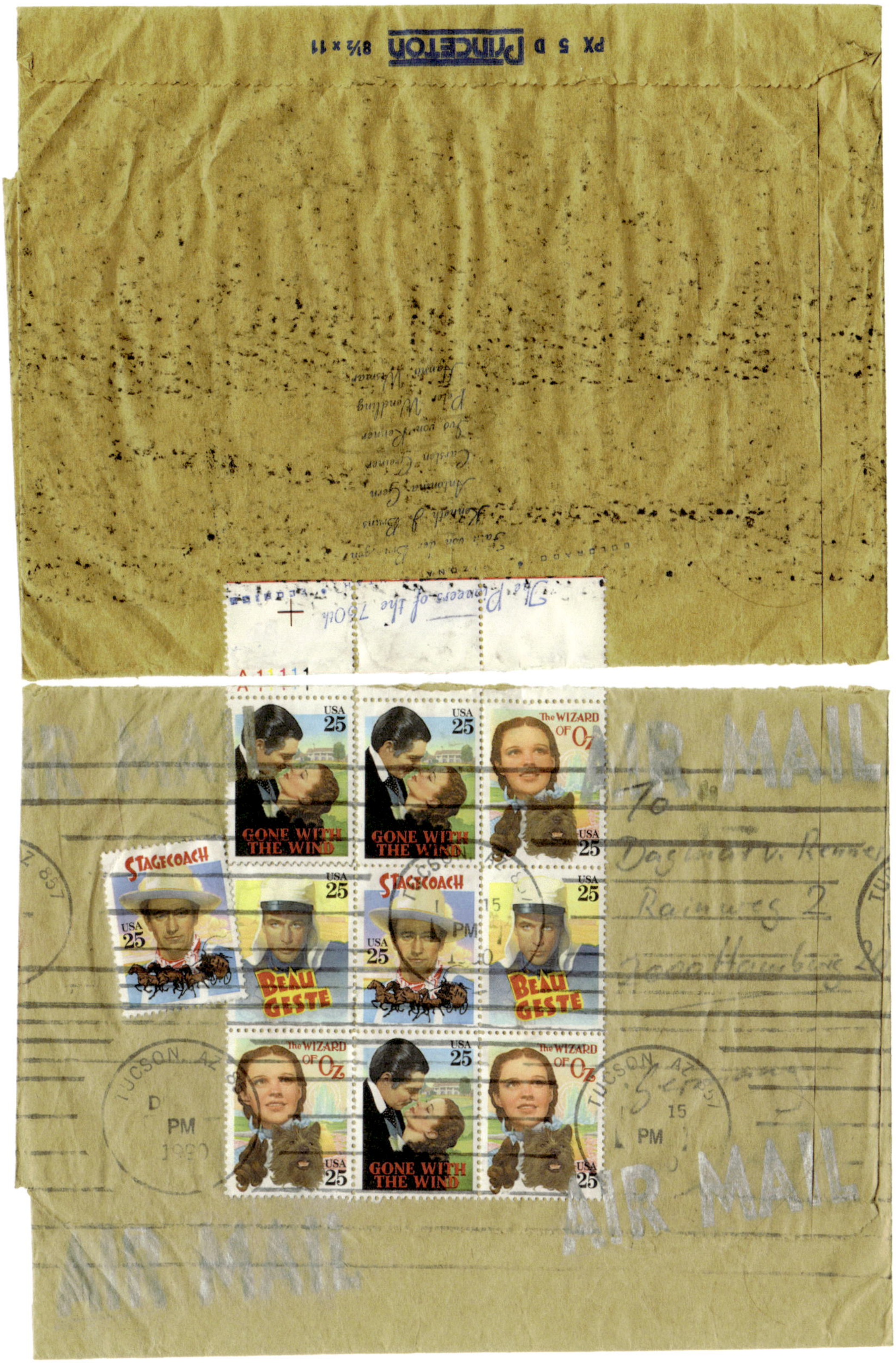

TUCSON

December 12th, 1990

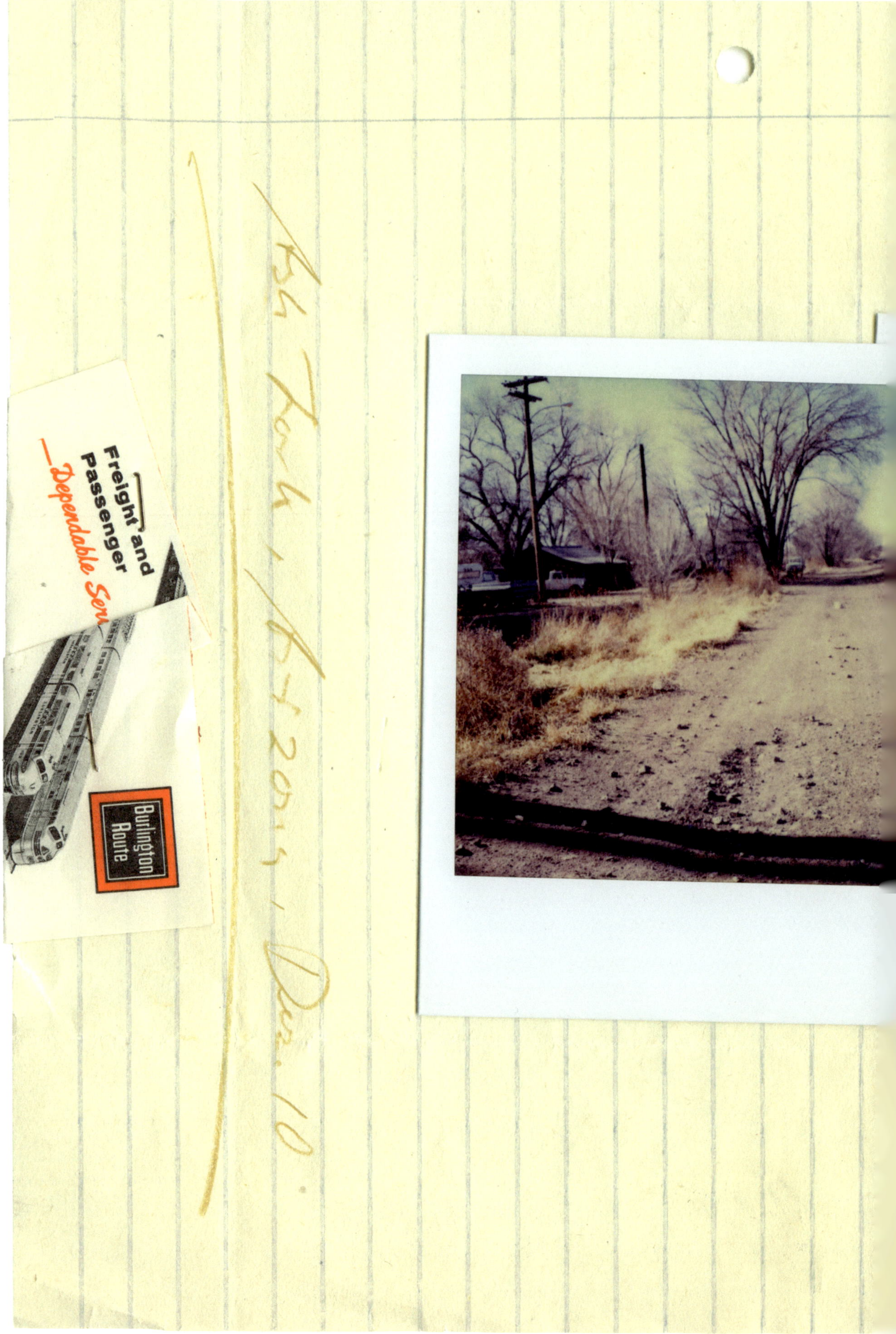
Ash Fork, AZ 2015, Dec. 10
Freight and Passenger
—Dependable
Burlington Route

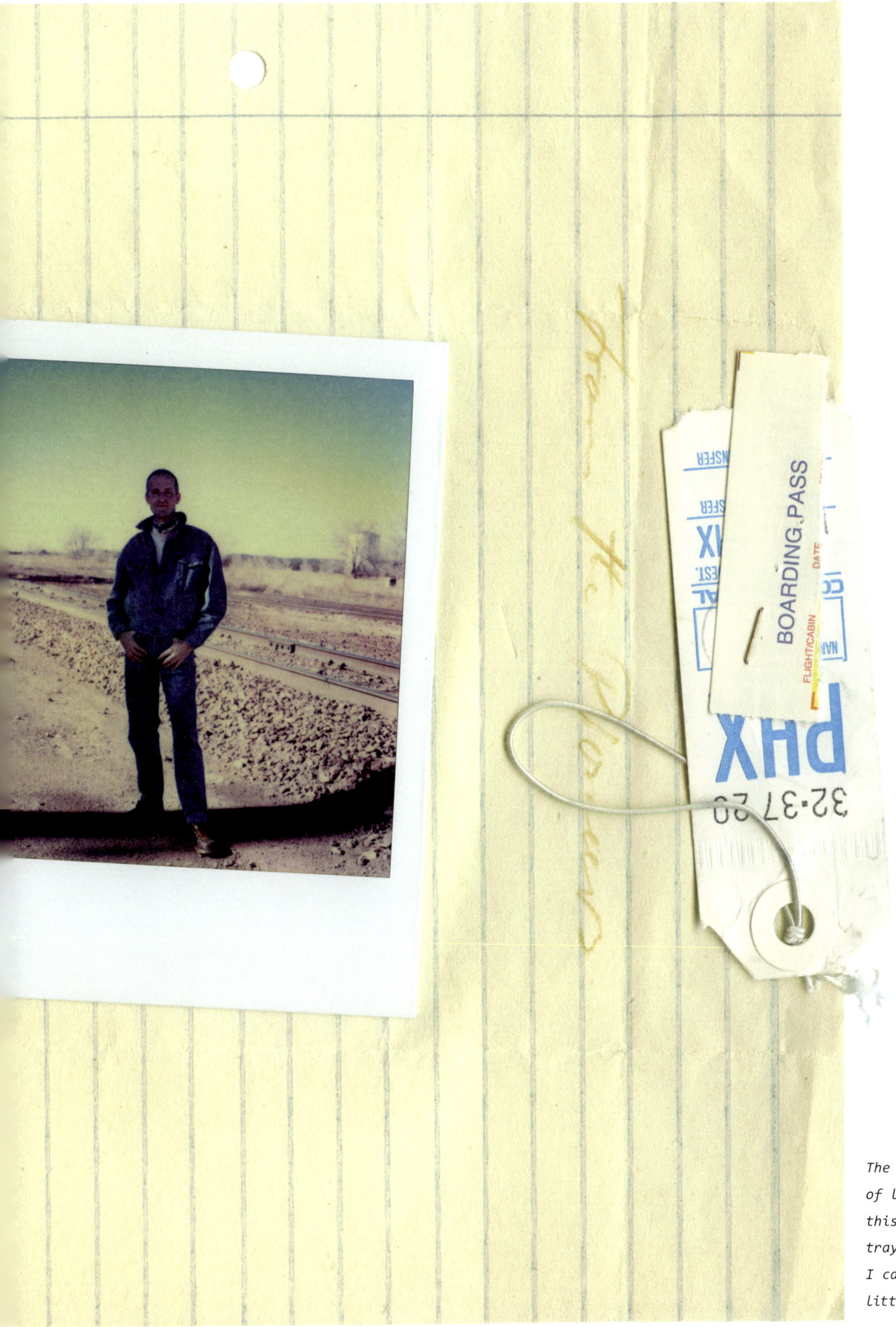

The large number of letters from this journey portray my longing. I call Cecil "the little peewee".

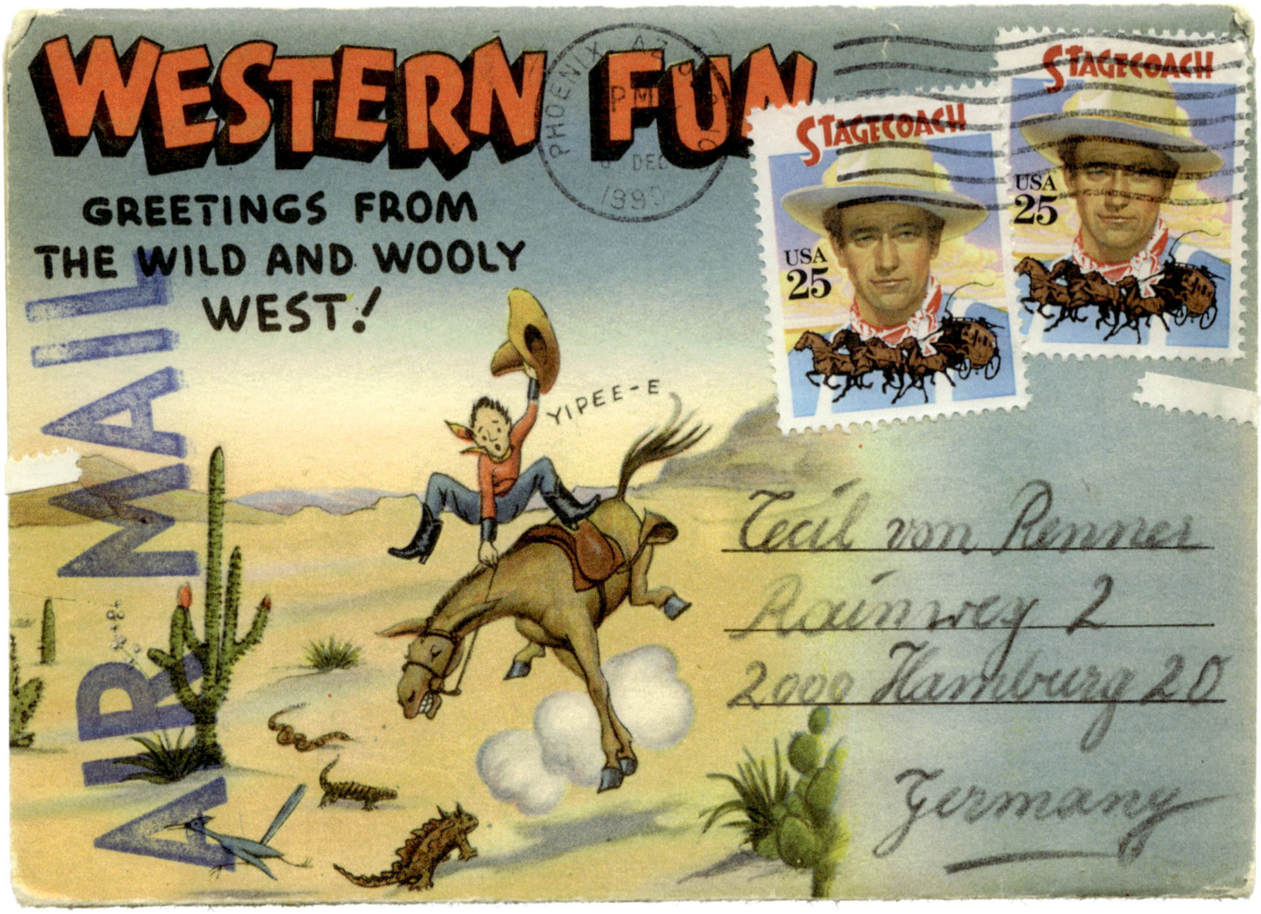
WESTERN FUN
GREETINGS FROM THE WILD AND WOOLY WEST!
YIPEE-E
STAGECOACH
USA 25
STAGECOACH
USA 25
AIR MAIL
Rainweg 2
2000 Hamburg 20
Germany

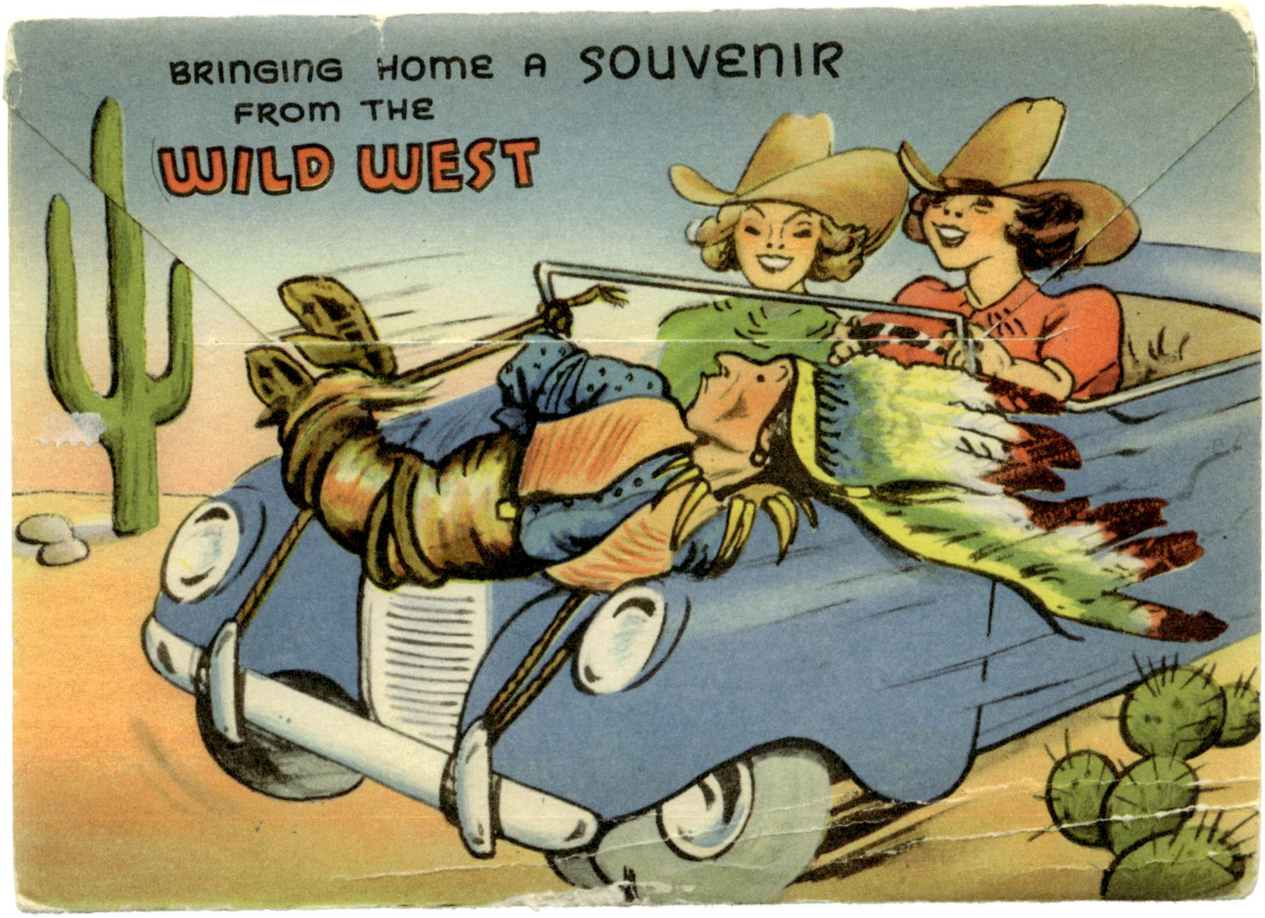
BRINGING HOME A SOUVENIR
FROM THE
WILD WEST

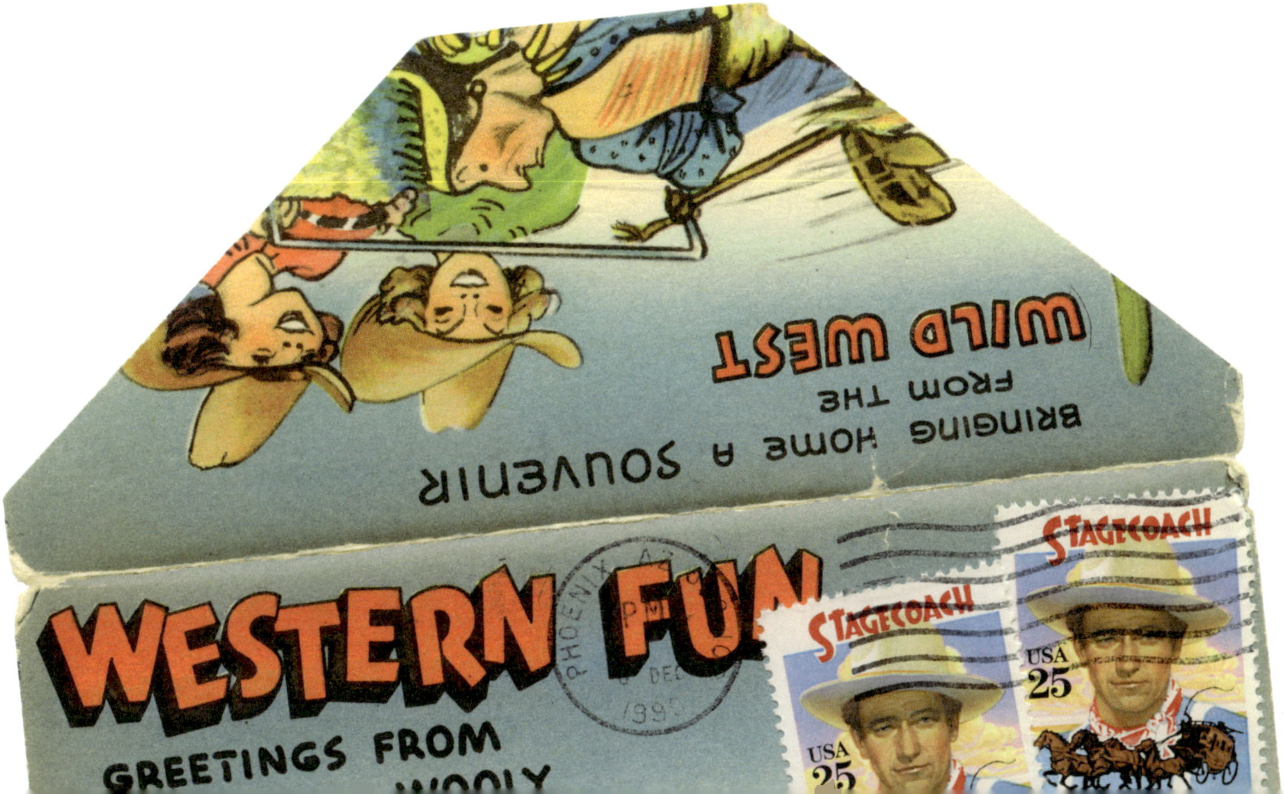
BRINGING HOME A SOUVENIR
FROM THE
WILD WEST
WESTERN FUN
GREETINGS FROM
STAGECOACH
USA 25
STAGECOACH
USA 25

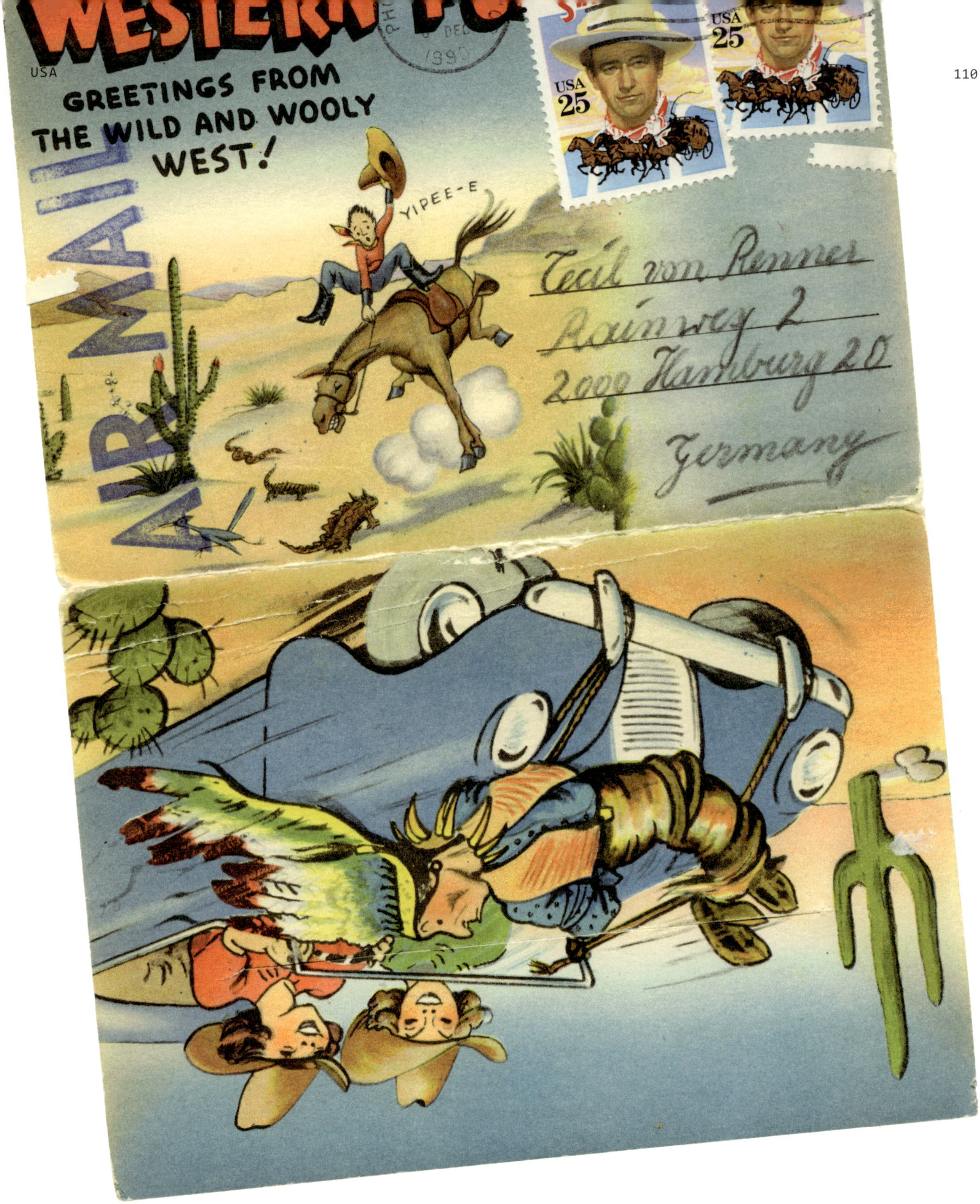
GREETINGS FROM
THE WILD AND WOOLY
WEST!
YIPEE-E
AIR MAIL
USA 25
USA 25
Rainweg 2
2000 Hamburg 20
Germany

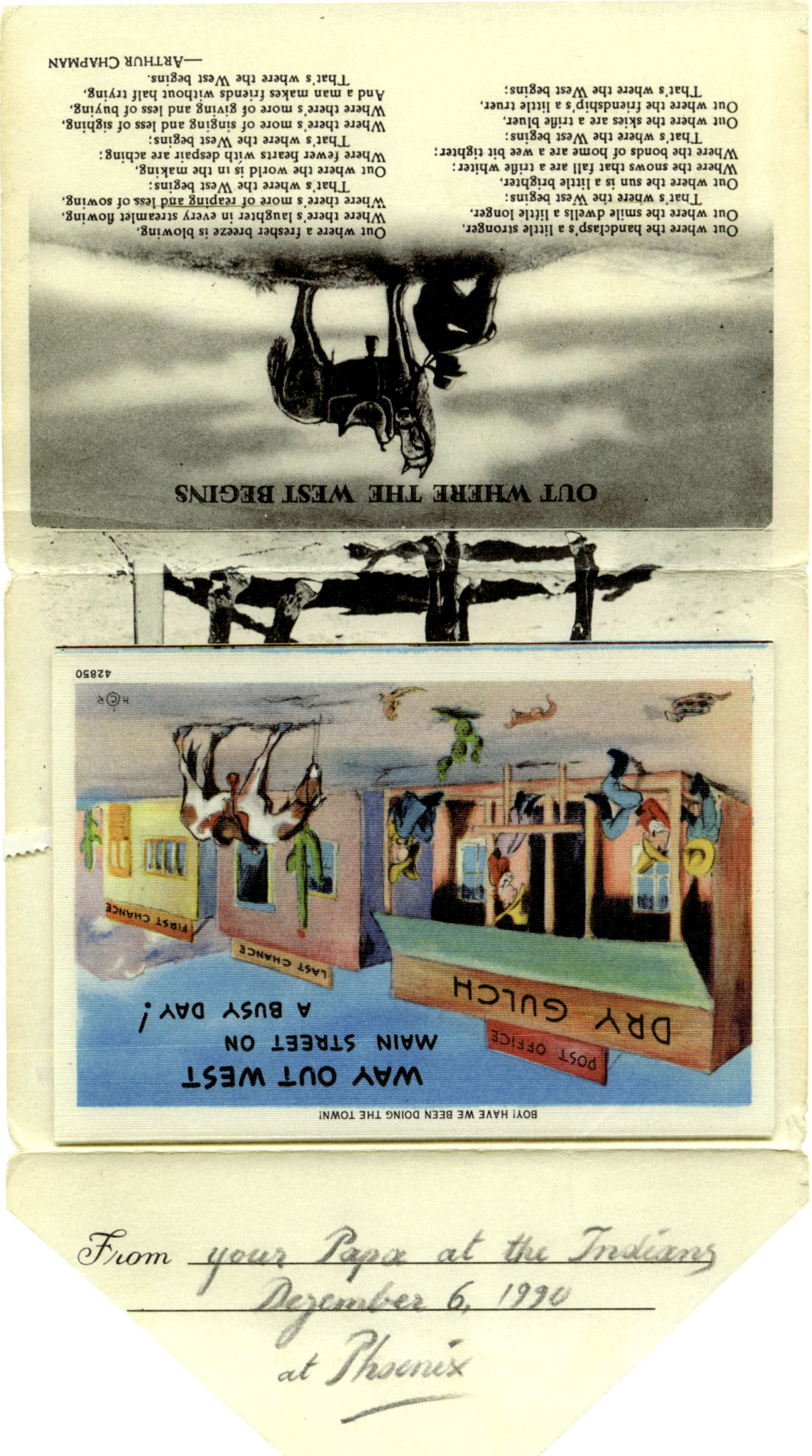
OUT WHERE THE WEST BEGINS
Out where the handclasp's a little stronger,
Out where the smile dwells a little longer,
That's where the West begins;
Out where the sun is a little brighter,
Where the snows that fall are a trifle whiter,
Where the bonds of home are a wee bit tighter;
That's where the West begins;
Out where the skies are a trifle bluer,
Out where the friendship's a little truer,
That's where the West begins.
Out where a fresher breeze is blowing,
Where there's laughter in every streamlet flowing,
Where there's more of reaping and less of sowing,
That's where the West begins;
Out where the world is in the making,
Where fewer hearts with despair are aching;
That's where the West begins;
Where there's more of singing and less of sighing,
Where there's more of giving and less of buying,
And a man makes friends without half trying,
That's where the West begins.
—ARTHUR CHAPMAN
42850
WAY OUT WEST
MAIN STREET ON
A BUSY DAY!
DRY GULCH
POST OFFICE
LAST CHANCE
FIRST CHANCE
BOY! HAVE WE BEEN DOING THE TOWN!
From your Papa at the Indians
Dezember 6, 1990
at Phoenix

Didn't fall for two days.

Among other places, the journey for Robinson Club takes us to Switzerland. I will never go location scouting on skis ever again. It could have been worse!

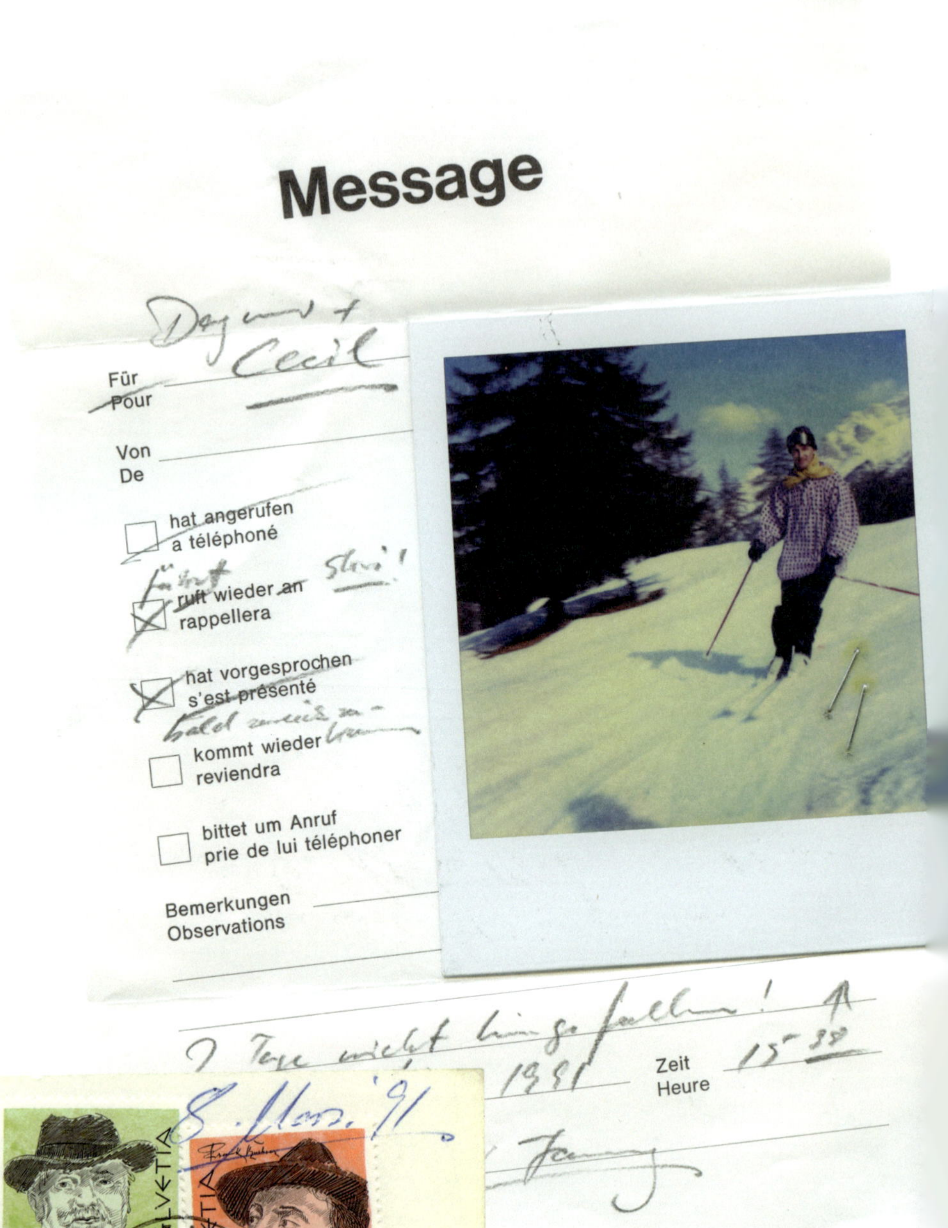

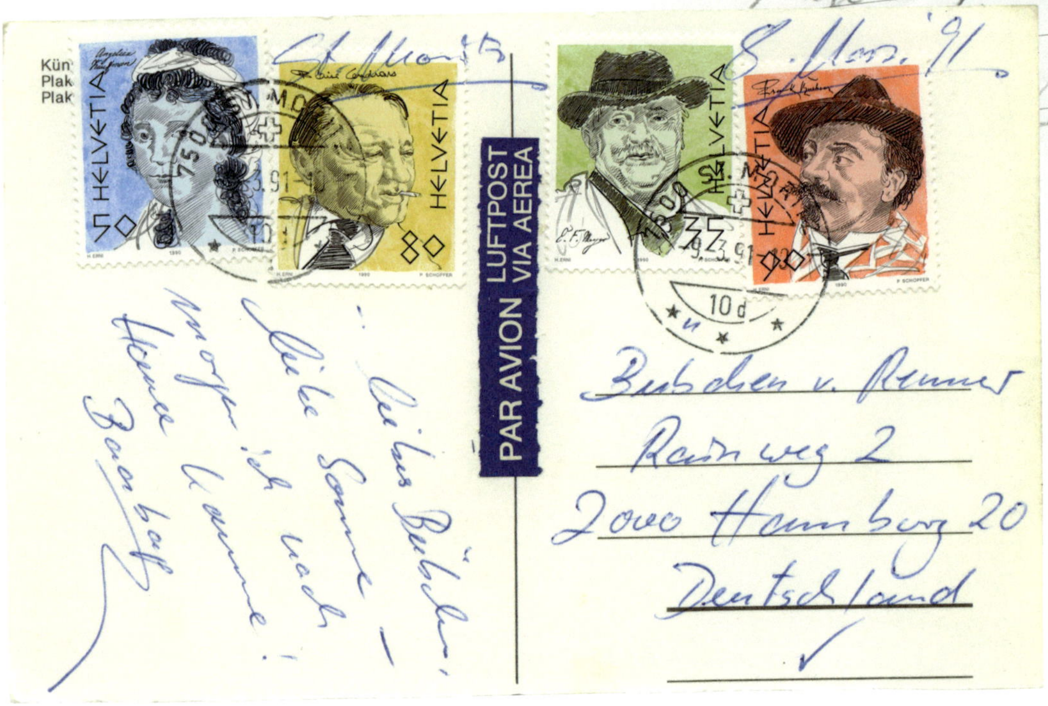

ST. MORITZ
March 9th, 1991

VULPERA

March 6th, 1991

-

Bunny on the other side!

(I neatly cut out the stamp using a scalpel and a magnifying glass).

Baabap says hello to the lovely bunny

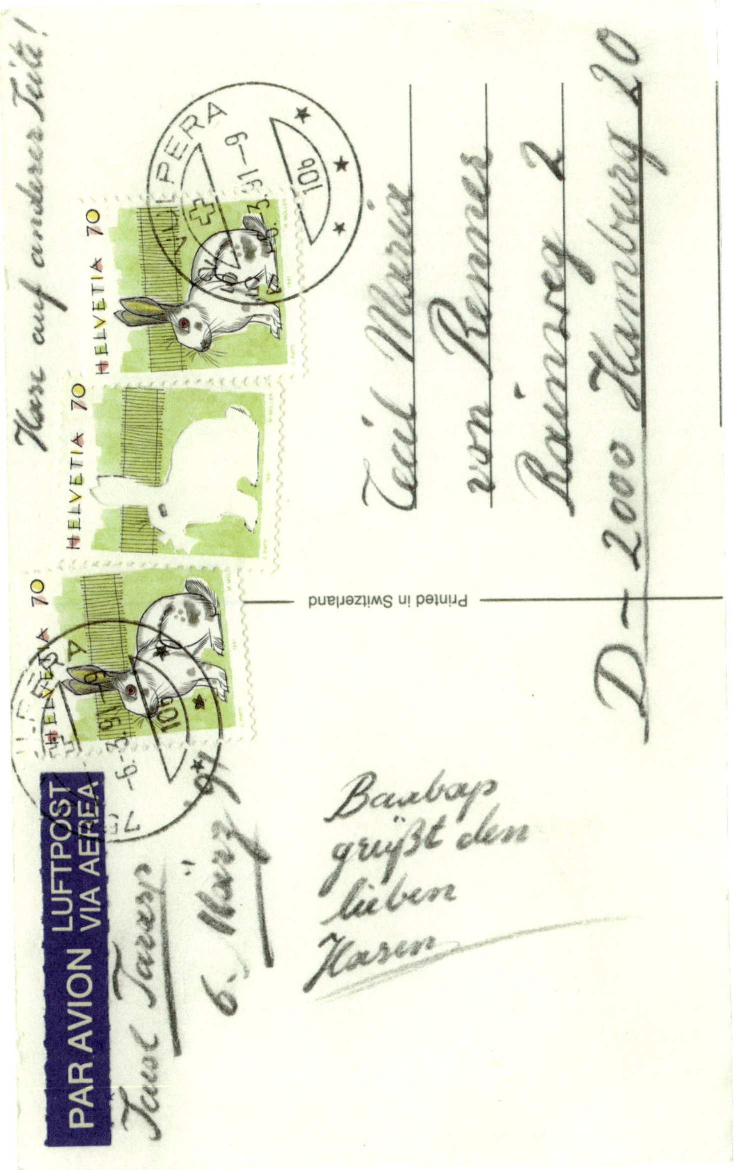

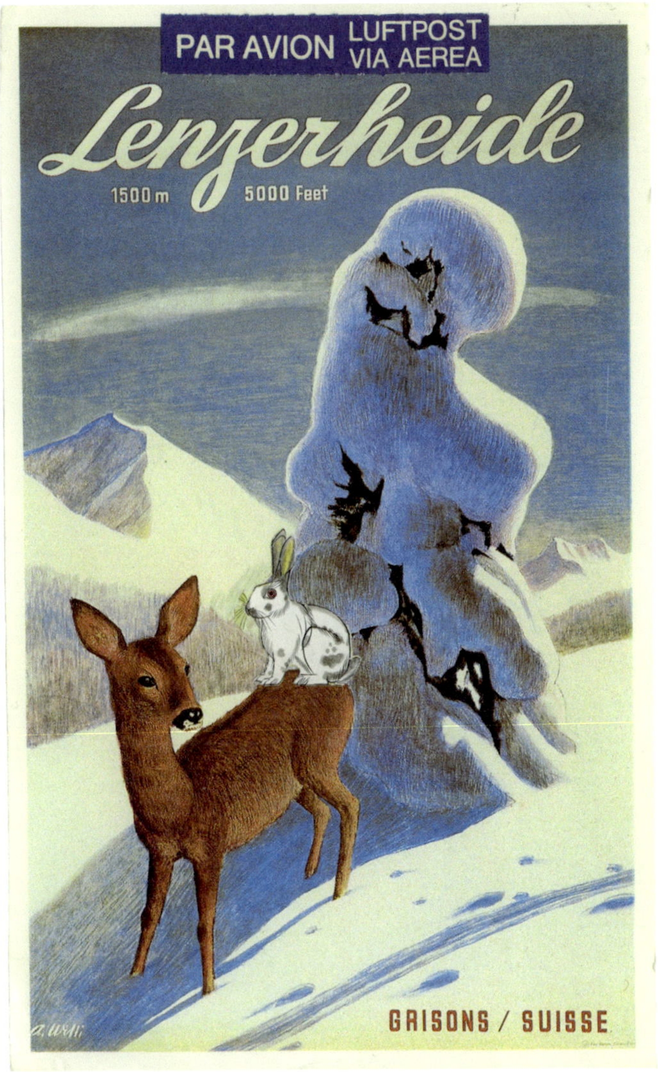

A journey for Aral to the formely barred country.

A photoshoot for Aral. As a stranger to the formerly German states, Bohemia and Moravia, which are situated beyond Saxony, form a piece of contemporary history for me. One day, Cecil will ask me what I mean …

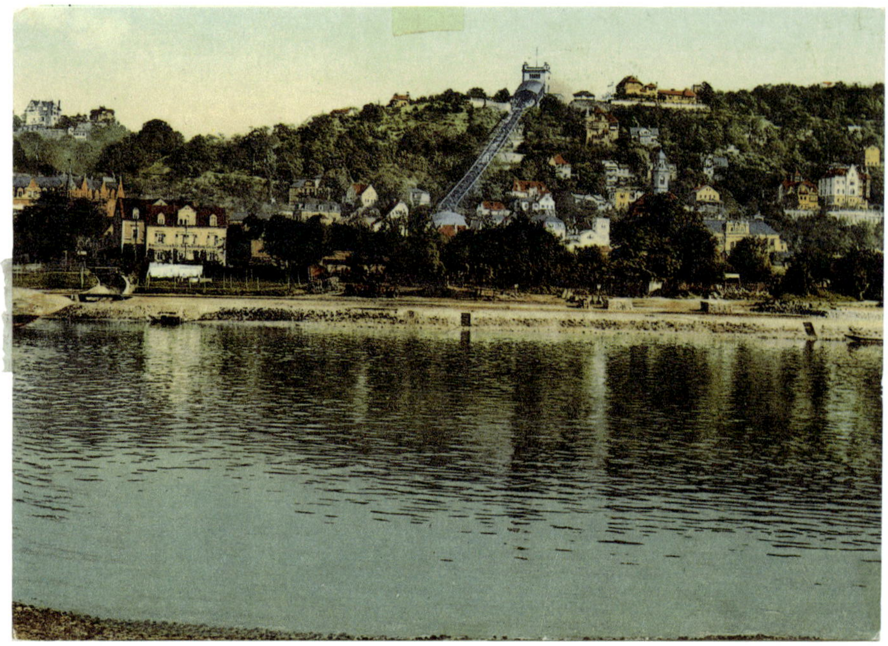

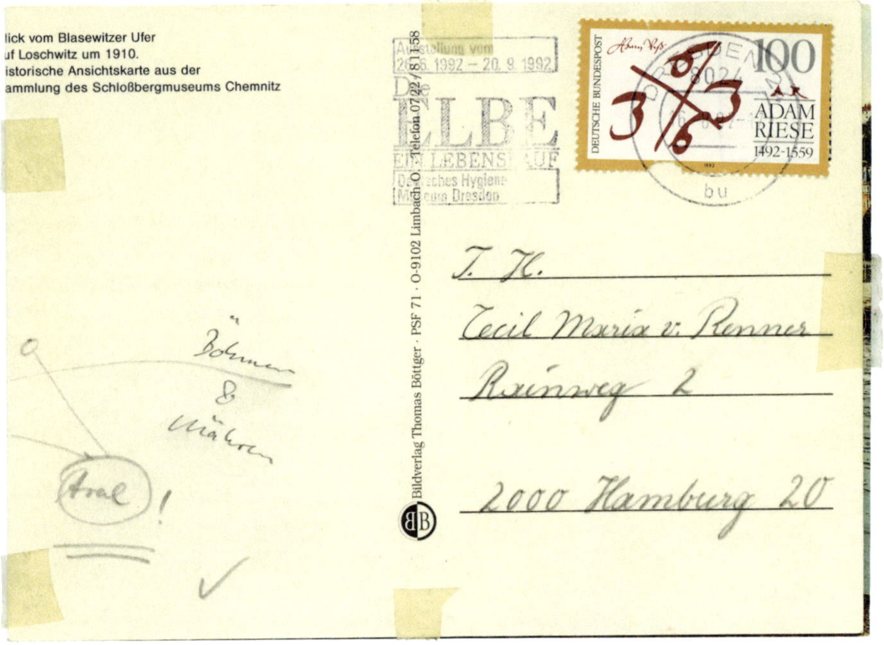

Rügen, 30. Juni '92

Kleines Bübchen, schau mal an,
wie der Pappi zaubern kann!
gestern noch am Mittelmeer,
zeig ich heut, wie schön es wär,
wenn die Tö Tö nicht nur mich
hier säh. Gruß an Mami und an Dich!

Dein Pappi

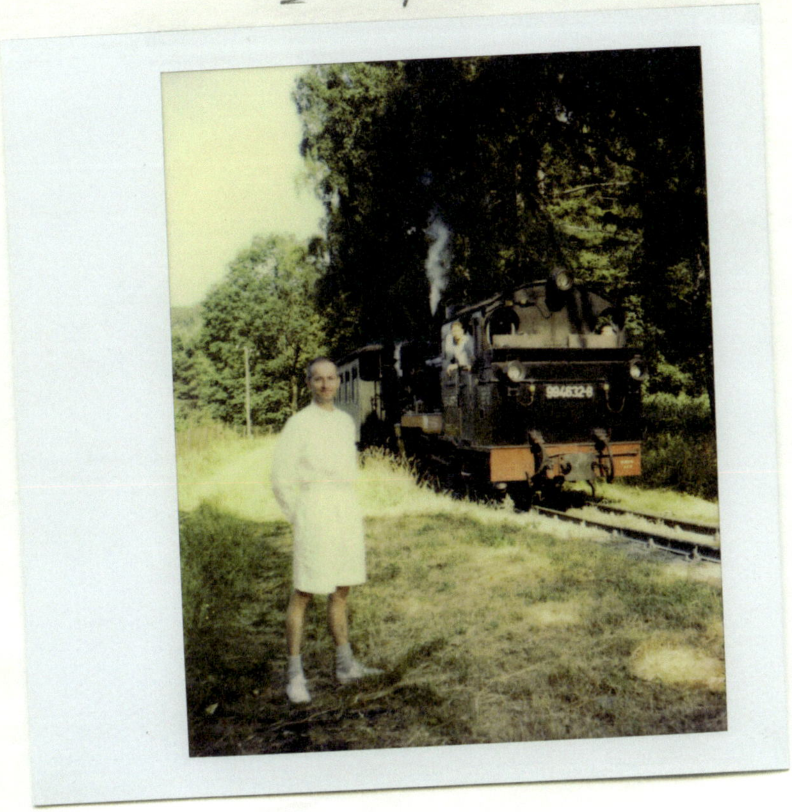

A letter from Rügen, from a VW photo shoot. We need a railway crossing in the background. That's how the picture of the locomotive came about. And, like my father, I try to infect Cecil with my love of railways. It's going to turn out to be Lego instead. Despite the Rudolf Steiner school.

RÜGEN
June 30th, 1992
–
Little peewee, have a look
at the photograph I took.
Yesterday still at the Côte d'Azur
it would be nice to have you here
now at this place with my new toy.
Say hello to Mami, boy!
Your Pappi.

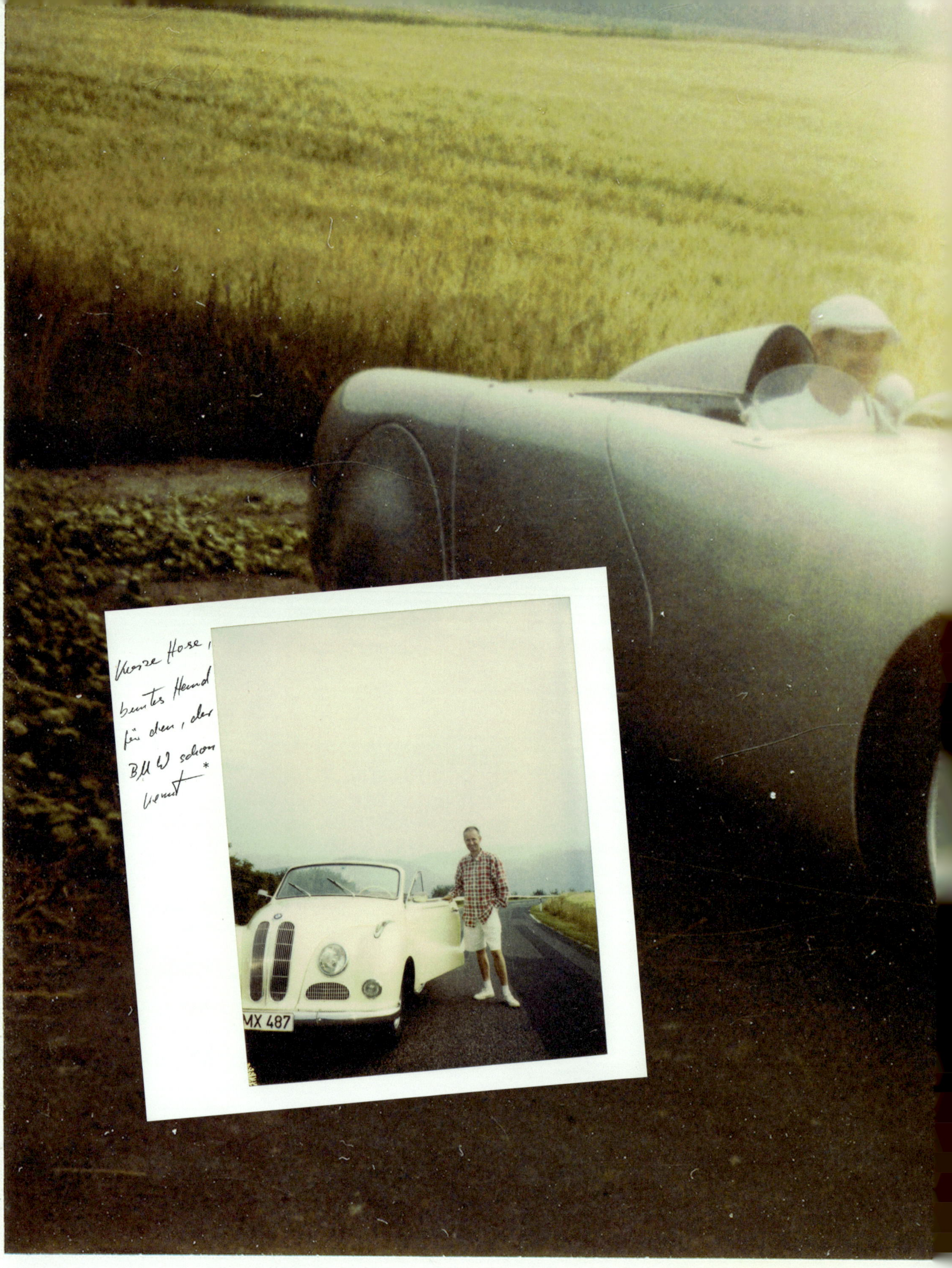

During the photo shooting for Aral, I'm sitting in one of three cars that I ever really desired as a man. Its price diminishes all my dreams.

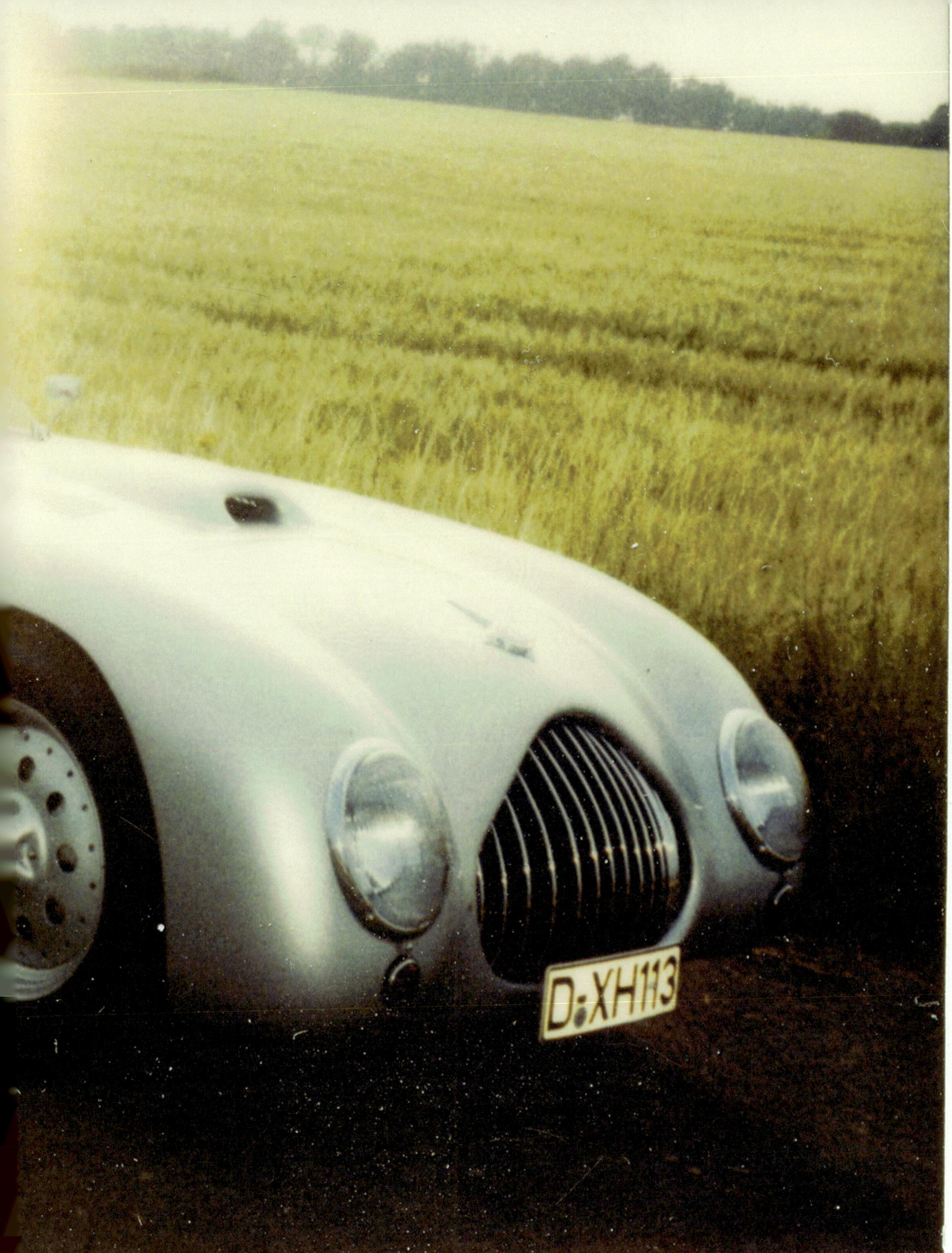
D-XH113

“We make the Italians as beautiful as our country” …

… is the title of the campaign. The aim is to show a couple clad in lingerie or swimming clothes, in places that make it look like they had just taken a tourist selfie where this is not allowed. For example, wearing pyjamas in the Cafe Greco in Rome.

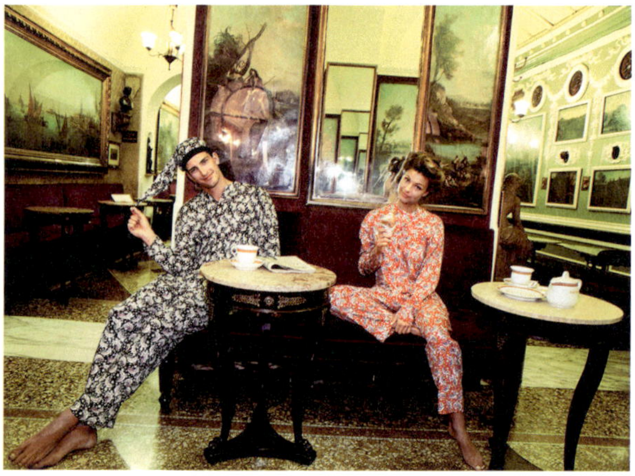

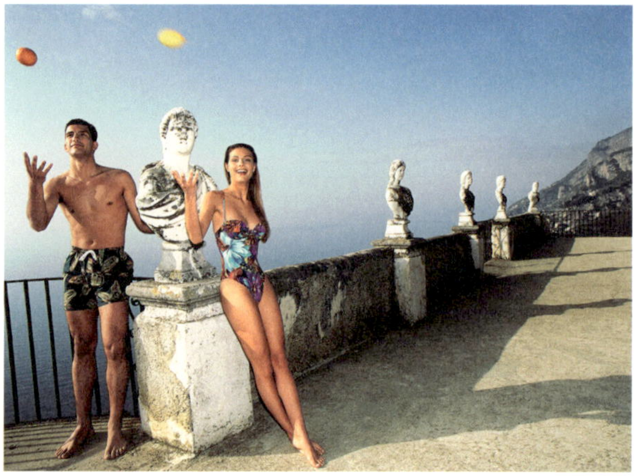

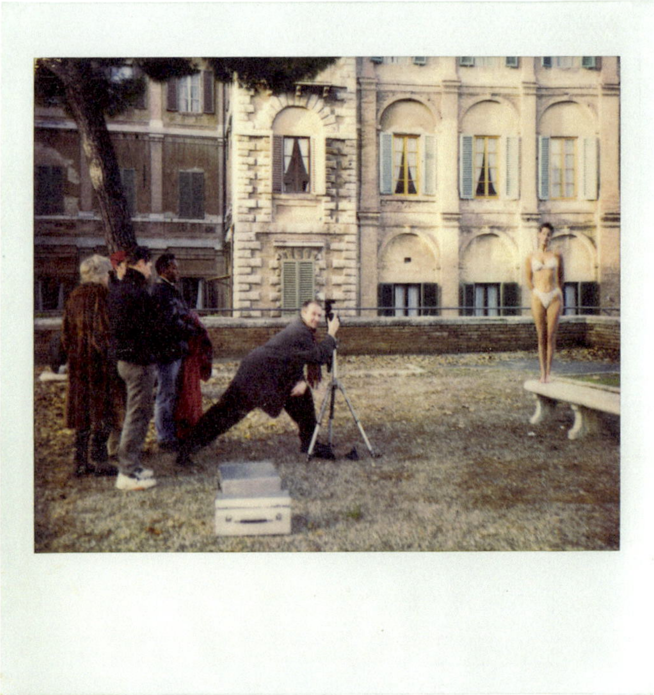

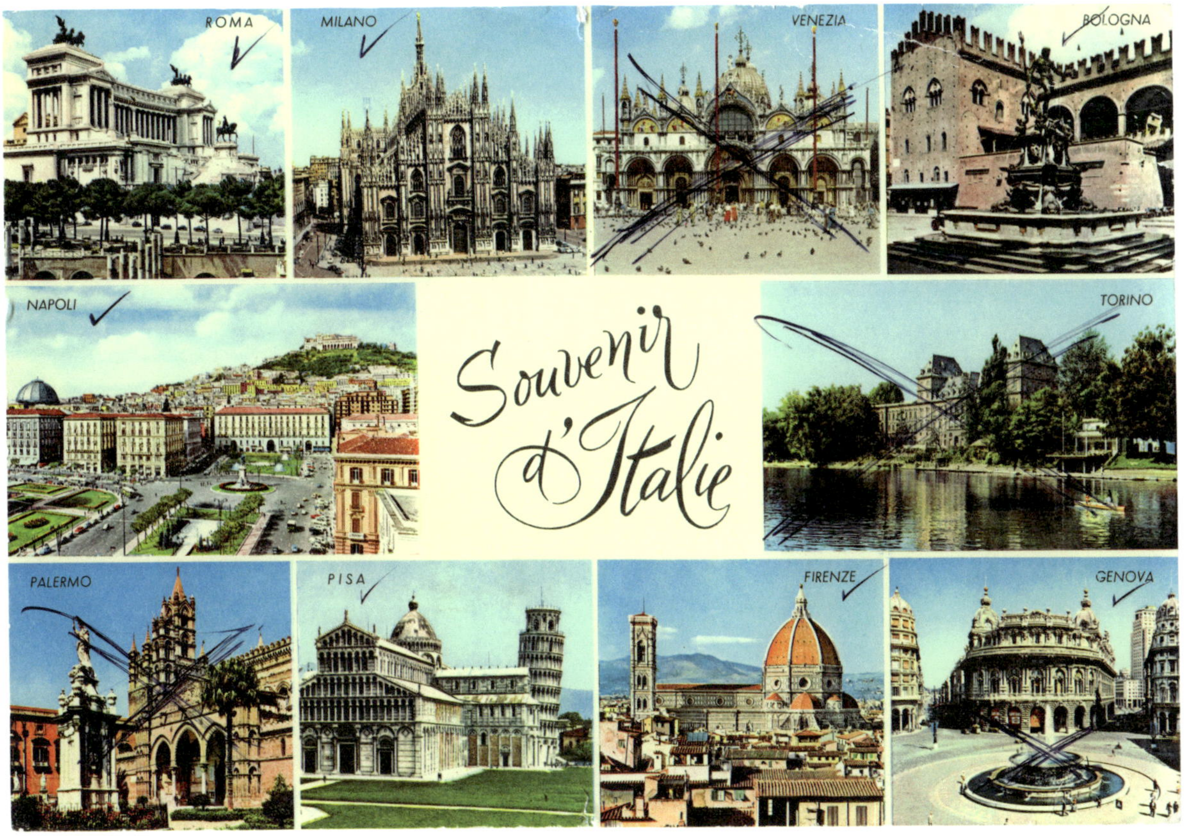

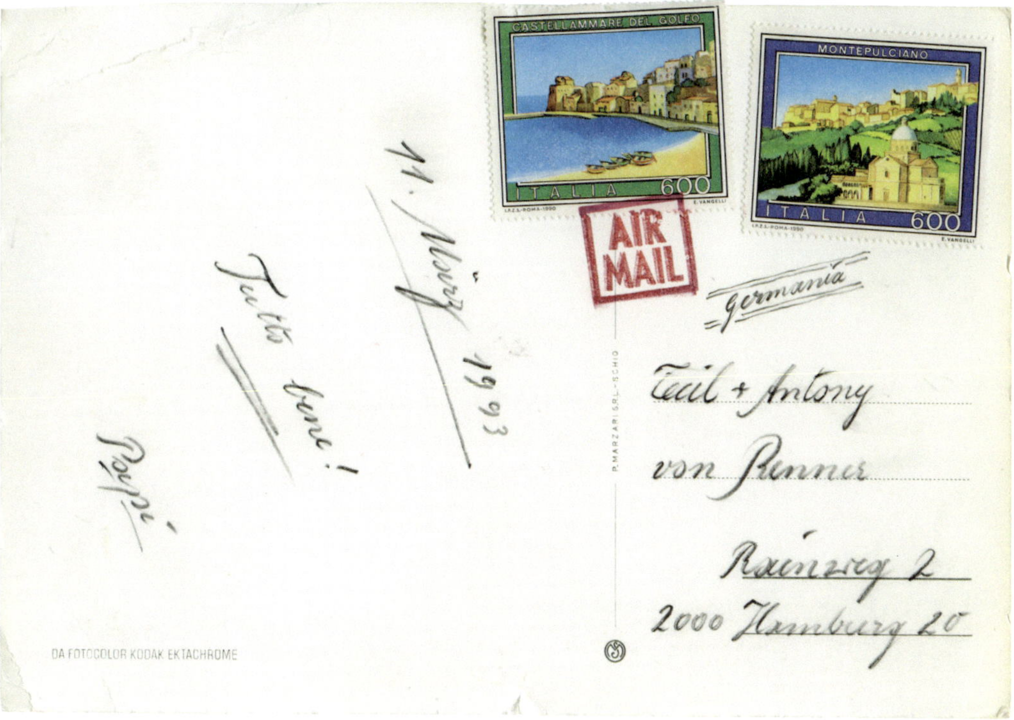

ITALY

March 11th, 1993

-

“Tutto bene!

Papi”

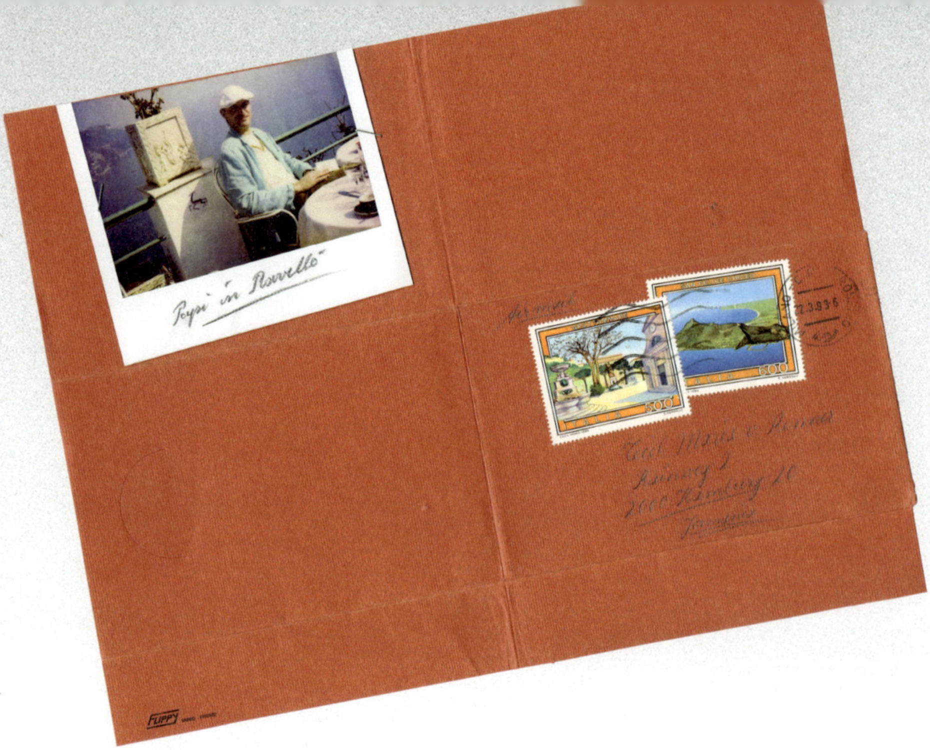

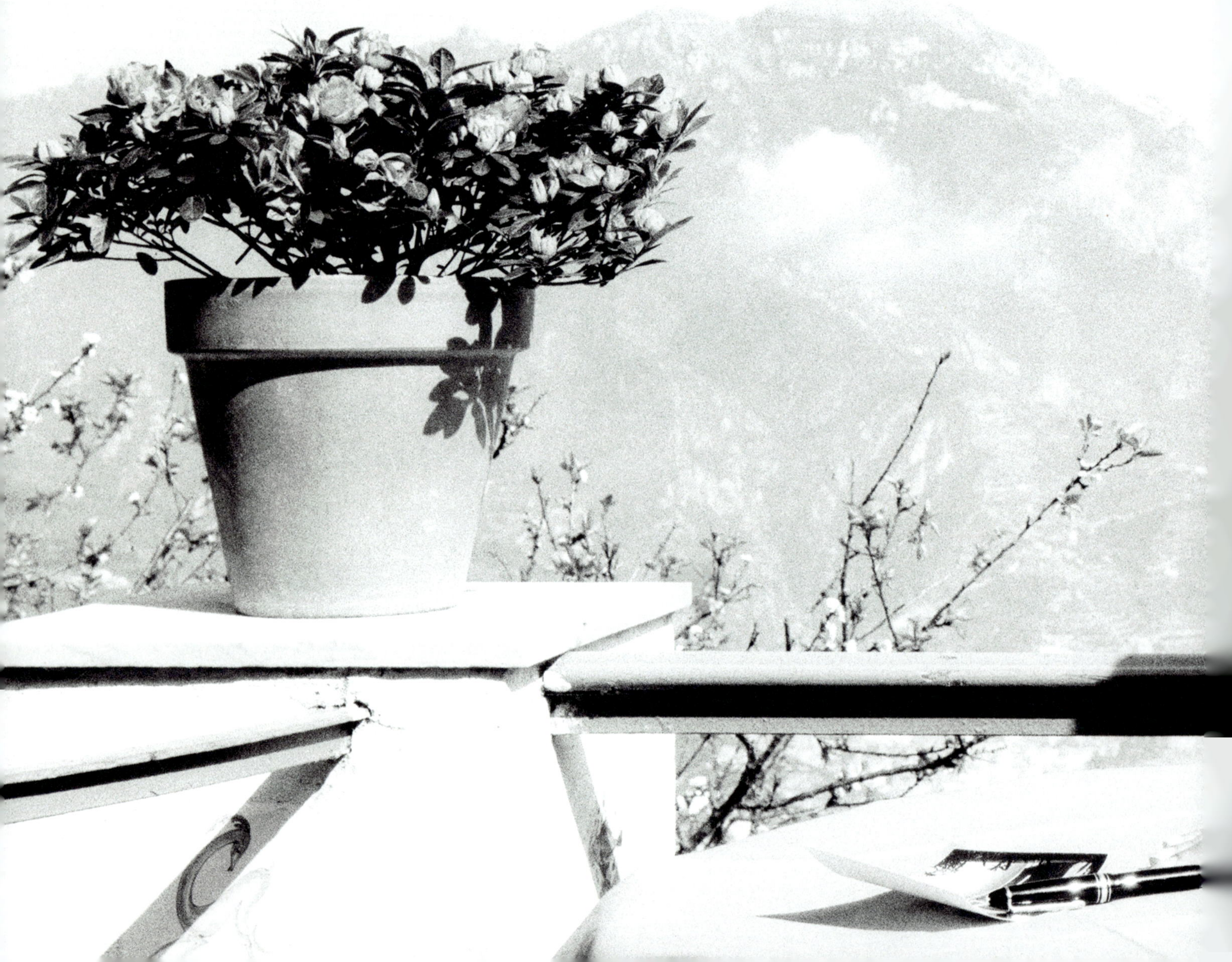

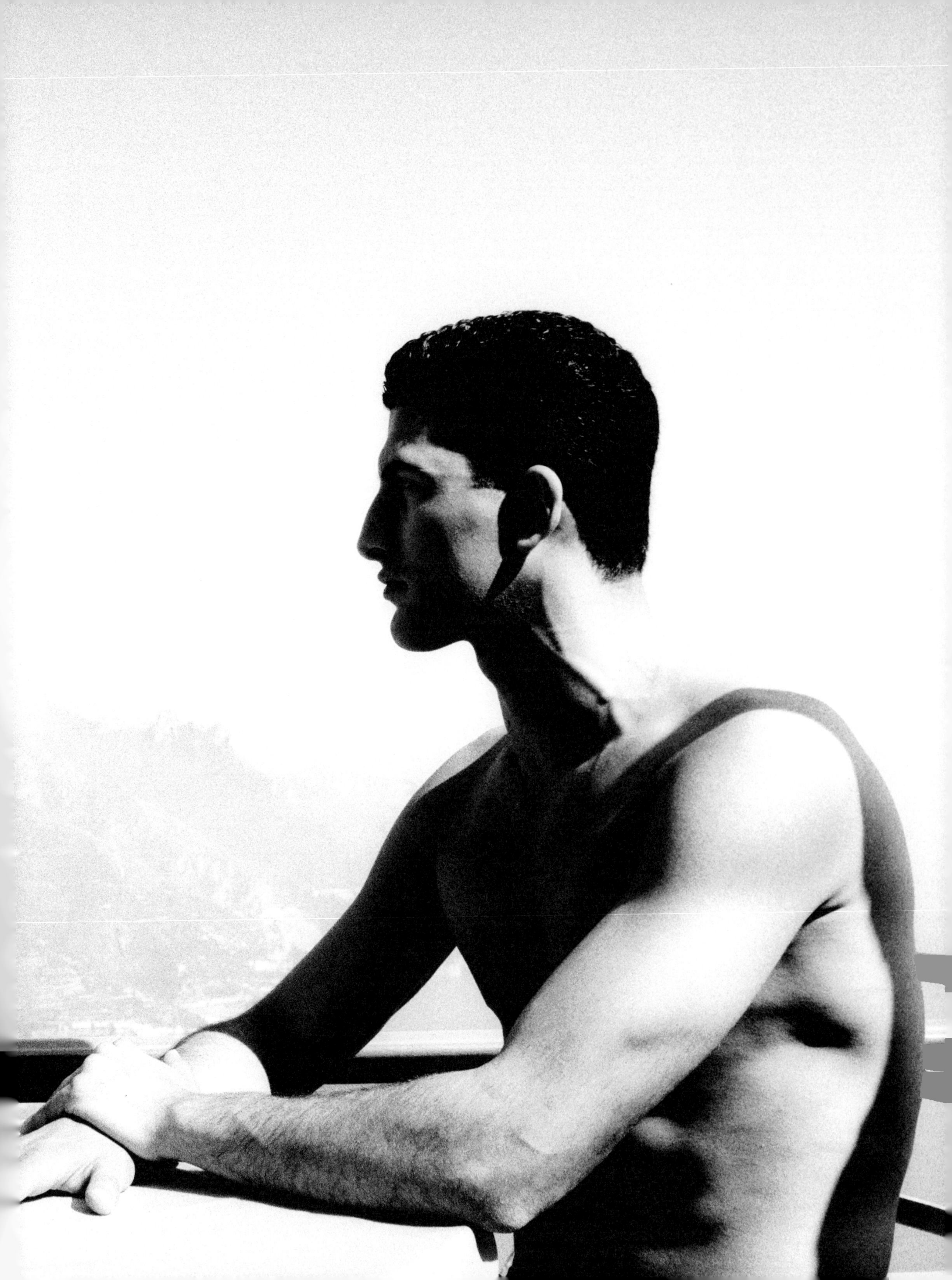

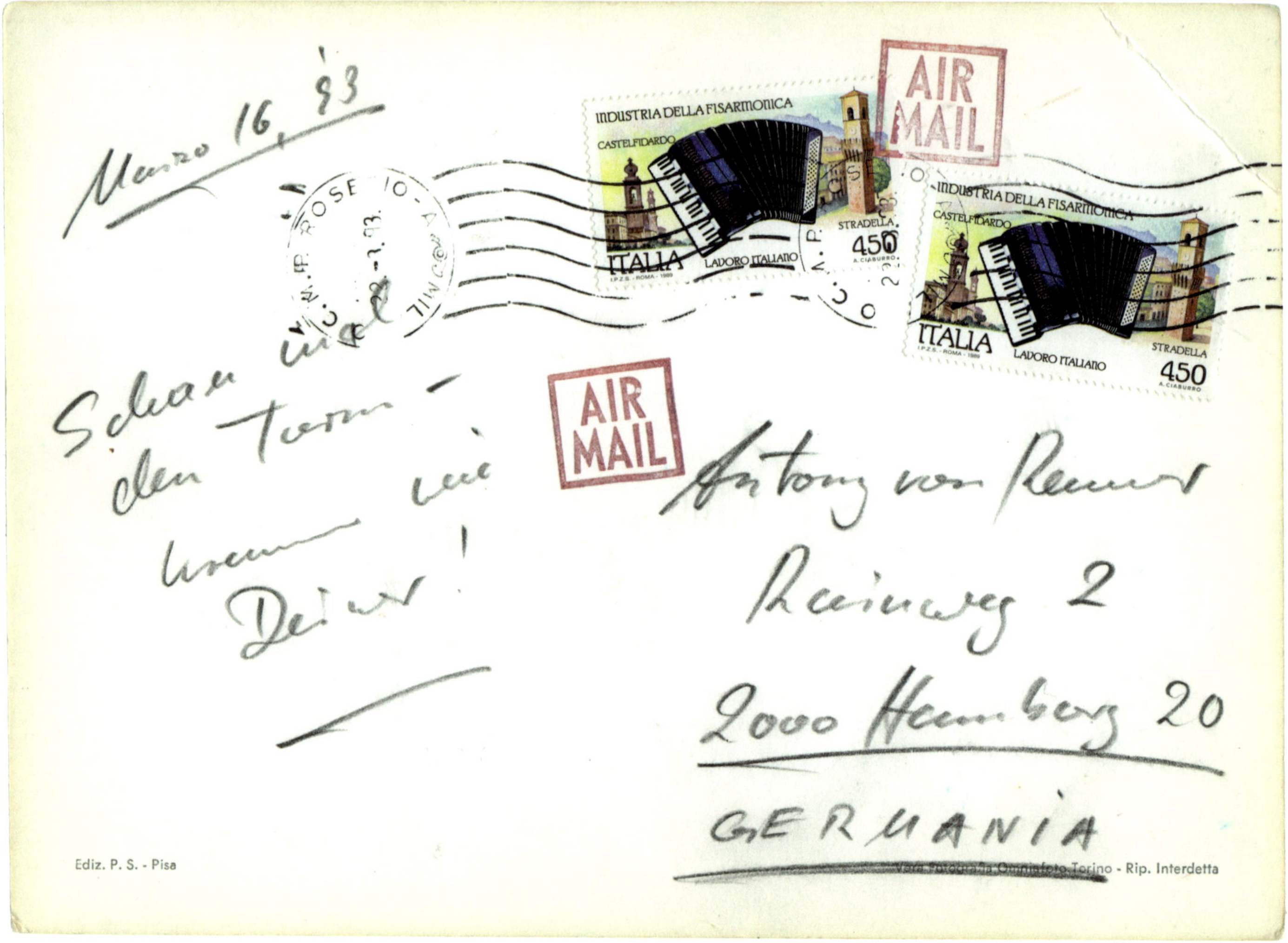

PISA
March 16th, 1993
-
Look at the tower -
crooked like yours!

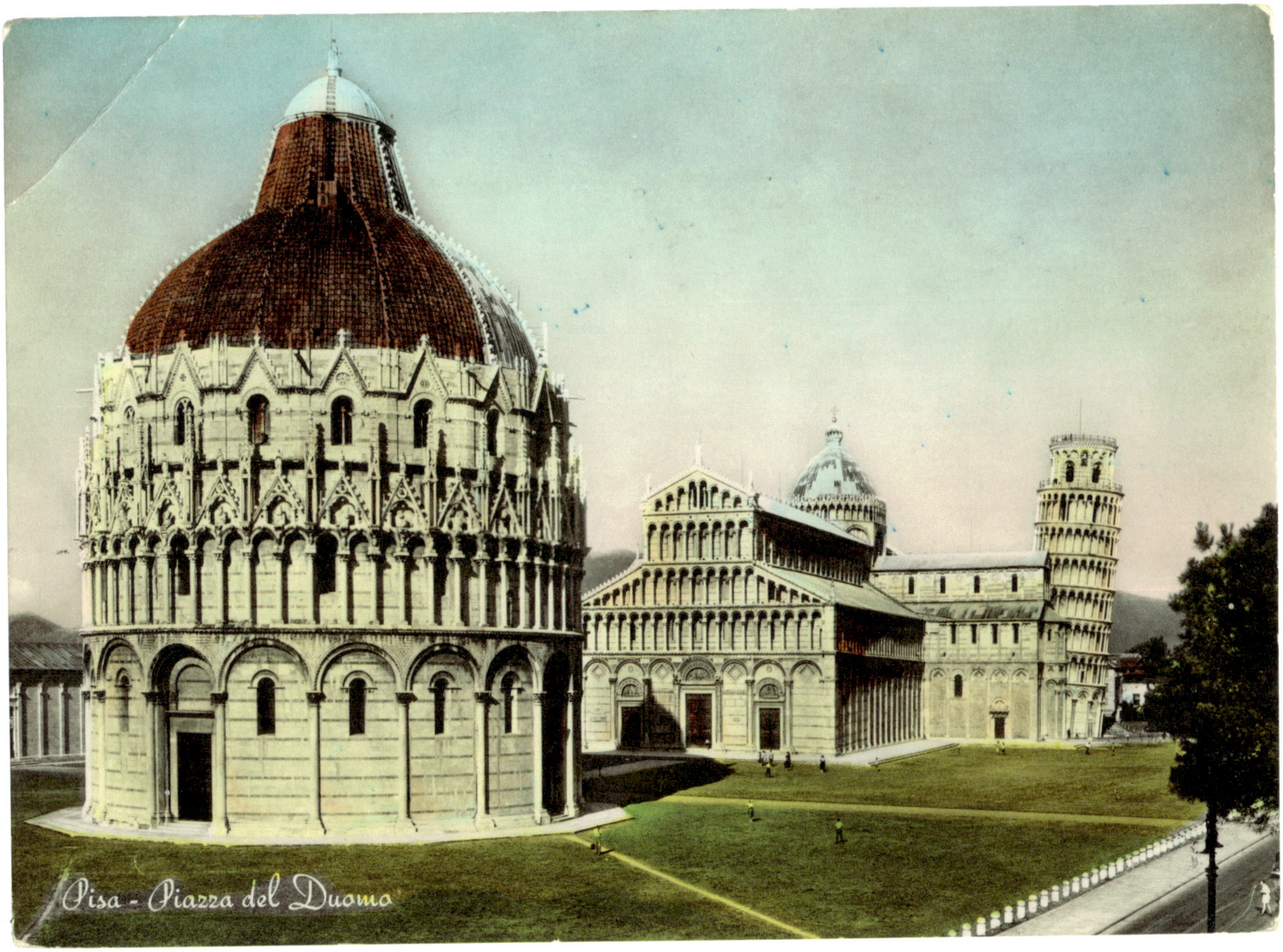
Pisa - Piazza del Duomo

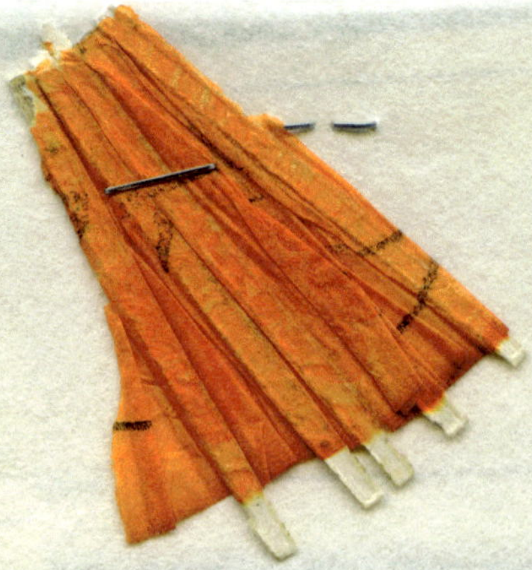

Ich liebe Dich

16.3.93

MU

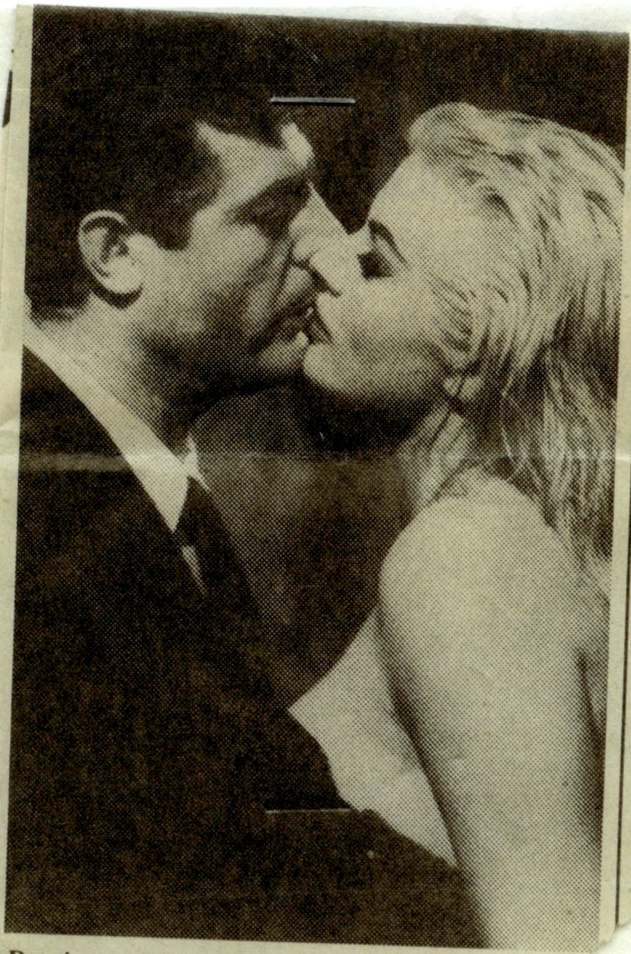

Due immagini storiche dalla «Dolce vita» di Fellini: a sinistra il bagno di Anita Ekberg n fontana, a destra il bacio con Mastroianni (dal libro «La dolce vita», a cura di Gianfranco Angelucci)

I

pu
ria
ro
to
pa
il
di

cho
e stre
wells,
ening
ar

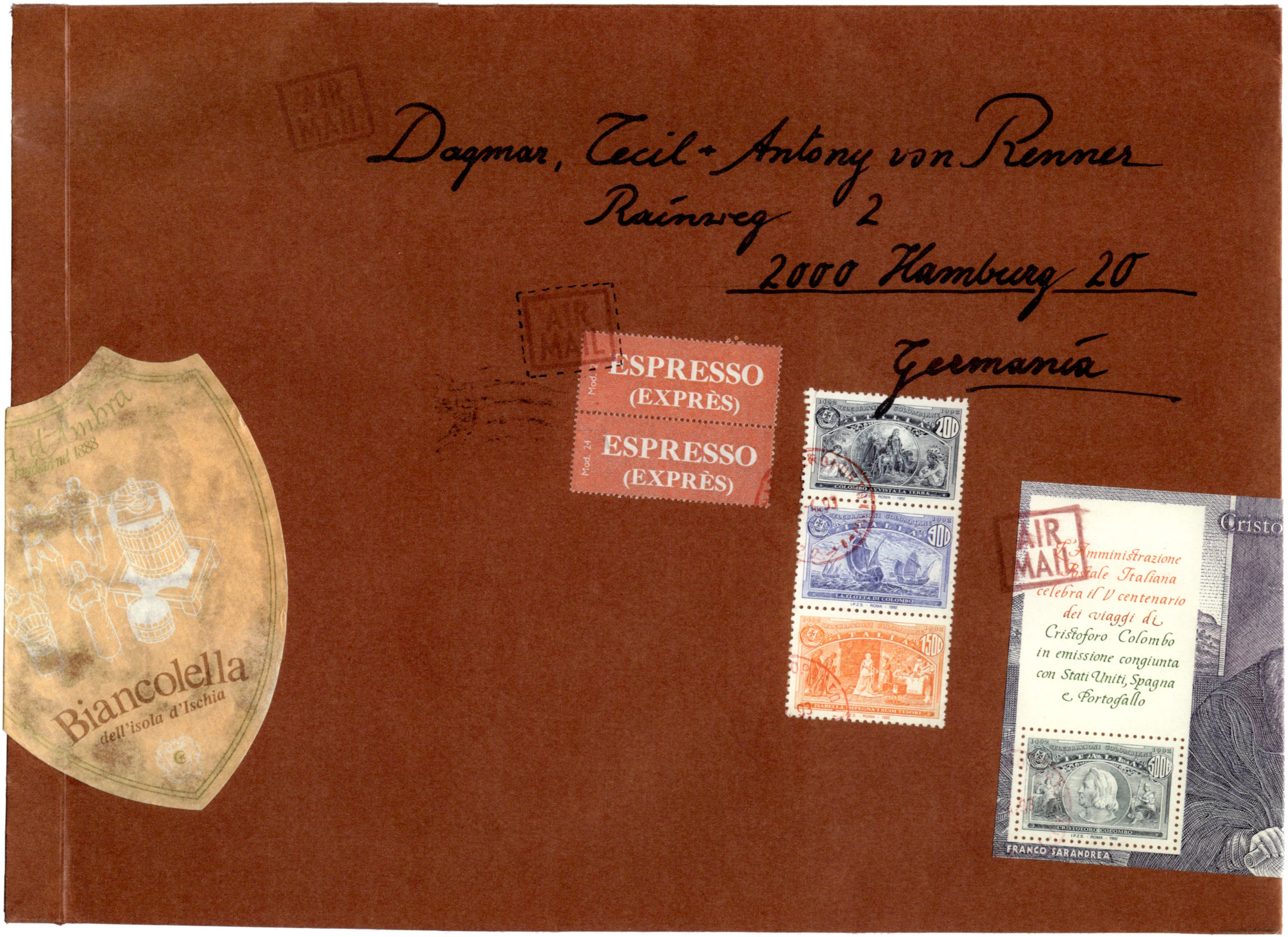
AIR MAIL
Dagmar, Cecil + Antony von Renner
Rainweg 2
2000 Hamburg 20
Germania
ESPRESSO
(EXPRÈS)
ESPRESSO
(EXPRÈS)
Mod. 24
L'Amministrazione
Postale Italiana
celebra il V centenario
dei viaggi di
Cristoforo Colombo
in emissione congiunta
con Stati Uniti, Spagna
e Portogallo
FRANCO SARANDREA
Biancolella
dell'isola d'Ischia

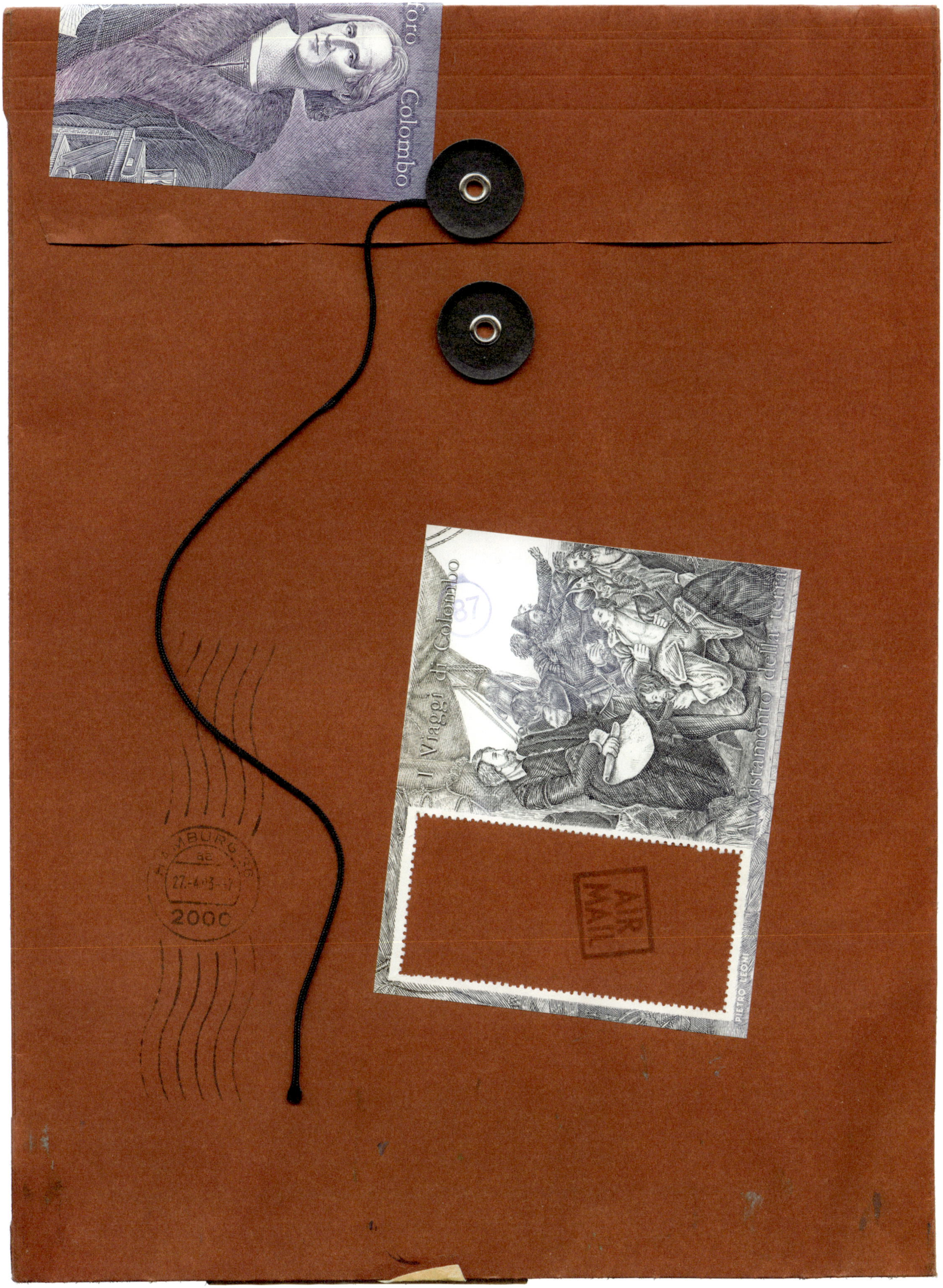
foro Colombo
I Viaggi di Colombo
Avvistamento della terra
PIETRO LEON
2000
AIR MAIL

Venison five times.

Aral requests a photo of a Mini pulling a mobile home over a mountain pass. Removing a wooden board and mounting a tow-bar to my VW Passat Variant officially makes the composition ready for use. During our tour to Switzerland, our agitated client calls to let us know he refuses to pay for anything, as he is familiar with the difficult weather situation in the Alps. And there is no snow, he says. Due to my research, we decide to go anyways, and take the picture within three hours: I calculate the mountains with a map and a compass in the evening fog, have the snow cleared the next morning and click! We have lunch when very slowly, like in a children's fairy tale, the snow begins to fall again. The next morning we inform the client that we are snowed in. Two days and two nights later, a special unit helps us cross the Grimselpass, which is closed off behind us for six months. The lunch and dinner menus read venison every day. Good venison days with good red wine can never be long enough …

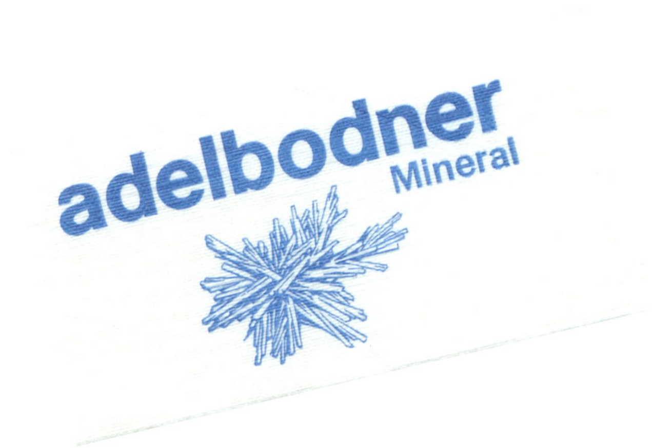

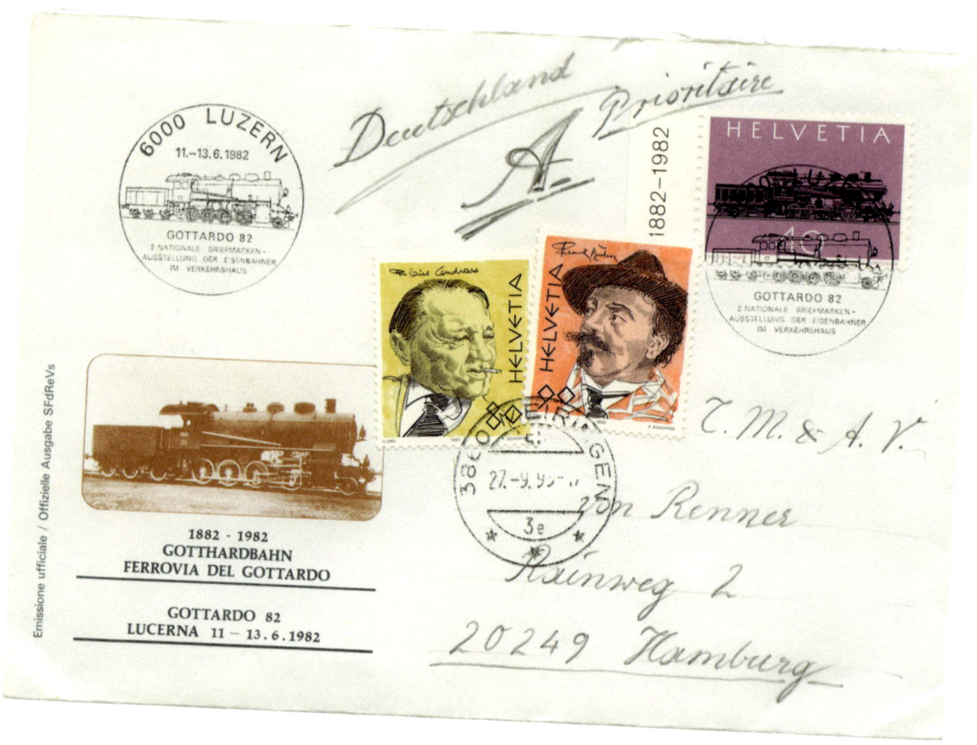

GRIMSELPASS
September 27th, 1993

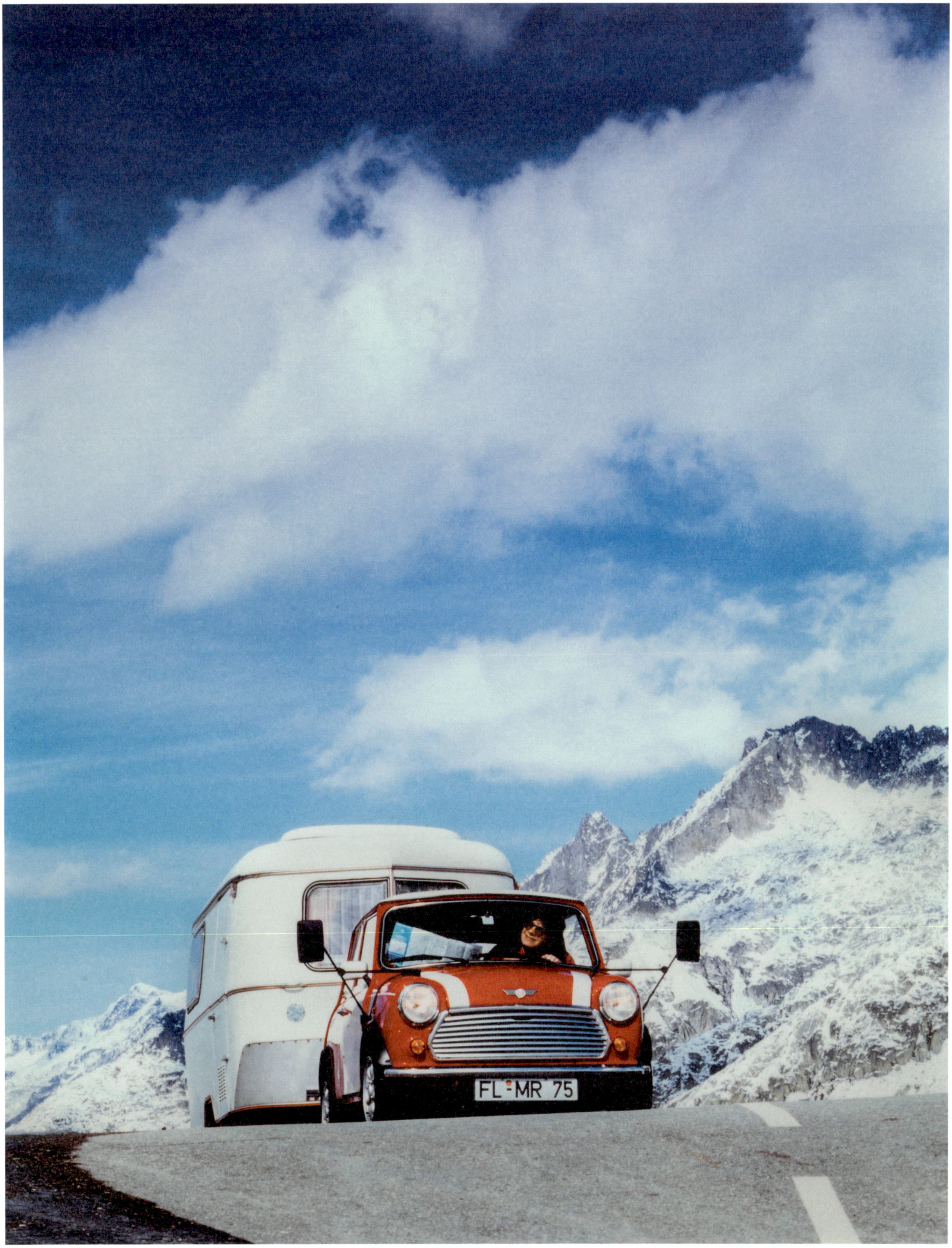
FL MR 75

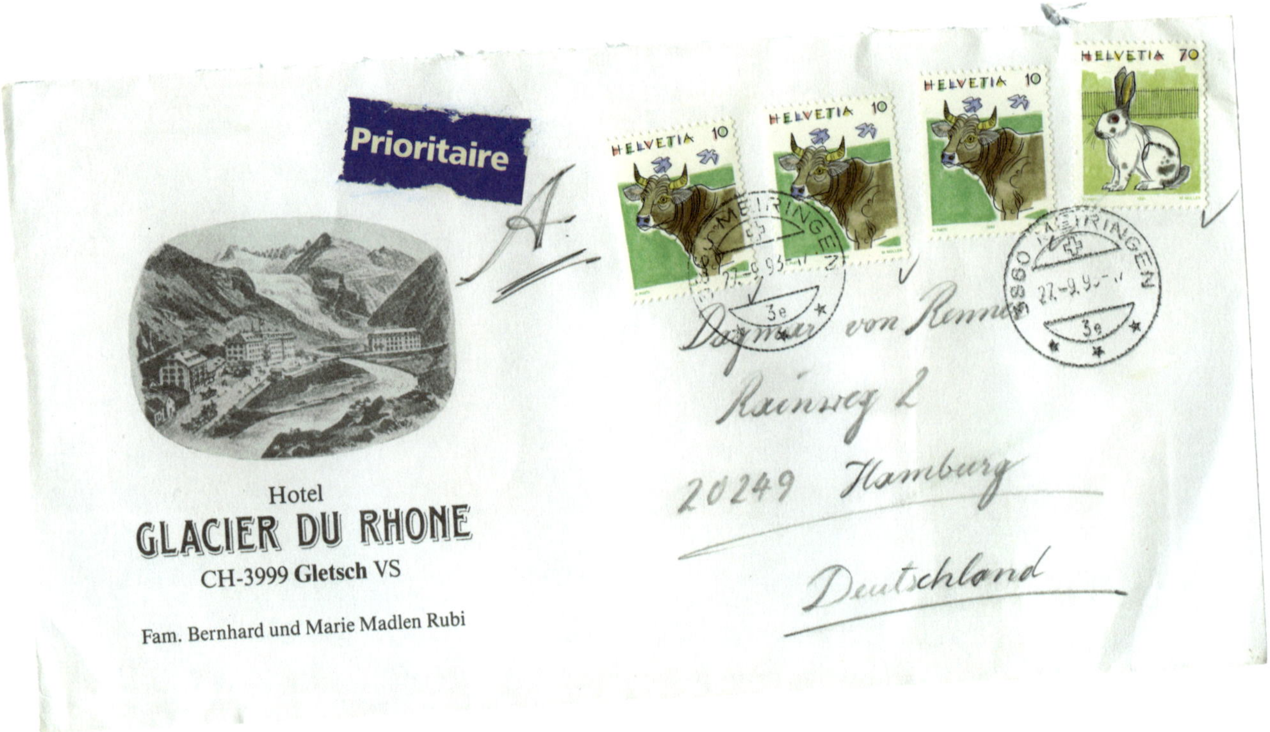

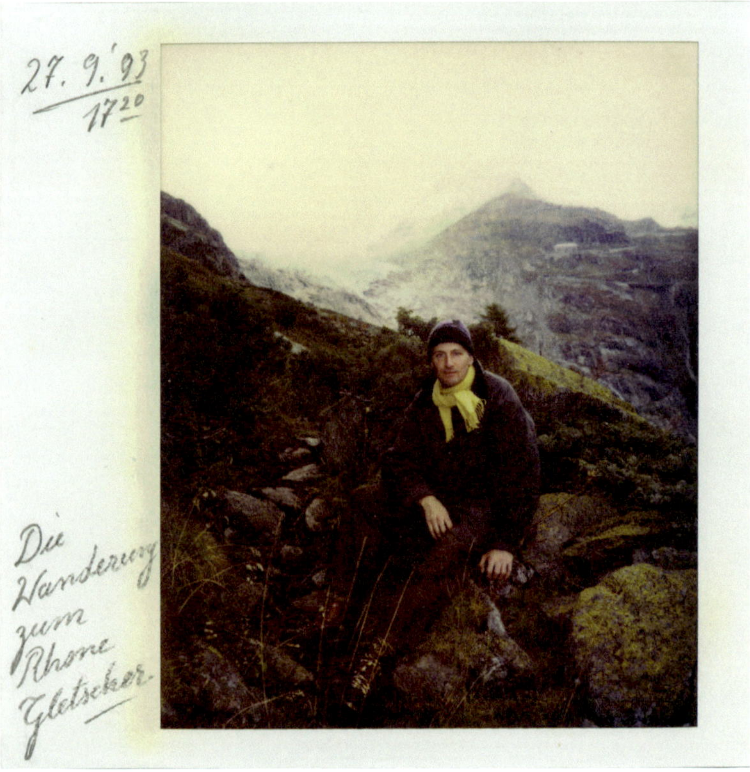

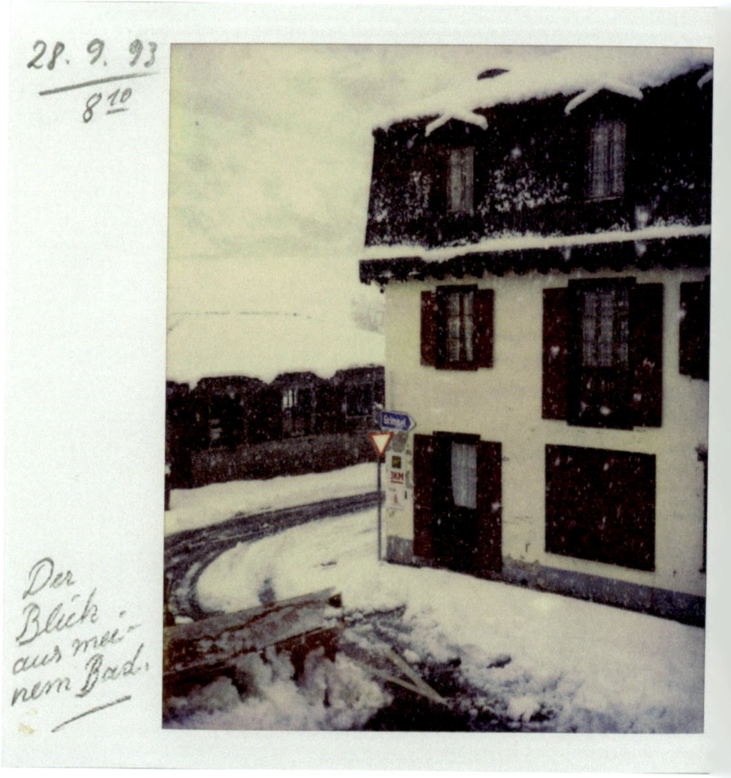

GRIMSELPASS

September 27th, 1993, 5:20 p.m.

-

The hiking tour to the Rhone glacier.

GRIMSELPASS

September 29th, 1993, 8:10 a.m.

-

The view from my bathroom.

"26 years later" means 26 years after I crossed the St. Gotthard from Hamburg towards Italy by bike.

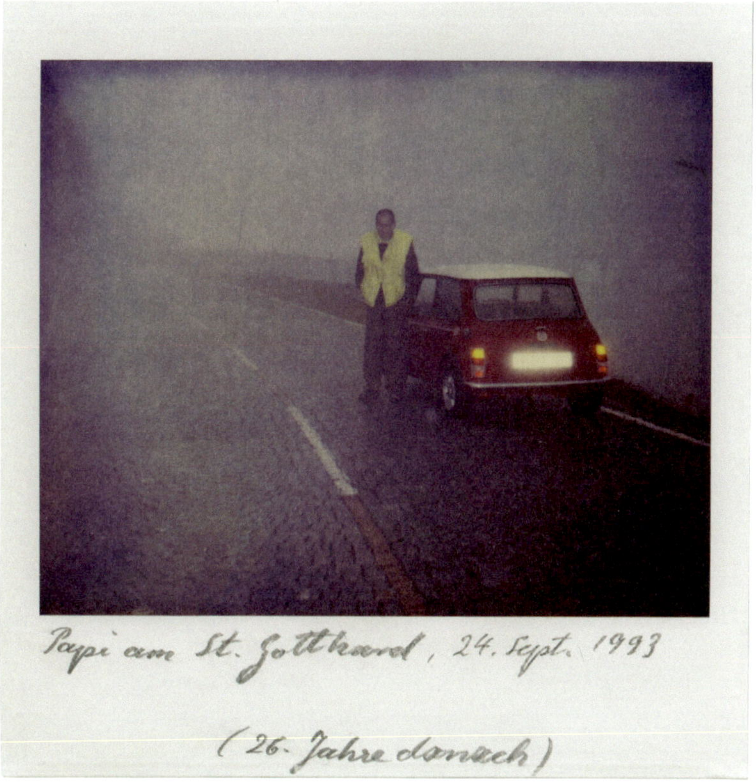

ST. GOTTHARD
September 24th, 1993
-
Papi at St. Gotthard, Sept. 24th, 1993
(26 years thereafter)

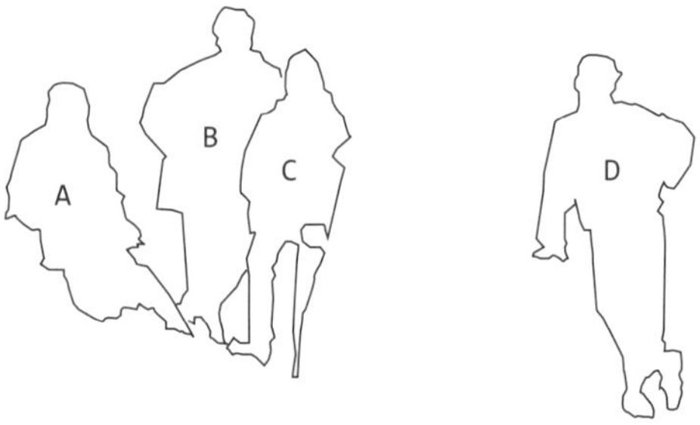

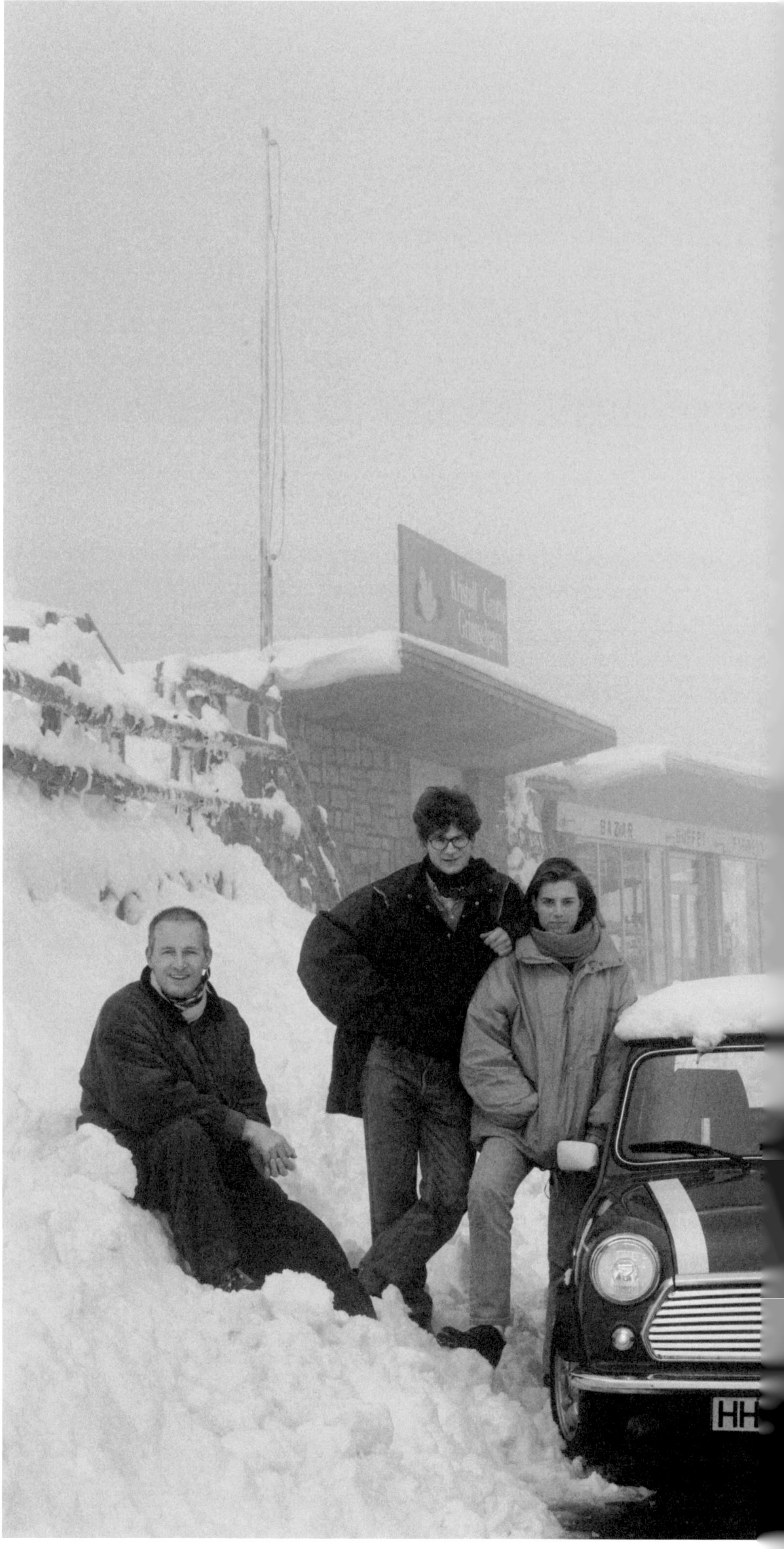

Group photo at the Grimselpass

A Me

B Martin Kaeswurm, assistant

C Annette Mieth, intern

D Wolfgang Stolten,
creative director

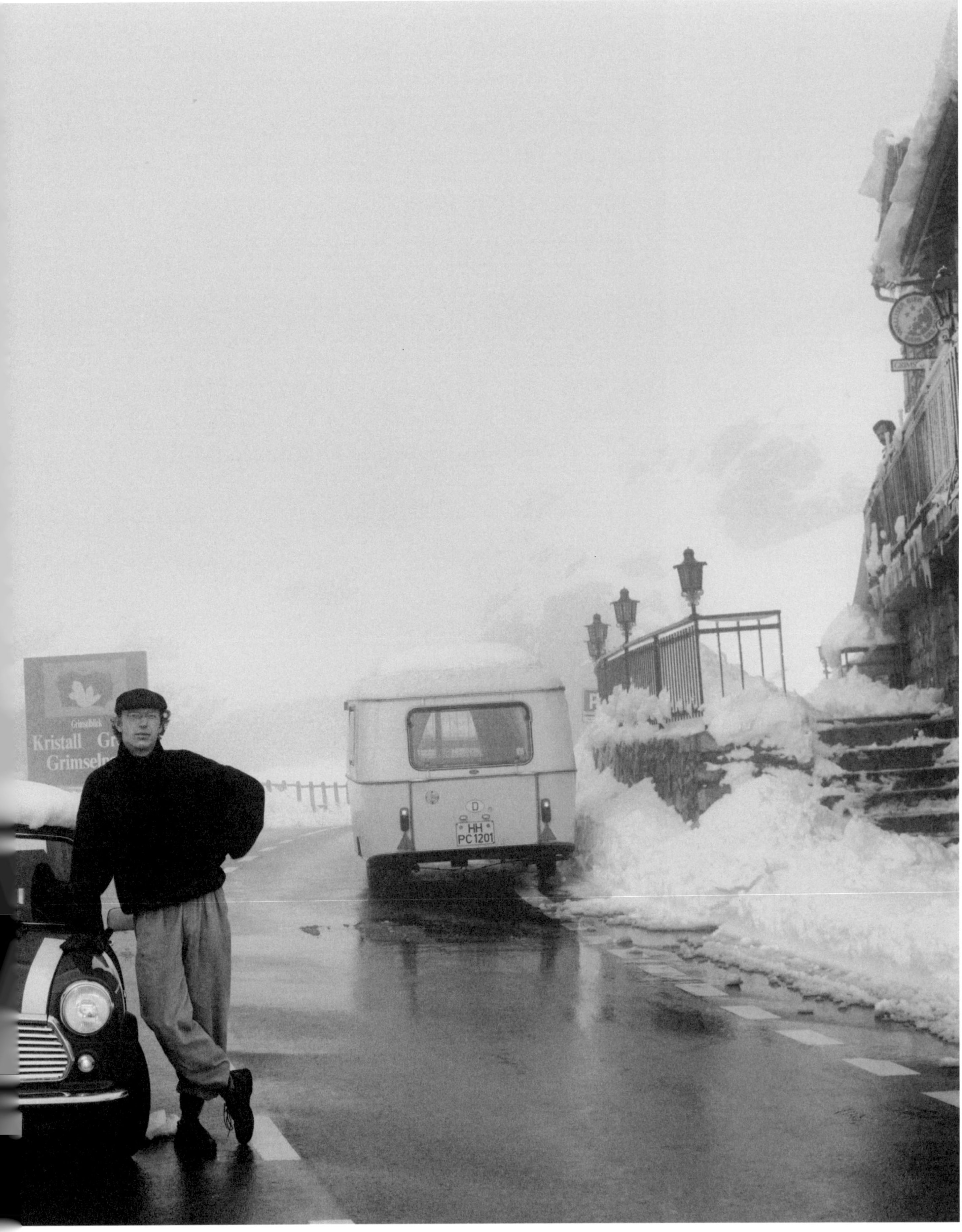
Kristall
D
HH
PC 1201

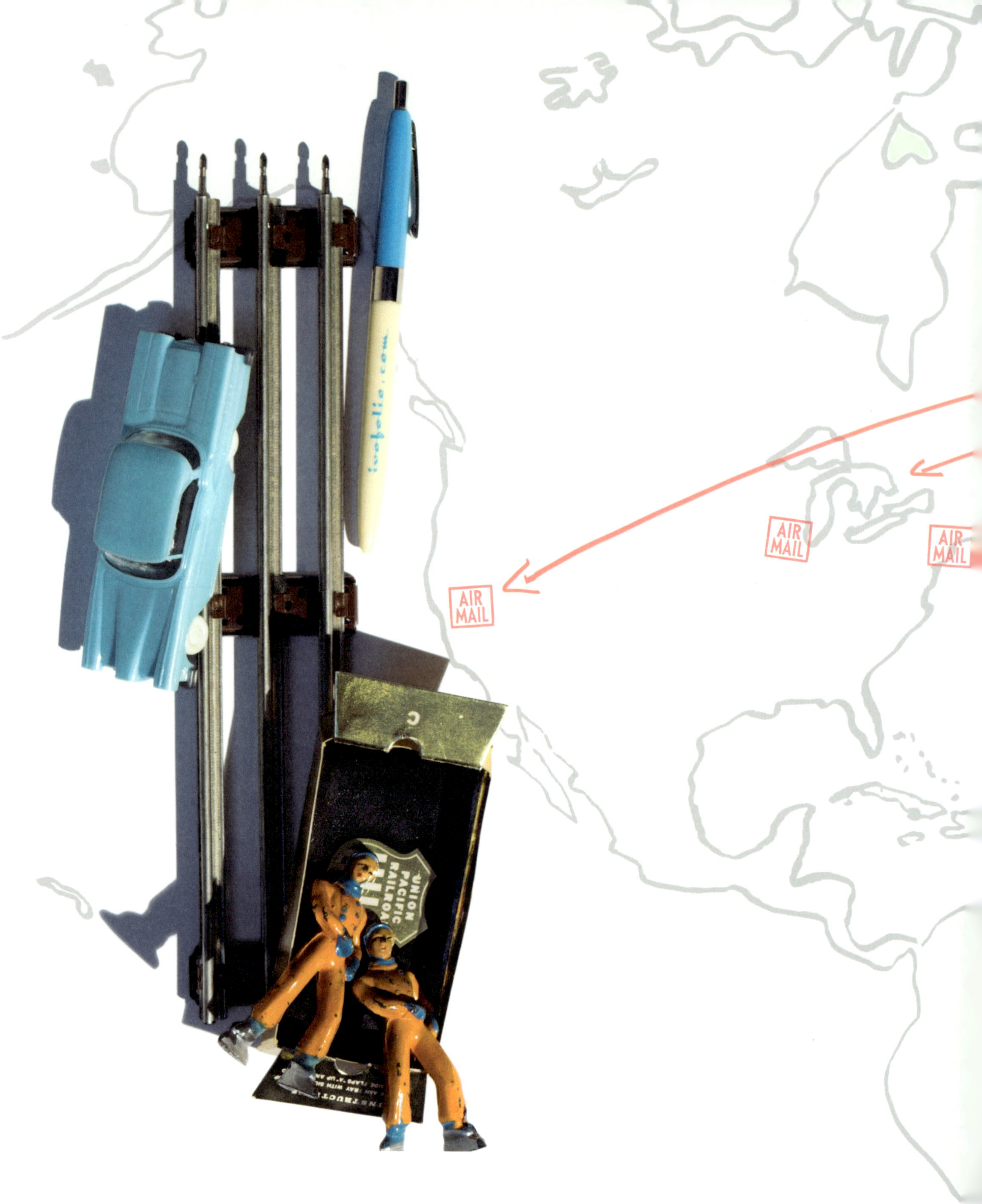
AIR MAIL
AIR MAIL
AIR MAIL

1994–1998
Belgique
Italia
USA
South Africa
España
Schweiz
France
England

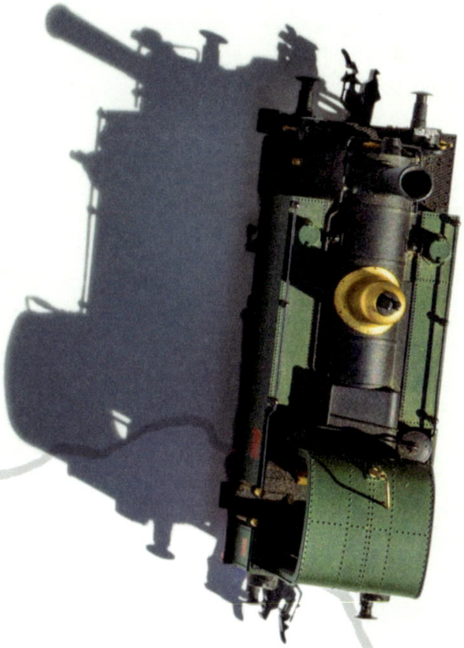

Brussels and Bulgari.

We are in Brussels to portray the Belgian representative of Bulgari. I send my two sons similar cards, for reasons of fairness.

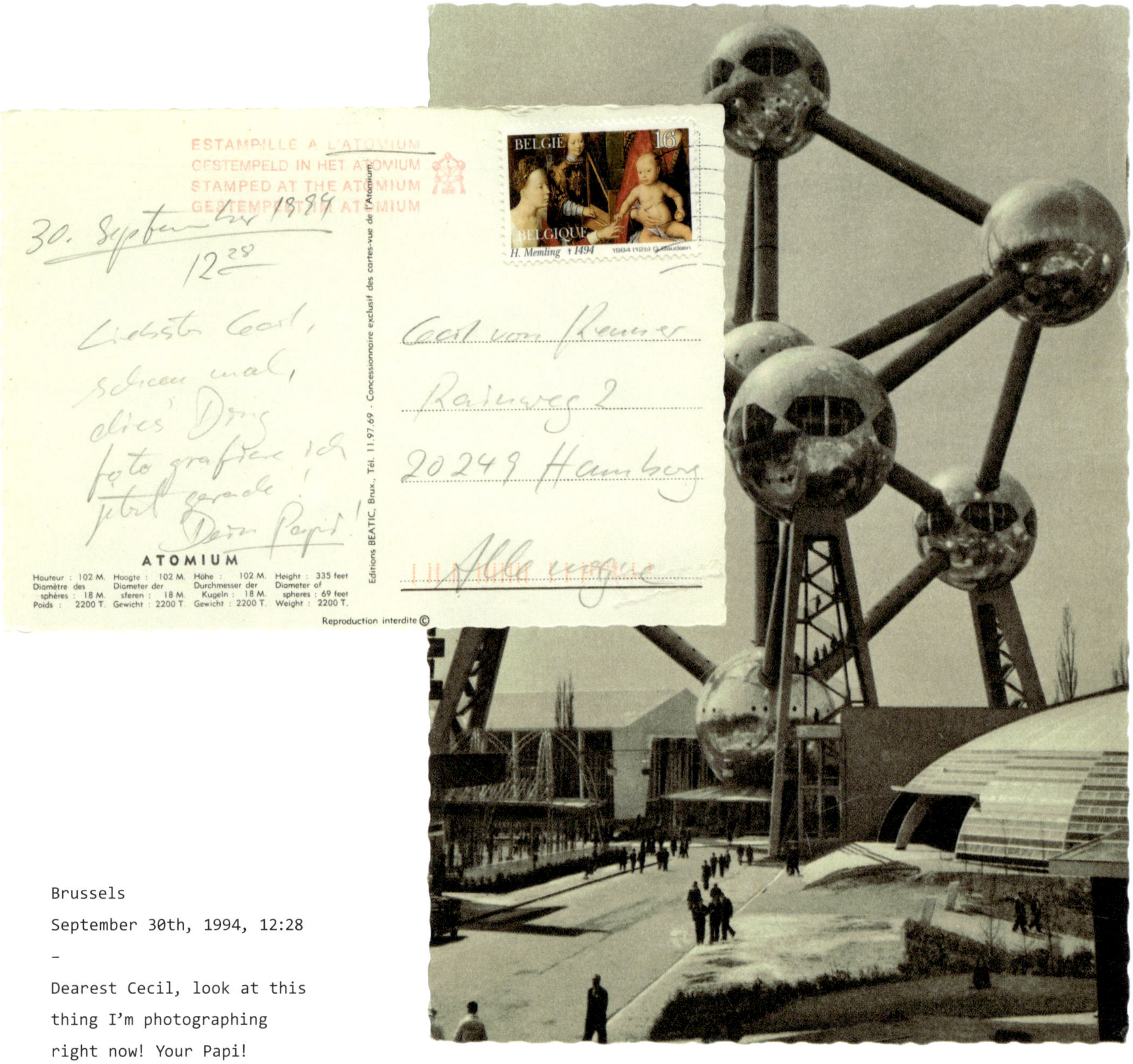

Brussels
September 30th, 1994, 12:28
–
Dearest Cecil, look at this thing I'm photographing right now! Your Papi!

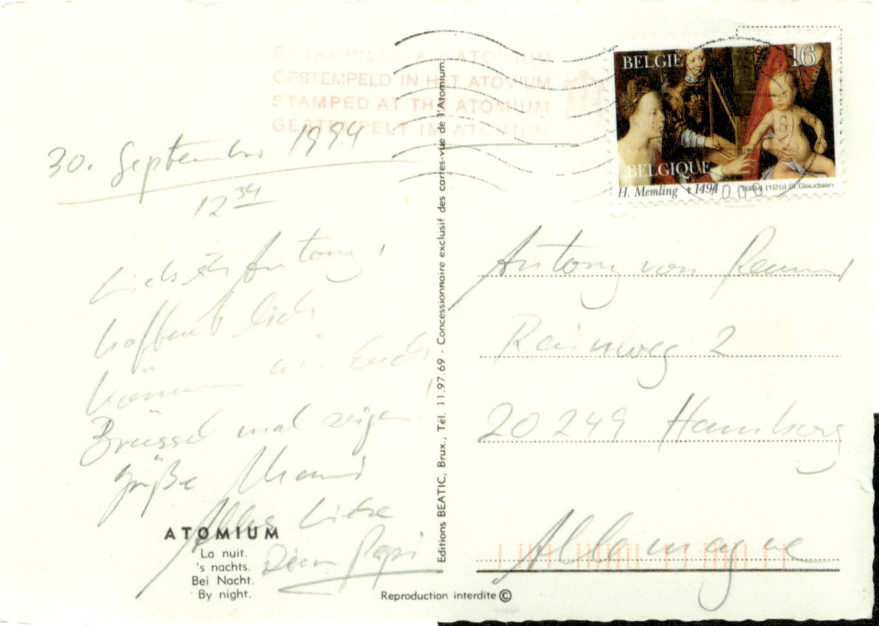

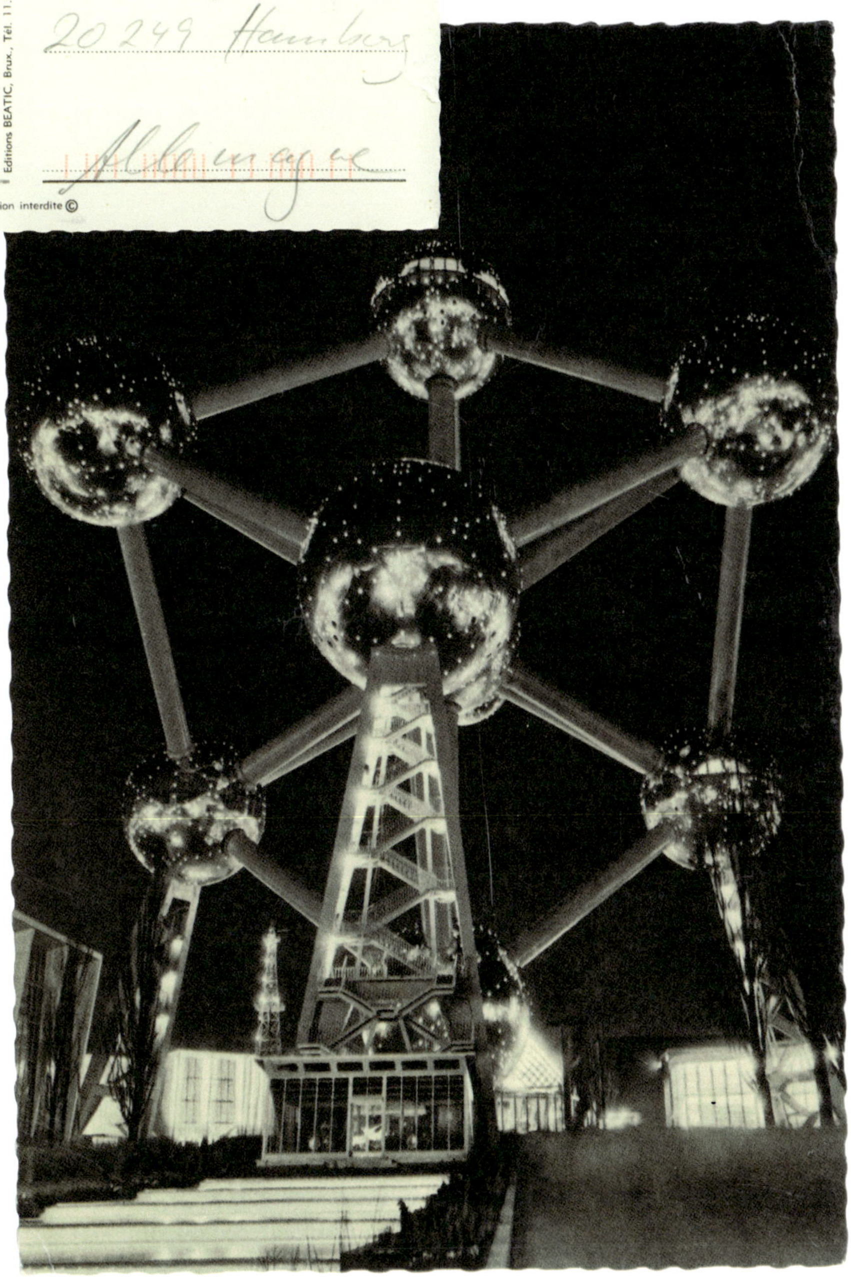

Brussels

September 30th, 1994, 12:34

–

Dearest Antony, I hope we can show you Brussels one day! Send my love to Mami. All the best, your Papi

»

I have never been to Brussels before. And I have never imagined the Atomium to be so impressive, inside and out. Some chicken walk onto the street from a bewildered garden right behind us. Belgium! The location of the European parliament. The world is still in order here.

«

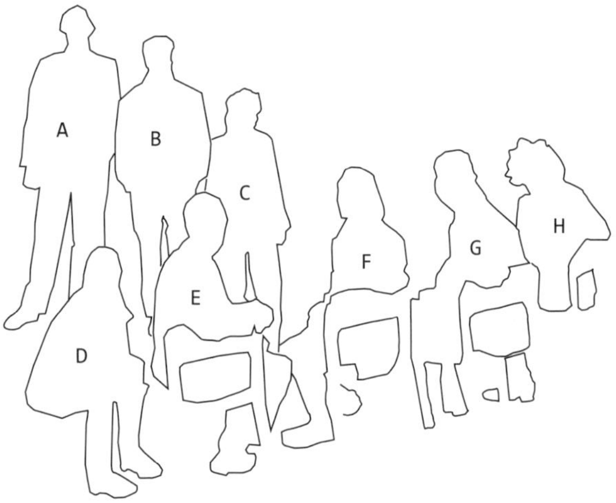

Group photo in Brussels

A Me

B Martin Kaeswurm, assistant

C Anne, intern

D Make-up artist

E Bulgari, distributor from Brussels

F Bulgari, client from Rome

G Art director

H Productioneer

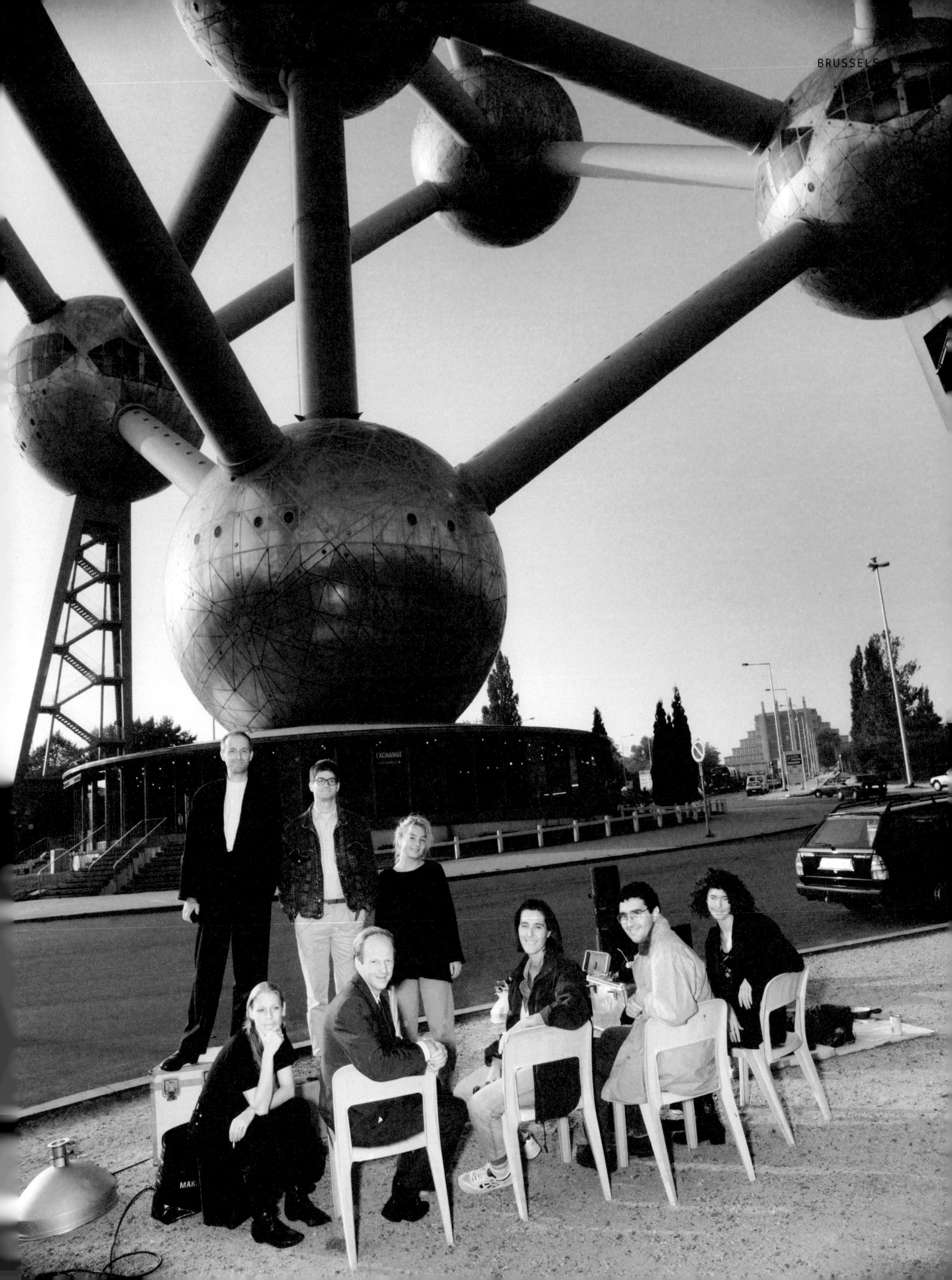
EXCHANGE

Sands®

HOTEL CASINO LAS VEGAS

Las Vegas

February 1994

KEN BRUNS
CONSUELO GöTZ
MARTIN KAESWURM
IVO VON RENNER
TOMMIE PINNOW

30.1.
'94

✓

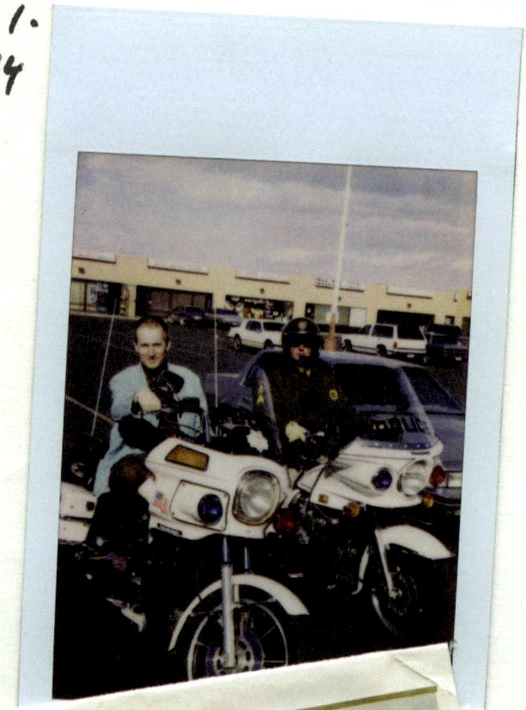

Concierge®

THE Sands
LAS VEGAS, NEVADA

SANDS HOTEL C… …GAS, NEVADA 89109
TOLL … 732-1047

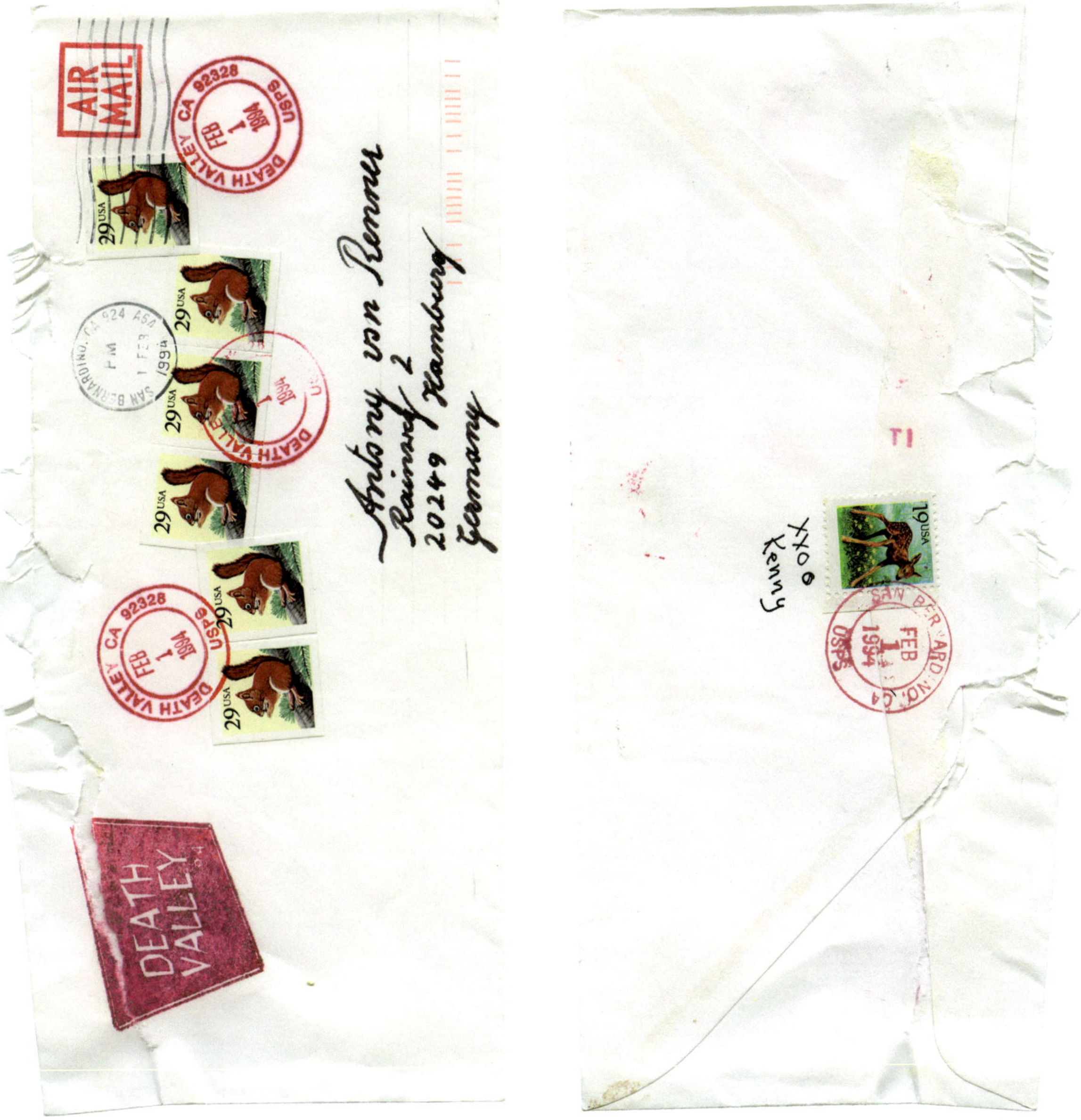

Antony receives the letter with the squirrel stamp and me on the motorcycle. 16 years later, he will have a Yamaha standing in the garden.

DEATH VALLEY
February 1st, 1994

USA

Thursday, February 3rd

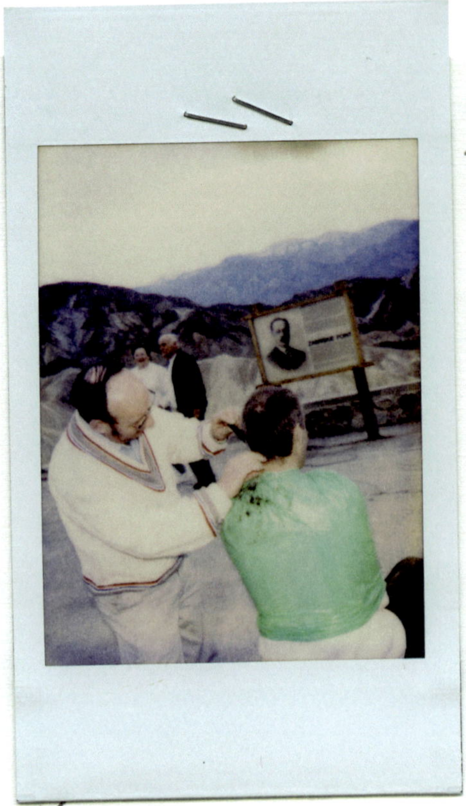

Hey Anthony,

This is the famous
Zabriskie haircut.
Done by a barber
from Upper State
New York!

Pappi!

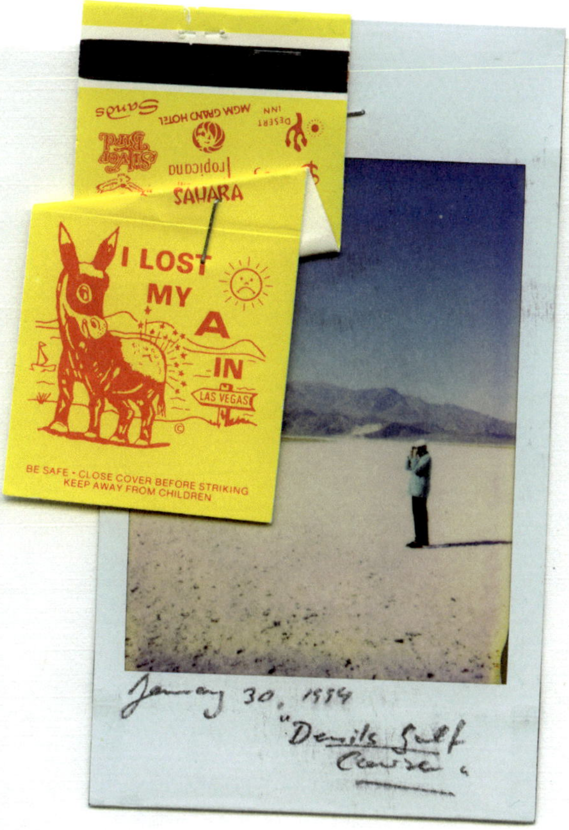

See you soon.
Daddy!

Furnace Creek Inn & Ranch Resort, P.O. Box 1, Death Valley, CA 92328 • 619-786-2345 • FAX 619-786-2307
TRADITIONAL HOSPITALITY SINCE 1876 BY Fred Harvey®

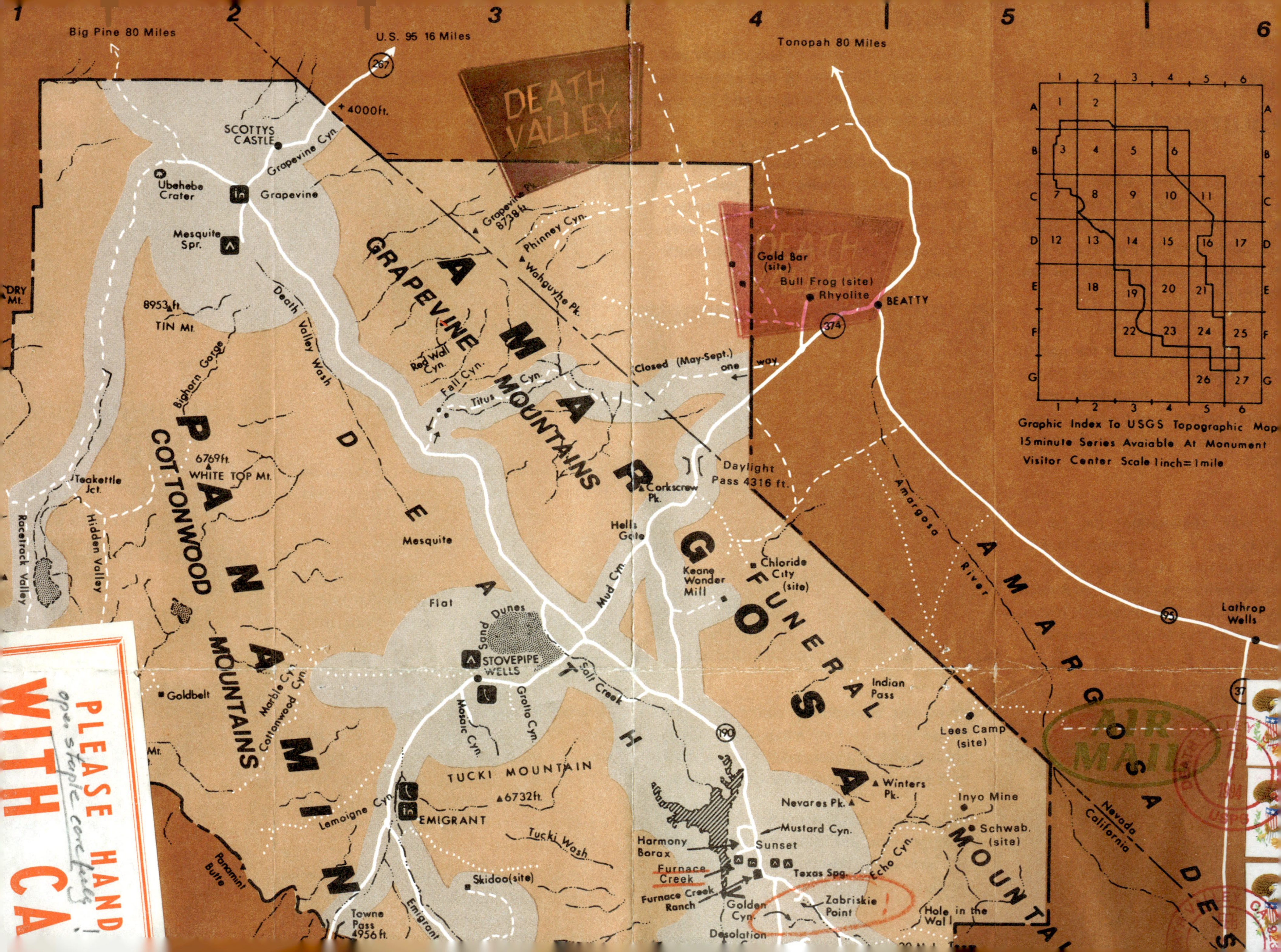
Big Pine 80 Miles
U.S. 95 16 Miles
Tonopah 80 Miles
DEATH VALLEY
+4000ft.
SCOTTYS CASTLE
Grapevine Cyn.
Ubehebe Crater
Grapevine
Mesquite Spr.
Grapevine Pk. 8738ft.
Phinney Cyn.
Wahguyhe Pk.
GRAPEVINE MOUNTAINS
AMARGOSA
Gold Bar (site)
Bull Frog (site)
Rhyolite
BEATTY
DRY Mt.
8953ft.
TIN Mt.
Death Valley Wash
Red Wall Cyn.
Fall Cyn.
Titus Cyn.
Closed (May-Sept.)
one way
Bighorn Gorge
PANAMINT
COTTONWOOD MOUNTAINS
6769ft.
WHITE TOP Mt.
DEATH VALLEY
Mesquite
Daylight Pass 4316 ft.
Corkscrew Pk.
Hells Gate
Teakettle Jct.
Racetrack Valley
Hidden Valley
Mud Cyn.
Keane Wonder Mill
Chloride City (site)
FUNERAL MOUNTAINS
Amargosa River
Lathrop Wells
Flat
Sand Dunes
STOVEPIPE WELLS
Salt Creek
Goldbelt
Marble Cyn.
Cottonwood Cyn.
Grotto Cyn.
Mosaic Cyn.
Indian Pass
Lees Camp (site)
TUCKI MOUNTAIN
6732ft.
Tucki Wash
Lemoigne Cyn.
EMIGRANT
Skidoo (site)
Winters Pk.
Nevares Pk.
Mustard Cyn.
Inyo Mine
Schwab. (site)
Harmony Borax
Sunset
Furnace Creek
Texas Spg.
Echo Cyn.
Furnace Creek Ranch
Golden Cyn.
Zabriskie Point
Hole in the Wall
Desolation
Panamint Butte
Towne Pass 4956 ft.
Emigrant
Mt.
Nevada
California
AMARGOSA DESERT
Graphic Index To USGS Topographic Map
15minute Series Avaiable At Monument
Visitor Center Scale 1inch=1mile
AIR MAIL
PLEASE HAND WITH CA
open staple carefully!

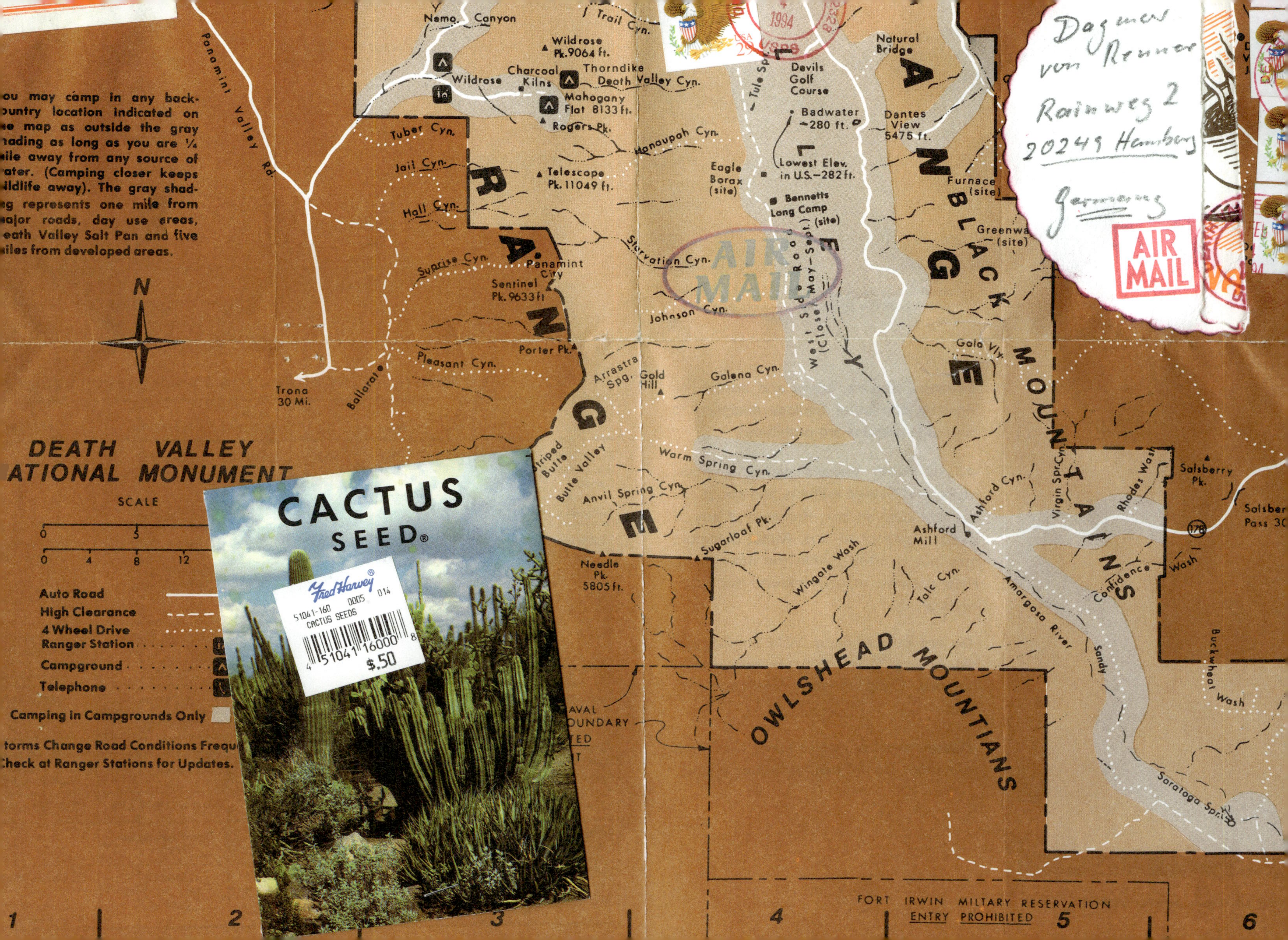

Dagmar von Renner
Rainweg 2
20249 Hamburg
Germany
AIR MAIL
AIR MAIL
DEATH VALLEY
ATIONAL MONUMENT
SCALE
Auto Road
High Clearance
4 Wheel Drive
Ranger Station
Campground
Telephone
Camping in Campgrounds Only
torms Change Road Conditions Frequ
Check at Ranger Stations for Updates.
ou may camp in any back-
ountry location indicated on
e map as outside the gray
hading as long as you are ¼
ile away from any source of
ater. (Camping closer keeps
ildlife away). The gray shad-
g represents one mile from
ajor roads, day use areas,
eath Valley Salt Pan and five
iles from developed areas.
N
CACTUS
SEED®
Fred Harvey
CACTUS SEEDS
$.50
PANAMINT RANGE
BLACK MOUNTAINS
OWLSHEAD MOUNTIANS
Panamint Valley Rd.
Trona 30 Mi.
Badwater −280 ft.
Lowest Elev. in U.S.−282 ft.
Dantes View 5475 ft.
Telescope Pk. 11049 ft.
Wildrose Pk. 9064 ft.
Sentinel Pk. 9633 ft.
Needle Pk. 5805 ft.
Amargosa River
FORT IRWIN MILITARY RESERVATION
ENTRY PROHIBITED

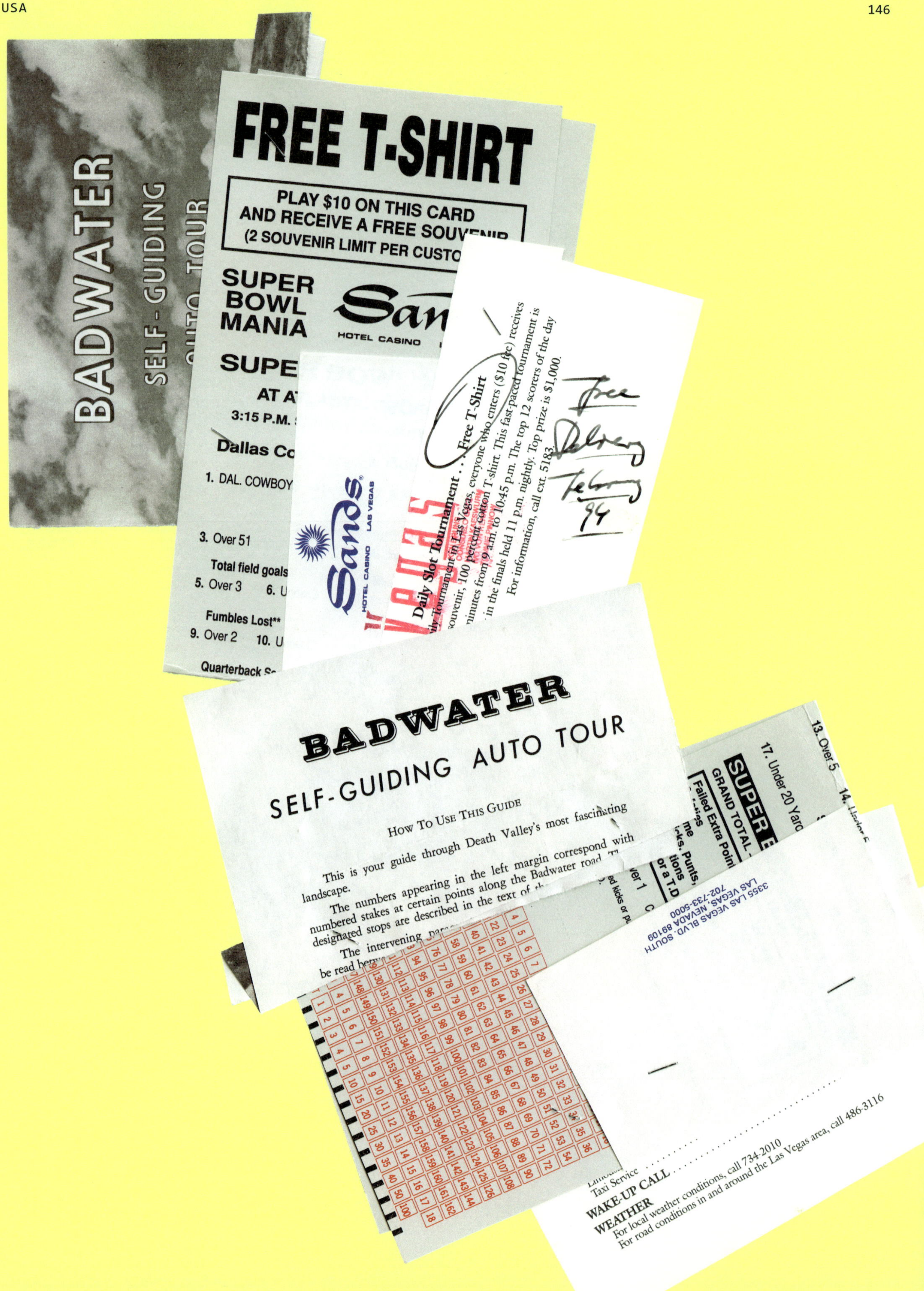
BADWATER
SELF-GUIDING
AUTO TOUR
FREE T-SHIRT
PLAY $10 ON THIS CARD
AND RECEIVE A FREE SOUVENIR
(2 SOUVENIR LIMIT PER CUSTO
SUPER
BOWL
MANIA
HOTEL CASINO
3:15 P.M.
Dallas Co
1. DAL. COWBOY
3. Over 51
Total field goals
5. Over 3
Fumbles Lost**
9. Over 2
Quarterback S
Sands
HOTEL CASINO LAS VEGAS
Daily Slot Tournament . . . Free T-Shirt
For information, call ext. 5183.
BADWATER
SELF-GUIDING AUTO TOUR
How To Use This Guide
This is your guide through Death Valley's most fascinating landscape.
The numbers appearing in the left margin correspond with numbered stakes at certain points along the Badwater road.
13. Over 5
17. Under 20 Yard
SUPER B
GRAND TOTAL
Failed Extra Point
3355 LAS VEGAS BLVD. SOUTH
LAS VEGAS, NEVADA 89109
702-733-5000
Taxi Service
WAKE-UP CALL
WEATHER
For local weather conditions, call 734-2010
For road conditions in and around the Las Vegas area, call 486-3116

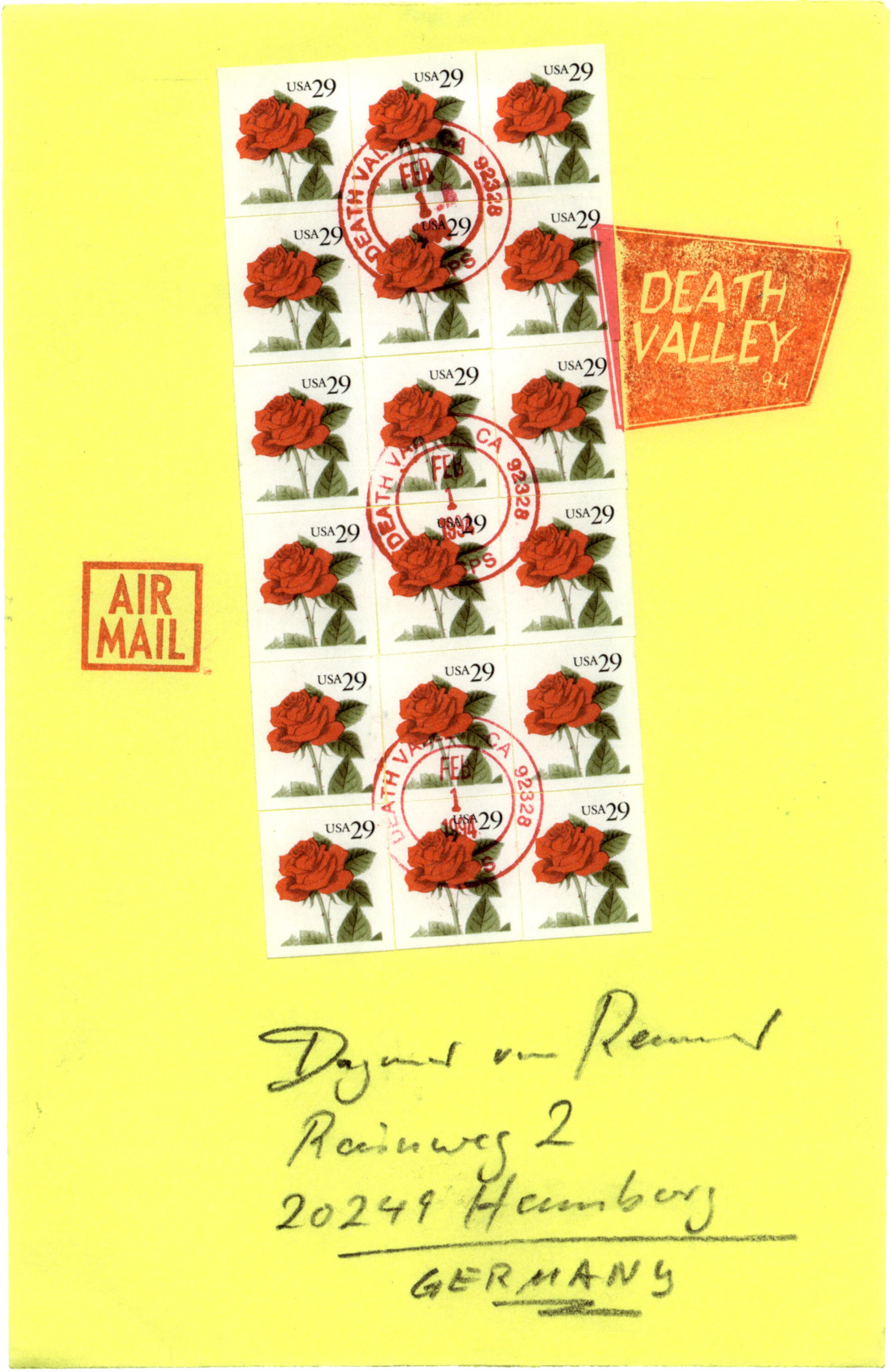

The "AIR MAIL" stamp comes from Arnfried Weiss. I create "DEATH VALLEY" and "Las Vegas" in Hamburg in advance.

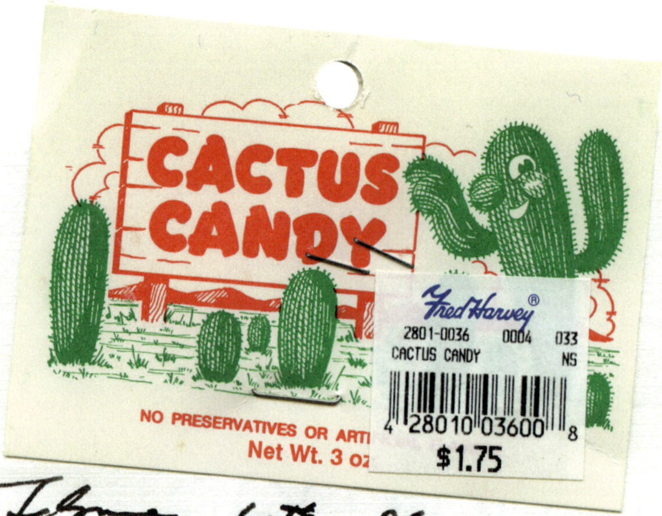

February 4th, 99

In love..

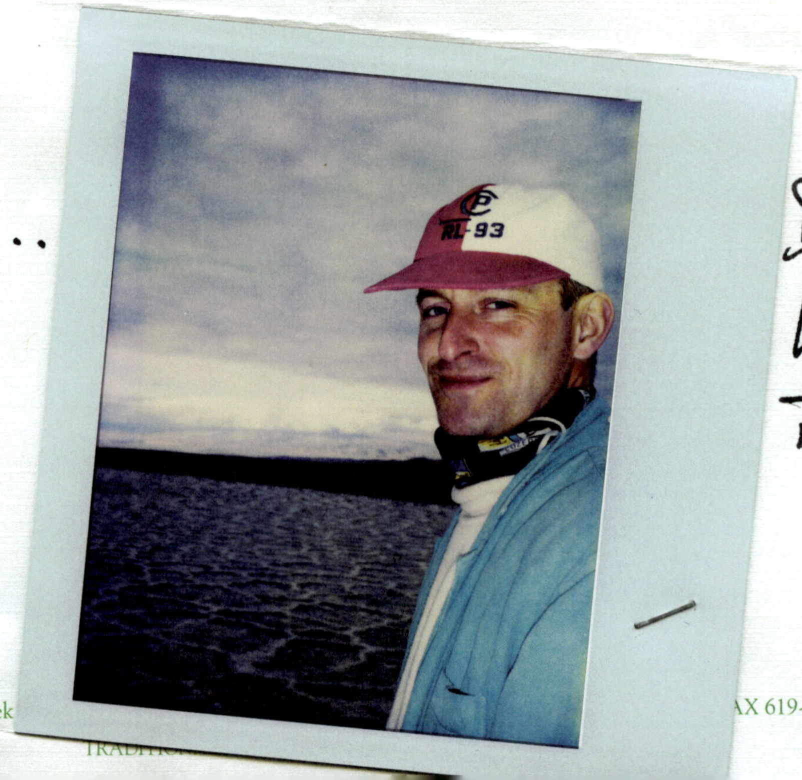

Death Valley

Furnace Creek … AX 619-786-2307

TRADITIO…

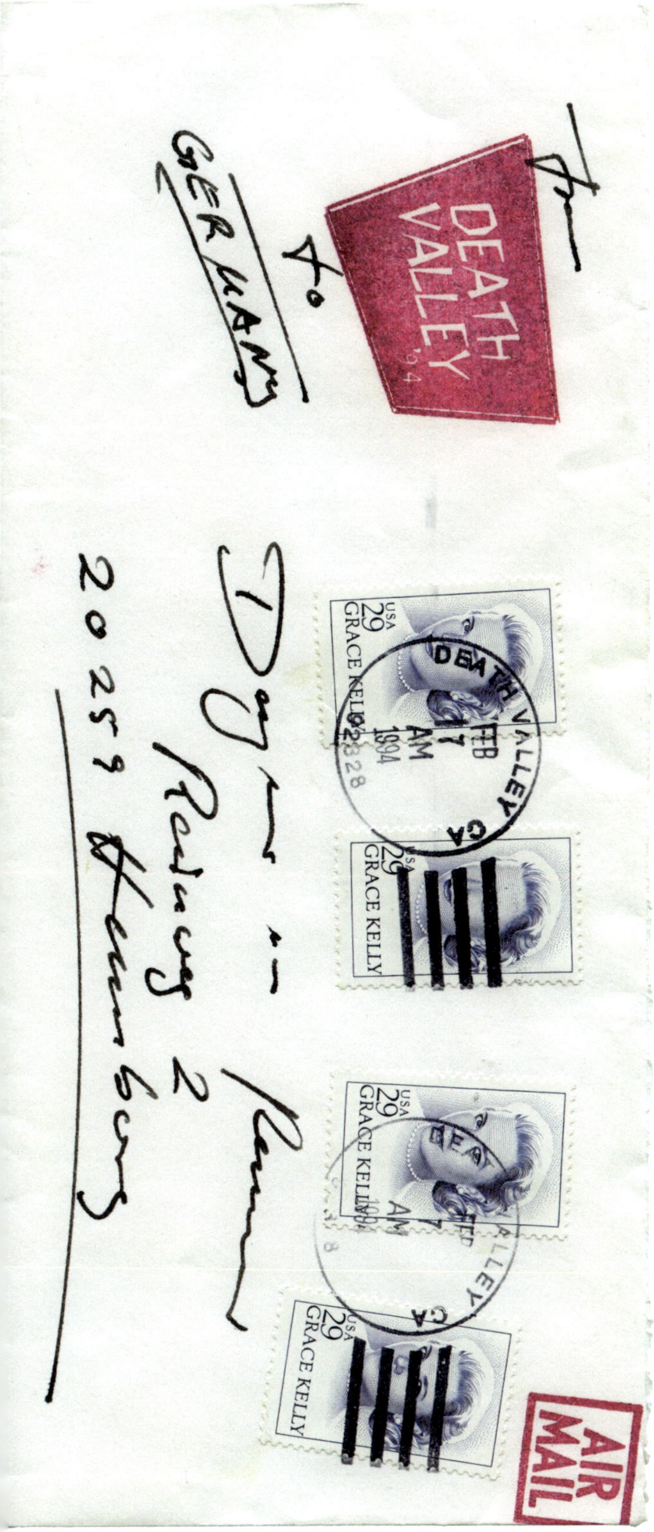

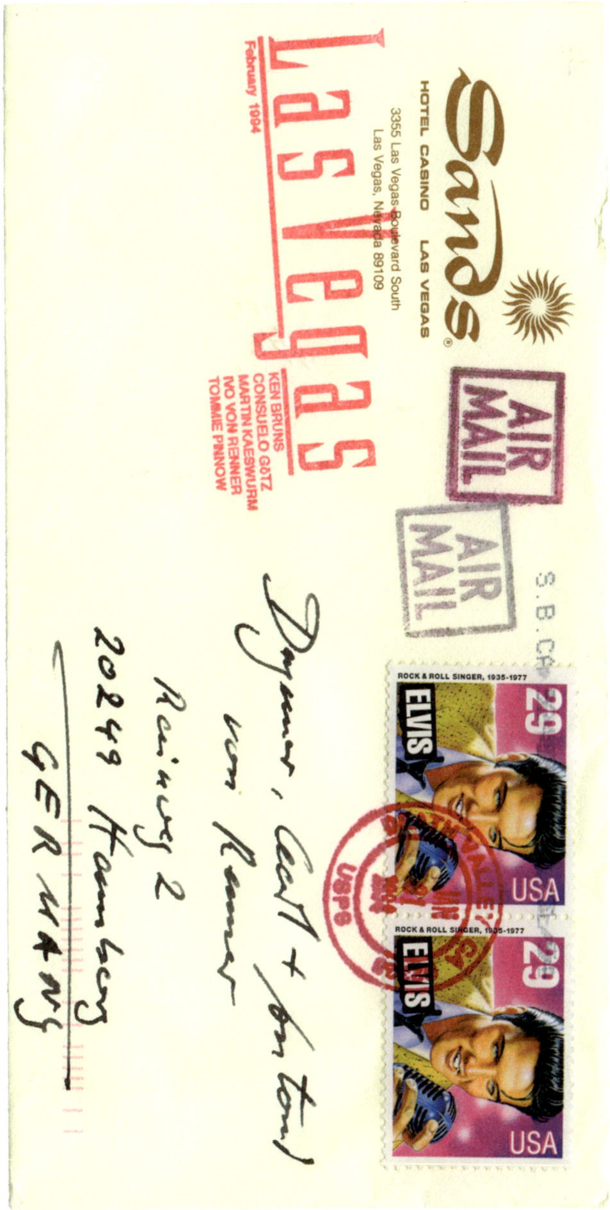

A year earlier, I had spent one hour waiting in line at the Islamorada, Florida post office for two sheets of Elvis stamps. Holding Cecil's hand – carrying him – holding his hand. This is a good opportunity for a father to lovingly explain queues to his four-year-old son. Although he said it took a long time, it didn't dampen his mood.

DEATH VALLEY
February 4th, 1994

Open-air haircut.

Death Valley has four rainy days per year on average, all in November. We experience nine of them in February. When Opel grants us another waiting day, the sky finally clears up in the evening. I brought my make-up artist Consuelo Götz along, to photograph a couple in front of a convertible. Just as she is cutting my hair on the part of the world which became famous in Michelangelo Antonioni's film "Zabriskie Point", an elderly gentleman introduces himself, a former barber in a place near the Hudson River, upstate New York. Without further ado, he takes over her tools. This is all documented for the ranger's photo album with his red plastic camera, closely watched by the female model Bernice Nussbaum.

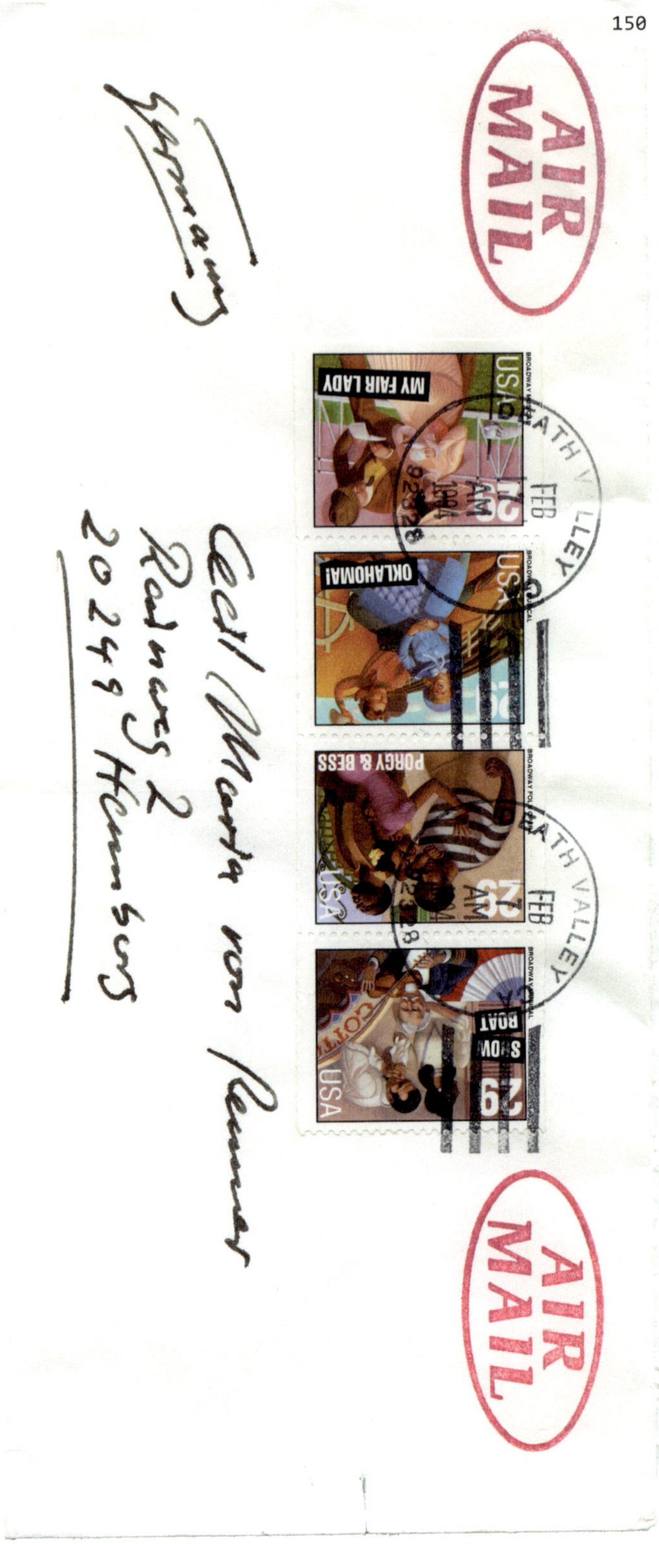

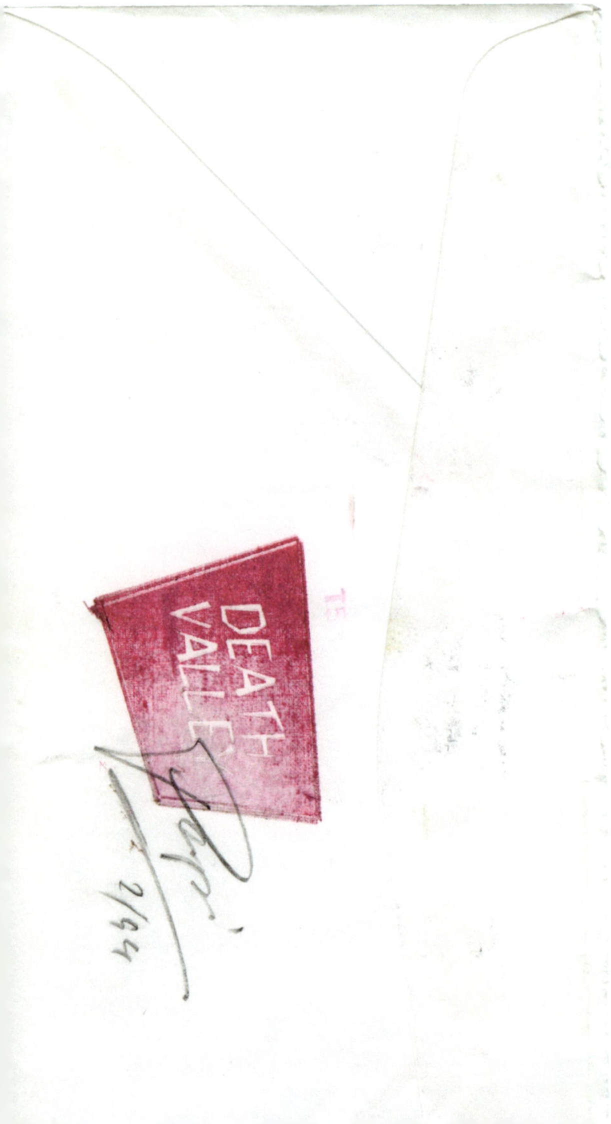

DEATH VALLEY

February 5th, 1994

–

"Zabriskie Point" Dear Cecil,

Mami says you asked for a picture of Papi. Alright, here you go.

Your Papi

February 5th '94

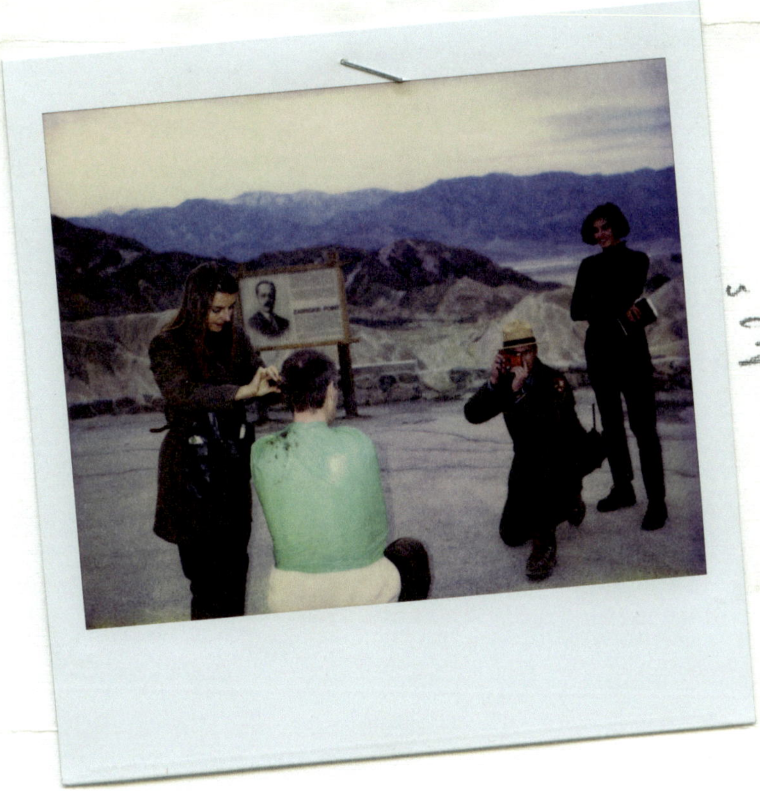

„Zabriski Point"

Liebste Cecil,
Mami sagt, Du möchtest ein Bild von Papi haben.

Nun sagt, Du hast es!

Dein Papi

Furnace Creek Inn & Ranch Resort, P.O. Box 1, Death Valley, CA 92328 • 619-786-2345 • FAX 619-786-2307
TRADITIONAL HOSPITALITY SINCE 1876 BY Fred Harvey®

Sands®

HOTEL CASINO LAS VEGAS

Las Vegas
February 1994
KEN BRUNS
CONSUELO GÖTZ
MARTIN KA…
IVO VON RE…NER
TOMMIE PIN…OW

There's something for everyone at the Sands Hotel

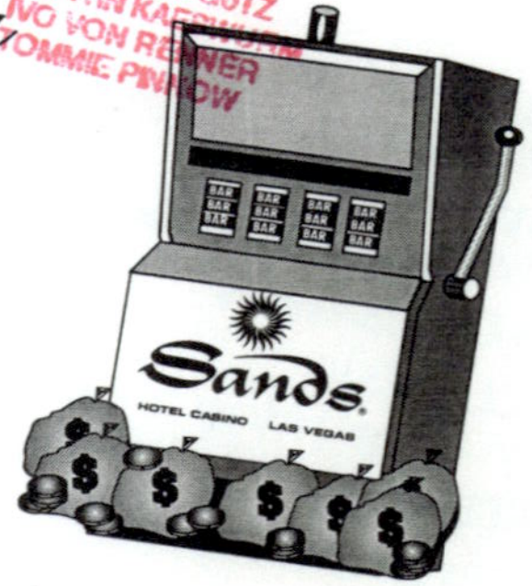

Sandsational Bonus Slot Club . . .

Join the Sandsational Bonus club where winners win more . . . guaranteed. Points are accumulated by the amount of coins that come out of the machine. Plus, customers who have a Sandsational Bonus Slot Club card will receive special discounts at the Sands. Sandsational Bonus is FREE . . . JOIN NOW! For information, call ext. 5574

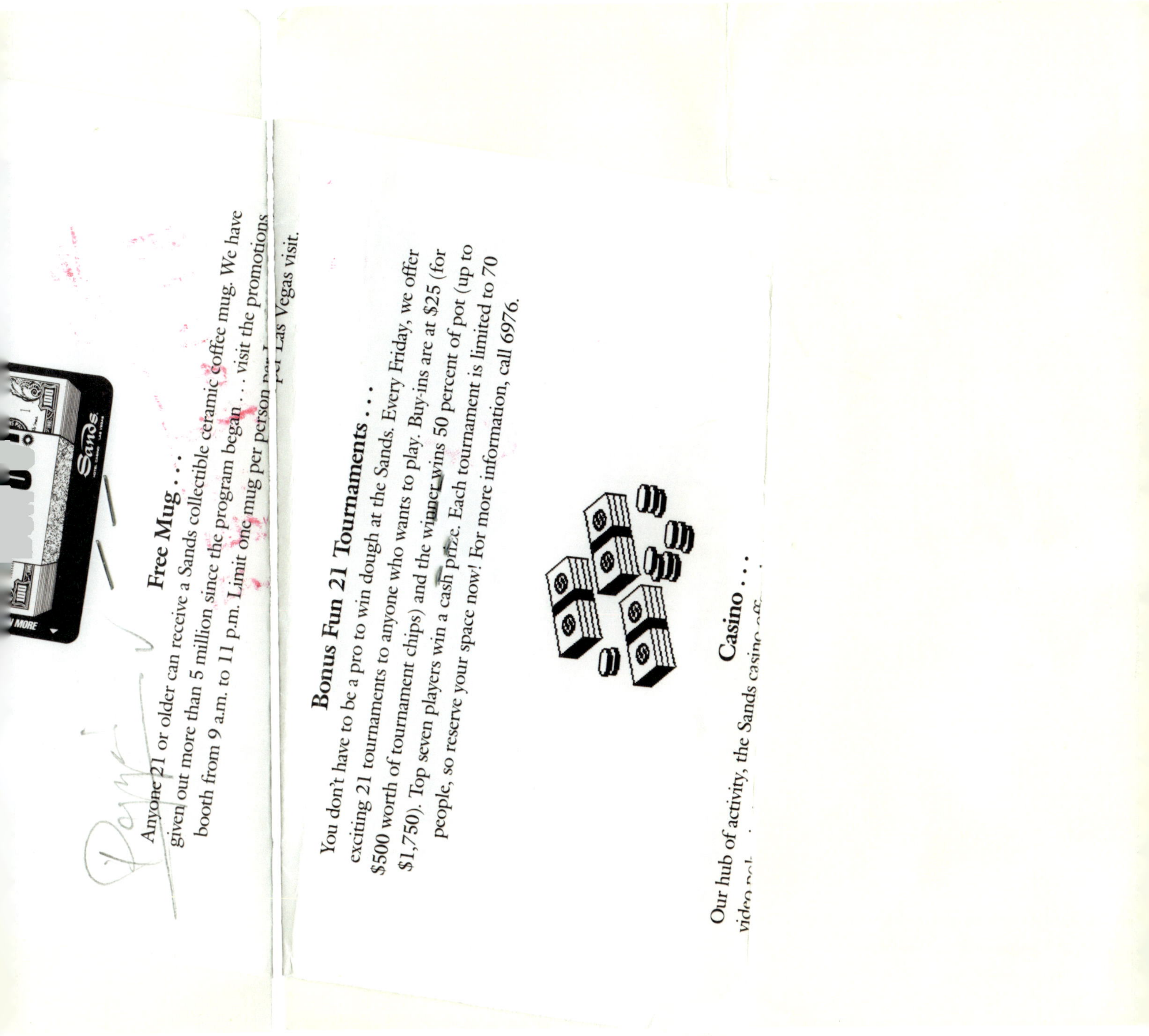

Free Mug . . .

Anyone 21 or older can receive a Sands collectible ceramic coffee mug. We have given out more than 5 million since the program began . . . visit the promotions booth from 9 a.m. to 11 p.m. Limit one mug per person per Las Vegas visit.

Bonus Fun 21 Tournaments . . .

You don't have to be a pro to win dough at the Sands. Every Friday, we offer exciting 21 tournaments to anyone who wants to play. Buy-ins are at $25 (for $500 worth of tournament chips) and the winner wins 50 percent of pot (up to $1,750). Top seven players win a cash prize. Each tournament is limited to 70 people, so reserve your space now! For more information, call 6976.

Casino . . .

Our hub of activity, the Sands casino

We spent two days developing films in Las Vegas after our return. I entered one dollar into the one-armed bandit per day – with no success.

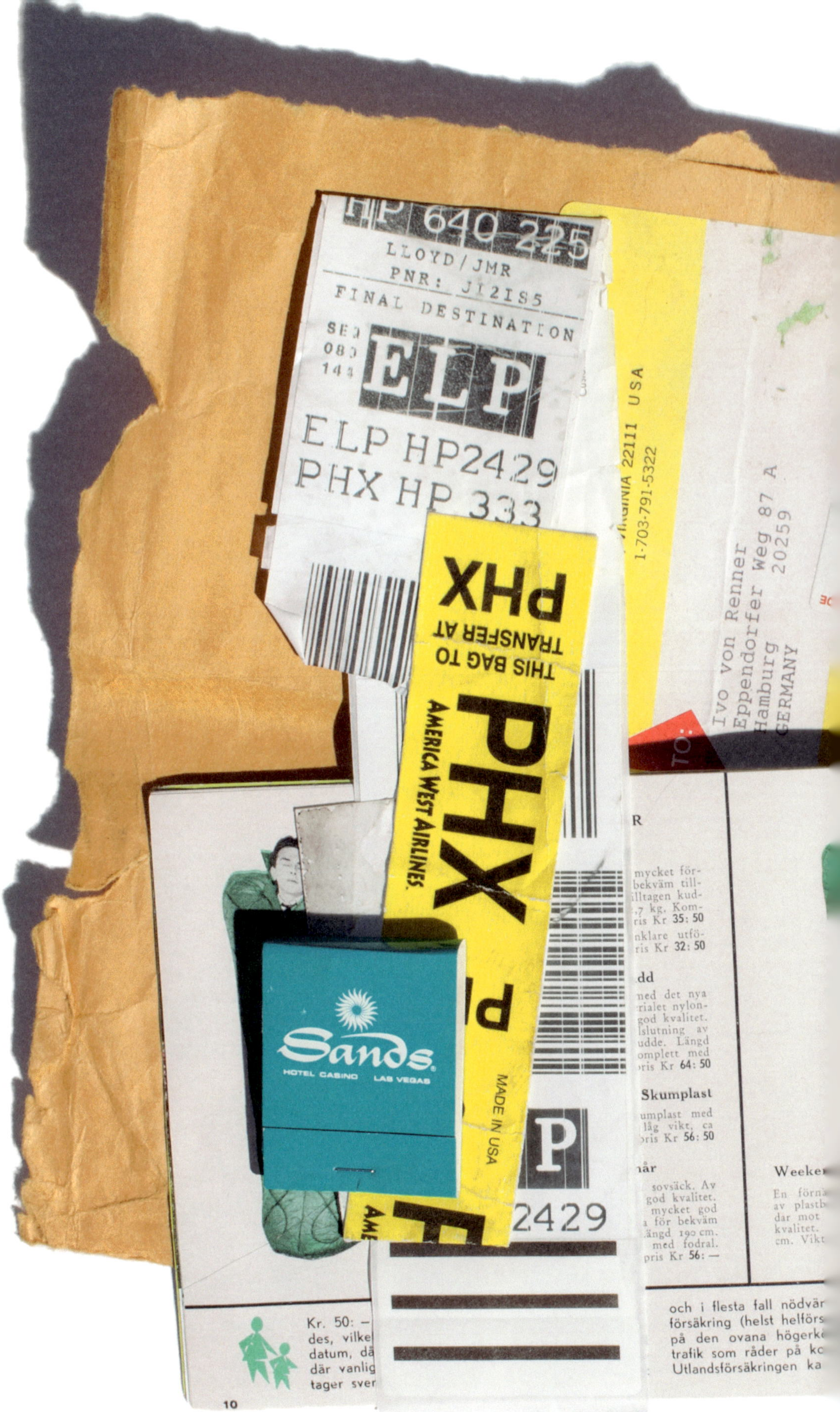
HP 640 225
LLOYD/JMR
FINAL DESTINATION
ELP
ELP HP2429
PHX HP 333
PHX
THIS BAG TO
TRANSFER AT
PHX
AMERICA WEST AIRLINES.
MADE IN USA
Sands
HOTEL CASINO LAS VEGAS
1-703-791-5322
USA
TO:
Ivo von Renner
Eppendorfer Weg 87 A
Hamburg 20259
GERMANY
Skumplast
2429
Weeken
10

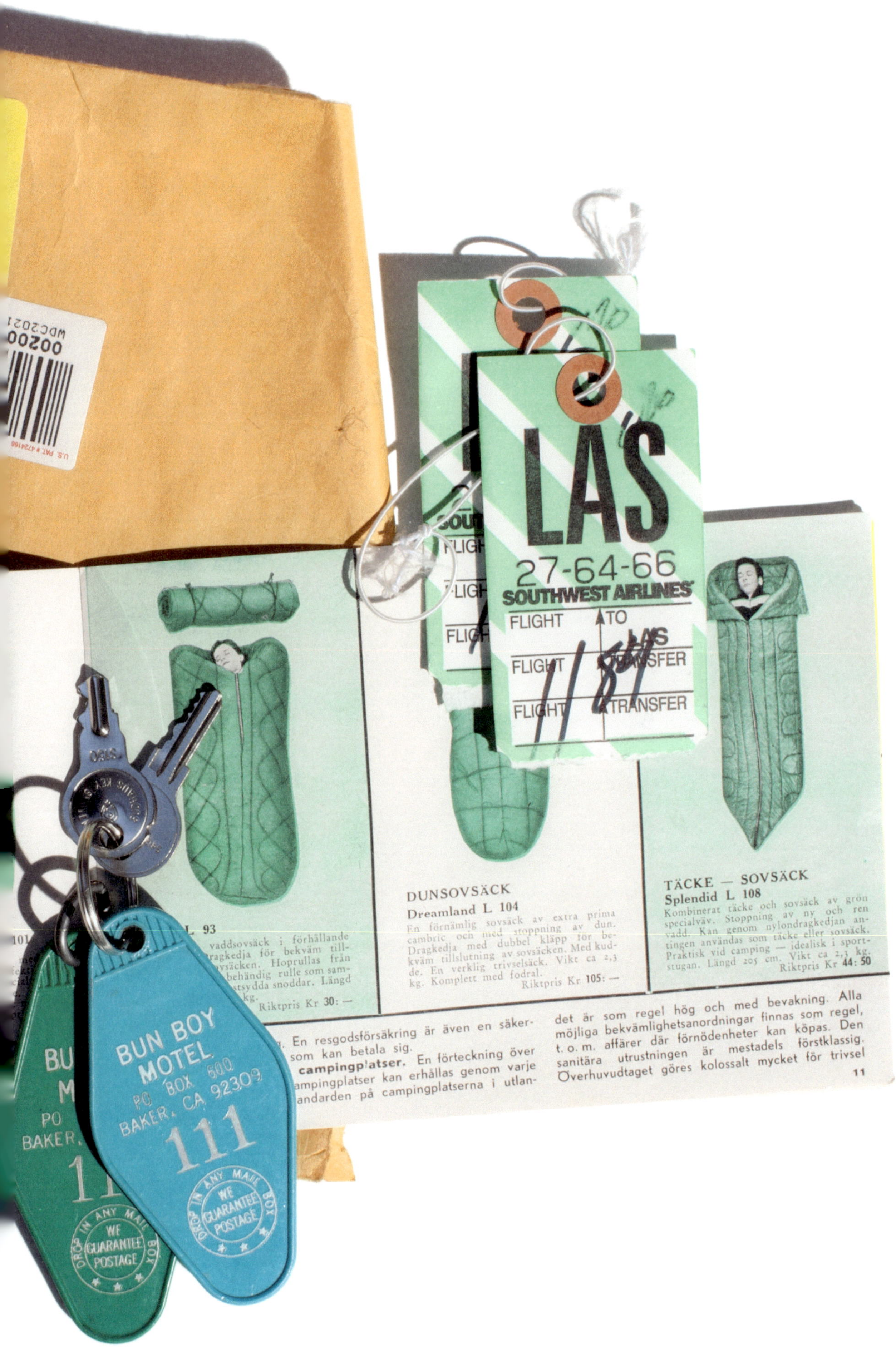
LAS
27-64-66
SOUTHWEST AIRLINES
FLIGHT
TO
FLIGHT
TRANSFER
FLIGHT
TRANSFER
DUNSOVSÄCK
Dreamland L 104
En förnämlig sovsäck av extra prima
cambric och med stoppning av dun.
Dragkedja med dubbel kläpp för be-
kväm tillslutning av sovsäcken. Med kud-
de. En verklig trivselsäck. Vikt ca 2,3
kg. Komplett med fodral.
Riktpris Kr 105: —
TÄCKE — SOVSÄCK
Splendid L 108
Kombinerat täcke och sovsäck av grön
specialväv. Stoppning av ny och ren
vadd. Kan genom nylondragkedjan an-
tingen användas som täcke eller sovsäck.
Praktisk vid camping — idealisk i sport-
stugan. Längd 205 cm. Vikt ca 2,3 kg.
Riktpris Kr 44: 50
L 93
vaddsovsäck i förhållande
behändig rulle som sam-
snoddar. Längd
Riktpris Kr 30: —
En resgodsförsäkring är även en säker-
som kan betala sig.
campingplatser. En förteckning över
campingplatser kan erhållas genom varje
andarden på campingplatserna i utlan-
det är som regel hög och med bevakning. Alla
möjliga bekvämlighetsanordningar finnas som regel,
t. o. m. affärer där förnödenheter kan köpas. Den
sanitära utrustningen är mestadels förstklassig.
Överhuvudtaget göres kolossalt mycket för trivsel
11
BUN BOY
MOTEL
PO BOX 500
BAKER, CA 92309
111
DROP IN ANY MAIL BOX
WE GUARANTEE POSTAGE

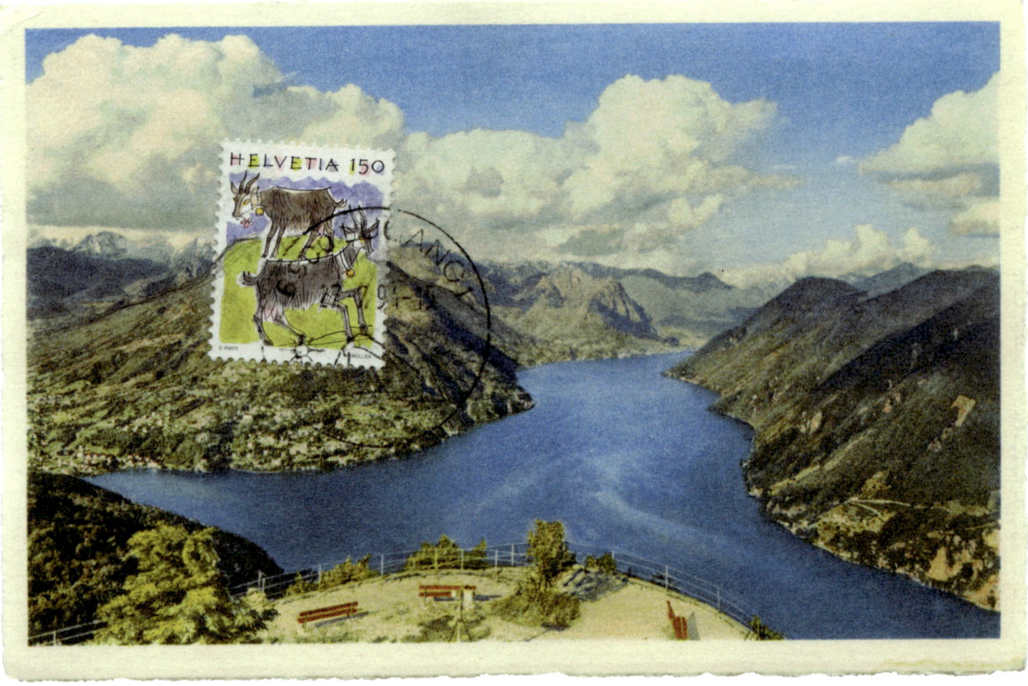

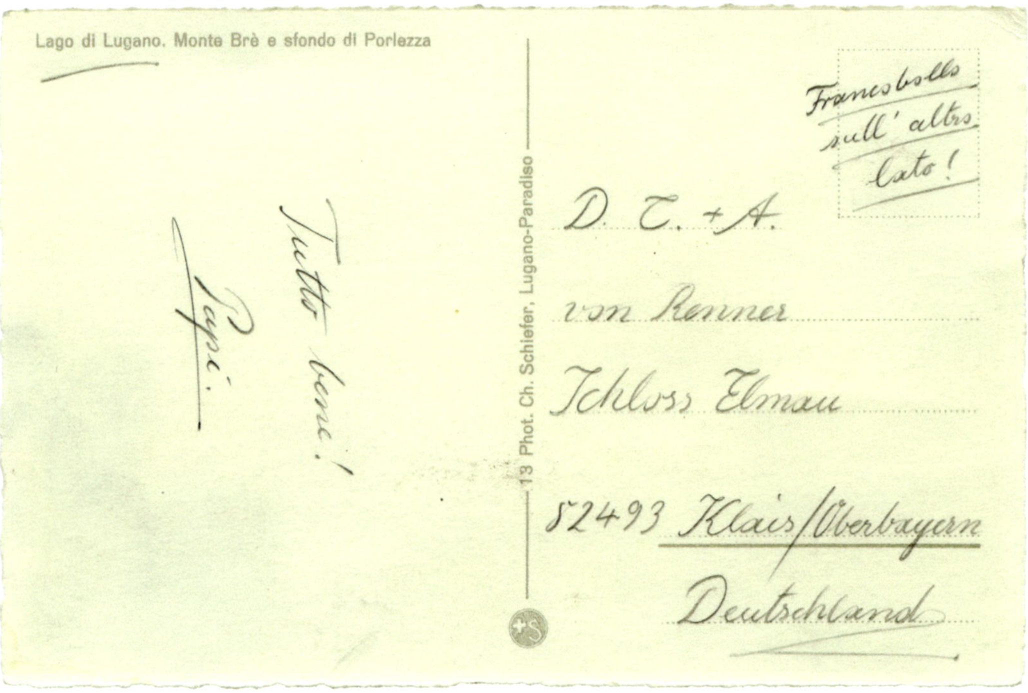

LUGANO

July 27th, 1994

–

"Tutto bene!

Papi"

The mud battle of Siena.

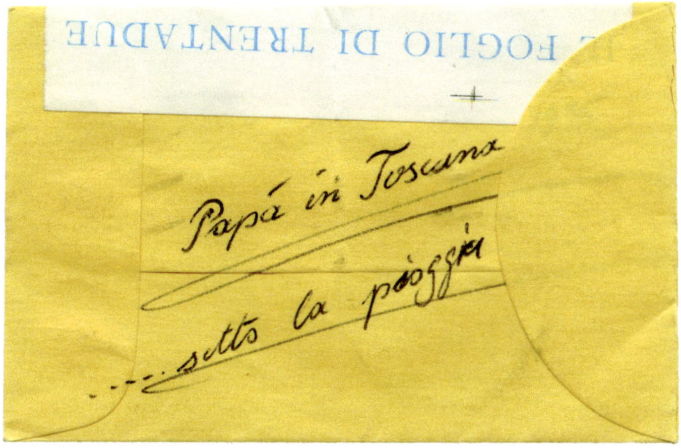

I mail my smallest letter of all time. We are in Tuscany, Italy for Volkswagen. Every sane Italian knows: it rains for three out of four weeks here in March. It turns into a single battle, fighting mud and clay. The VW Bully is pulled by a tractor, which is pulled by an even larger tractor. Finally, we heave a Passat onto a field by crane. The sticky lumps of clay on our wellies make it almost impossible to walk. I sit in a car, sketching the surrounding landscape. The photographer grabs a pen. Motivated by the young souls of the children.

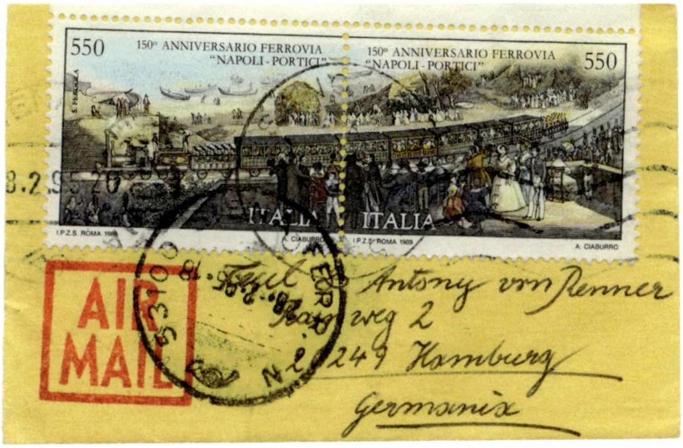

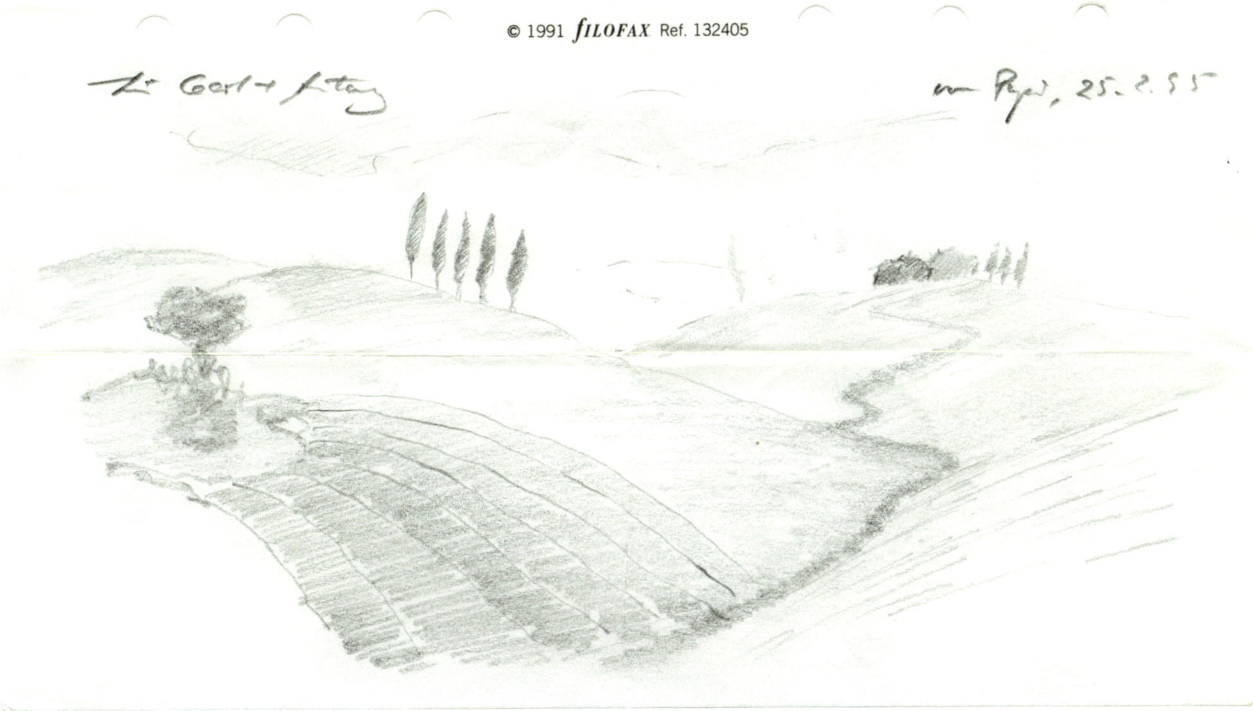

SIENA
February 8th, 1995
–
“Papá in Toscana sotto la pioggia.”

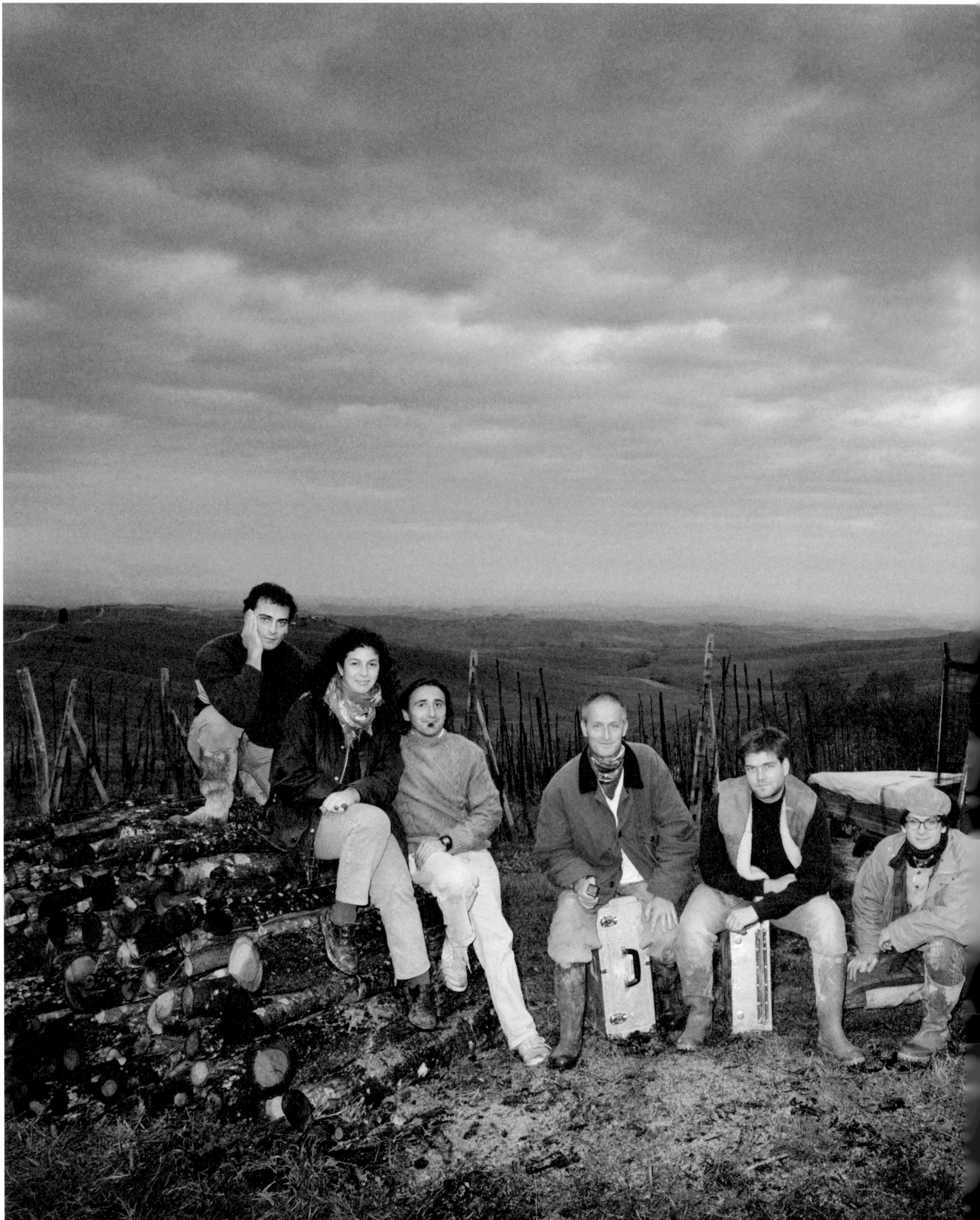

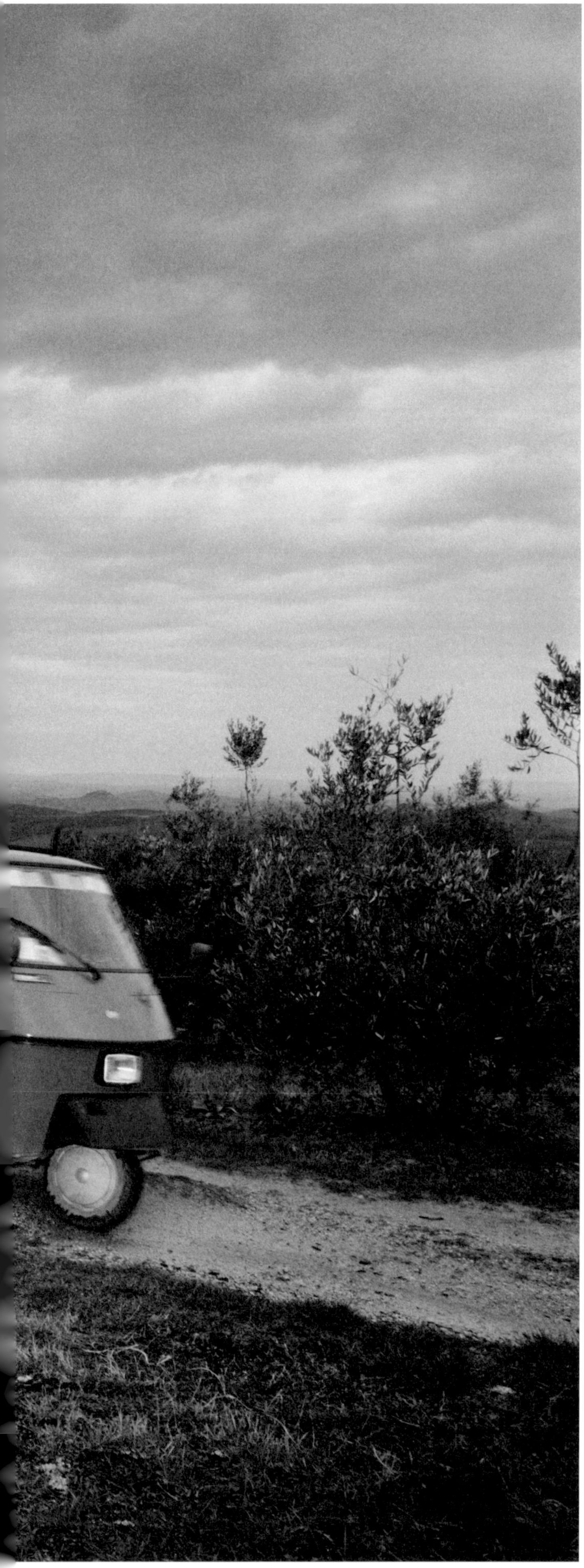

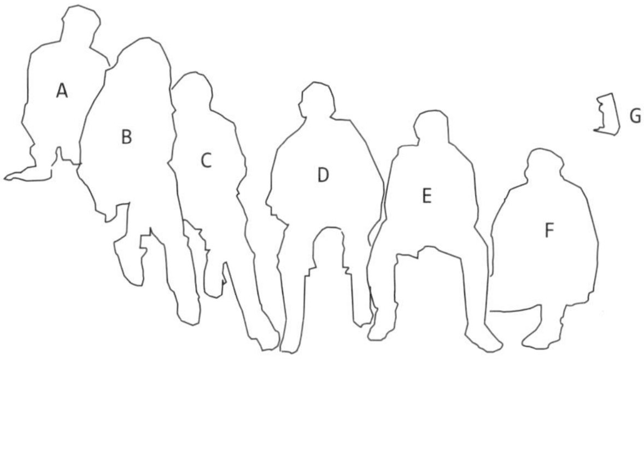

Group photo VW Tuscany
March 1st, 1995

A Model
B Art director
C Location manager
D Me
E Martin Luther, assistant
F Martin Kaeswurm, assistant
G Massimo, the Piaggio driver

America is calling.

I start to photograph for US advertising agencies from 1995 onwards. I travel to New York eleven times in 1997.

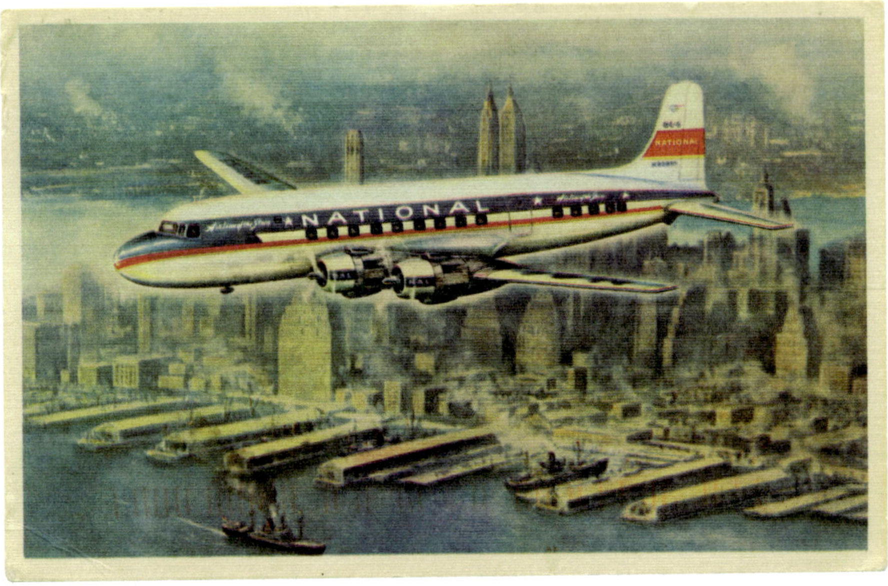

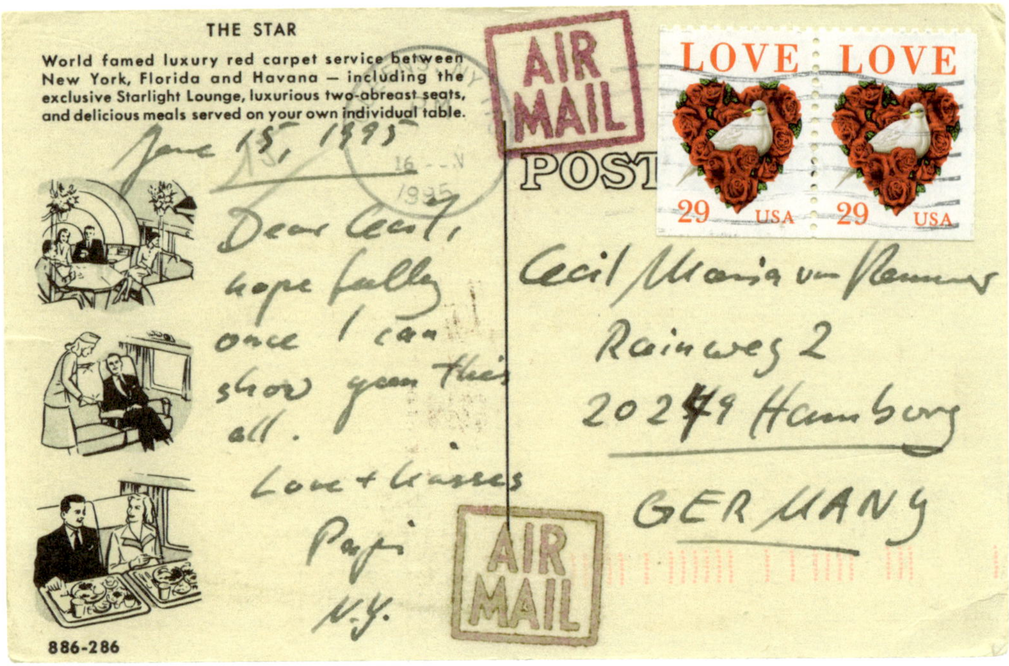

NEW YORK
June 15th, 1995
–
“hopefully
once I can
show you this
all.
Love + Kisses
Papi
N.Y.“

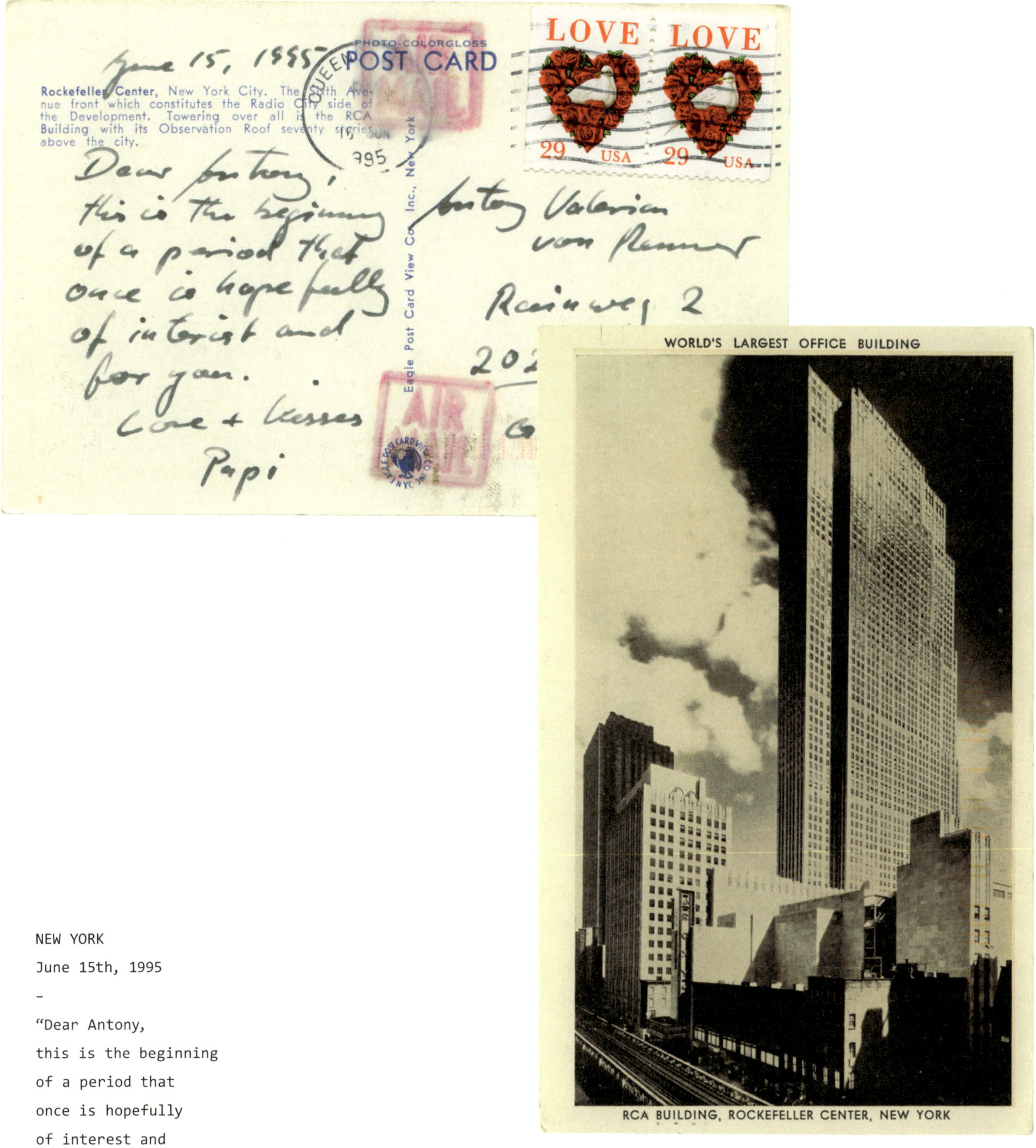

NEW YORK
June 15th, 1995
–
“Dear Antony,
this is the beginning
of a period that
once is hopefully
of interest and
for you.
Love + Kisses
Papi”

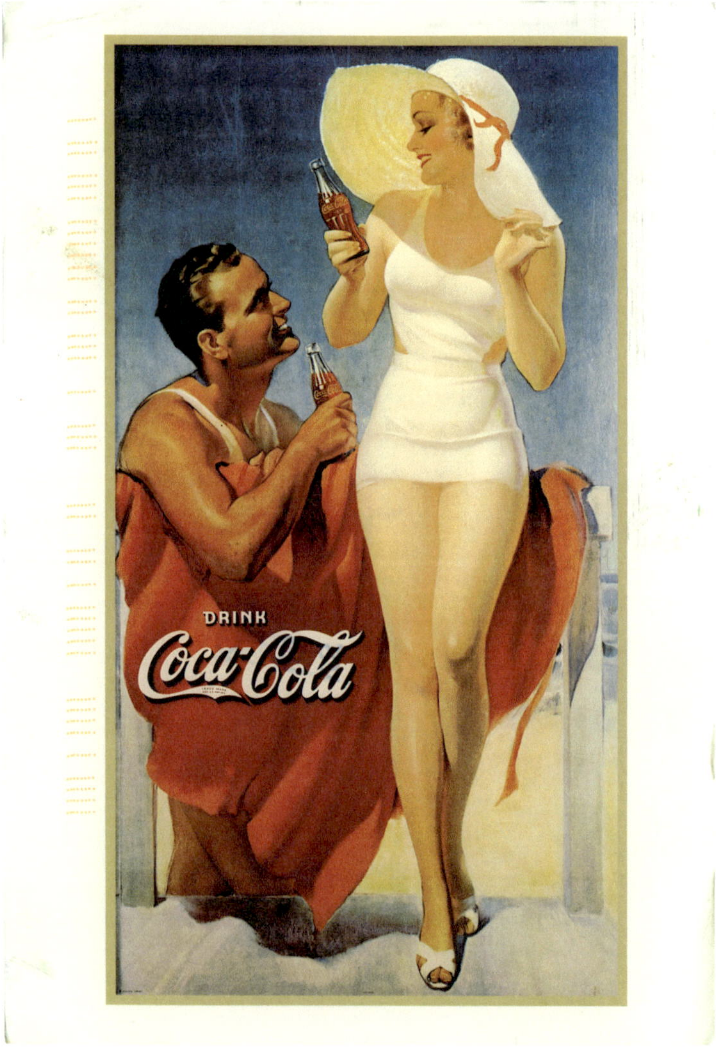

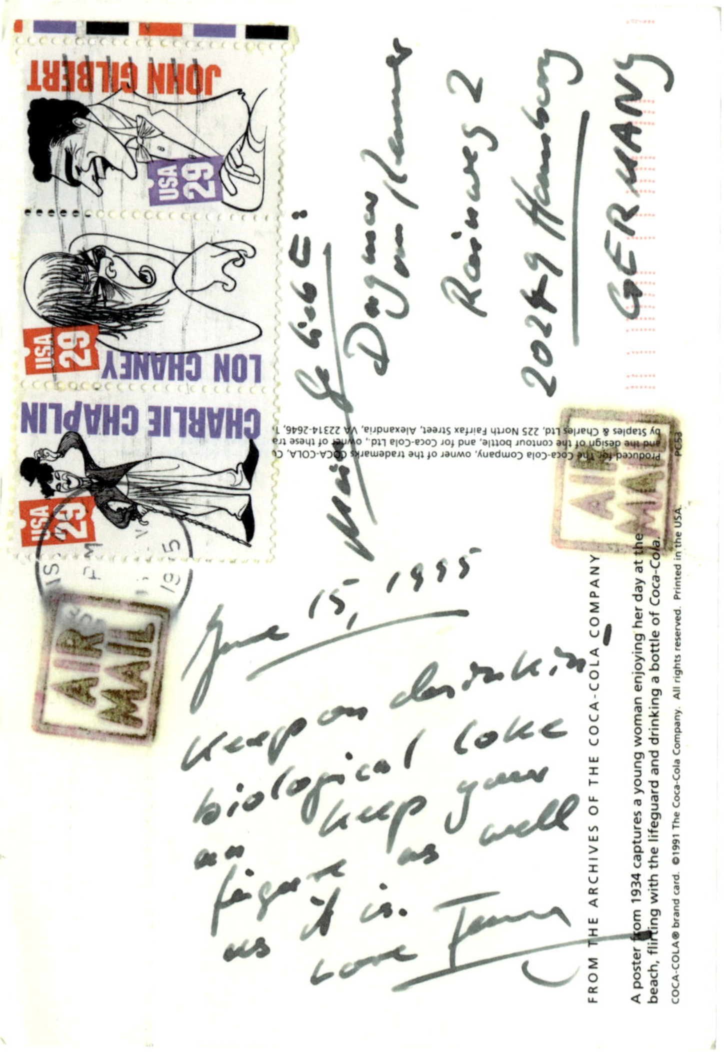

My English "needs spelling".
But the content is correct.

NEW YORK
June 15th, 1995
-
"My love:
Keep on drinkin'
biological Coke and
keep your figure as
well as it is.
Love Funny"

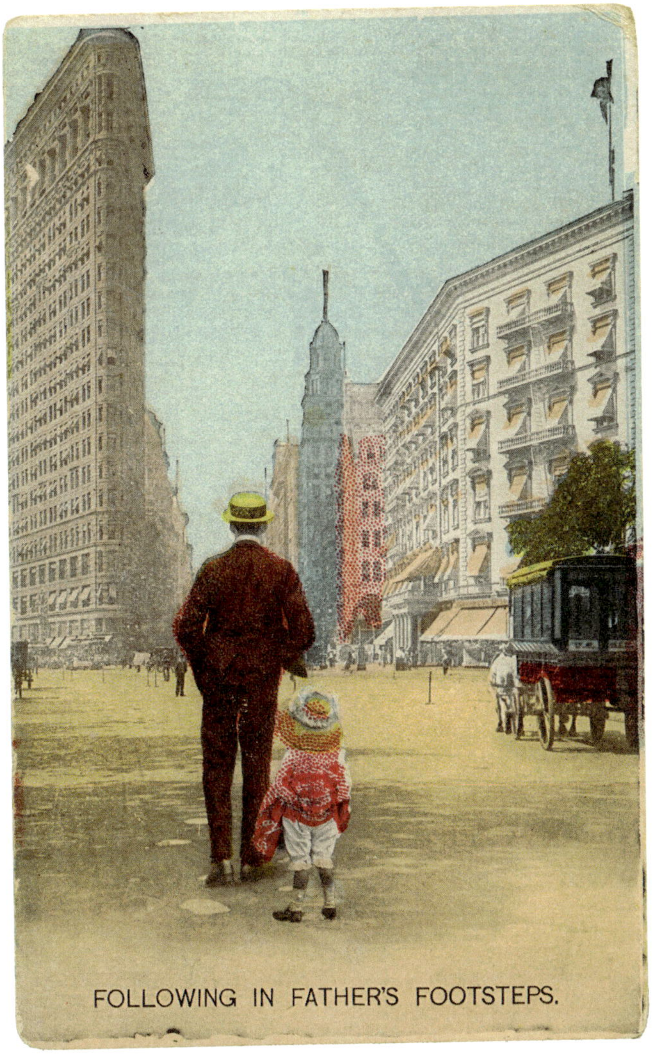

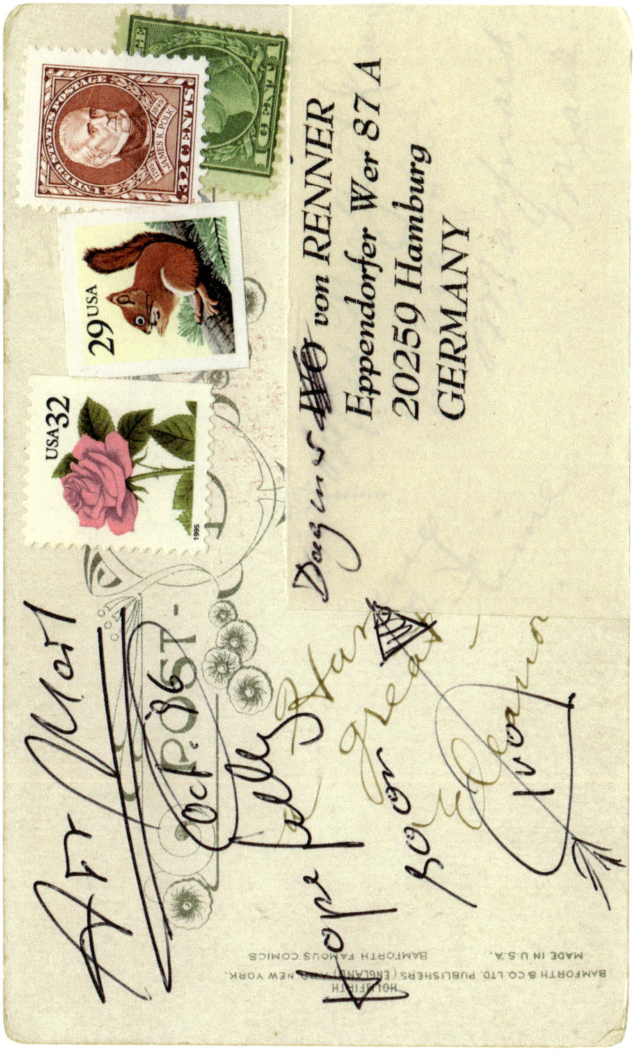

NEW YORK

June 10th, 1995

–

“Air Mail

Hopefully soon.

Ivo”

Today Spanish.

The relaunch of the Mercedes Vito brings us to Spain in 1995. This demands secret places, and we are asked to attract as little attention as possible. We drink where Hemingway used to drink, and photograph ourselves accordingly, wearing berets.

During this journey Antony, who will turn three in two days, invents the incoherent pet name "Butter-crap-ear", while fooling around with me on the telephone. The team greets me with this verbal outpour every morning for the rest of the trip.

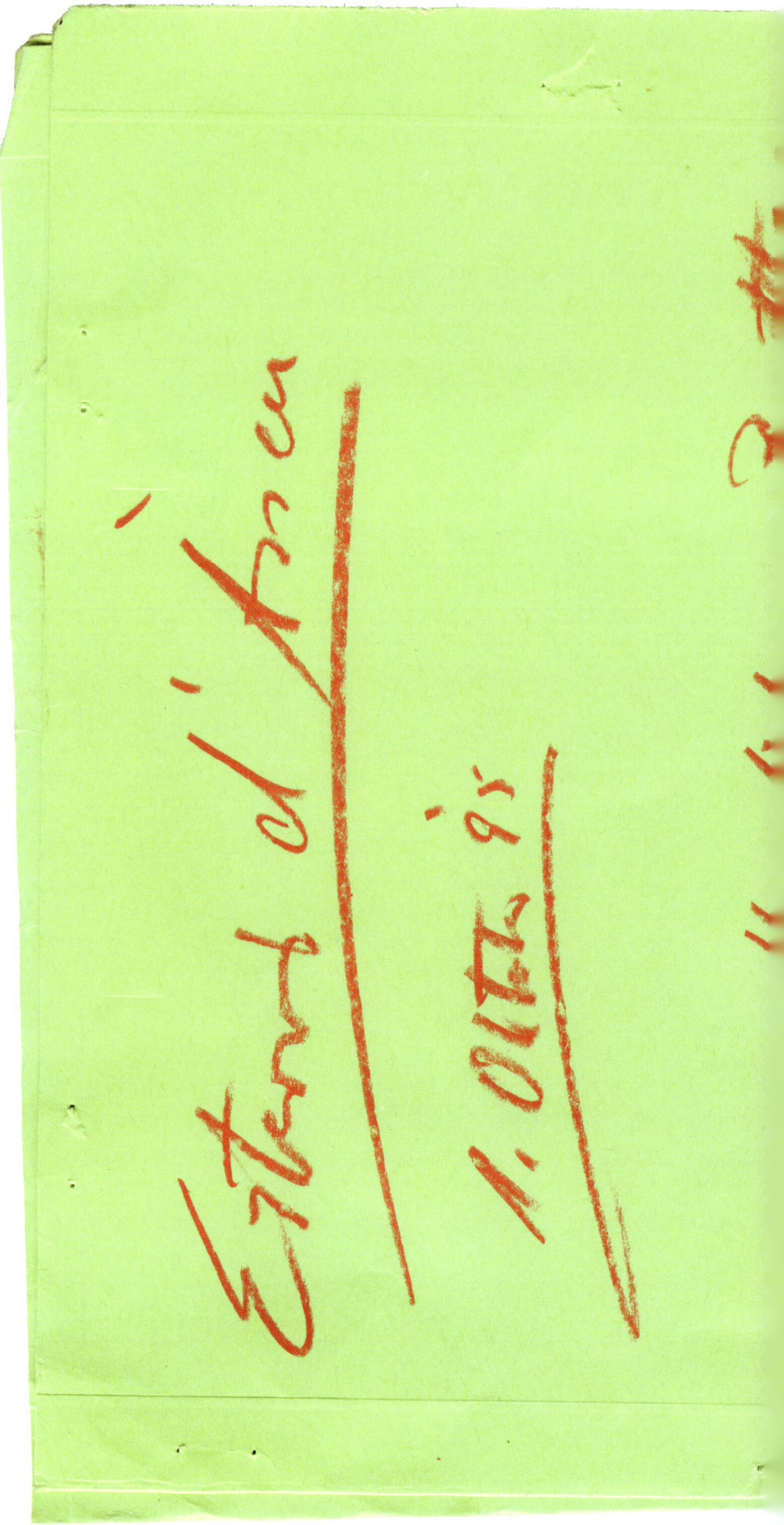

BENASQUE
October 1st, 1995
-
My dear Buttercrapears. It's really doop here, and we are waiting for our nom-nom. We will photograph some sheep, a tractor + a Mercedes tomorrow. We are proud. Papi!
(I quote Antony's pronunciation here)

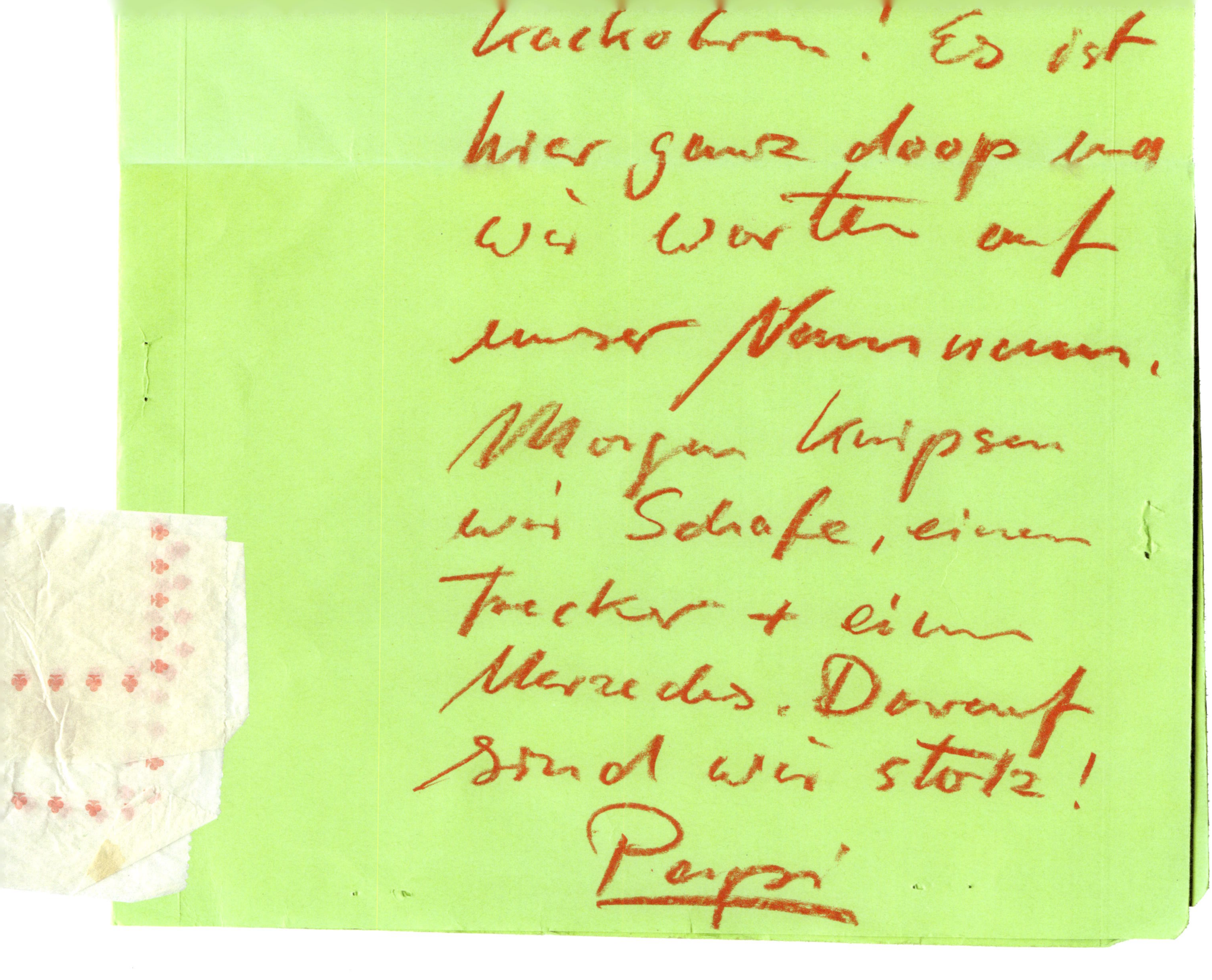

kackoben! Es ist hier ganz doof und wir warten auf unser Abendessen.
Morgen knipsen wir Schafe, einen Trecker + einen Mercedes. Darauf sind wir stolz!
Papi

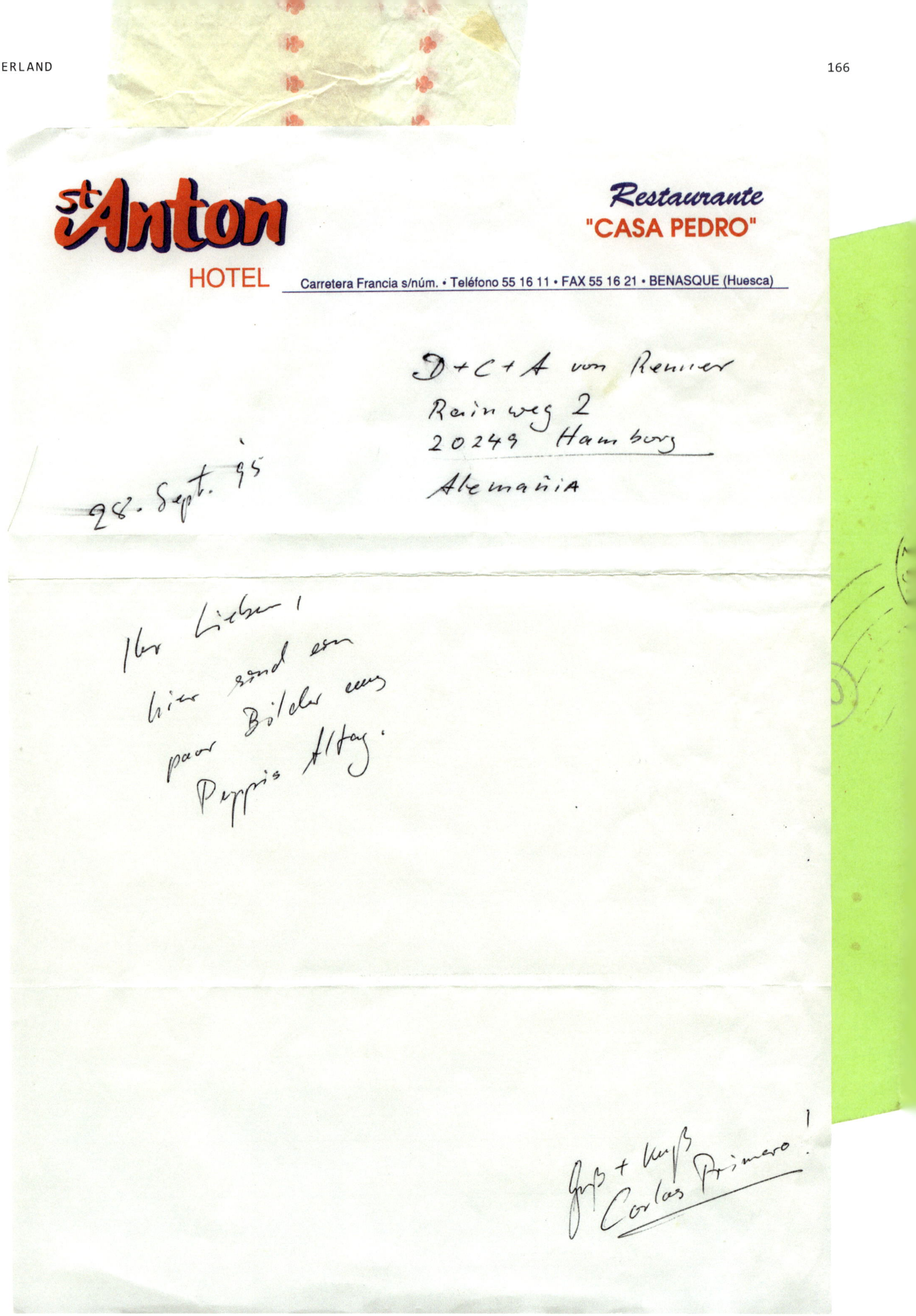

St Anton HOTEL

Restaurante "CASA PEDRO"

Carretera Francia s/núm. • Teléfono 55 16 11 • FAX 55 16 21 • BENASQUE (Huesca)

D+C+A von Renner
Rainweg 2
20249 Hamburg
Alemania

28. Sept. 95

Ihr Lieben!
hier sind ein
paar Bilder aus
Peppis Alltag.

Gruß + Kuß
Carlos Primero!

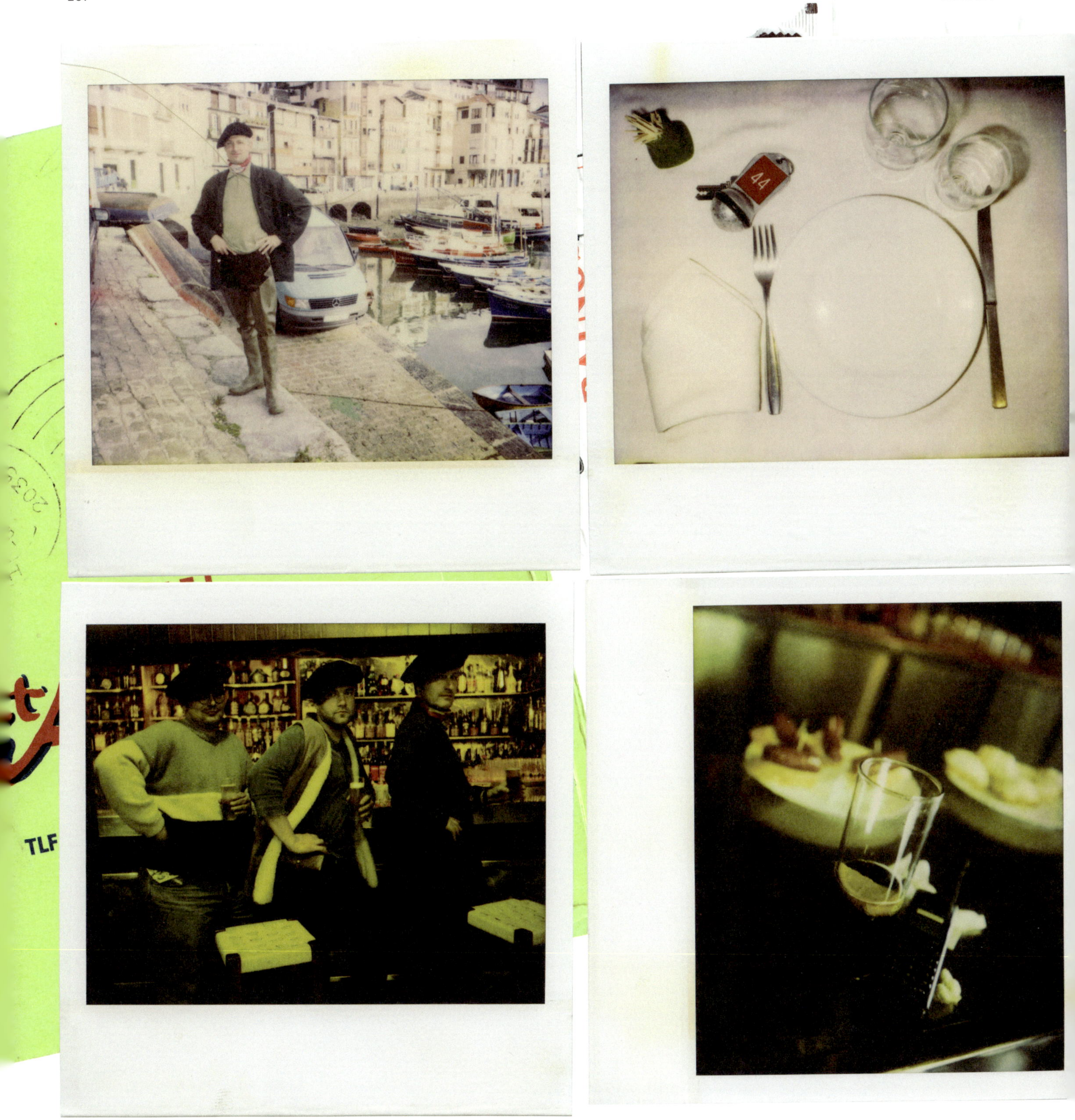

BERMEO
September 28th, 1995
-
Dear ones, here are a few pictures from Pappi’s daily routine.

I get to fly to South Africa in 1996 for the travel agency TUI. It's everything but "oh great, you get to fly to Cape Town". Not at all. It's 9°C at the beach during the day, and the nights are really cold. I sleep in two pairs of trousers and my travel jacket. The guest house isn't prepared for these temperatures, and thus doesn't have a heating system. Due to cold fingers, I only send one postcard from this trip.

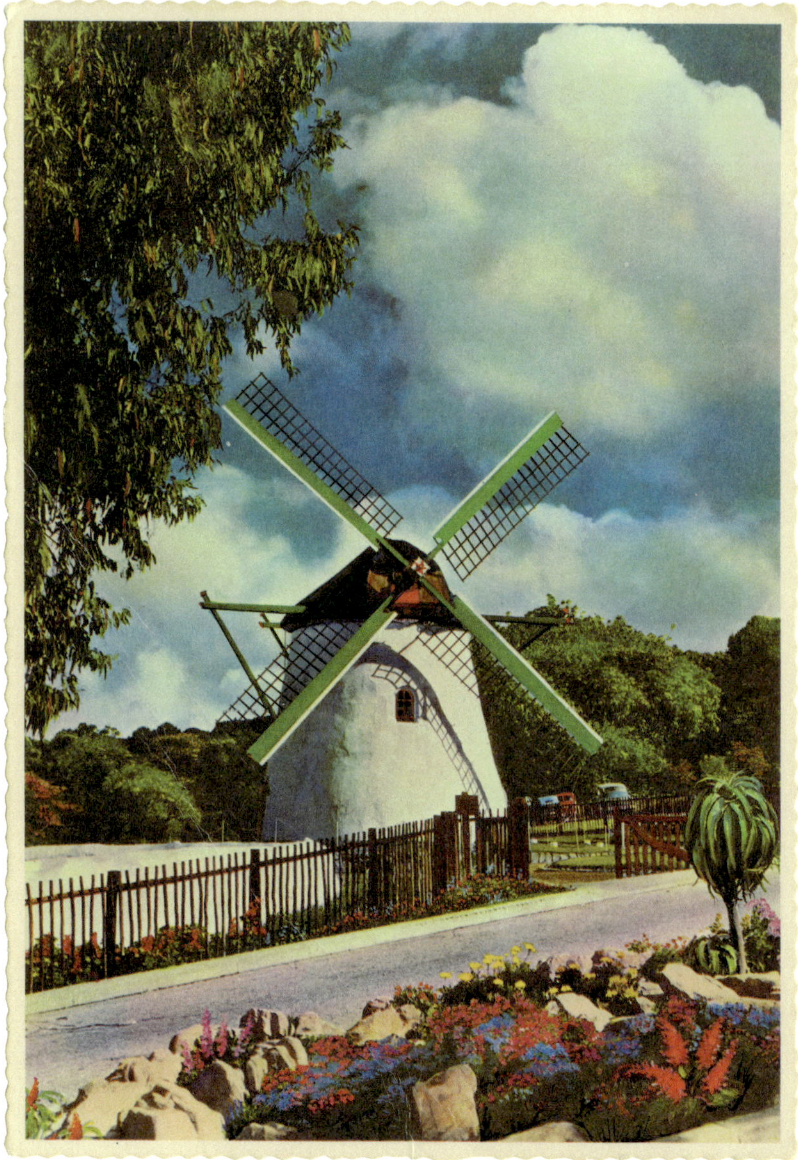

I'm freezing and would rather come back home straight away.

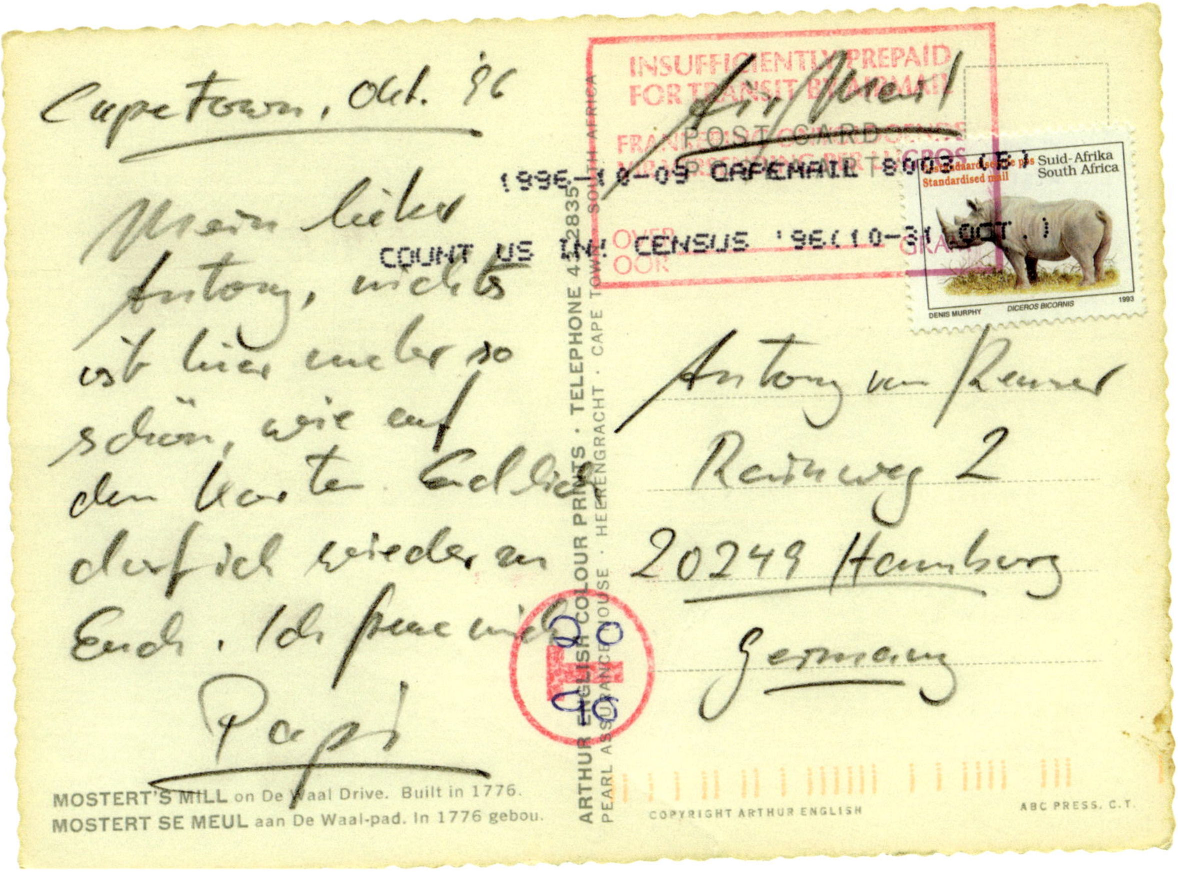

CAPE TOWN
October 9th, 1996
-
My dear Antony,
nothing is as beautiful here as
it is on the postcards. Finally,
I get to come home to you.
I can't wait.
Papi

The reference of the Hell Gate Bridge in NY is meant to remind Antony that we have the same bridge hanging on our wall, made of iron at a scale of 1:87. A trainee discovered it for me during a nightly drive through Aalborg, Denmark years ago. It is 2.40m in length.

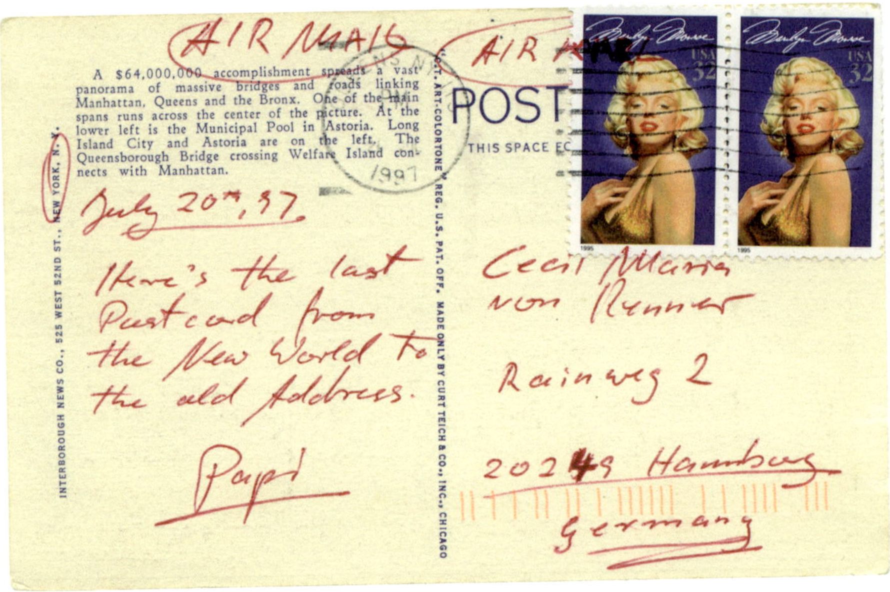

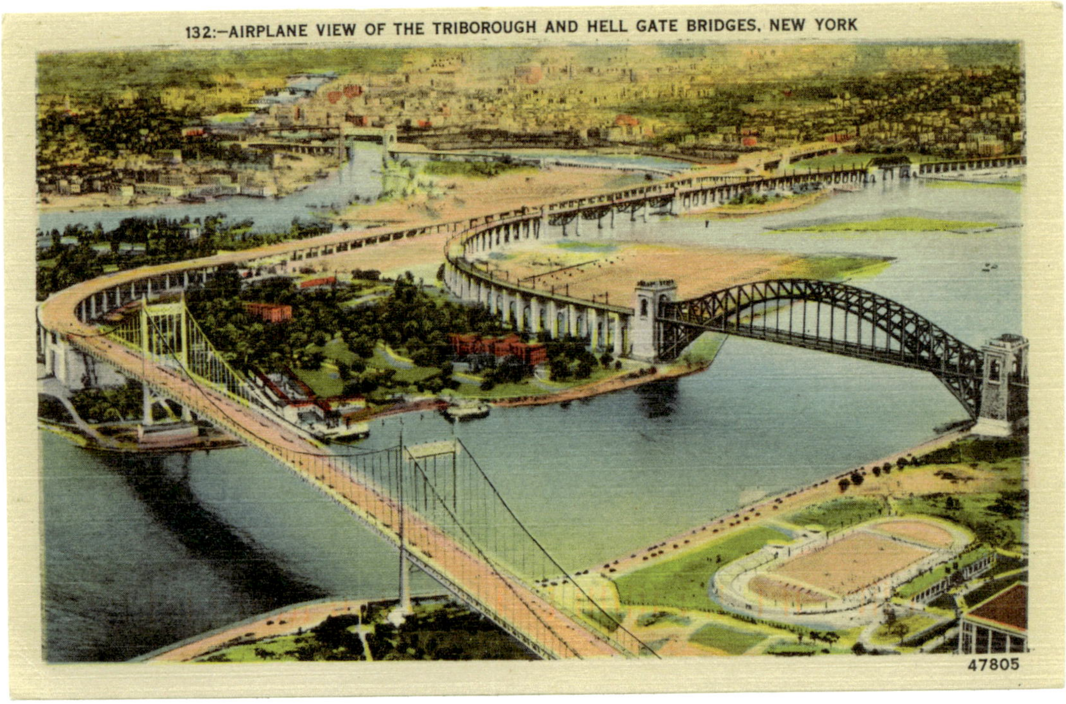

NEW YORK
July 20th, 1997
-
Here's the last
Postcard from
the New World to
the old Adress.
Papi

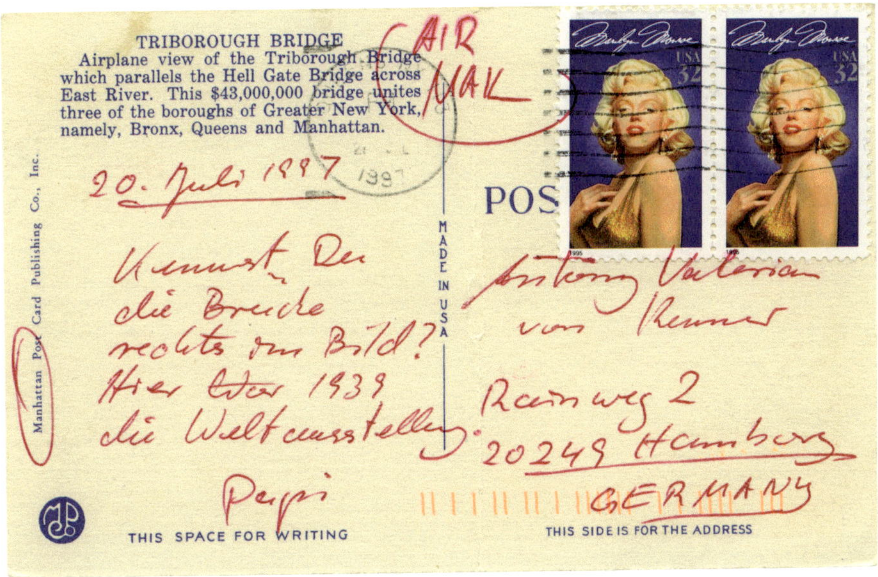
TRIBOROUGH BRIDGE
Airplane view of the Triborough Bridge which parallels the Hell Gate Bridge across East River. This $43,000,000 bridge unites three of the boroughs of Greater New York, namely, Bronx, Queens and Manhattan.

AIR MAIL

20. Juli 1997

Kennst Du die Brücke rechts im Bild? Hier war 1939 die Weltausstellung.

Papi

Antony Valerian von Renner
Rainweg 2
20249 Hamburg
GERMANY

Manhattan Post Card Publishing Co., Inc.

MADE IN USA

POS

THIS SPACE FOR WRITING

THIS SIDE IS FOR THE ADDRESS

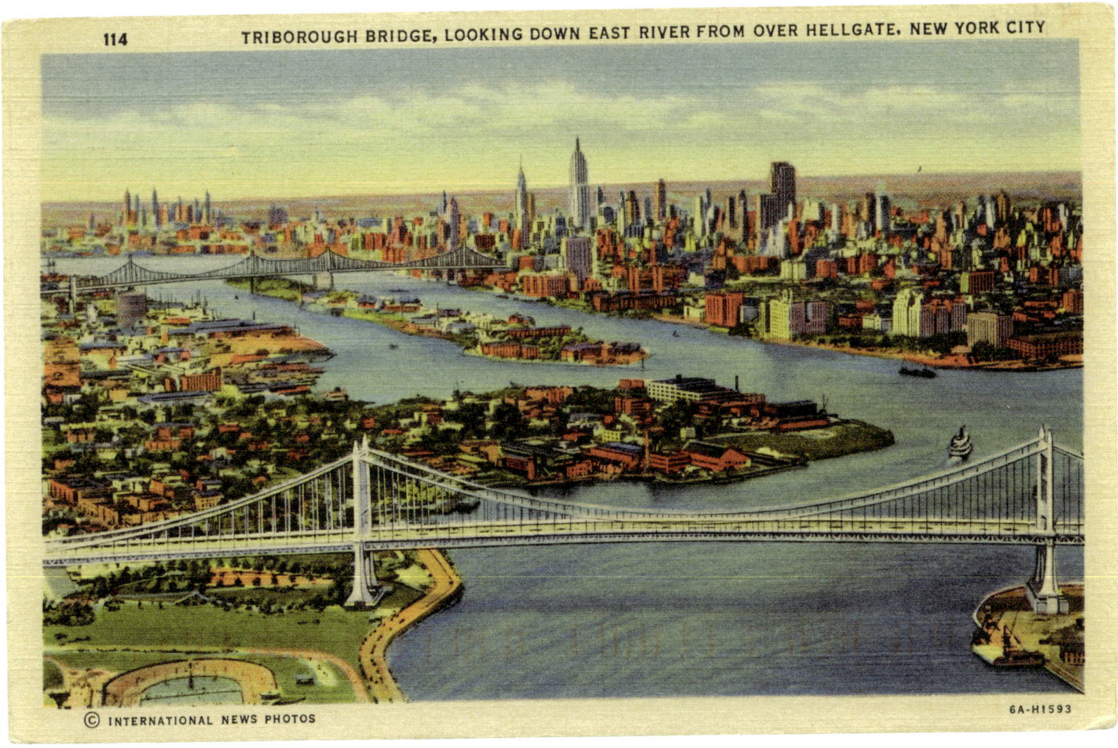

NEW YORK

July 20th, 1997

–

Do you recognise the bridge on the right? The world exhibition took place here in 1993.

Papi

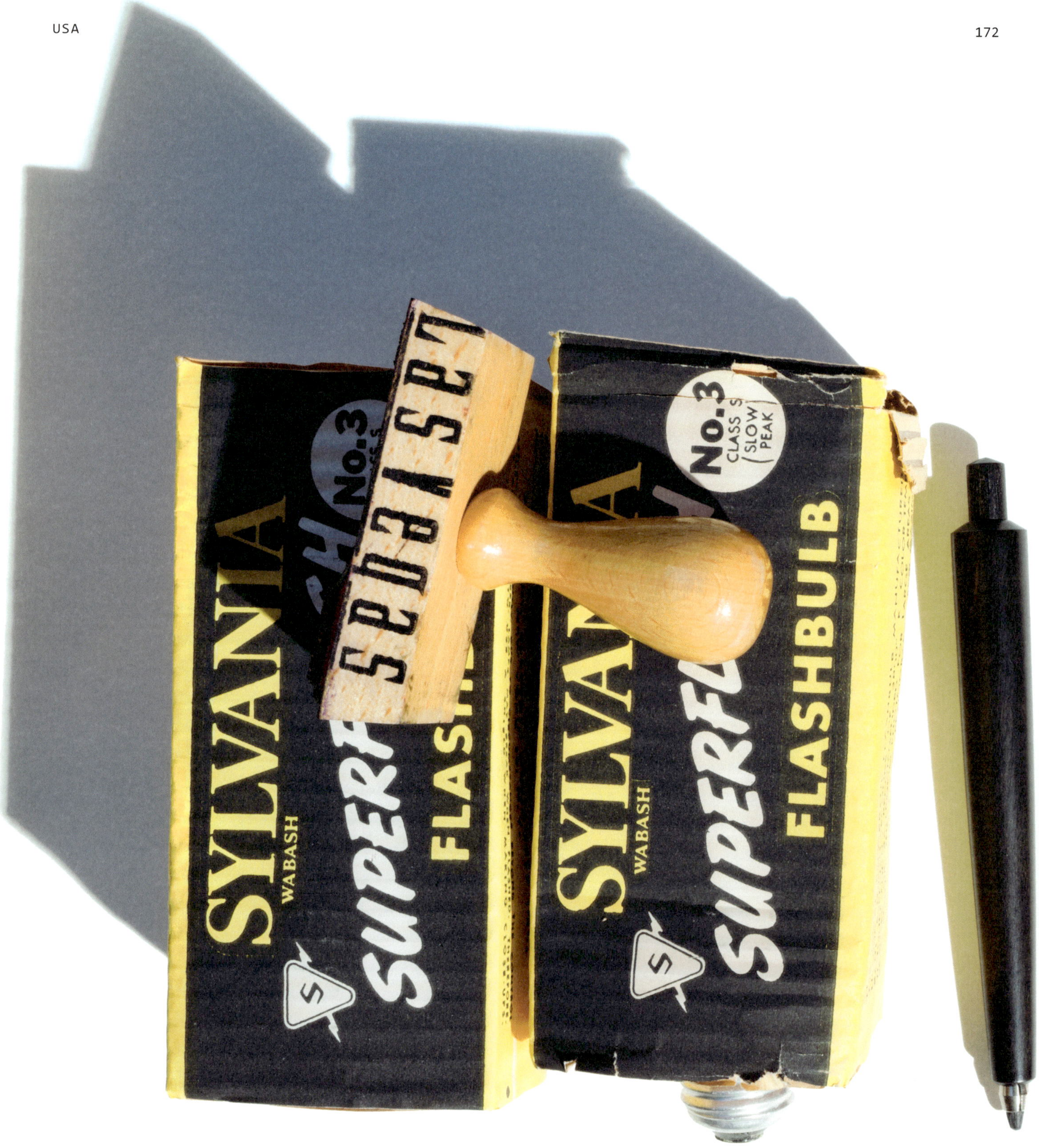
SYLVANIA
WABASH
No. 3
CLASS S
SLOW
PEAK
FLASHBULB

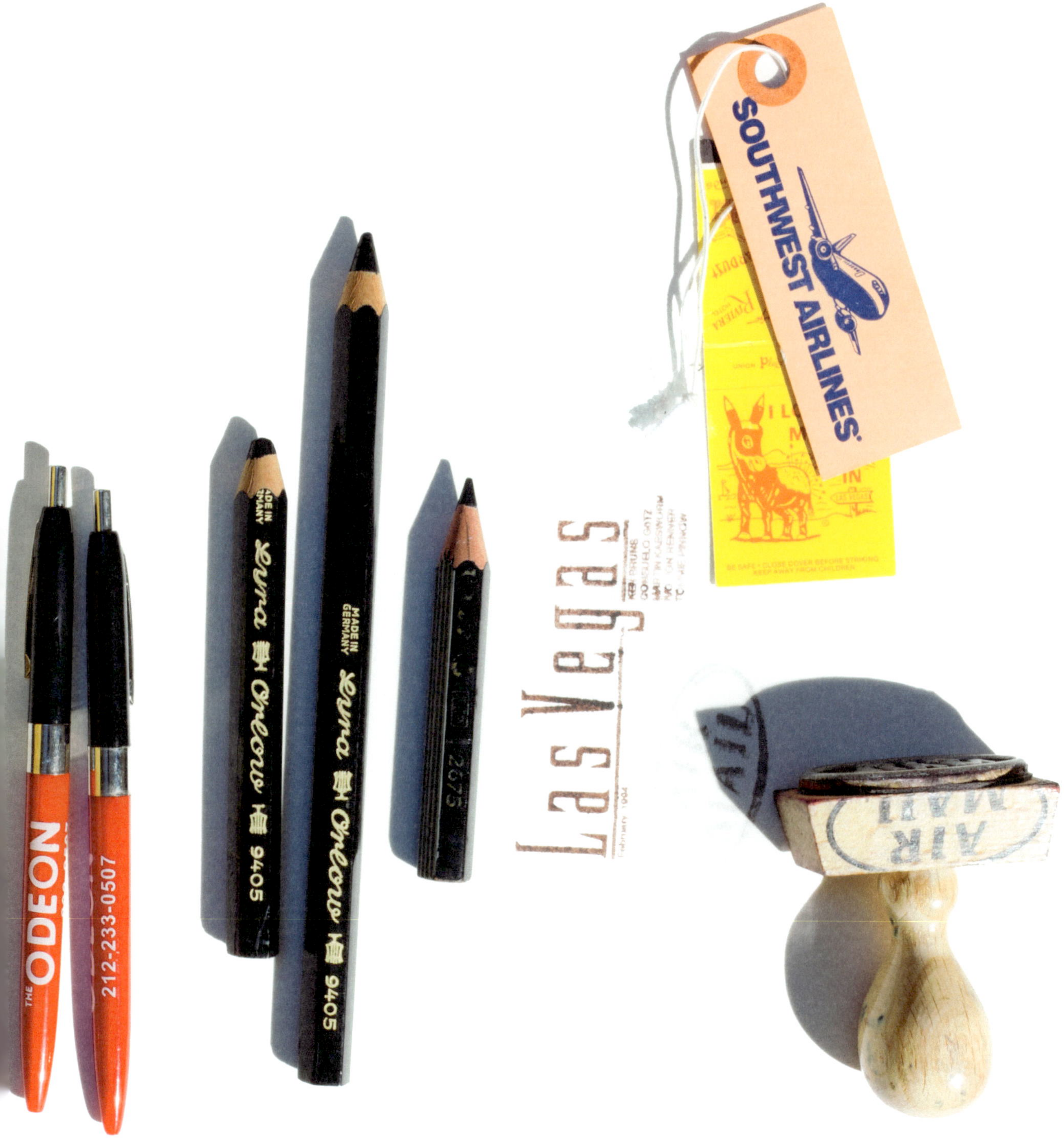

Brought along or taken home. I take the 1994 “Las Vegas” stamp along again on this trip.

Breakfast at the Detroit River.

I feel privileged to be able to work where car photography was basically invented. Mickey McGuire's studio is still there, and the cupboards are full of slides showing enormous sets, that were only recently made into a book. I eat ribs for the first time. Braised for 24 hours. I would like to stay there, although the city's full tragedy is visible.

My assistant Jeremy and I are sitting at the breakfast table in our hotel's junior suite, overlooking the Detroit River and Canada.

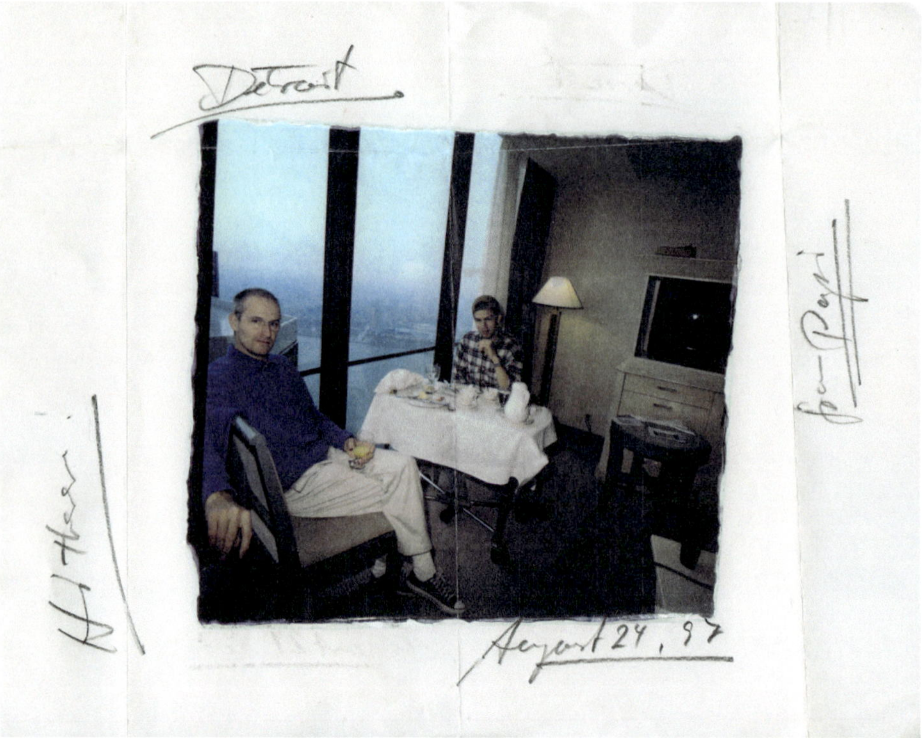

DETROIT
August 24th, 1997
-
"Hi there!
from Papi"

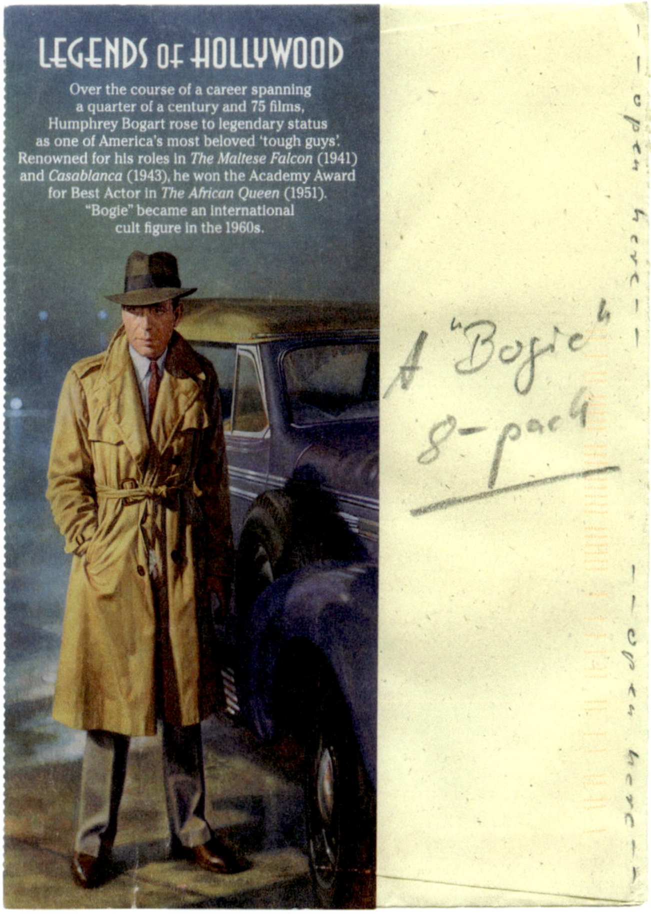

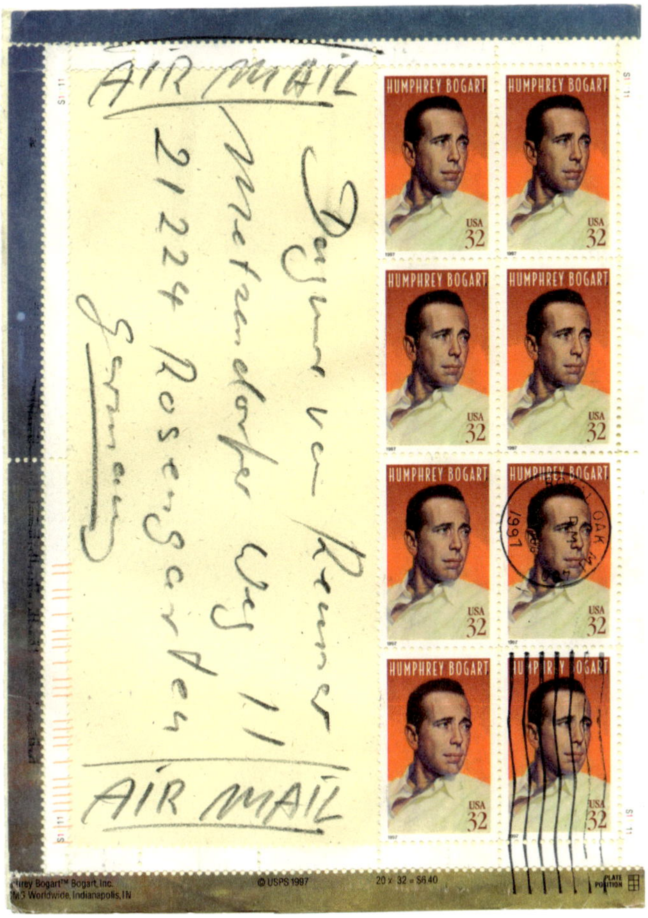

DETROIT

August 24th, 1997

–

"A 'Bogie'

8-pack"

Good bye, Nice!

Nokia: the trips to Nice have been replaced by America. It's the last attempt to get people into a warm atmosphere in February. All my photography colleagues fly to South Africa afterwards. Of course, I brought the postcard for Cecil along with me from my archive. My stamp supply is slowly running out.

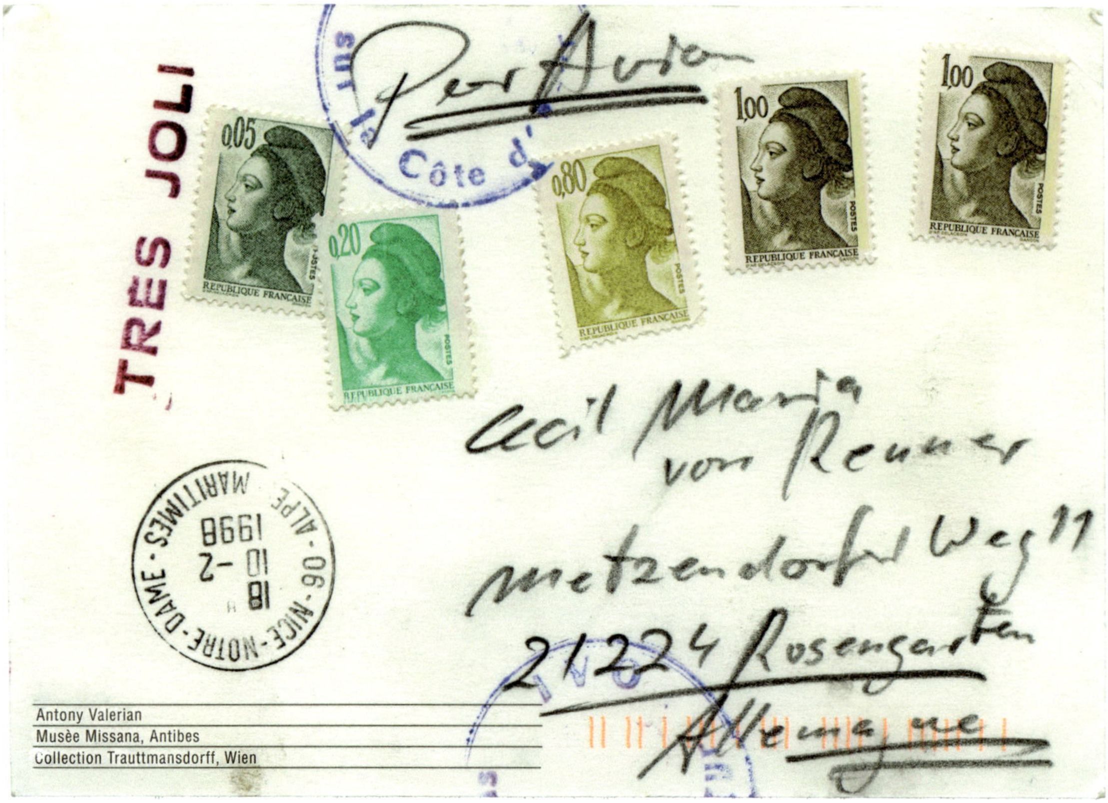

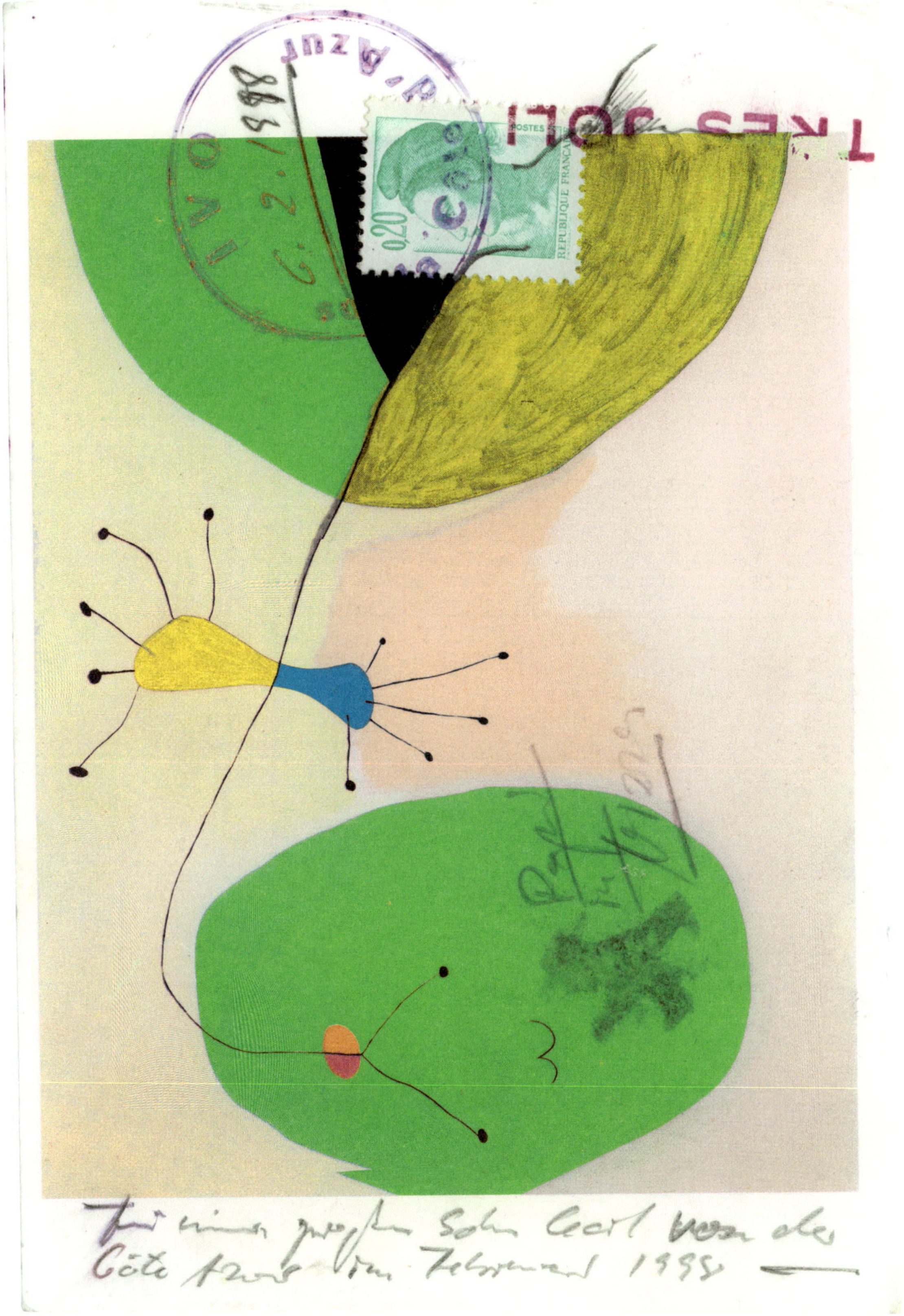

CÔTE D'AZUR

February 10th, 1998

–

For my big son Cecil, from the Côte d'Azur in February 1998

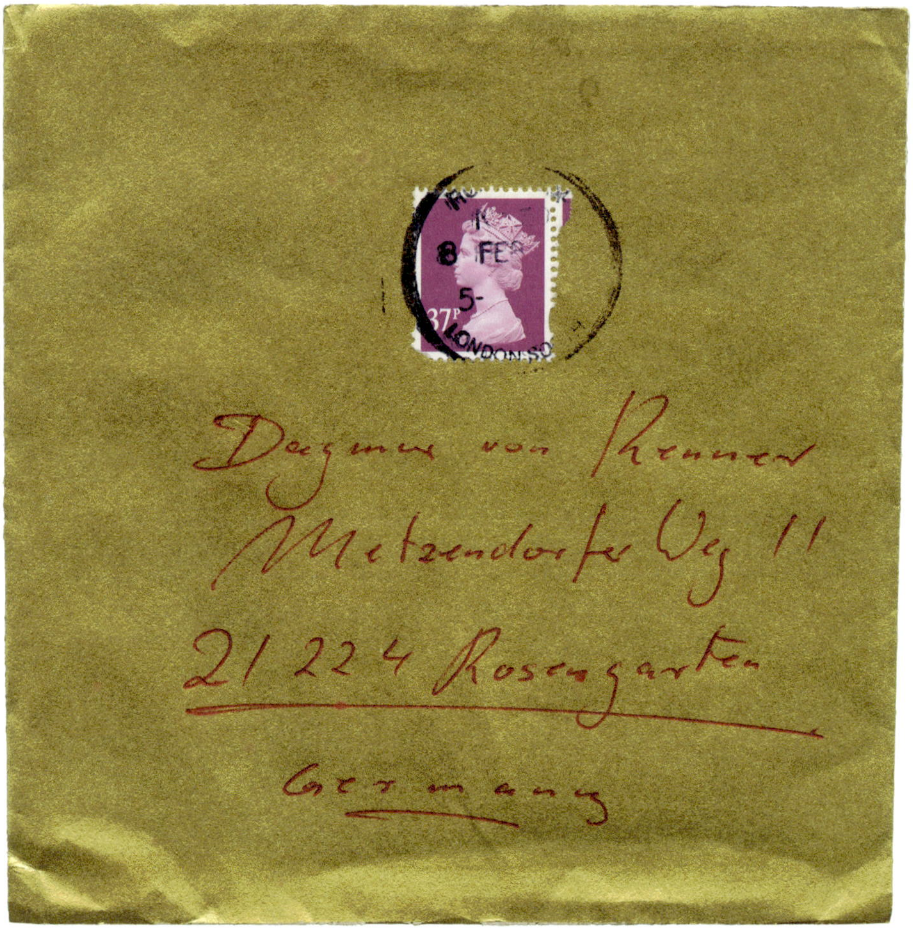
37p
8 FEB
LONDON
Metzendorfer Weg 11
21224 Rosengarten
Germany

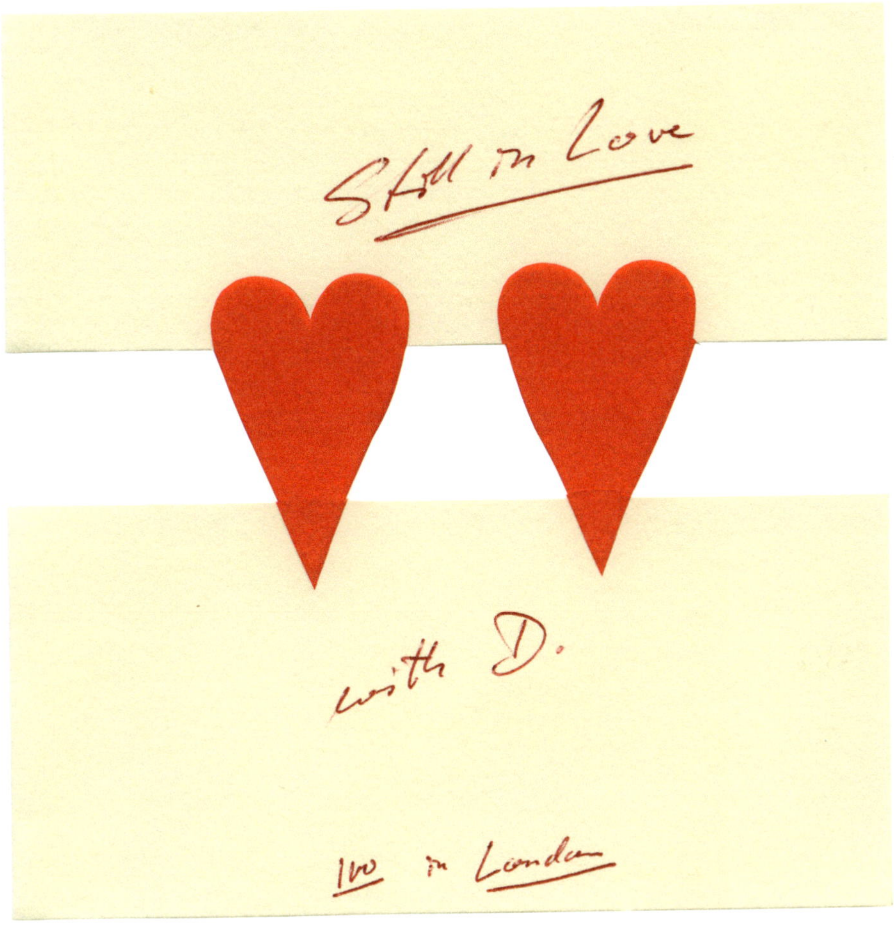
Still in Love
with D.
Ivo in London

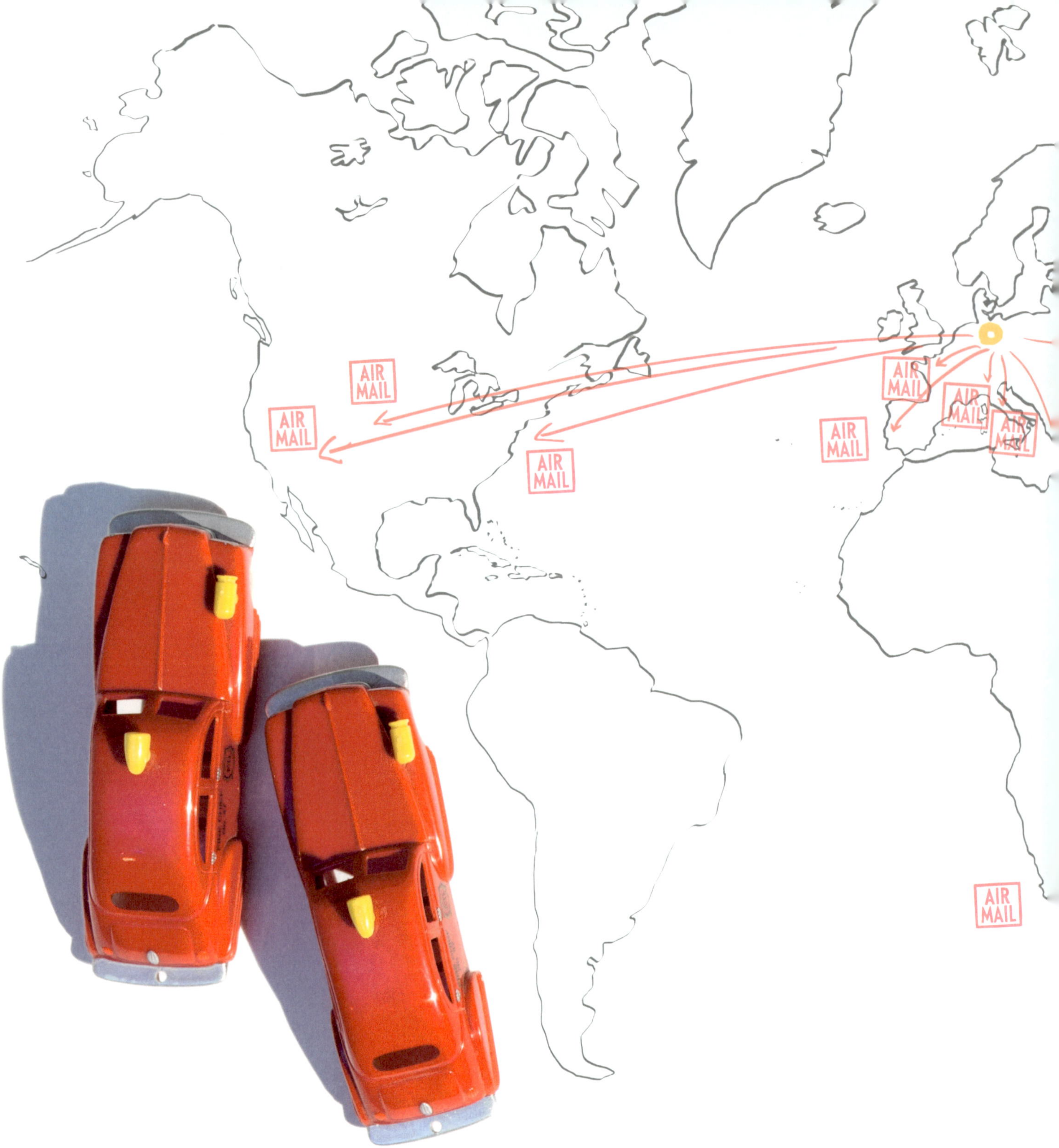

USA, Belgique, Portugal, Schweiz, Italia, South Africa, China

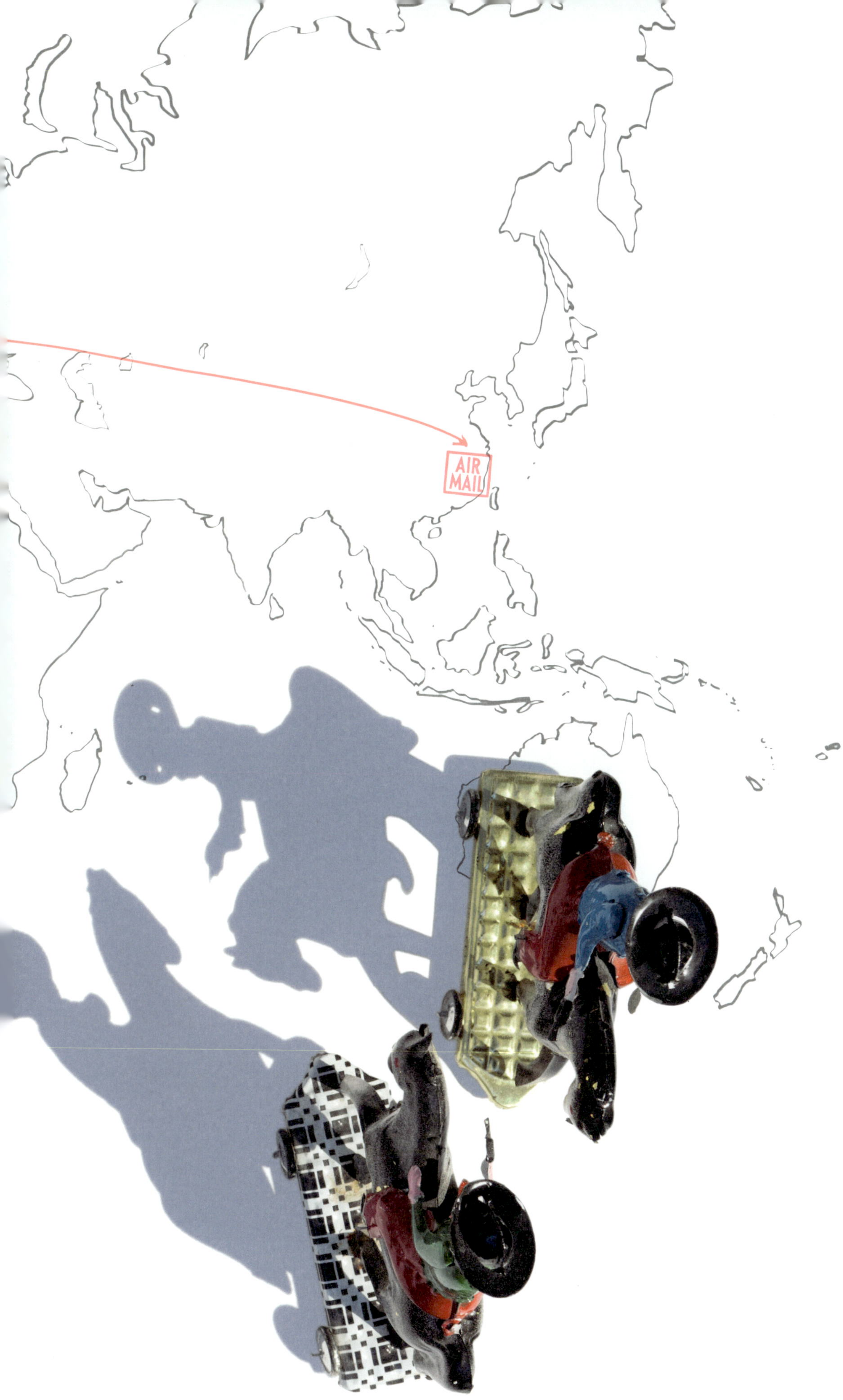
AIR
MAIL

He was James Bond.

This trip brings us a postcard showing UFOs, as well as this group picture. For Mercedes Vito we photograph two base jumpers while they jump from a rock ledge. On our departure day, we decide to drive for an hour to the Arches National Park in Moab, Utah, and do something that all tourists do: snap pictures of ourselves.

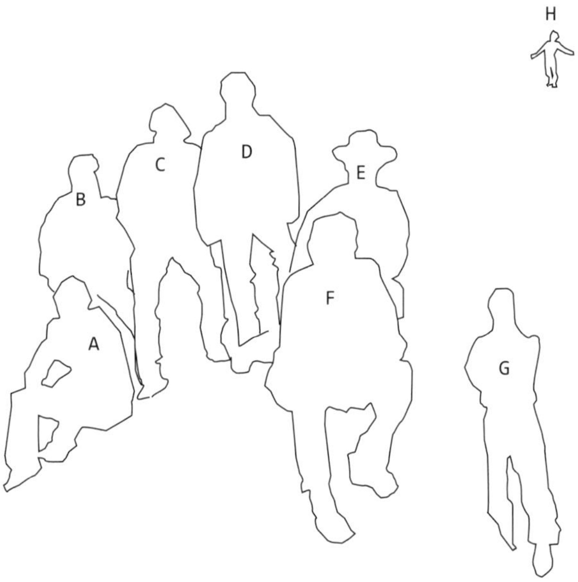

Group photo with the crew

A Jan Rincklake van Endert, assistant
B Jim Mattingly, location scout
C Eric Hofstetter, producer
D Tom Sanders, the most famous base jumper and stuntman of all time, who has played a part in many James Bond films
E Stefan Leick, art director
F Me
G Second base jumper
H Third base jumper

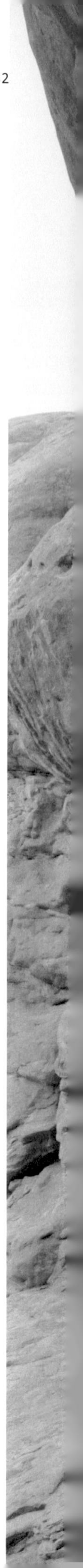

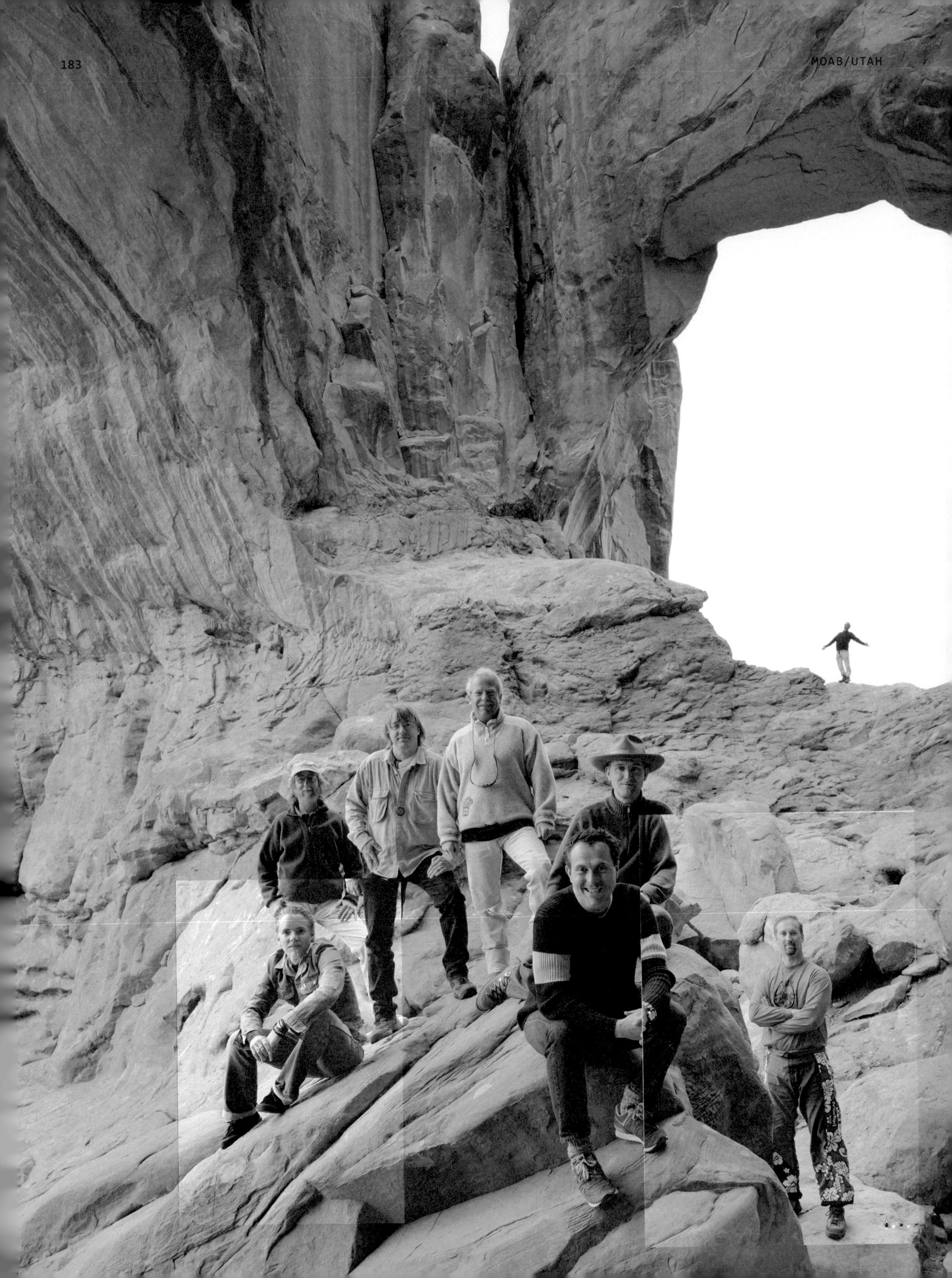

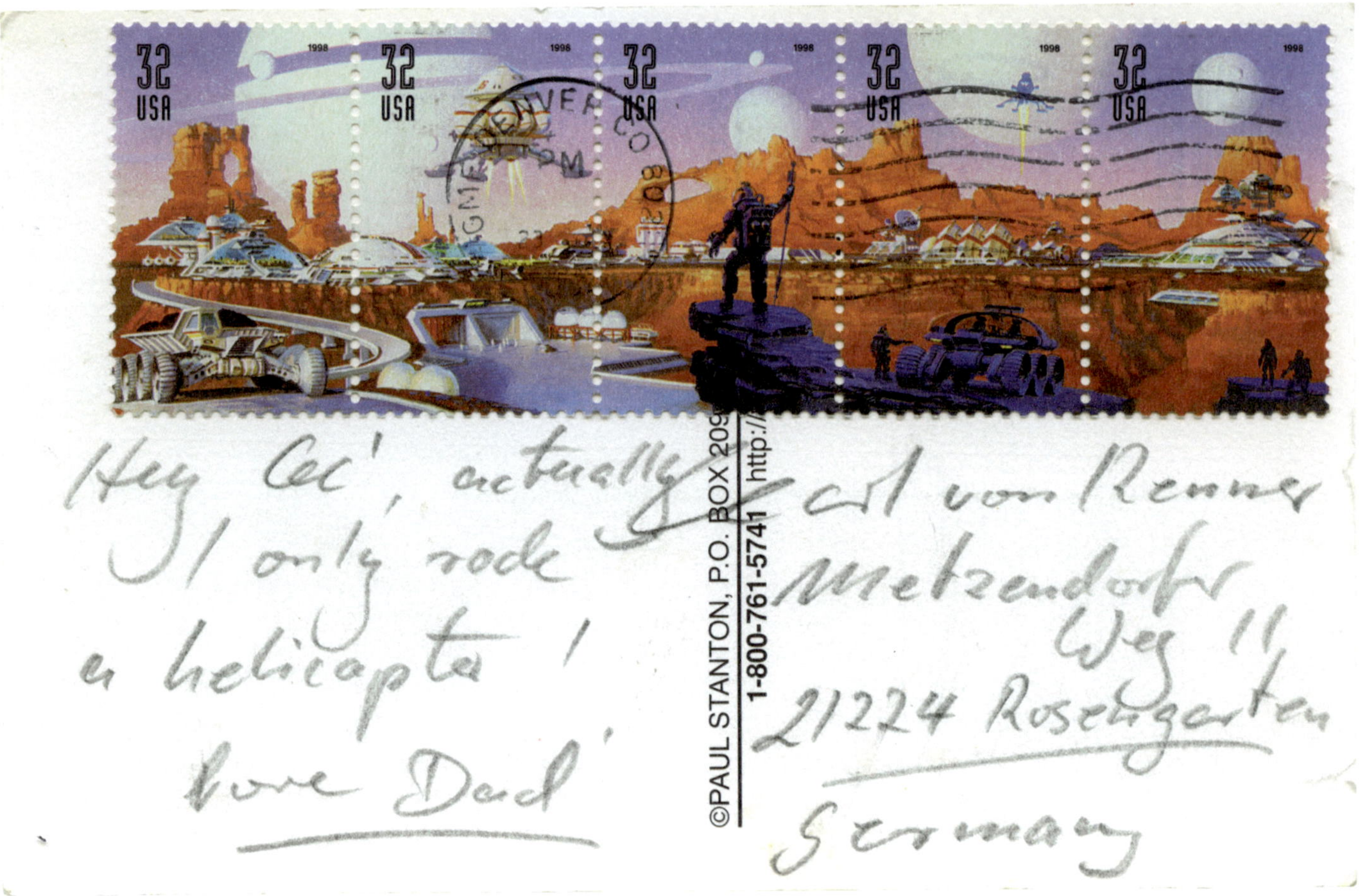

MOAB, UTAH

July 15th, 1995

–

“Hey Cec’, actually

I only rode

a helicopter!

Love Dad”

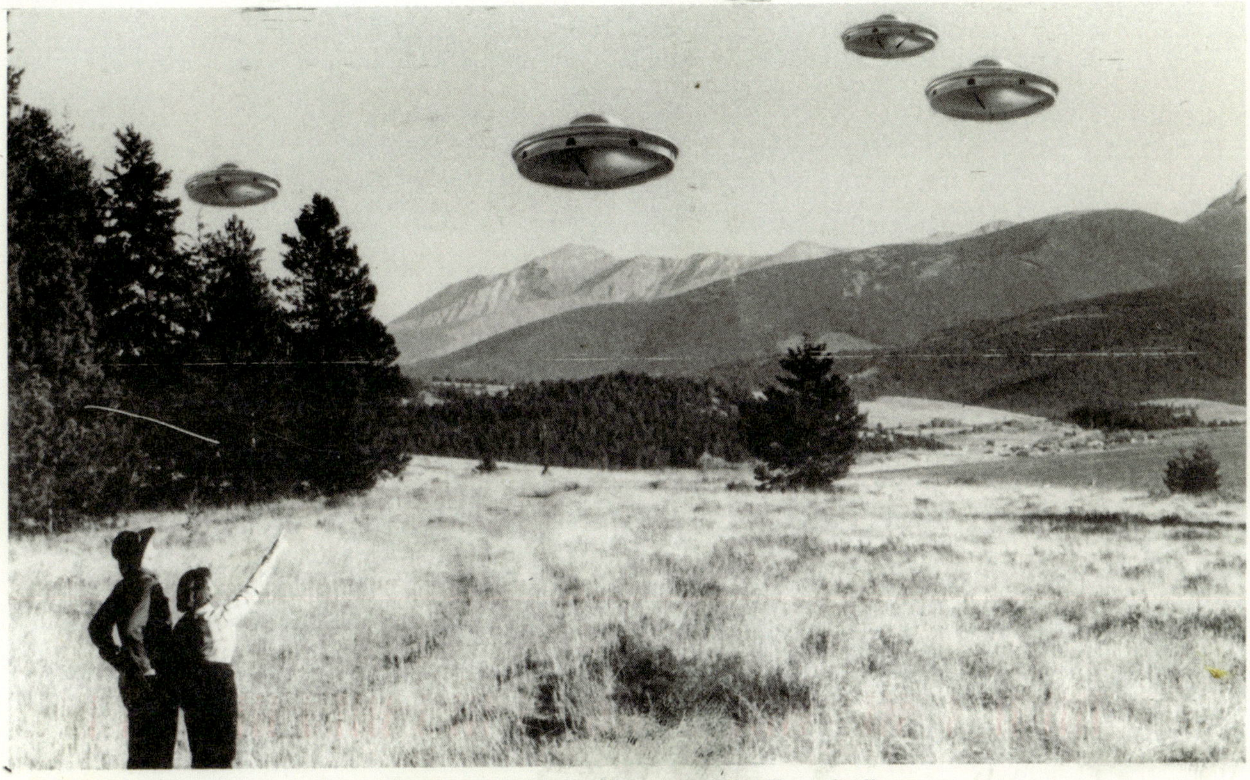

"More Californians, No Doubt"

Denver, Dalia Street.

Moab, Utah for Mercedes. We have our films developed in Denver on our return journey. The waiting time drives me to the outskirts of the city, which give the impression of having seen better days.

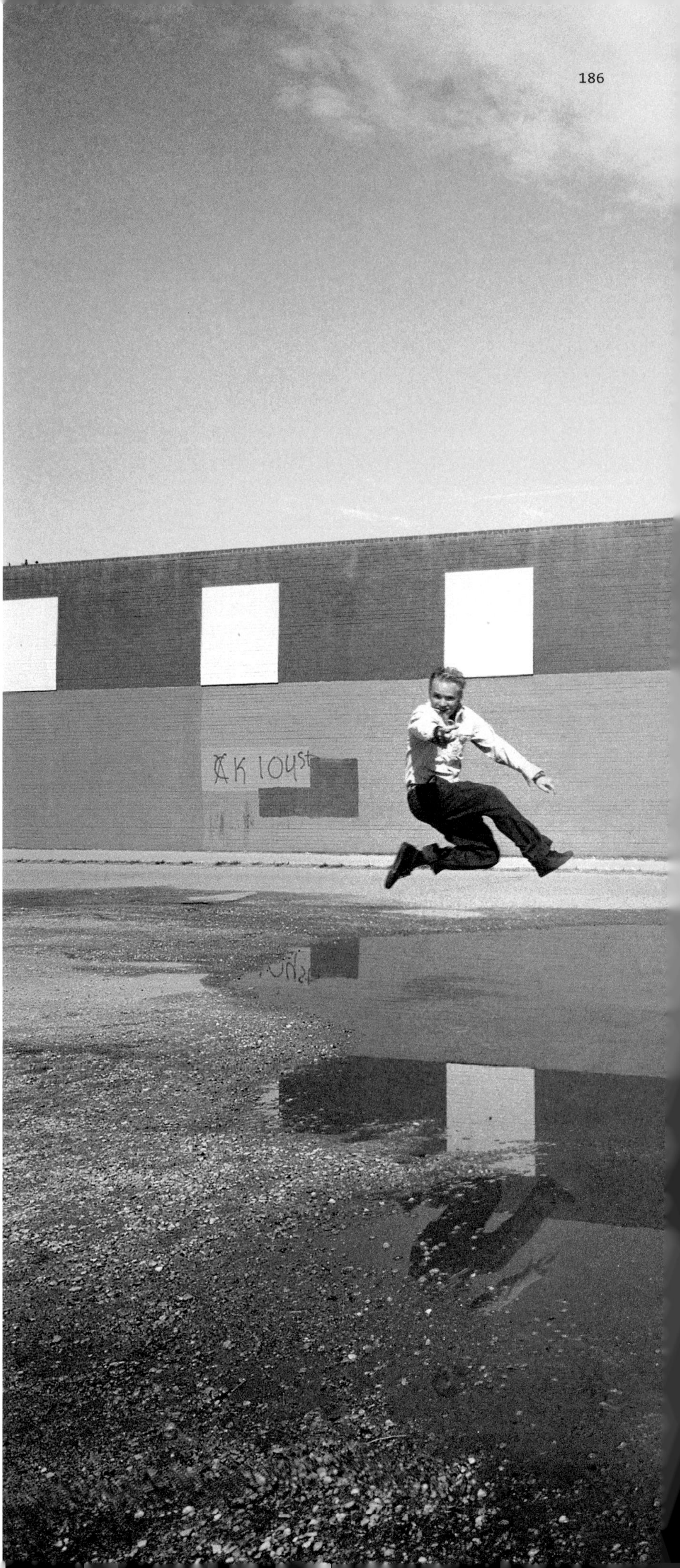

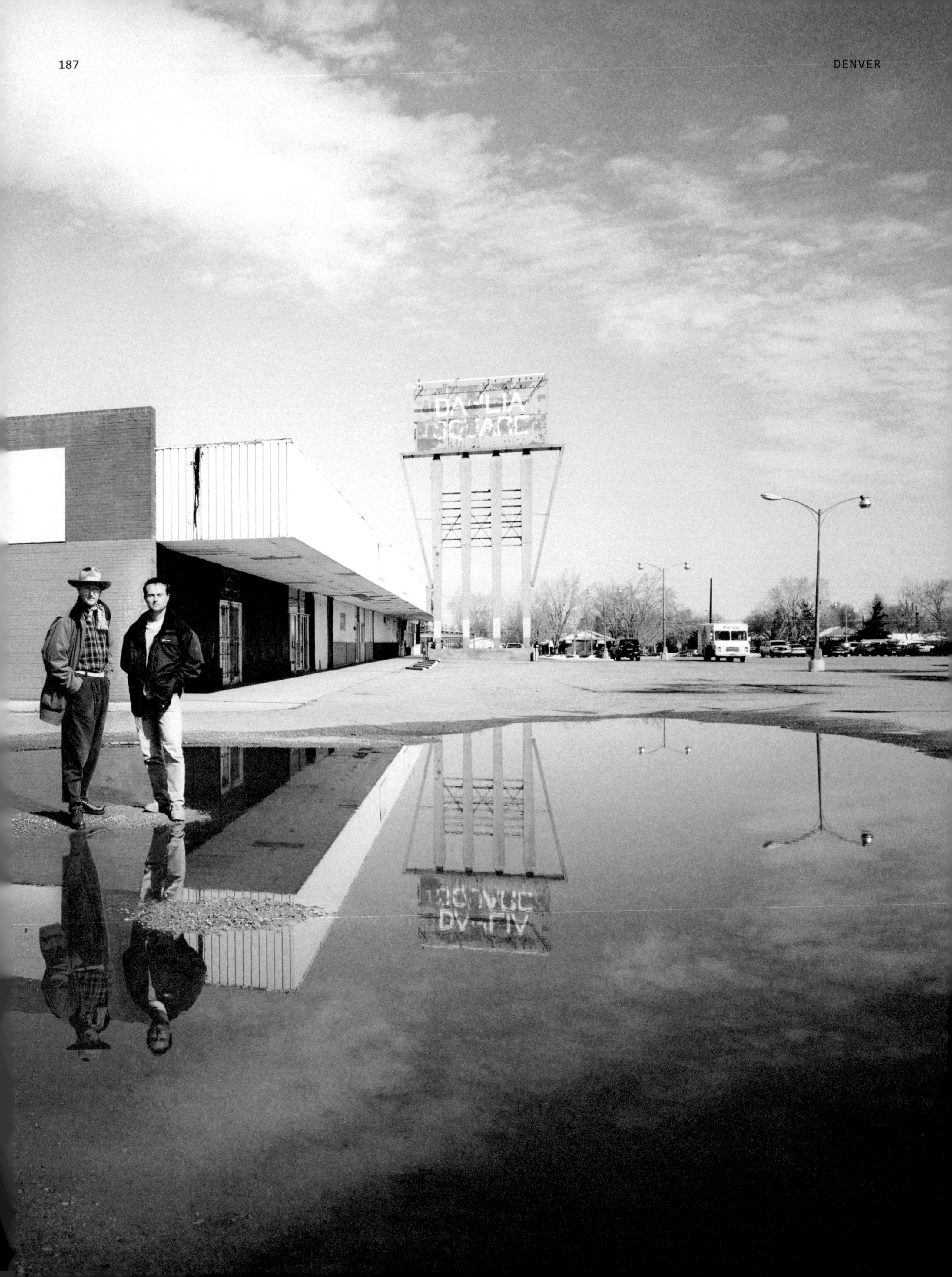

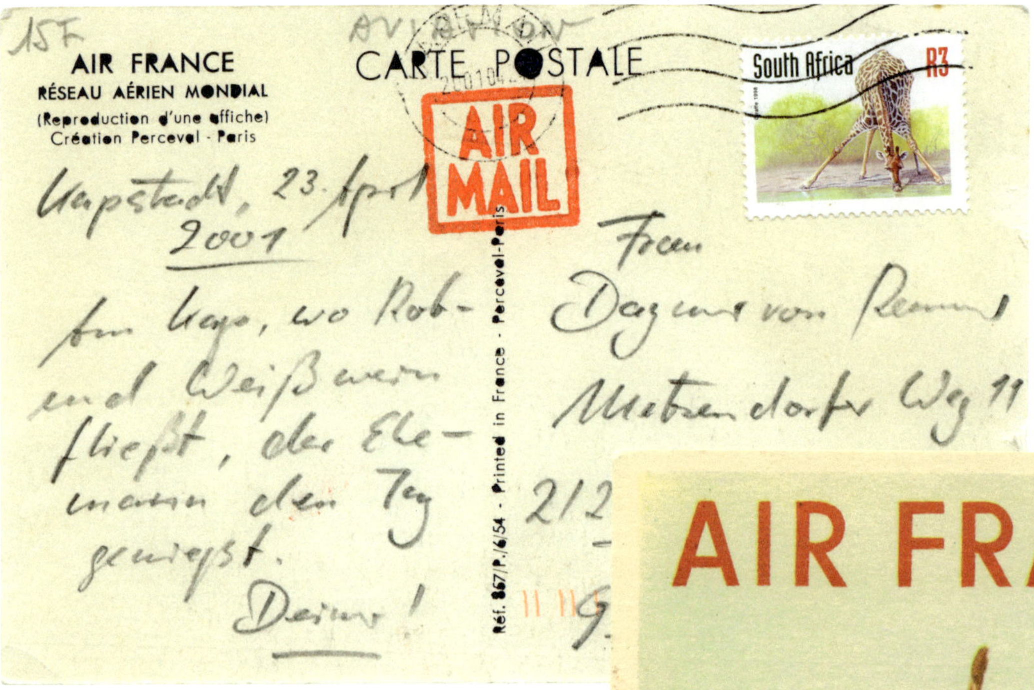

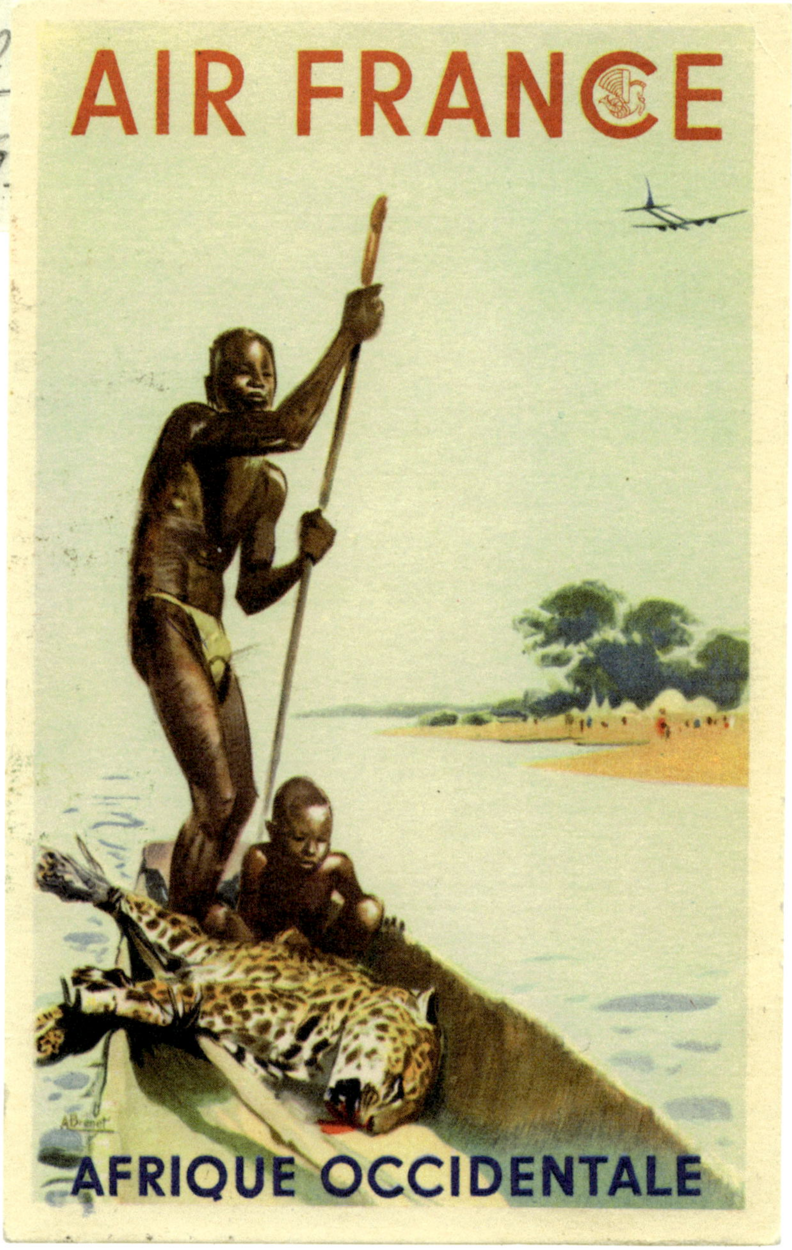

CAPE TOWN

April 23rd, 2001

–

At the Cape where red and white wine flow, the husband enjoys the day. Yours!

Okt. 1

Wo Afrika ein Ende hat . . .

Da ist sie ja wieder, die Dose mit diesen schwarzen Krümeln, die dem Nichtgourmet die Welt bedeuten. Ein letztes Mal sage ich Kaviar. Auf dem Rückflug wird sich der FirstClass Flieger der Seafood Platter zuwenden. Die Nacht kommt. Ich bin wie Boris Becker: Ich kann im Flugzeug schlafen. Der Jumbo neigt seine Nase gen Kapstadt; die eintönige Farblosigkeit will nicht enden; das Wetter ist bewölkt. Noch prägt mich das Gefühl, Mallorca wäre schöner gewesen. Ein paar Worte mit Euch, die die Welt umspannen, aus der Nase meines Riesenvogels während der Zwischenlandung in Johannesburg mahnen mich, wie fern - wie nah Ihr seid.

1. Oktober - Kalt! Es ist kalt, daß das pinkeln zur Suchaktion wird. Die guten Zeiten scheinen vorbei. Alles sieht ein wenig aus, als hätte der Verlust des Geschmackes der 70iger Jahre nie ein Ende gefunden. Eine schlecht kopierte Broschüre sagt: "Capetown- the new Miami" . Ja wenn man schreibt was man hört was einer sagt der einen kennt . . . . ! Wenn's nach Miami doch nur nicht so weit wär. Neuste Meldung: 19:54 Uhr, 8 Grad Celsius. Vorhersage für morgen früh: 6 Grad. Gottseidank kühlt es noch ab. Und dann treiben wir zum Sonnenaufgang Kinder und Eltern für die Werbung an den Strand, wie einst die Buren die Neger. Was sie nicht umbringt, macht sie wenigstens krank. In mir brennt eine ungestillte Sehnsucht nach Mallorca.

CAPE TOWN
October 1st,
2001

Where Africa comes to an end … This trip to South Africa is an improvement.

It's so cold that peeing becomes a search operation.

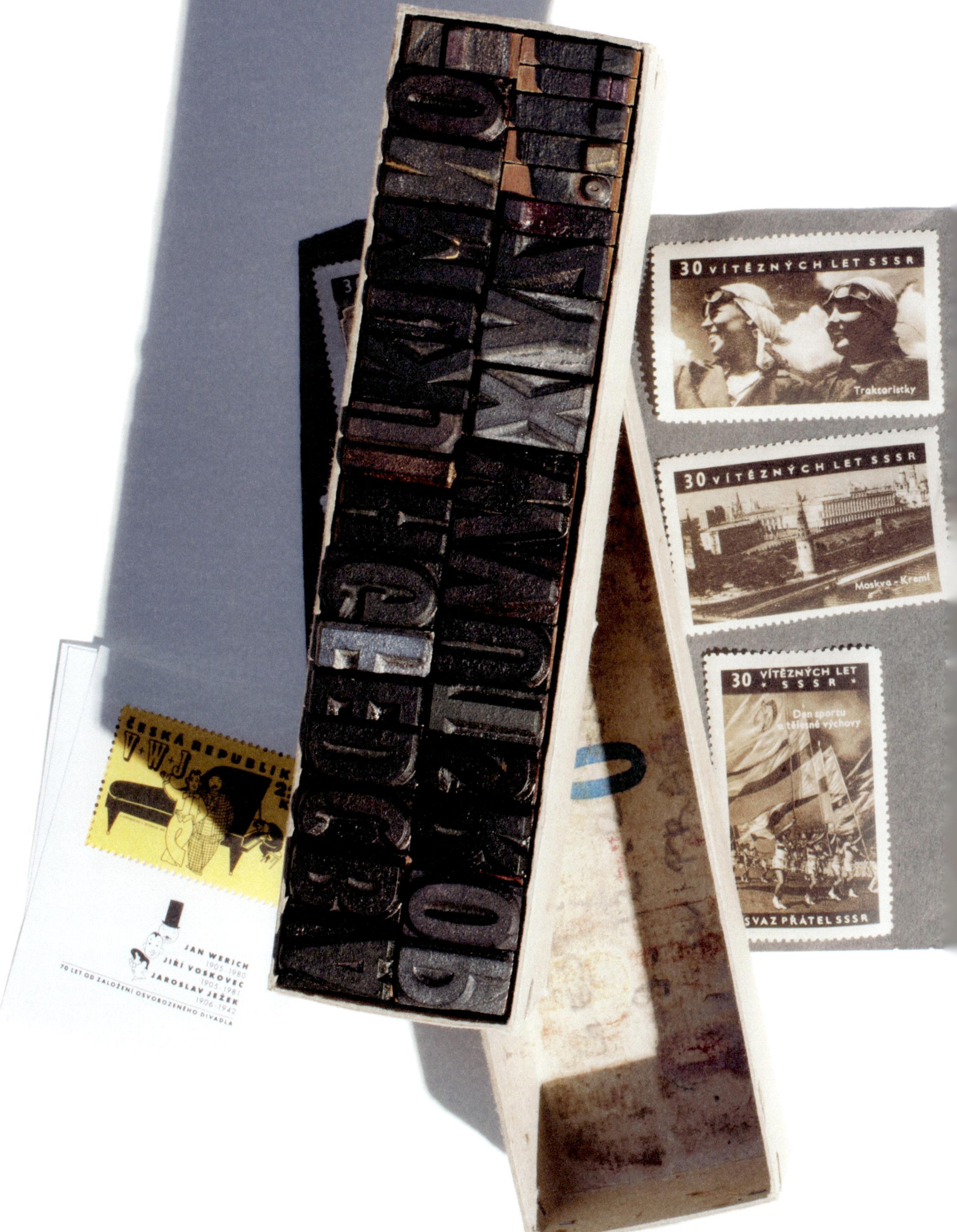
30 VÍTĚZNÝCH LET SSSR
Traktoristky
30 VÍTĚZNÝCH LET SSSR
Moskva - Kreml
30 VÍTĚZNÝCH LET SSSR
Den sportu a tělesné výchovy
SVAZ PŘÁTEL SSSR
V+W+J
JAN WERICH
1905–1980
JIŘÍ VOSKOVEC
1905–1981
JAROSLAV JEŽEK
1906–1942
70 LET OD ZALOŽENÍ OSVOBOZENÉHO DIVADLA

For a smoke to Prague.

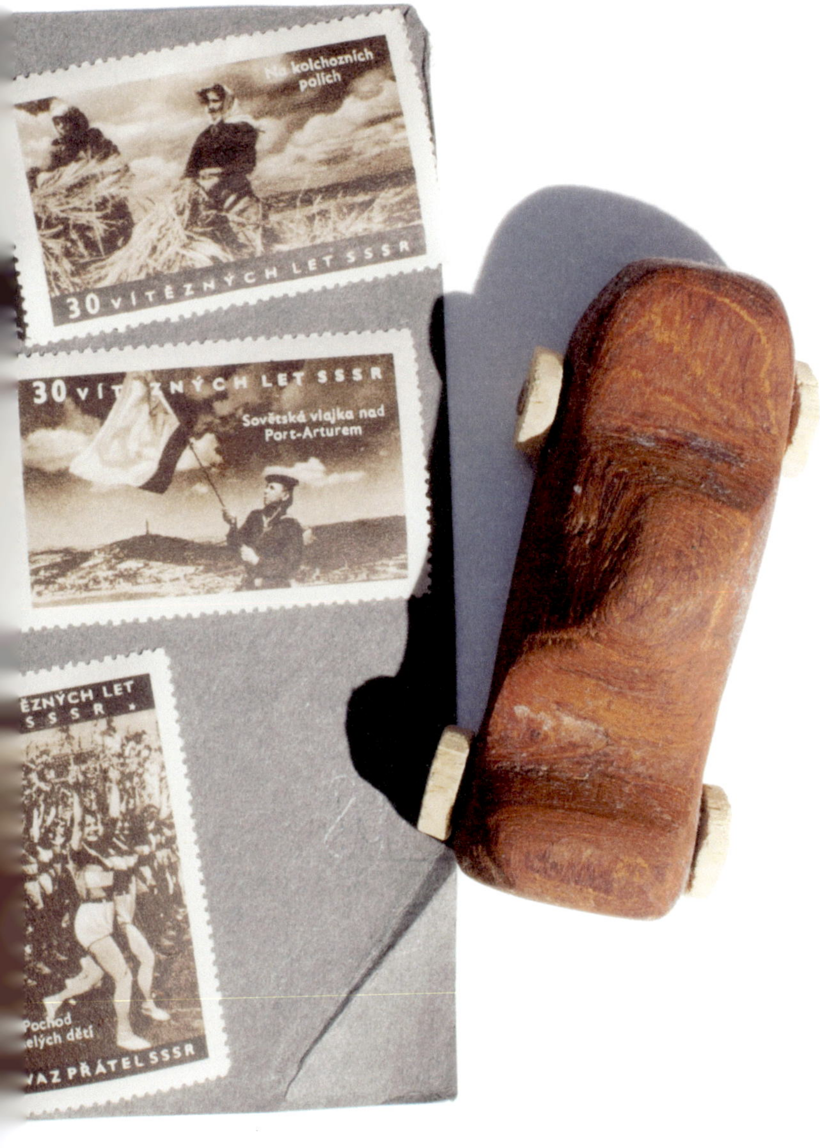

During my third trip to the Czech Republic, in Prague Libor Korman gives me the rubber stamp alphabet of his professor from Cologne. The brown stamps come from an anti-quarian shop in Prague, and Antony gives me the wooden car when I arrive home. This is the quality of cars that can only come from Rudolf Steiner Schools! The lack of time prevents me from writing a card.

"God protect our Pirelli building" is a reference to September 11th. Approximately one year later, a sports plane flies into that building, as well. The Pirelli building is a reminder of the fact that big design and architecture were at home in Italy.

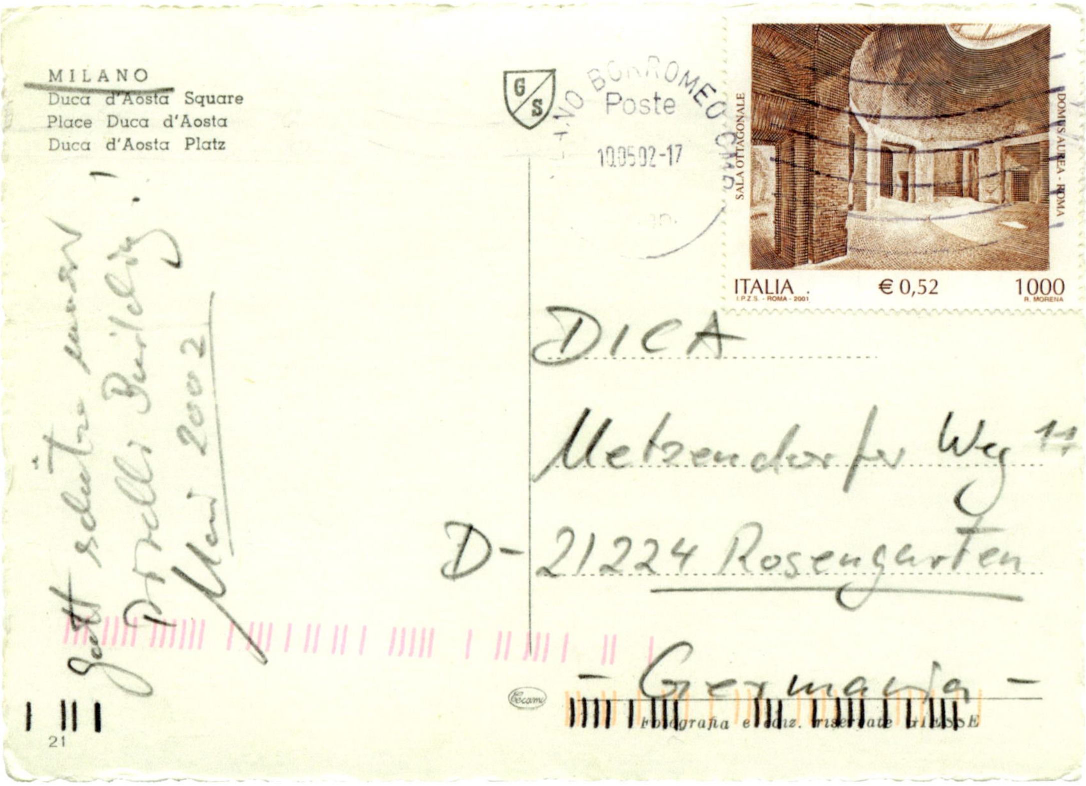

MILANO
May 2002
-
God protect our
Pirelli building!

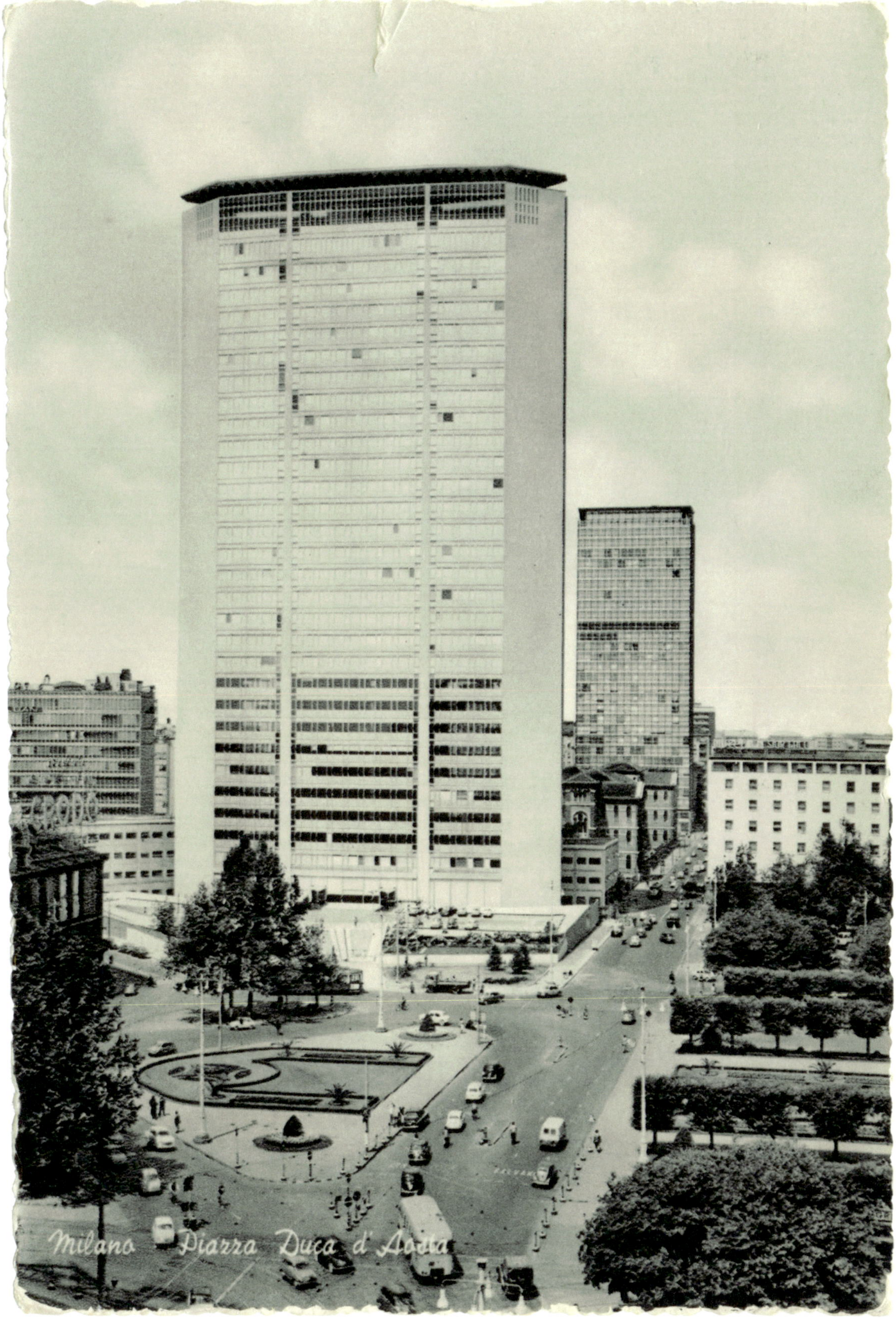
Milano Piazza Duca d'Aosta

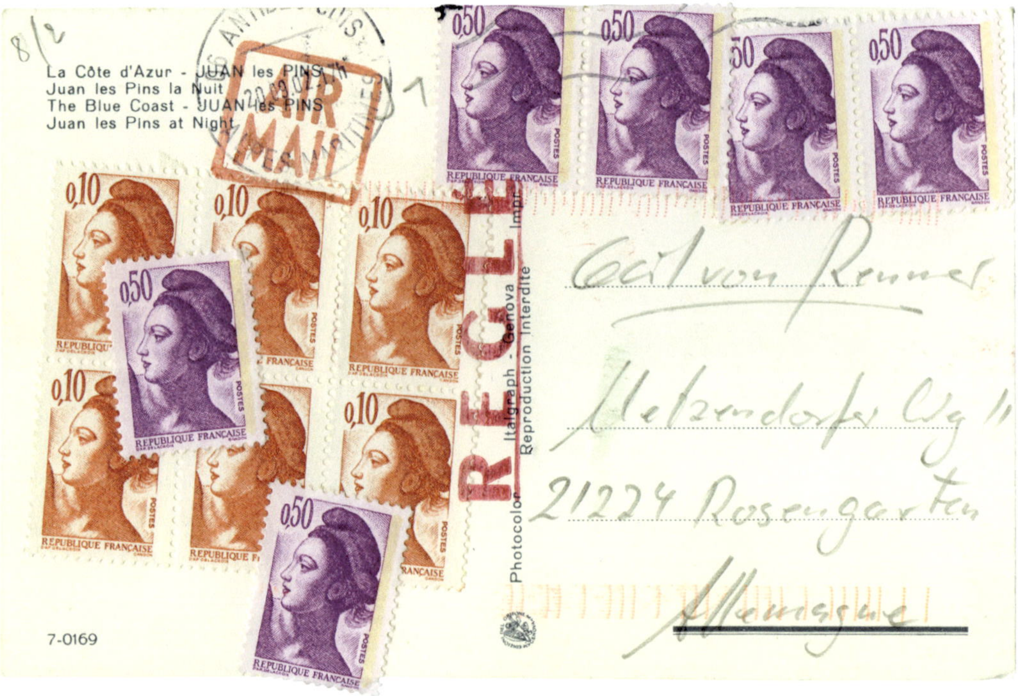
La Côte d'Azur - JUAN les PINS
Juan les Pins la Nuit
The Blue Coast - JUAN les PINS
Juan les Pins at Night
AIR MAIL
Photocolor Italgraph - Genova Impr.
Reproduction interdite
7-0169
21224 Rosengarten
Allemagne

06.121.02 SAINT-JEAN-CAP-FERRAT
(Alpes-Maritimes)
Le Port et la plage
AIR MAIL
20.09.02.17h
PIZZA
IVO
Sept. 19 2002
sur la Côte d'Azur
A
NIZZA
✻ Photo véritable ✻
21224 Rosengarten
Allemagne

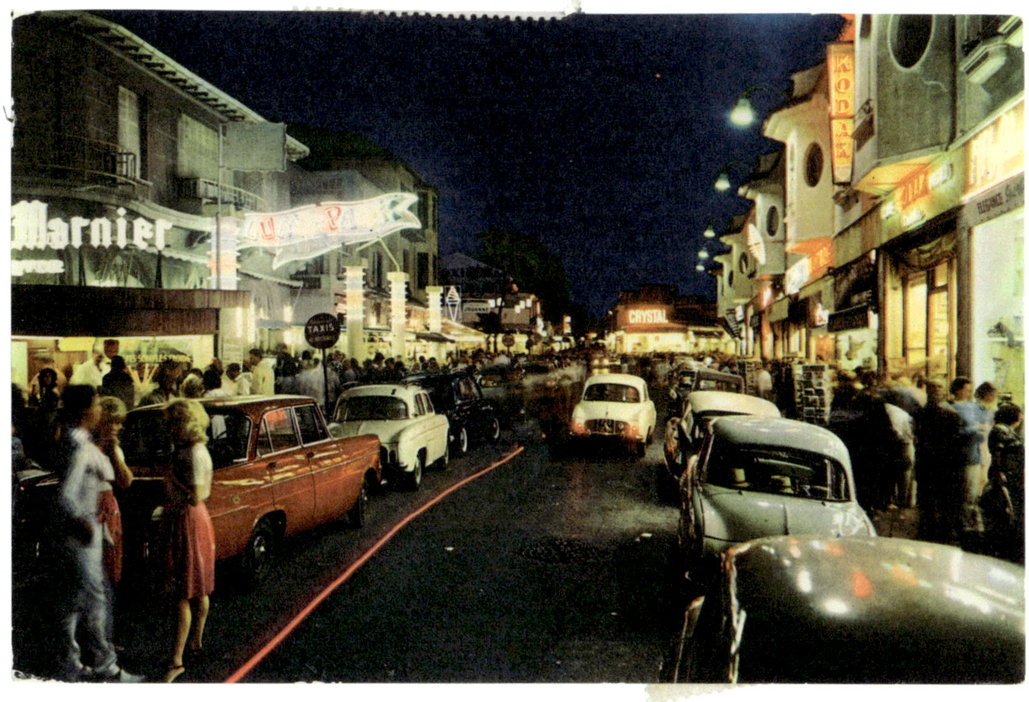
Marnier
TAXIS
CRYSTAL
KODAK

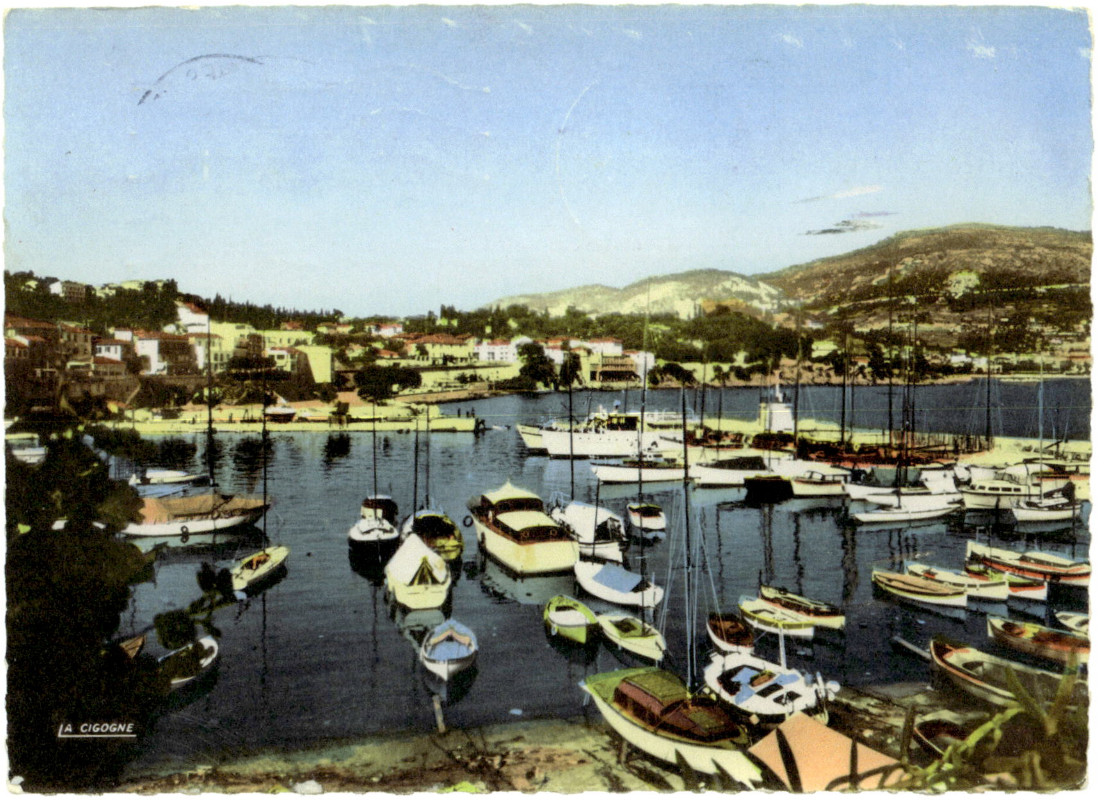
LA CIGOGNE

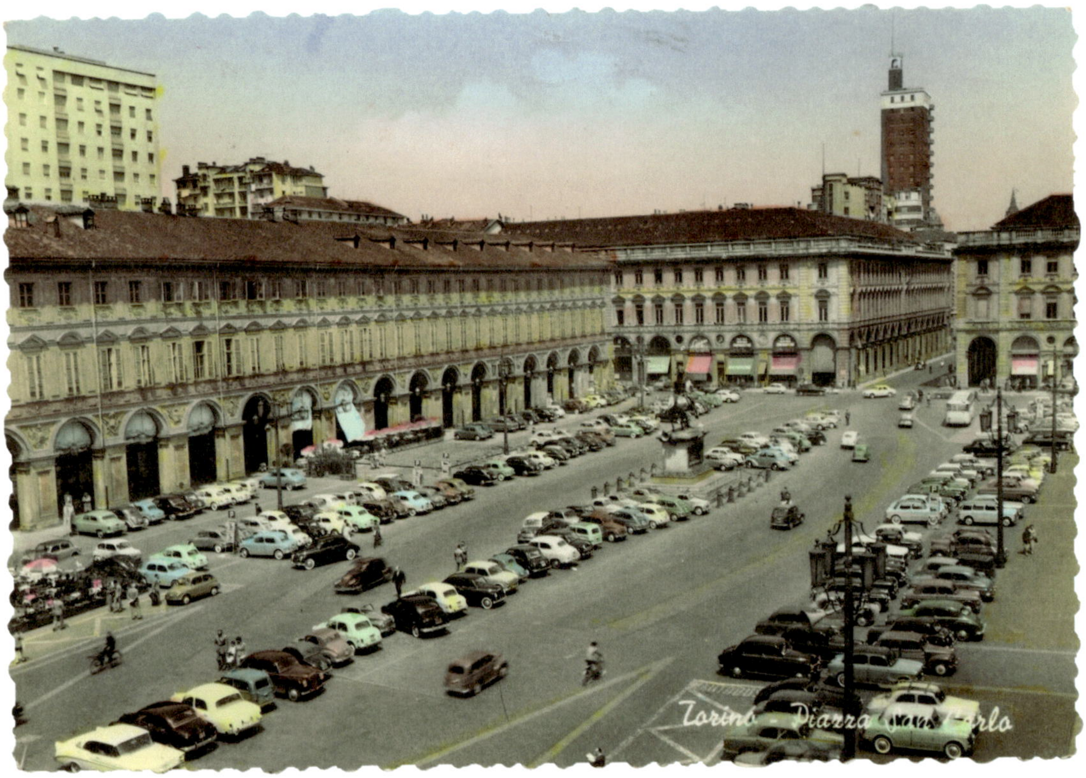

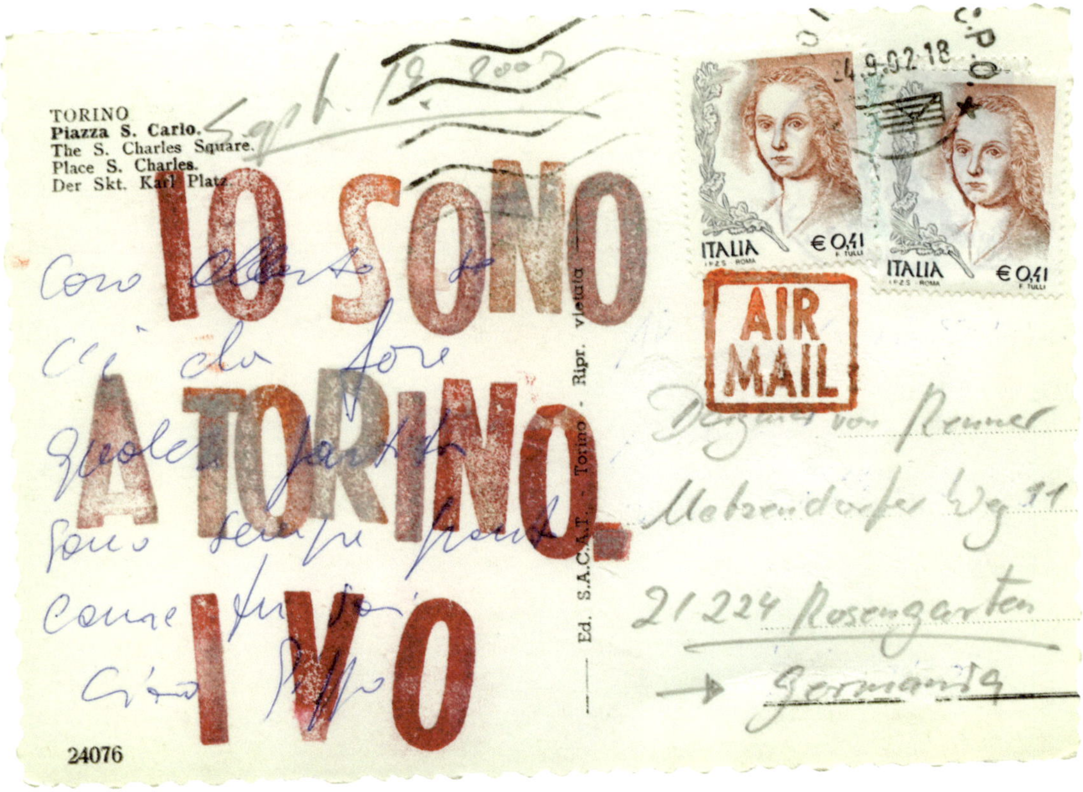

TURIN

September 19th, 2002

-

I am in Torino. Ivo

We are still on the same trip. Afterwards, I follow my family to Sicily for a vacation. In the past three months, I have experienced 23 countries and climate zones. Despite my complete exhaustion, I create numerous postcards. The travel case for rubber stamps, coloured ink pads and pencils has grown a little.

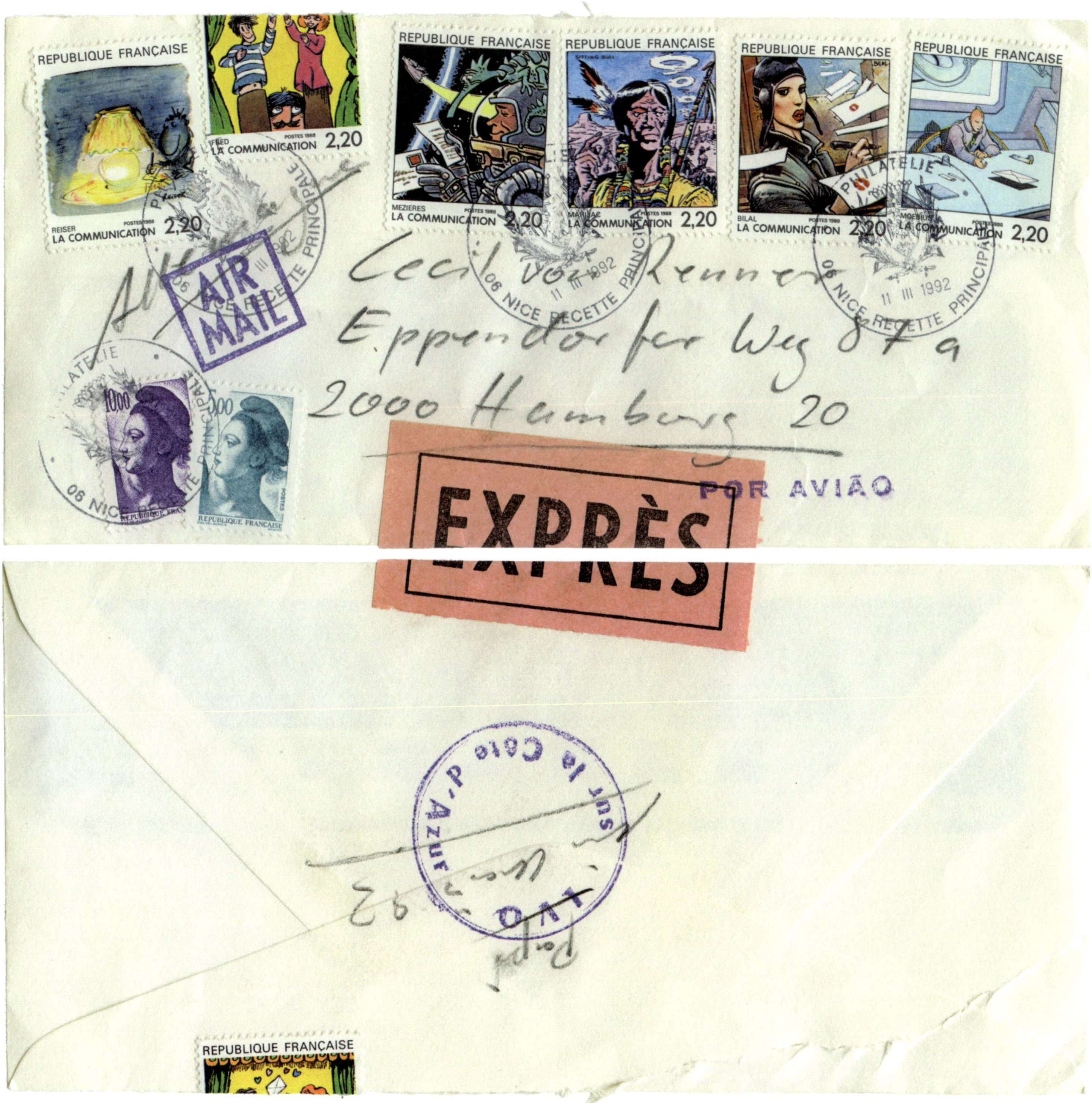

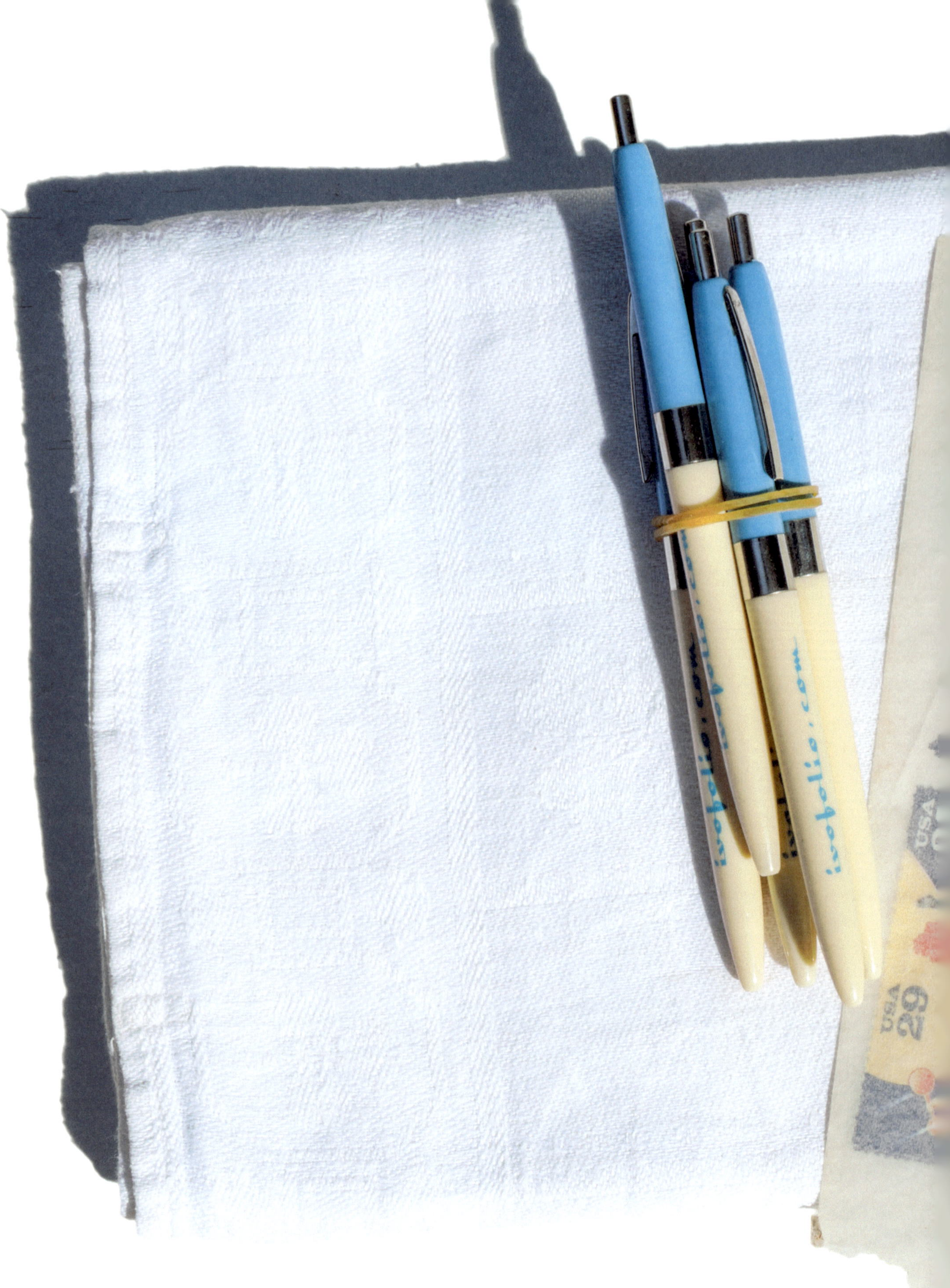
USA
29

CIRCUS
USA
29

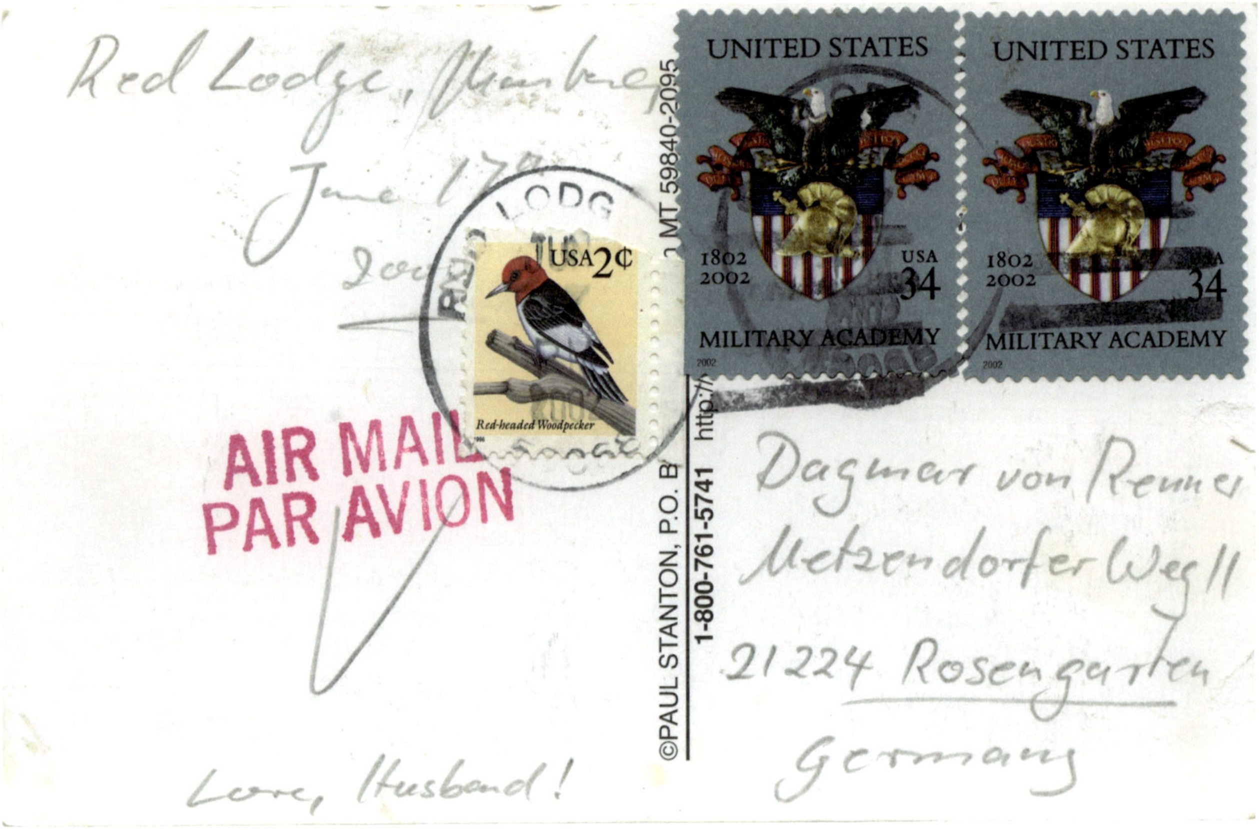

MONTANA

June 17th, 2002

–

“Red Lodge, Montana

Love, Husband!”

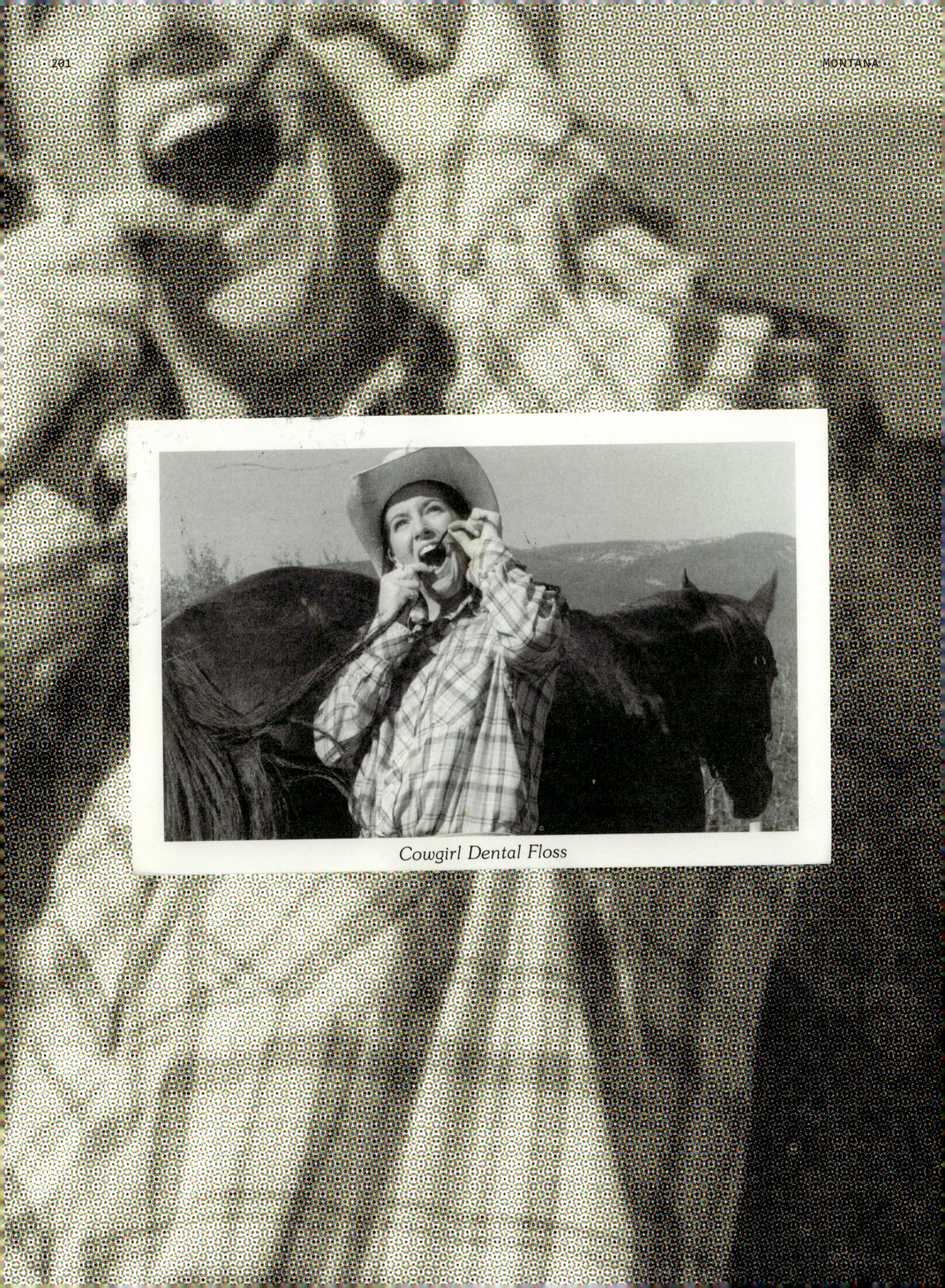
Cowgirl Dental Floss

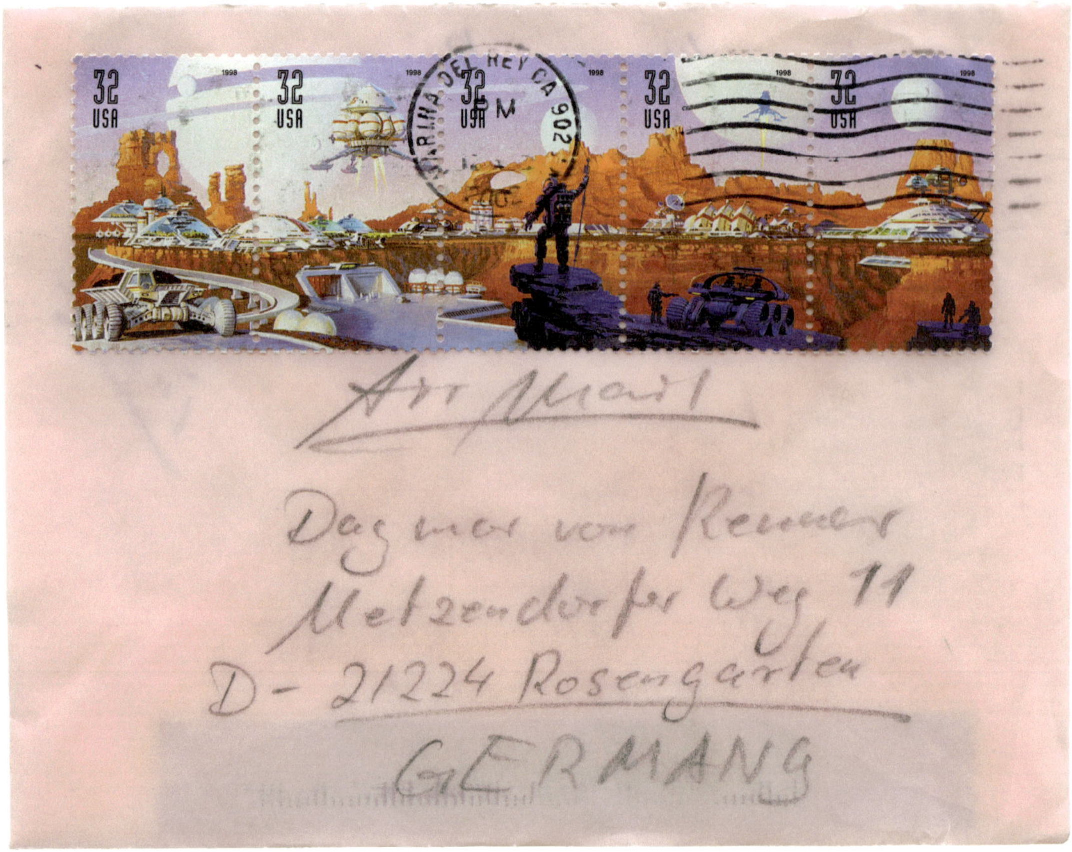
32 USA
Air Mail
Dagmar von Renner
Metzendorfer Weg 11
D-21224 Rosengarten
GERMANY

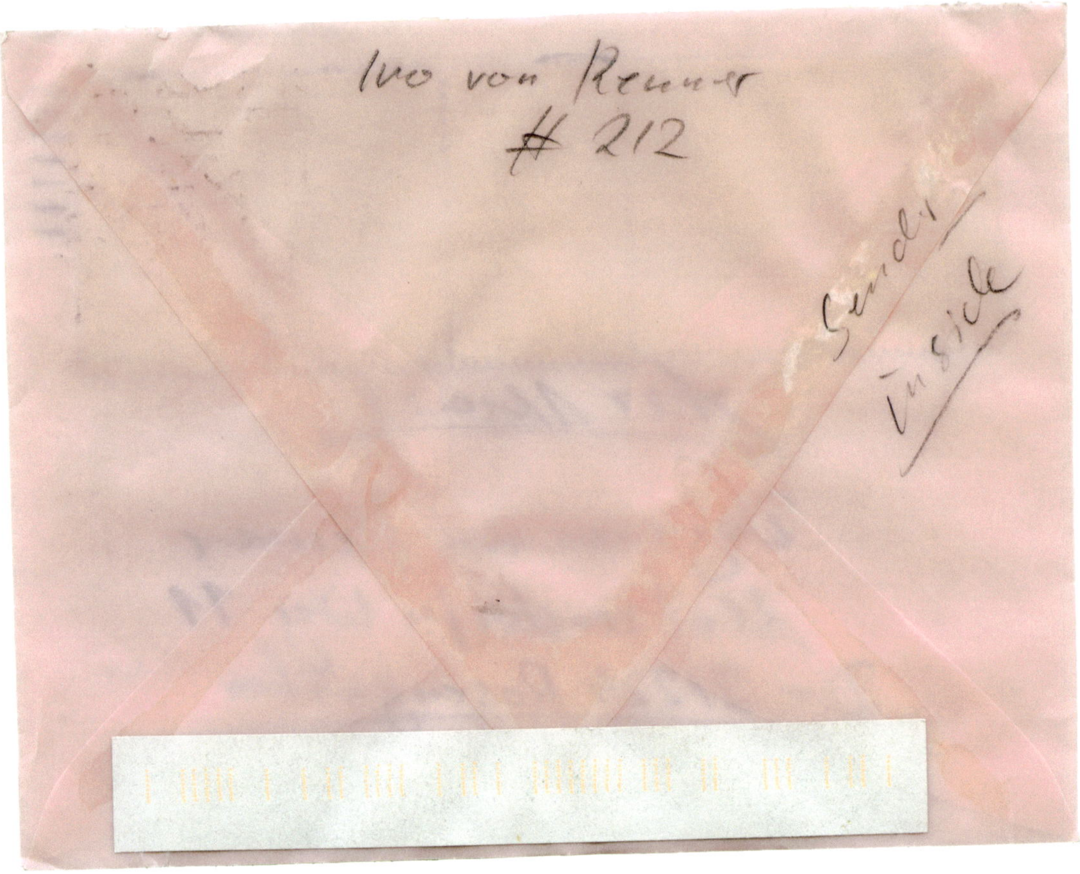
Ivo von Renner
212
Sender inside

A typical case of schedule miscalculation:
There are 96 working hours between Sunday and Sunday. But this is still completely within the range of normality. A brochure for the Toyota MR2 brings me to Montana. Freezing rain at 4000 metres above sea level, and 60 cm of snow melting per day at the same time. Seen just yesterday, no longer existent today. You never stop learning.

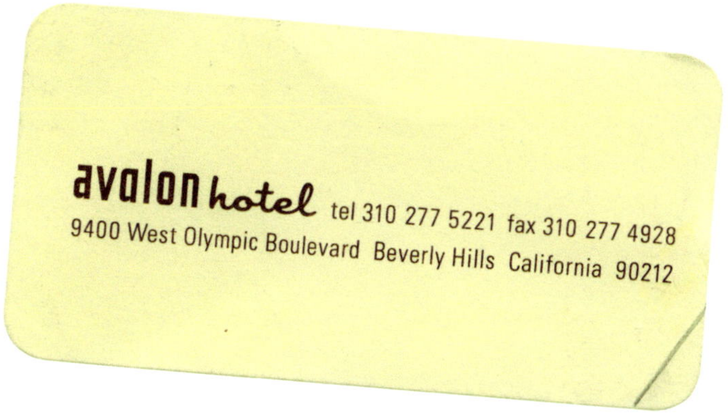

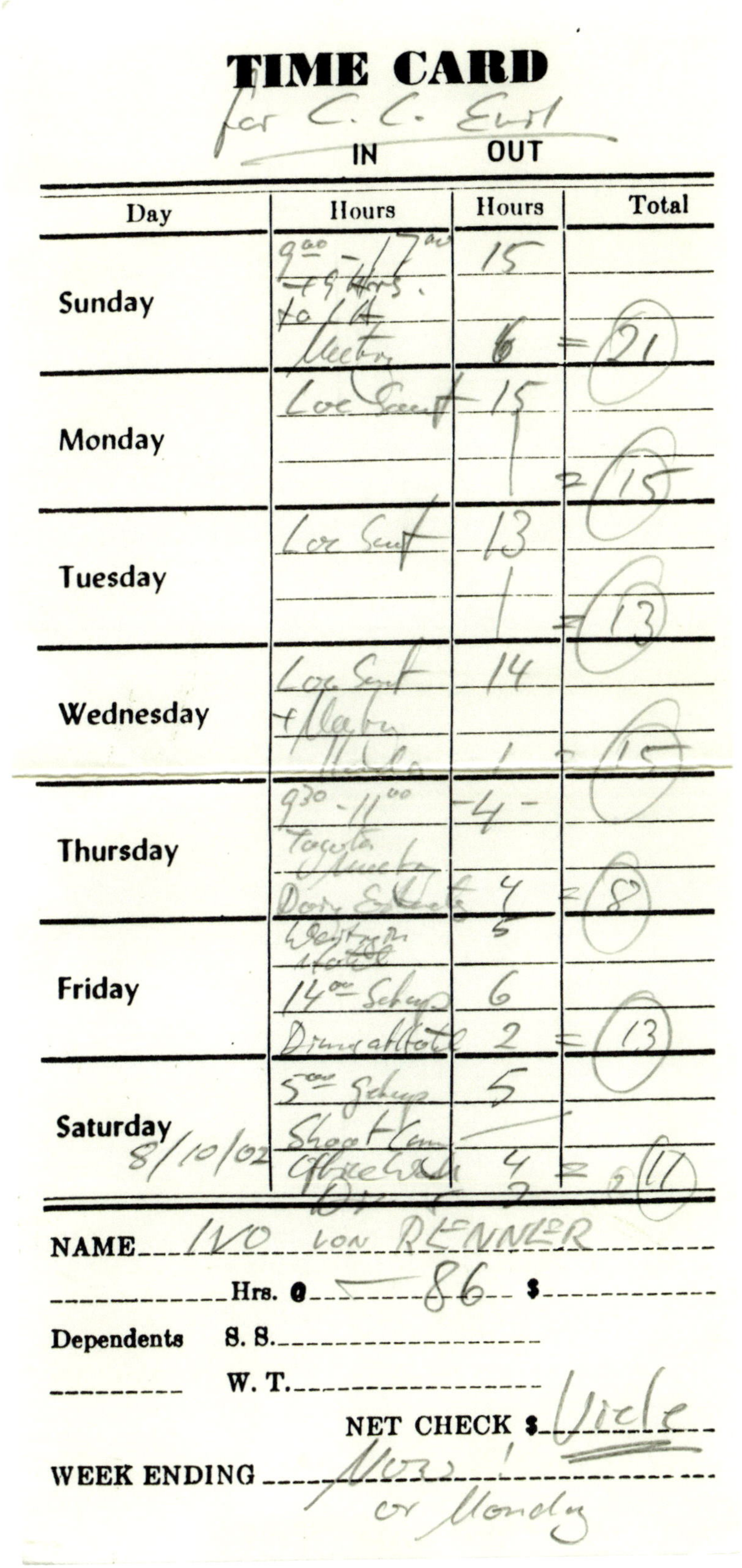

TIME CARD

for C. C. Ewl

Day	IN Hours	OUT Hours	Total
Sunday	9⁰⁰ – 17⁰⁰	15	
		6	= 21
Monday		15	
			= 15
Tuesday		13	
			= 13
Wednesday		14	
		1	= 15
Thursday	9³⁰ – 11⁰⁰	4	
	Toyota	4	= 8
Friday		5	
	14⁰⁰	6	
		2	= 13
Saturday 8/10/02	5⁰⁰	5	
		4	= 11

NAME IVO von RENNER

Hrs. @ 86 $

Dependents S. S.

W. T.

NET CHECK $

WEEK ENDING or Monday

RED LODGE
August 10th, 2002

Only Vegas.

My two assistants and I fly to Las Vegas for three and a half weeks in 2002, in order to develop a 23-motif campaign. It's called "What happens here – stays here" – Only Vegas. On the second night, I find a little book from the 50s showing the sights of the city. I make cards out of all pages of the book, and try to send one home every day. Almost – I'm back to 16-hour working days, and there isn't always enough time to write cards.

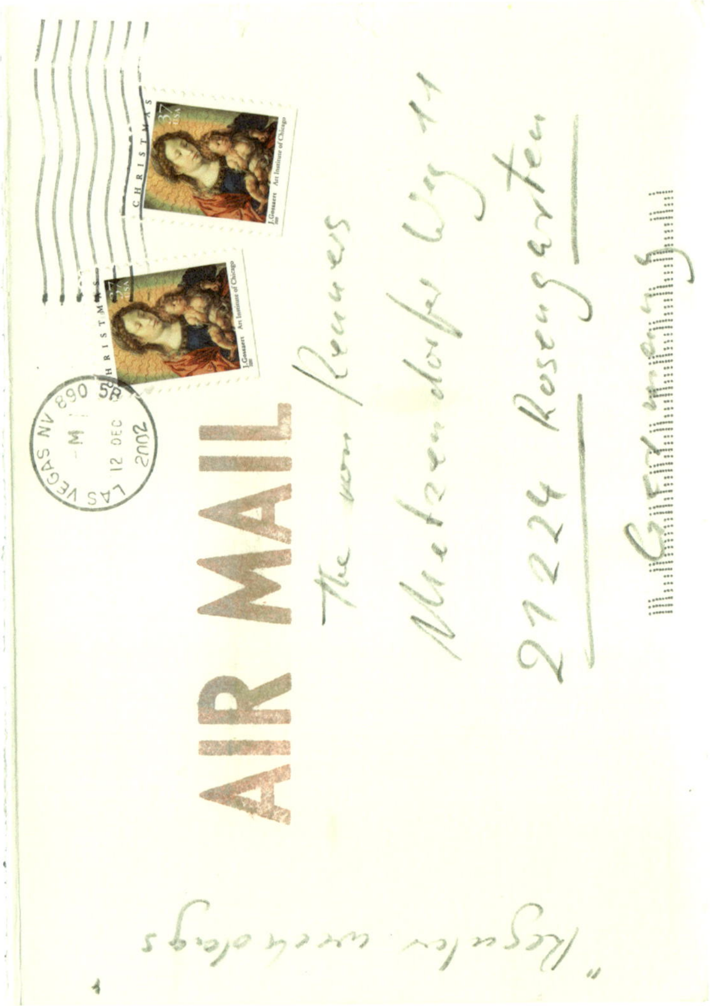

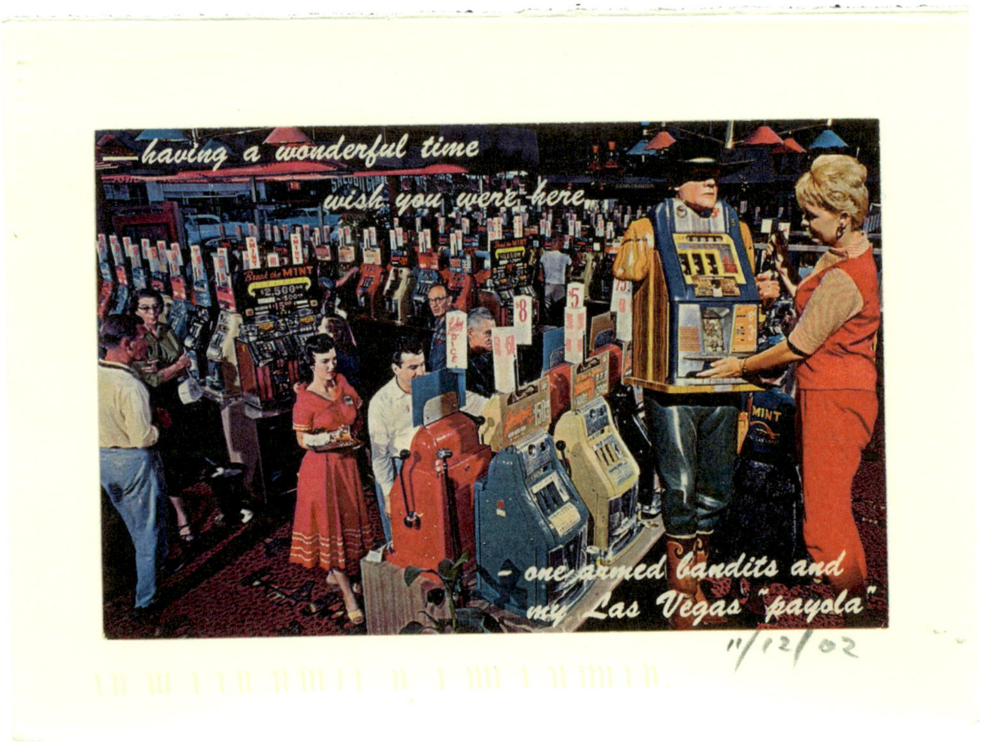

LAS VEGAS
November 12th, 2002
–
"Regular weekdays"

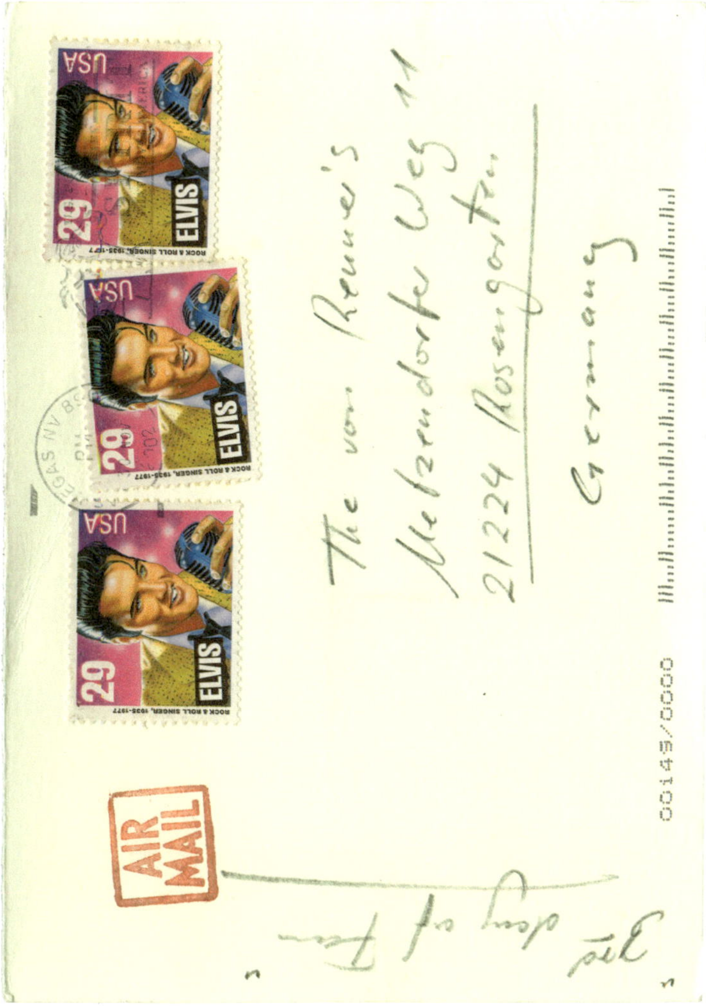

By the way, it's the first time we scout locations in a city in which we walk through 39 km of hotel corridors and halls for three days. It has become apparent that valet parking takes up more time than walking to the hotels.

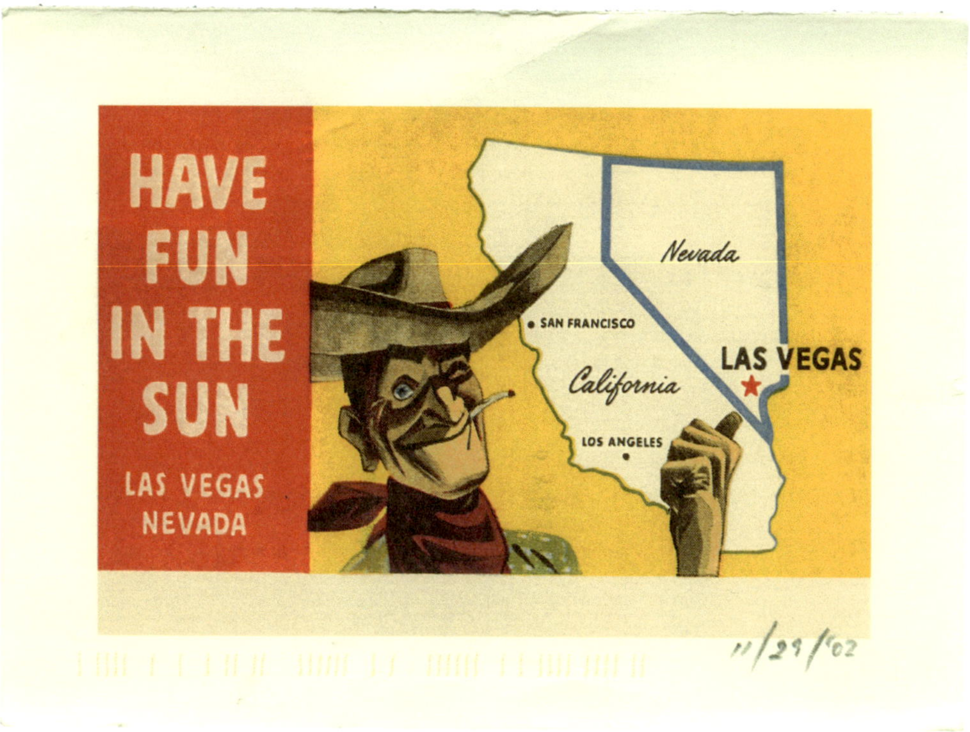

LAS VEGAS

November 29th, 2002

–

"3rd day of Fun"

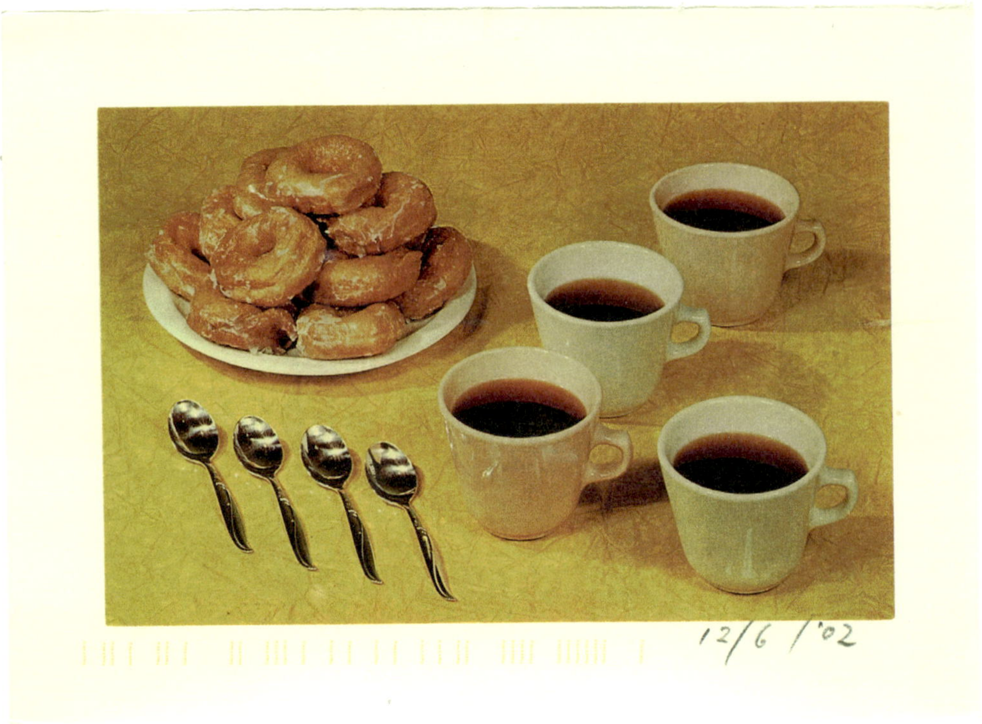

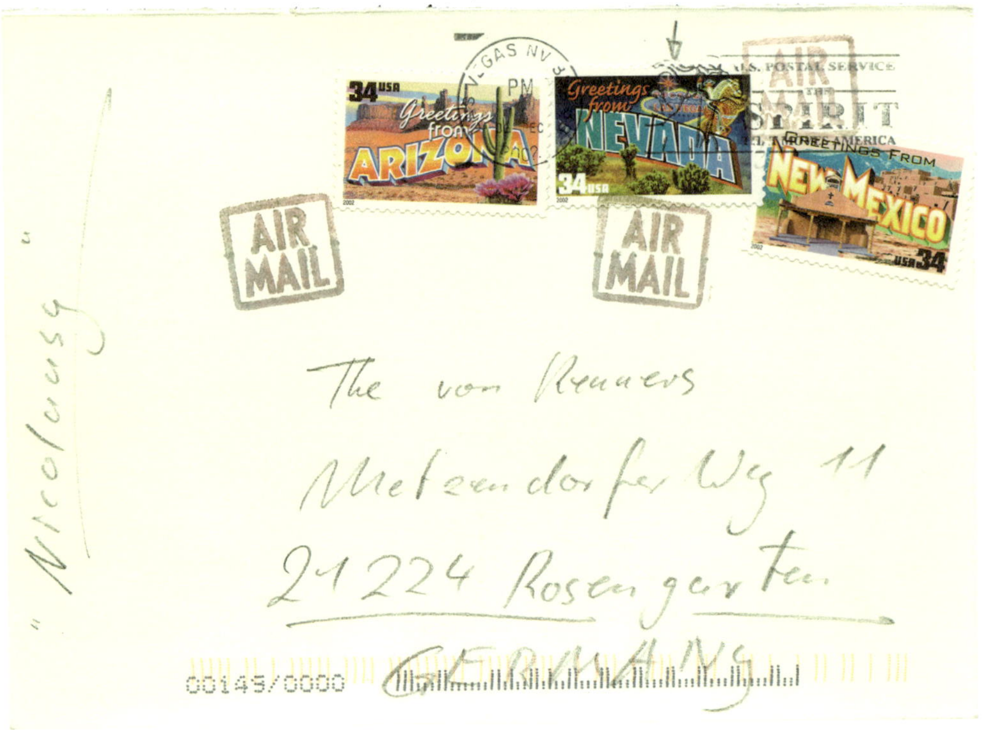

LAS VEGAS

December 6th, 2002

–

“Nicolausy”

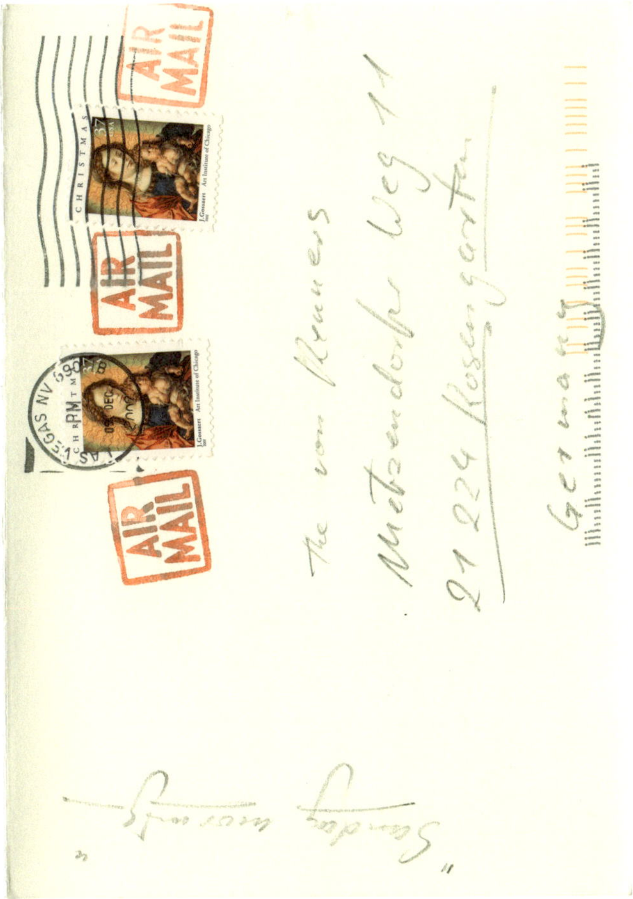

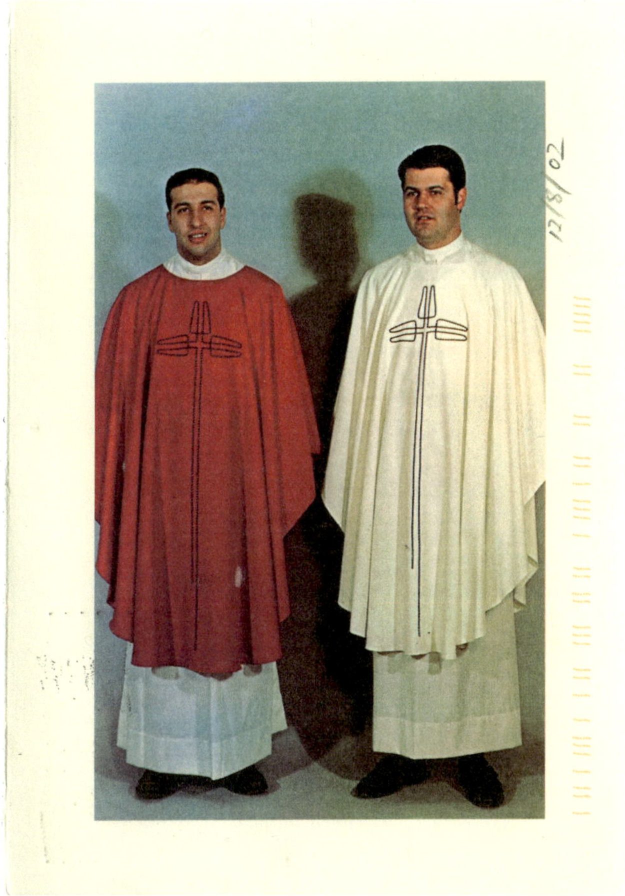

LAS VEGAS

December 8th, 2002

–

“Sunday morning”

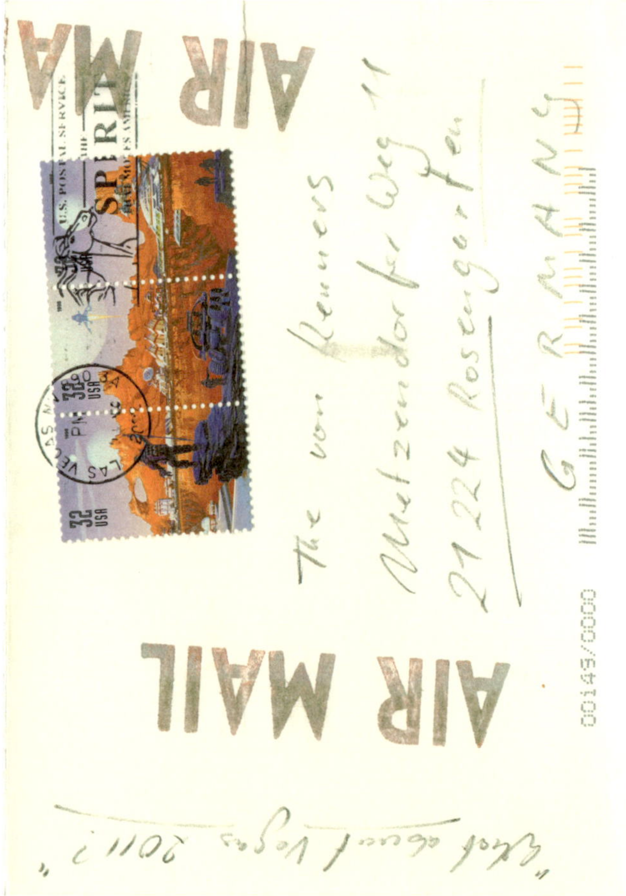

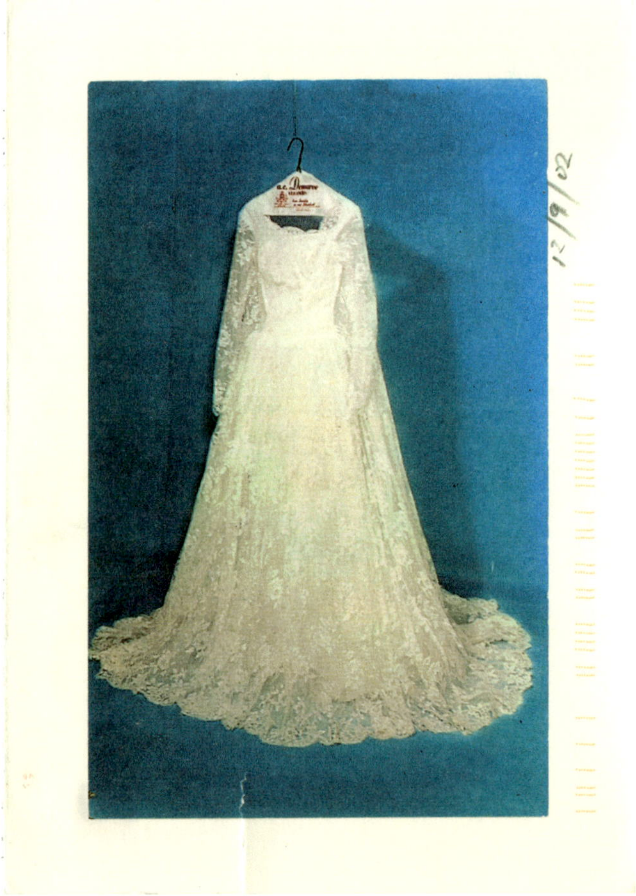

LAS VEGAS

December 9th, 2002

–

“What about Vegas 2011?”

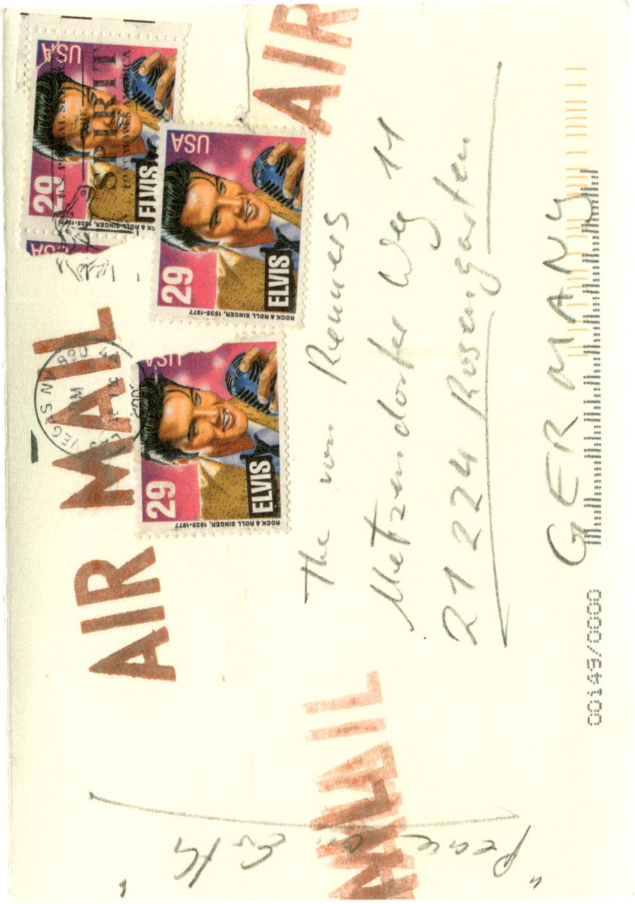

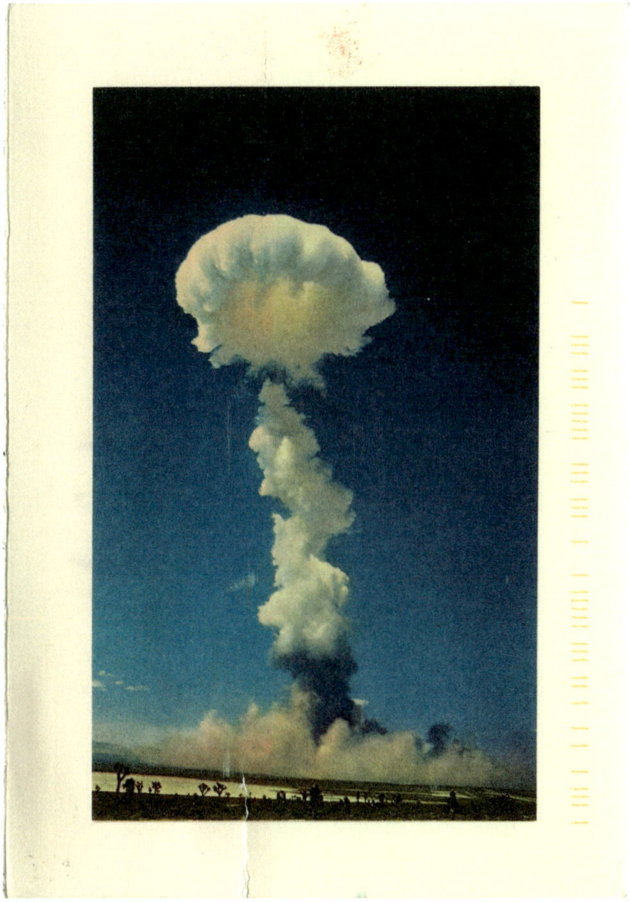

LAS VEGAS

December 10th, 2002

-

“Peace on earth”

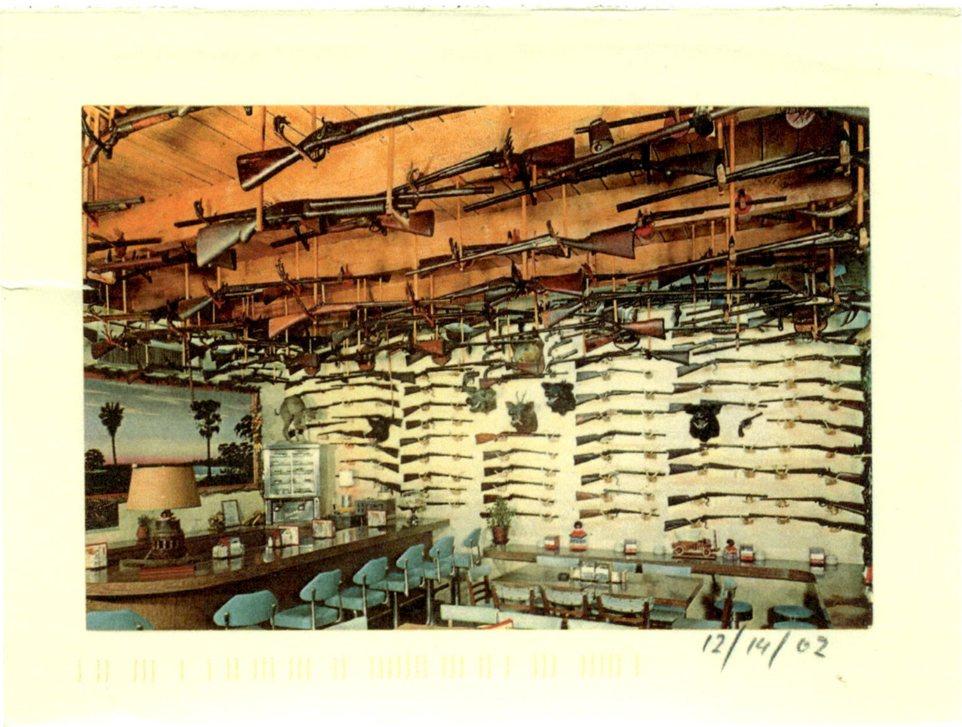

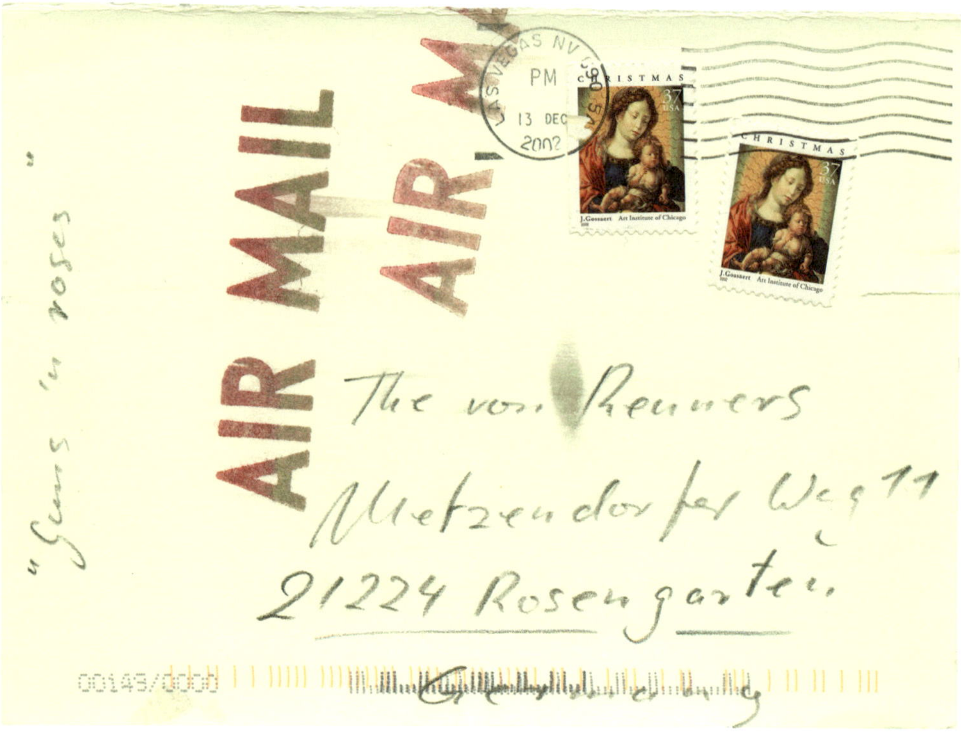

LAS VEGAS

December 13th, 2002

–

“Guns ’n roses”

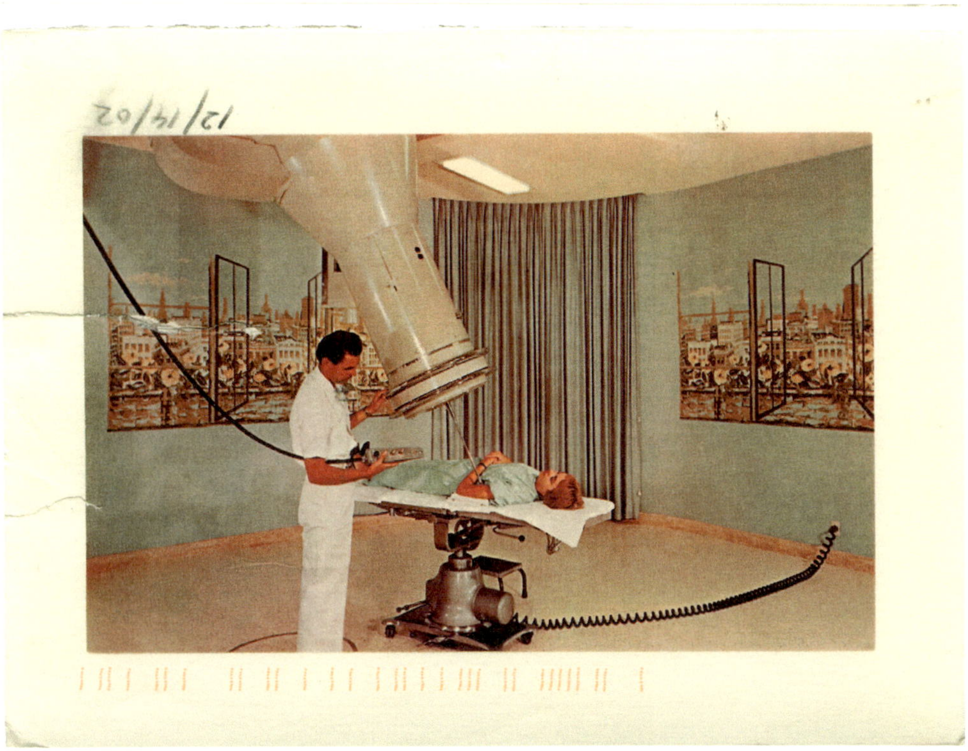

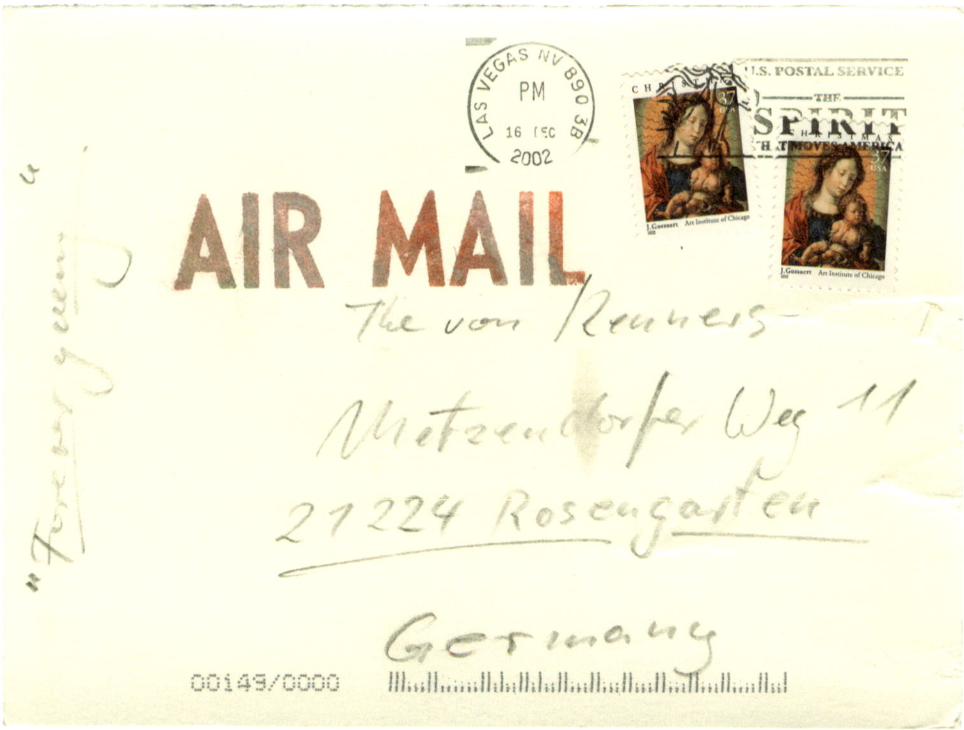

LAS VEGAS

December 14th, 2002

–

“Forever young”

Portugal, where I am at home.

I fly to Lisbon 16 times between 2003 and 2011. In the beginning, I am caught up making short films, which upstages my writing of cards.

– and then there's a poem about the erika, a species of flowering heather, which originates from a long mountain ascent in the Estrela Mountains of Portugal. Antony always begins reciting this poem when he wants to embarrass me in front of Dagmar. I never finished it …

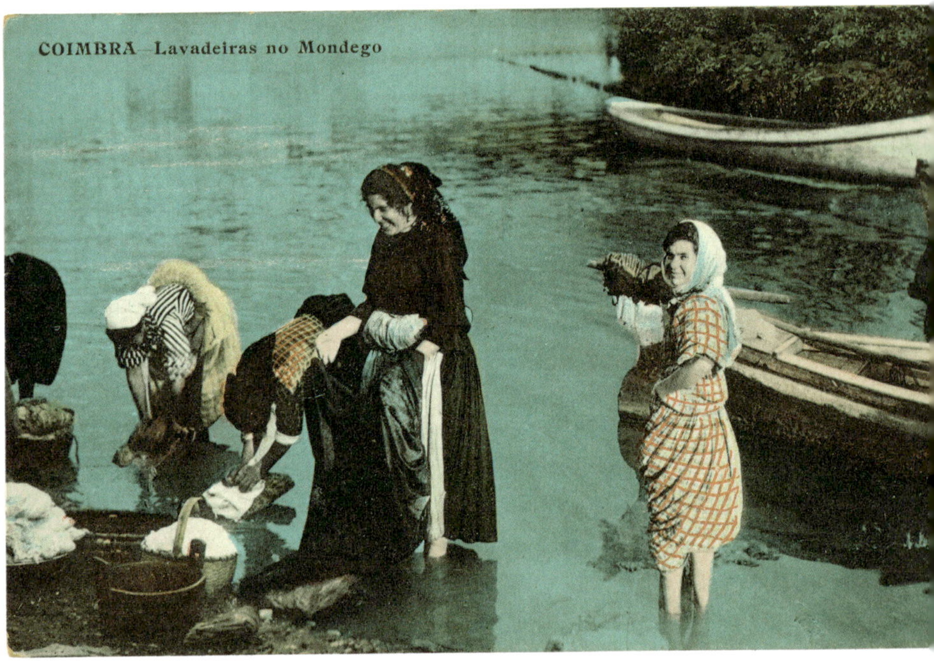

»
Erika lies in the grass, Peter leans against a tree. They brought along a blanket, and Peter …
«

PORTO
June 7th, 2005
–
Why? and
who is Erika!?
f.

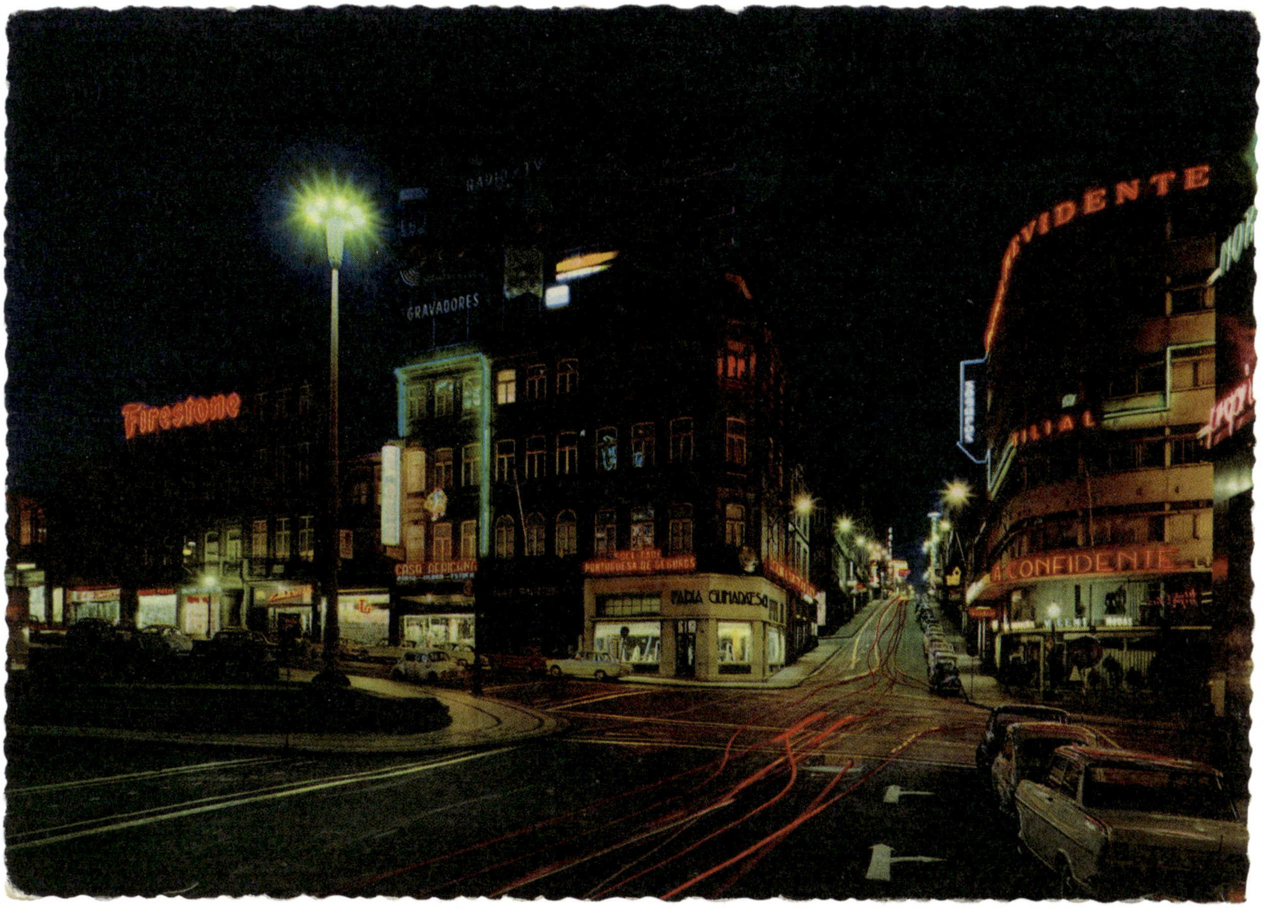

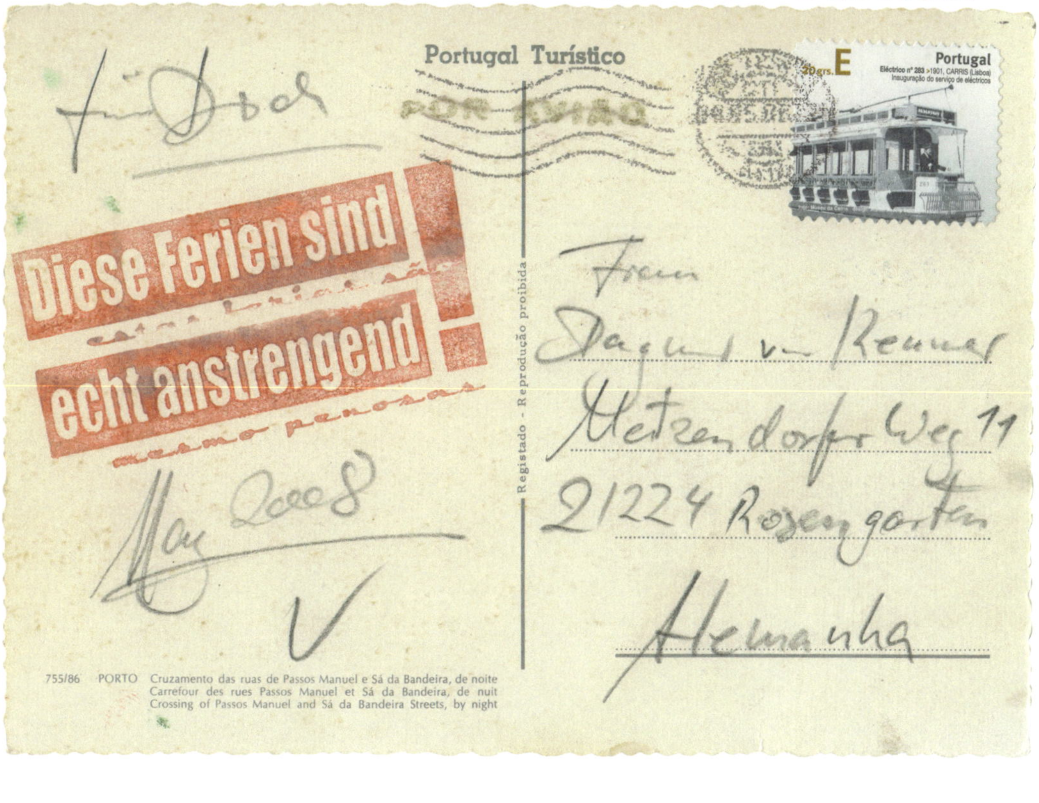

PORTO
June 22nd, 2005
–
This vacation is
really tiring!
May 2008

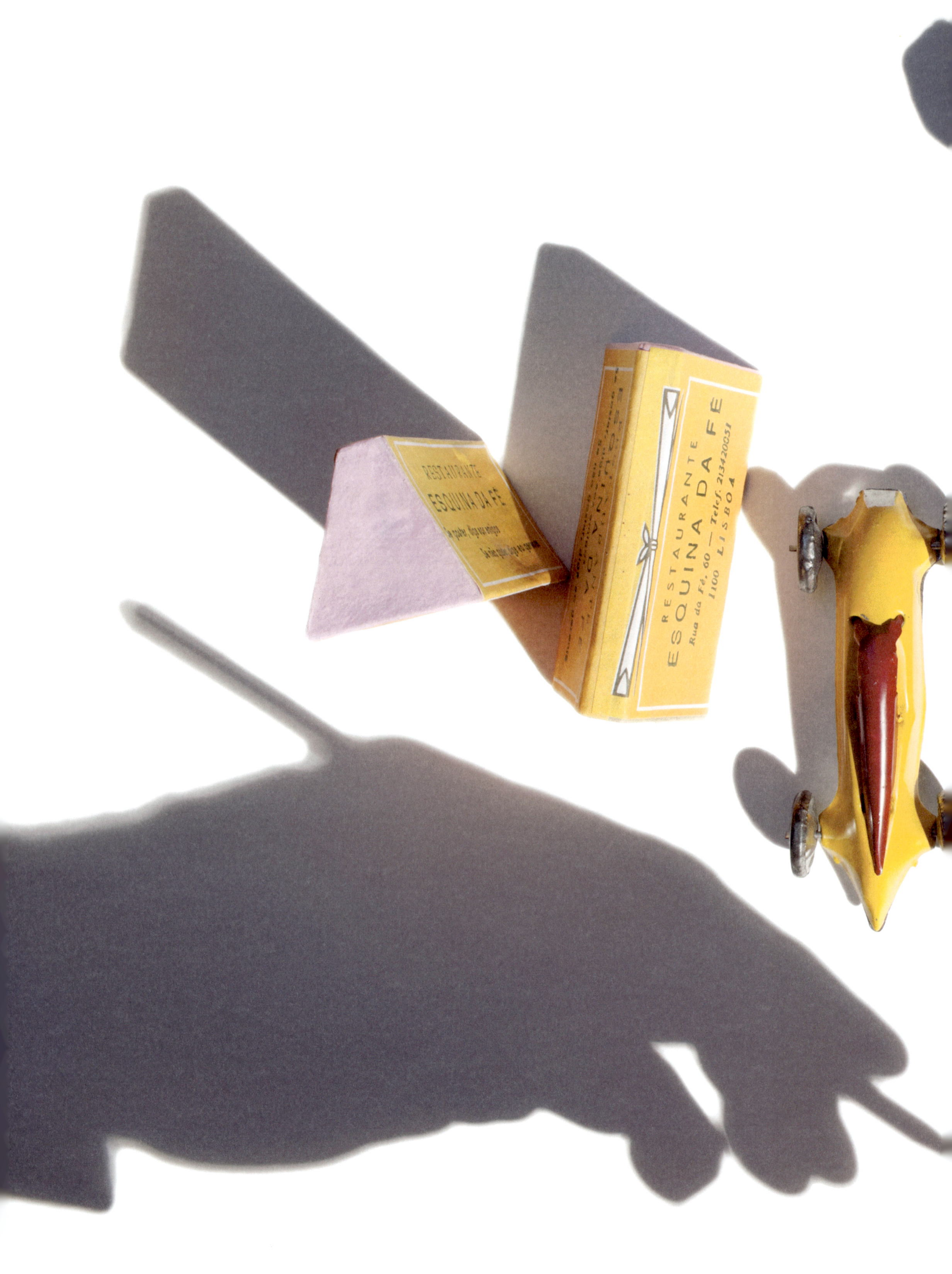
RESTAURANTE
ESQUINA DA FÉ
RESTAURANTE
ESQUINA DA FÉ
Rua da Fé, 60 — Telef. 213420051
1100 LISBOA

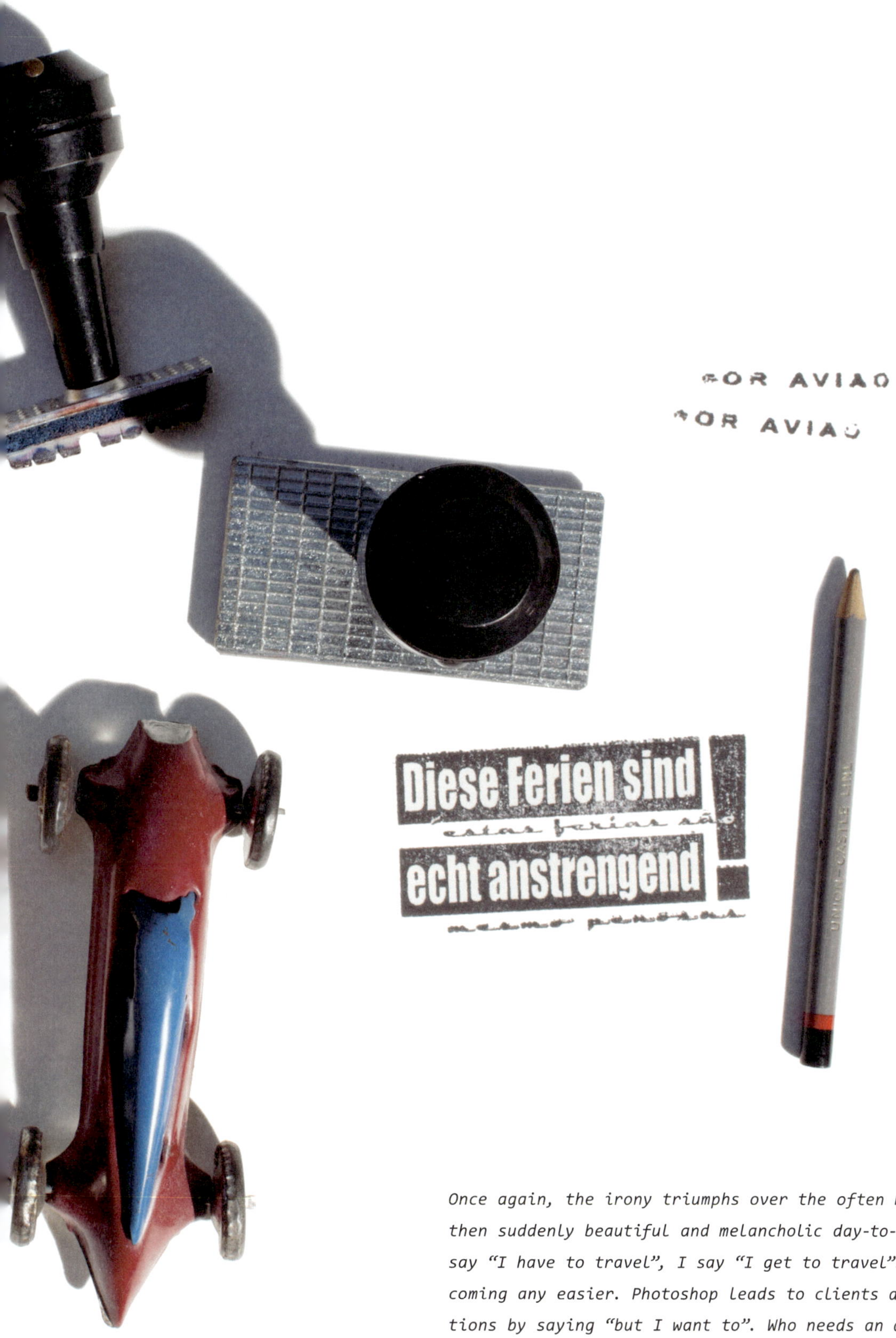

Once again, the irony triumphs over the often bizarre, exhausting and then suddenly beautiful and melancholic day-to-day work life. I no longer say "I have to travel", I say "I get to travel". But the jobs aren't becoming any easier. Photoshop leads to clients arguing for their corrections by saying "but I want to". Who needs an advertising agency, when we can all do everything ourselves via Facebook on our mobiles. But the stamps were made by me. And all the little trifles, manifested on cards for eternity …

The "POR AVIAO" stamp comes from an old stationery store, the racing cars are from a revived toy manufactory and the tooth picks come from my favourite cantine, Esquina da Fé in Lisbon.

The card I use here comes from an antiquarian shop in Prague, and has already been used. I am currently looking for agents in New York.

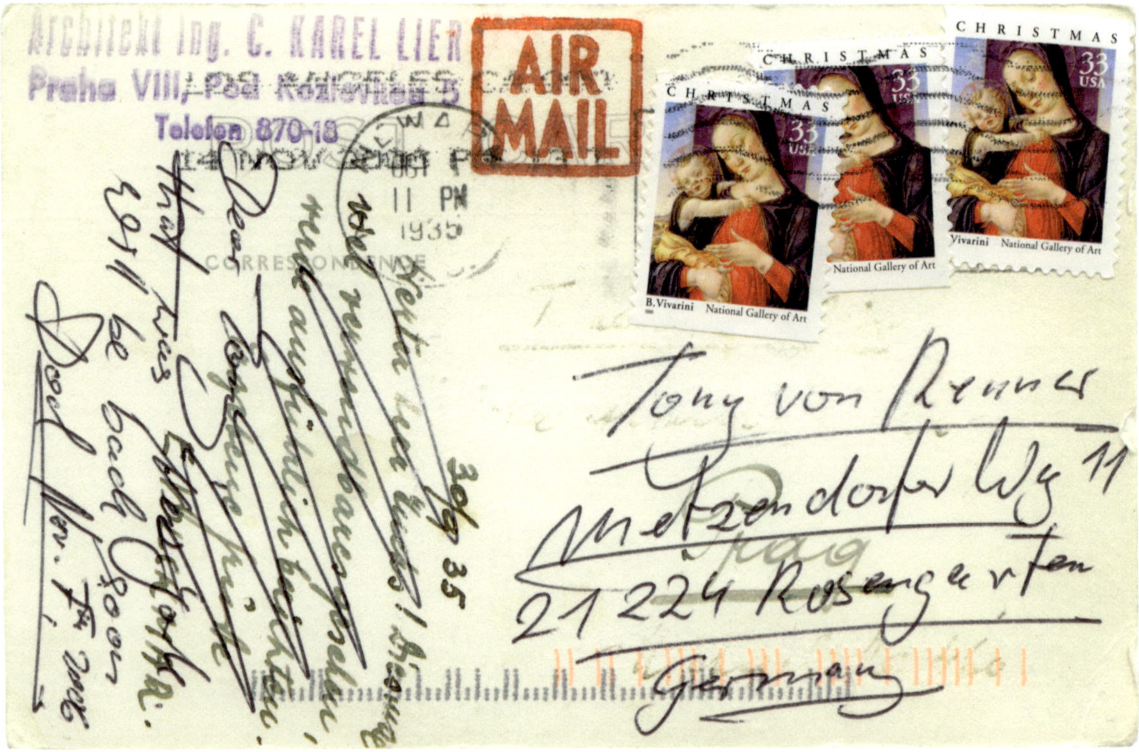

NEW YORK
July 24th, 2006
-
“Dear Tony,
that was New York.
Will be back soon. Dad”

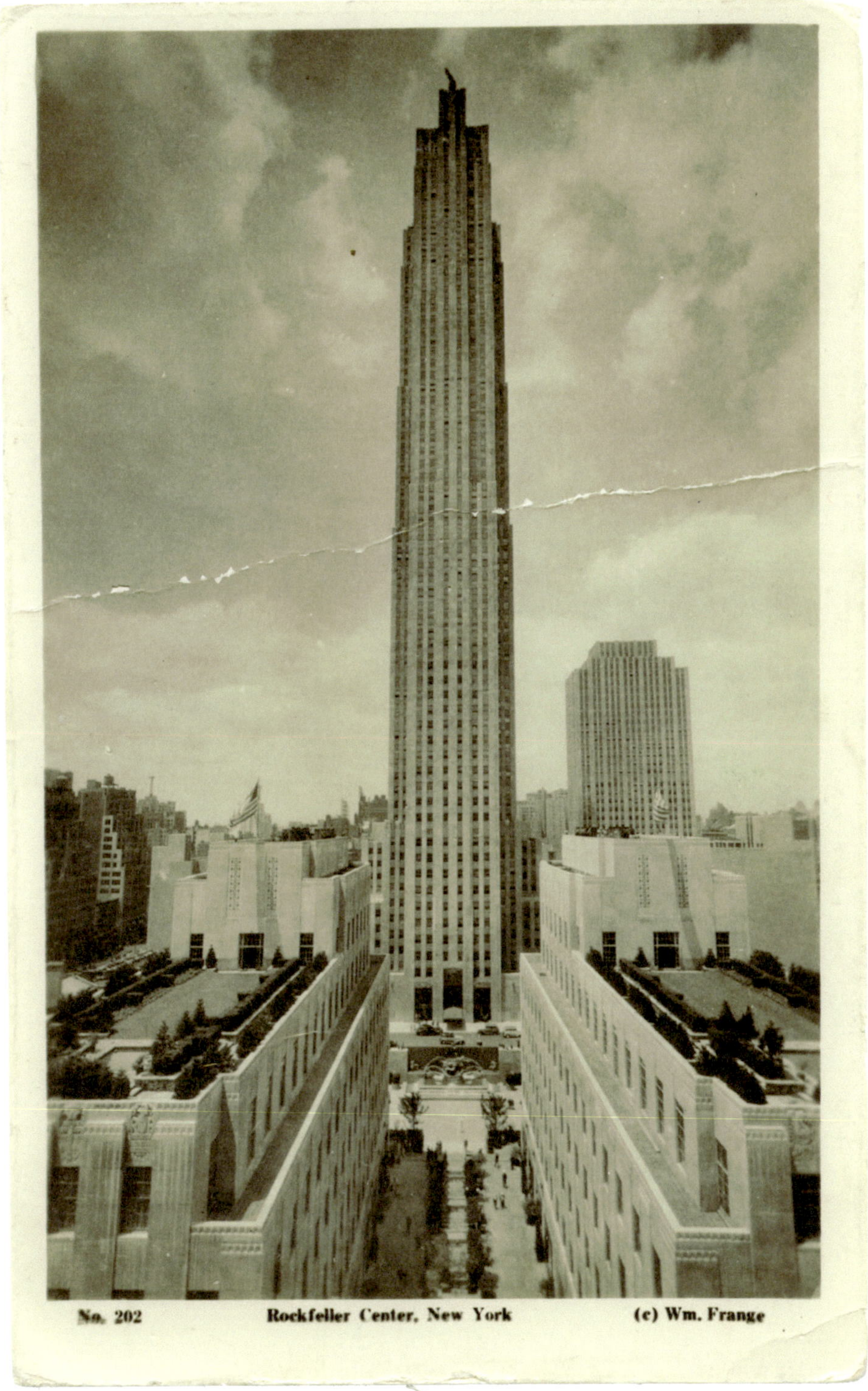
No. 202
Rockfeller Center, New York
(c) Wm. Frange

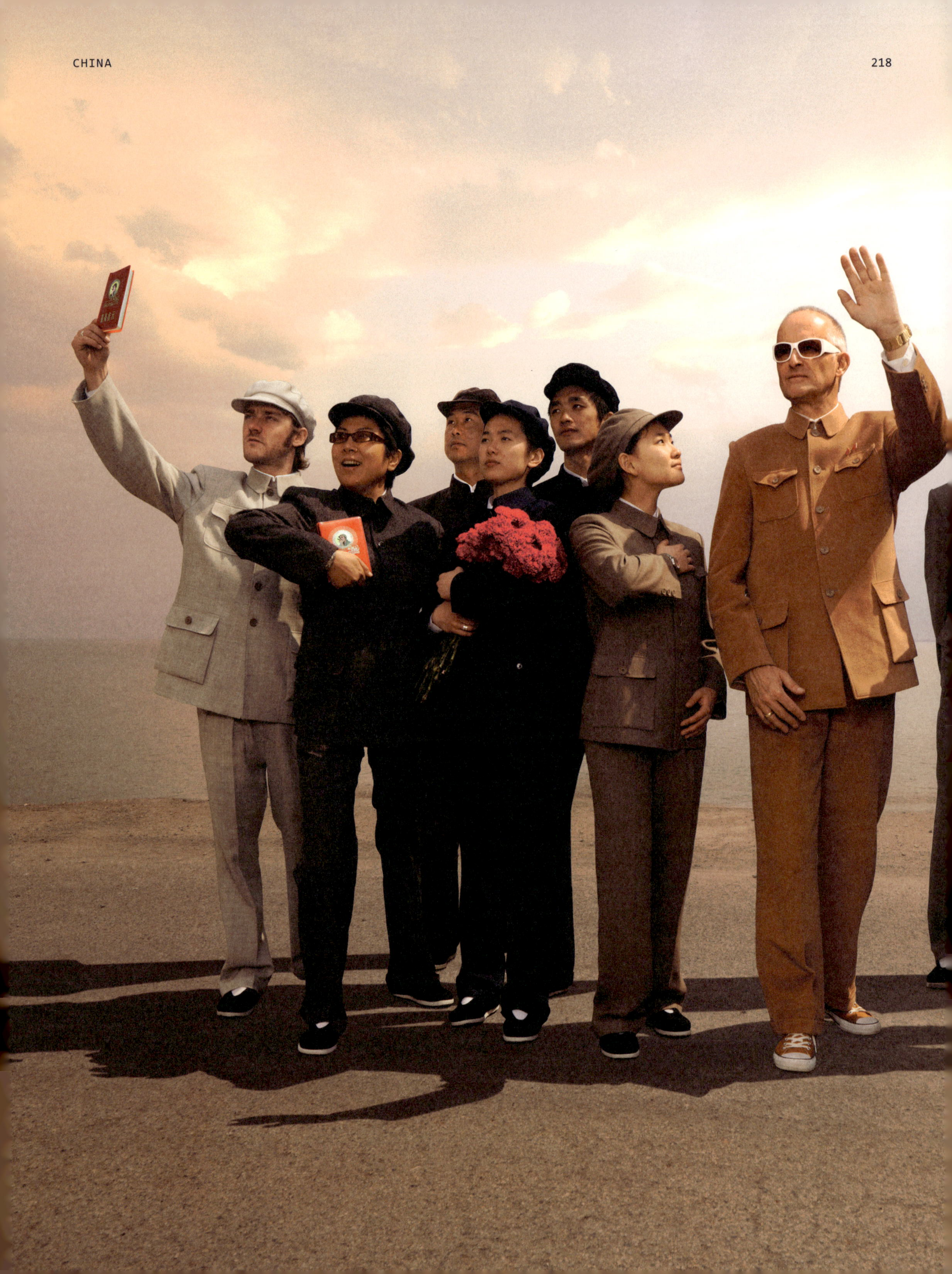

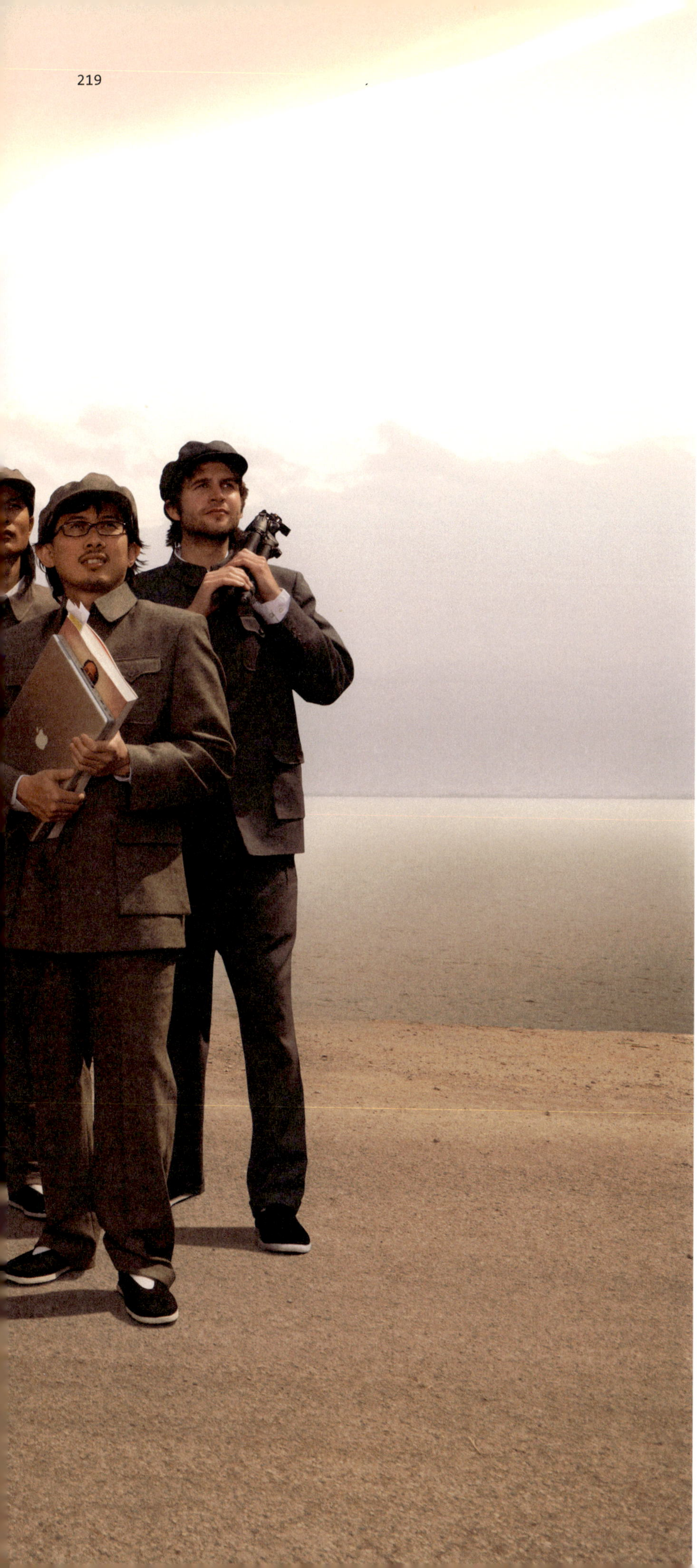

Group photo with the crew during a job for Toyota in China, 2007

A Manuel Ferrigato, assistant
B Lulu, producer
C Yang Yi, local producer
D Nuo Wang, production assistant
E Wang Hui, production assistant
F Mona Yao, production assistant
G Me
H Xiao Long, production assistant
I Colin Lai, head of production and owner
J Daniel Meyer, assistant

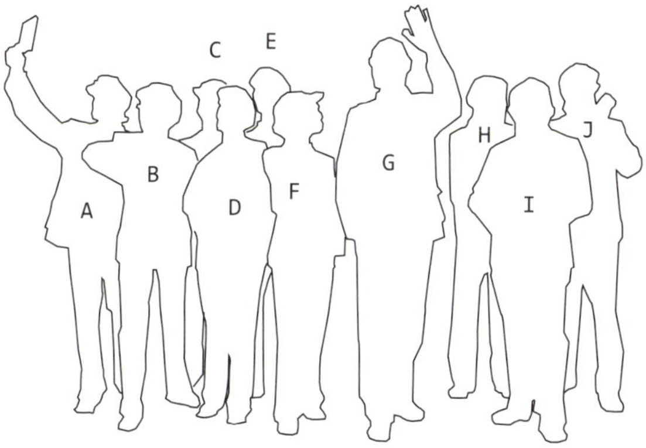

I'm a chameleon.

Mail arrives from China by e-mail. I can't find a single old postcard. I search for anything from Maoist China, and any possible achievements from the point of view of those times. To no avail. Slightly pixelated films are generated by an older Nikon model, which I edit, set to music, and send to my family via the Internet.

Toyota China compiles a brochure, which is meant to cover all four seasons: from pictures of snow to motifs of green, summery trees.

We drive 7000 km by car in seven weeks, visit Beijing three times, Shanghai four and drive the route from the mountains north of Shangri-La to an area south of Kunming twice in zigzag. No day has less than 18 hours. Had we planned to travel like this, it would have been doomed to disaster. When you experience it as we did, it's a rush of pure emotions.

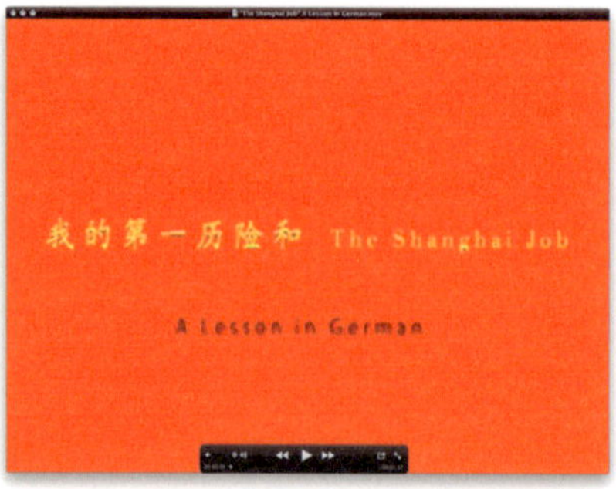

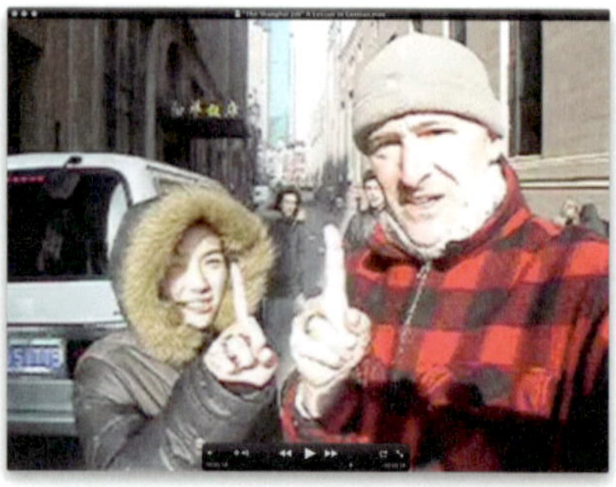

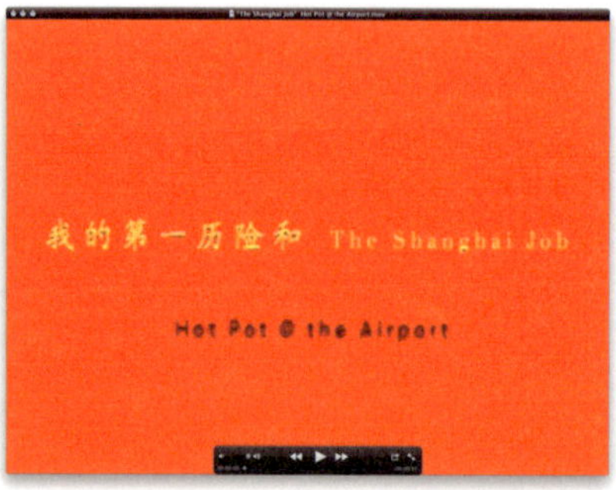

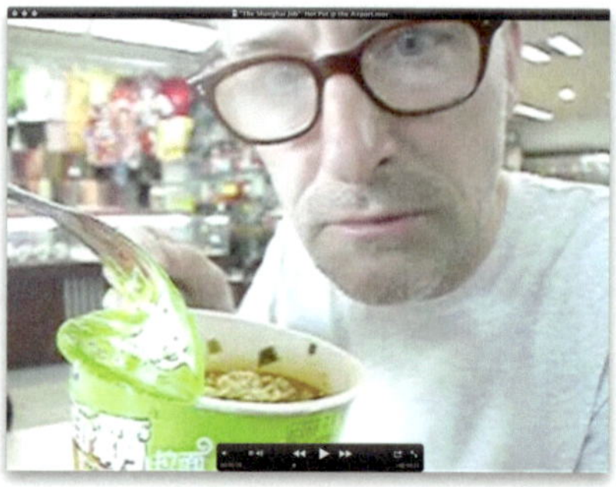

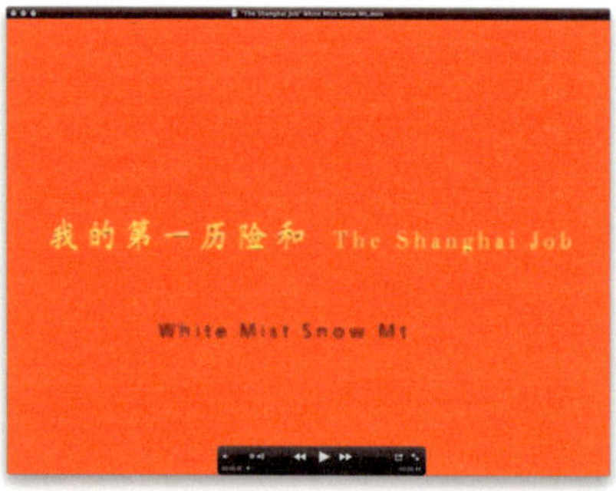

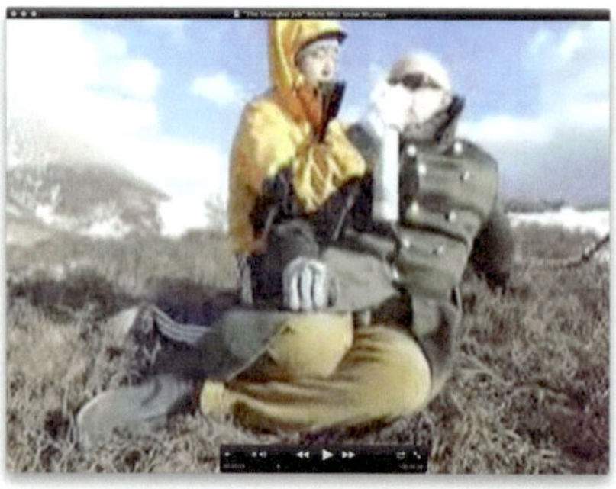

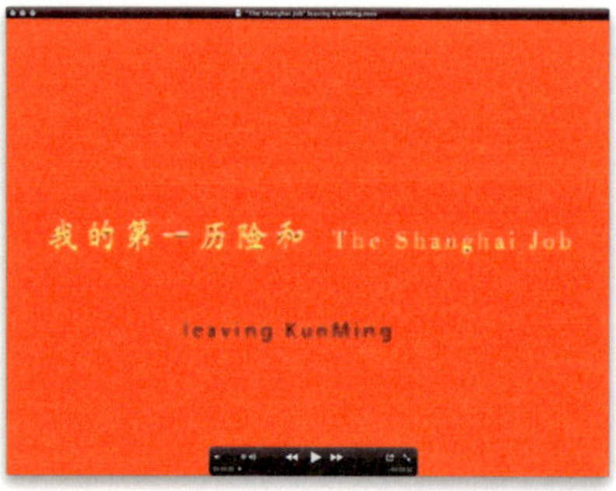

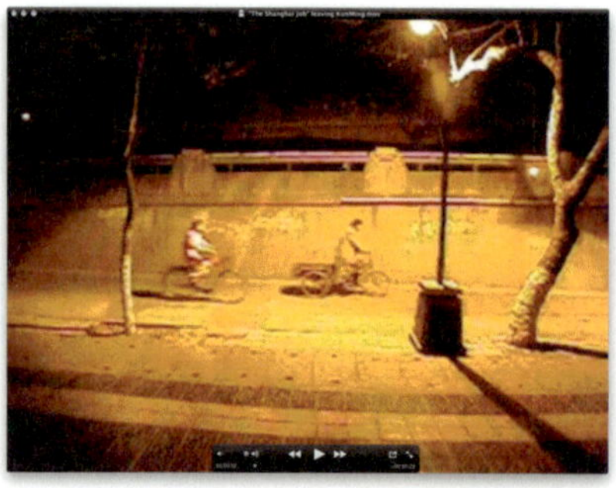

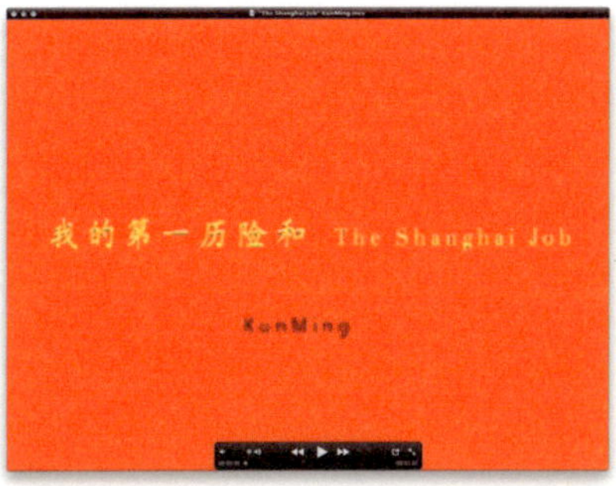

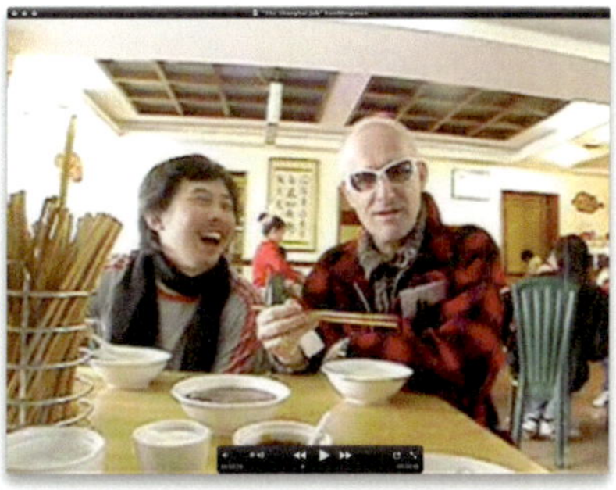

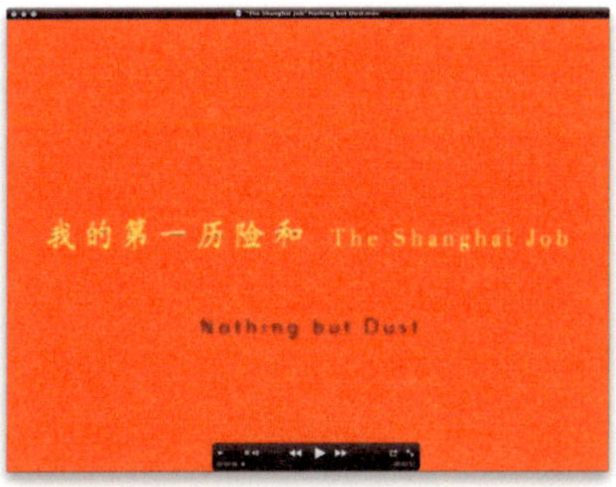

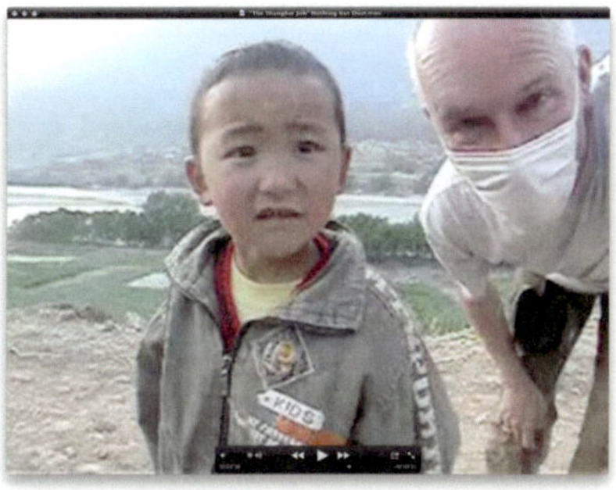

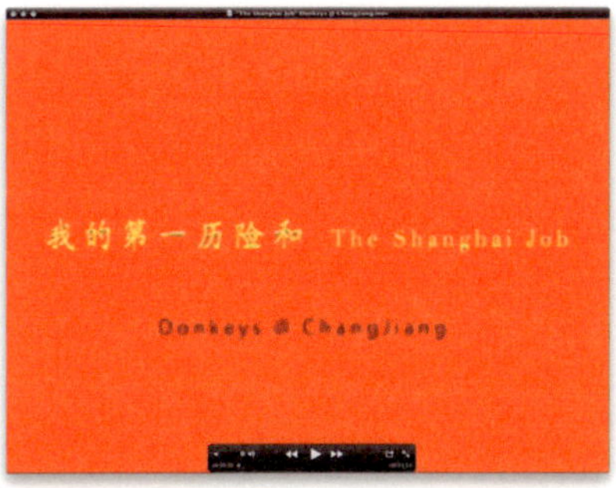

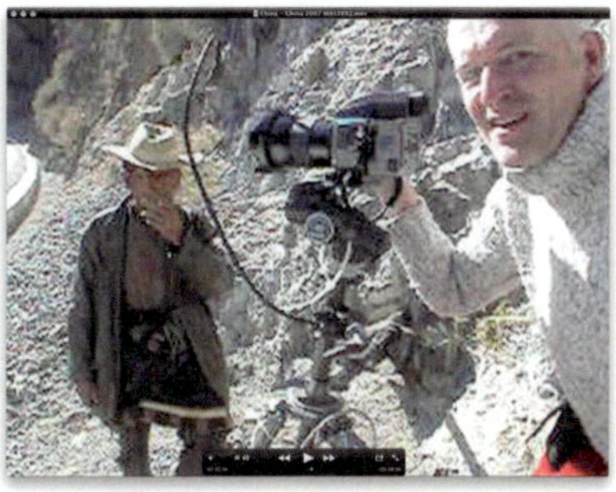

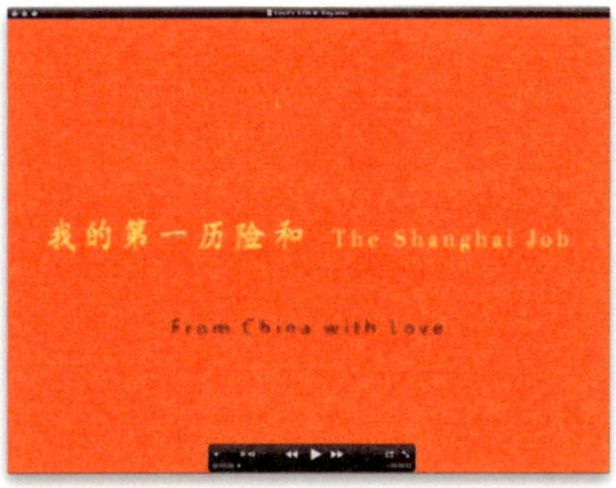

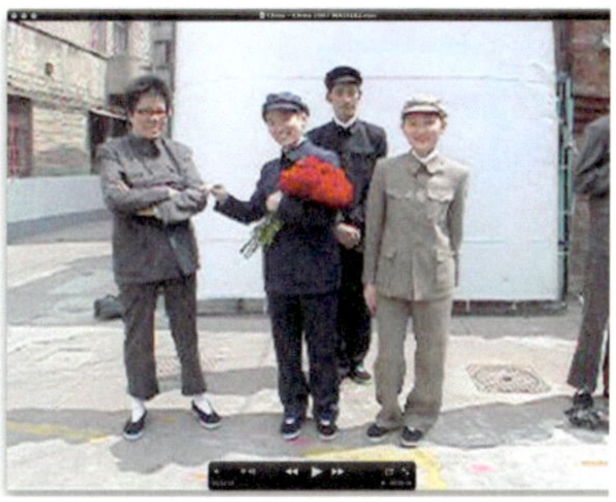

CHINA
March 9th –
April 8th, 2007

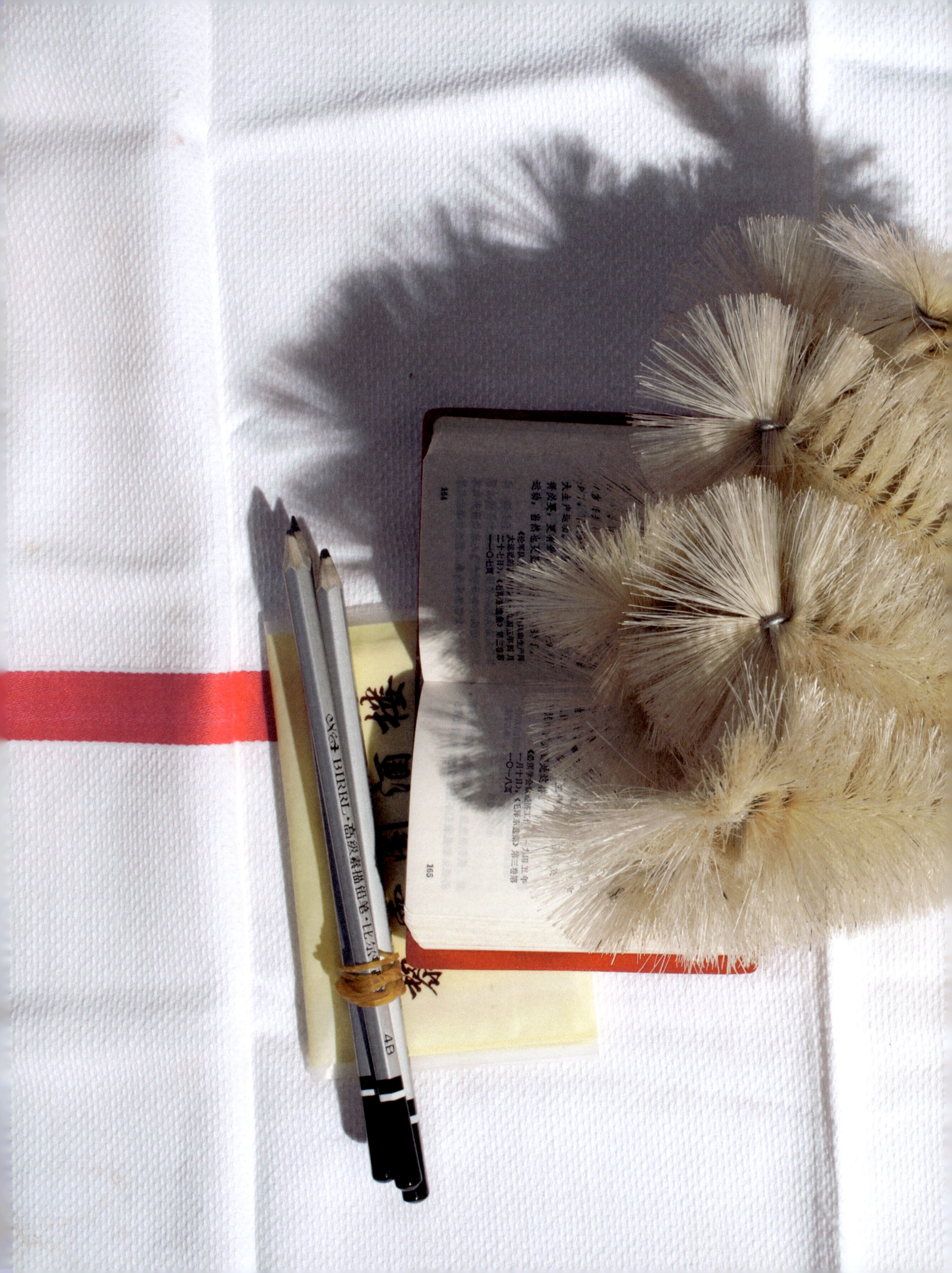
BIRRL·高级素描铅笔
4B

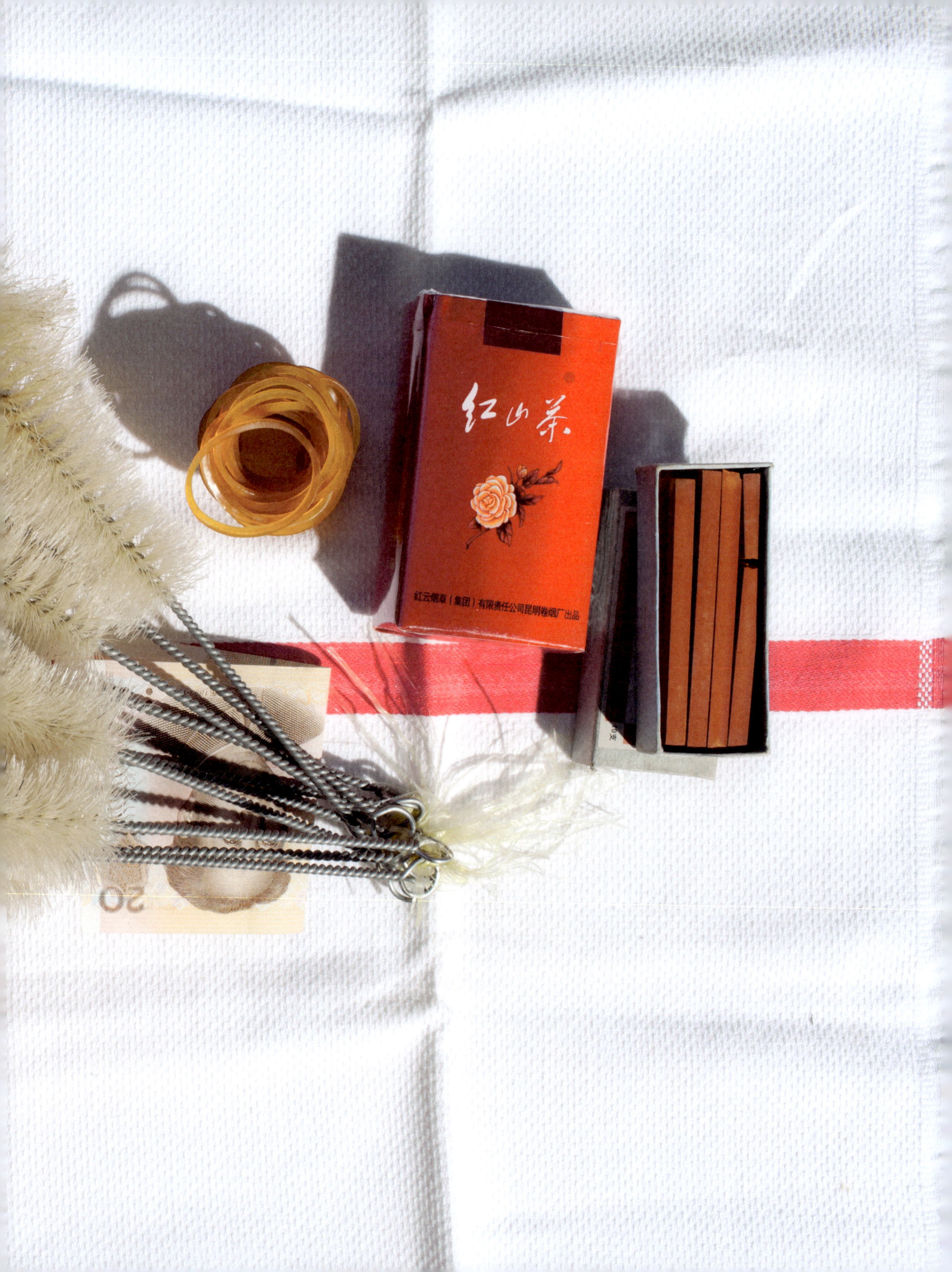
红山茶
红云烟草（集团）有限责任公司昆明卷烟厂出品
20

Full steam ahead!

Oliver Moarefi brings us to Australia in 2008 to shoot the new Viano. And I treat myself the second time to a steam locomotive. We are Mercedes, we are allrounders. At least it looks like it …

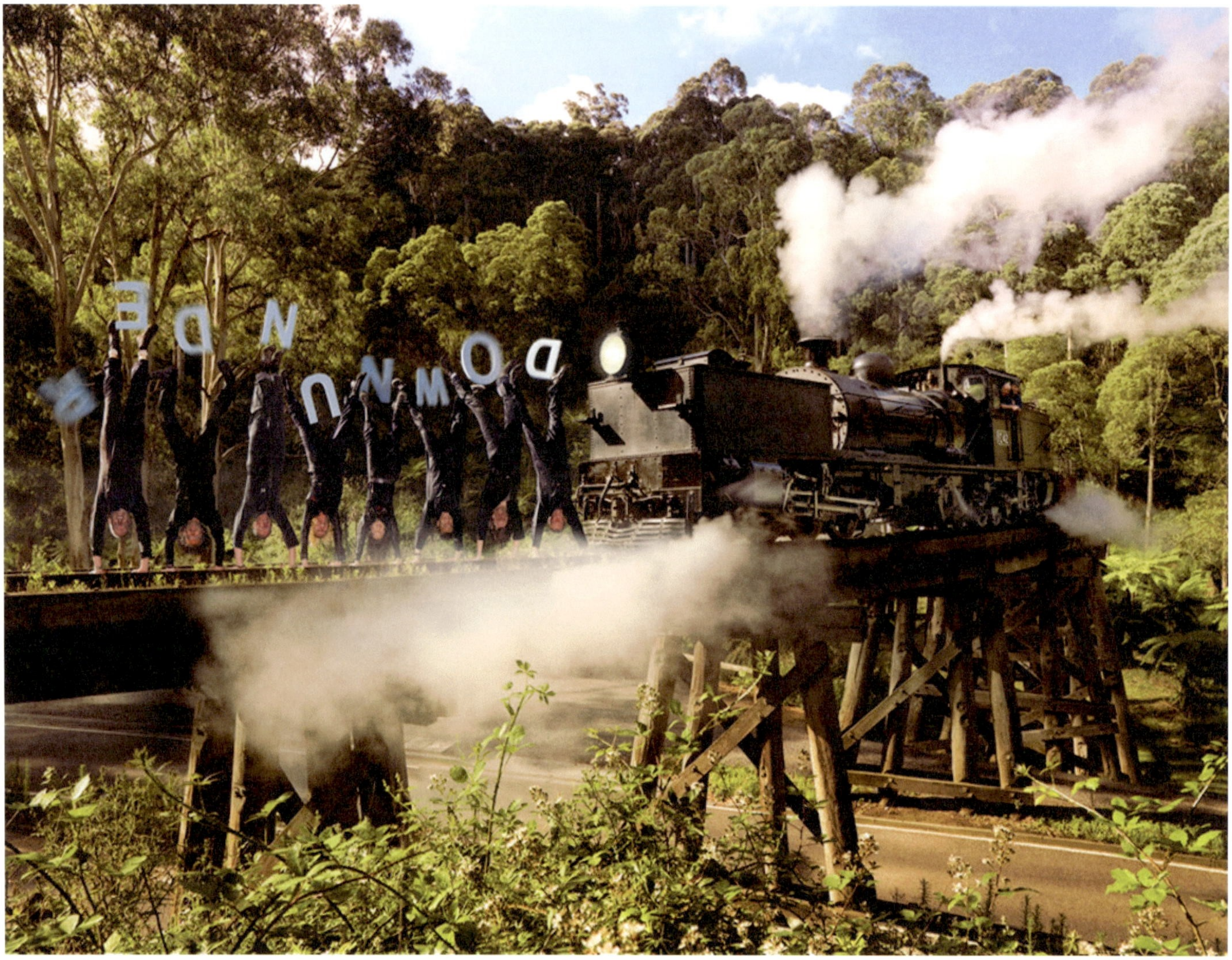

Group photo with the crew in Australia

A Me
B Oliver Moarefi
C Kevin McGrath
D Lilly Dawson
E Lana
F Siu Bun Mok
G Florian Schüppel
H Thomas Anderson

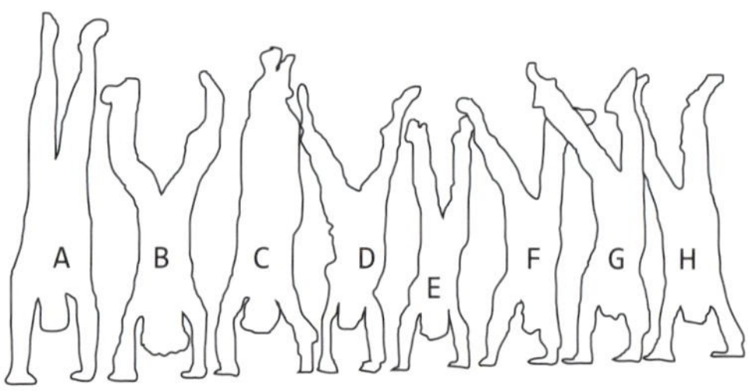

MELBOURNE
November 2008

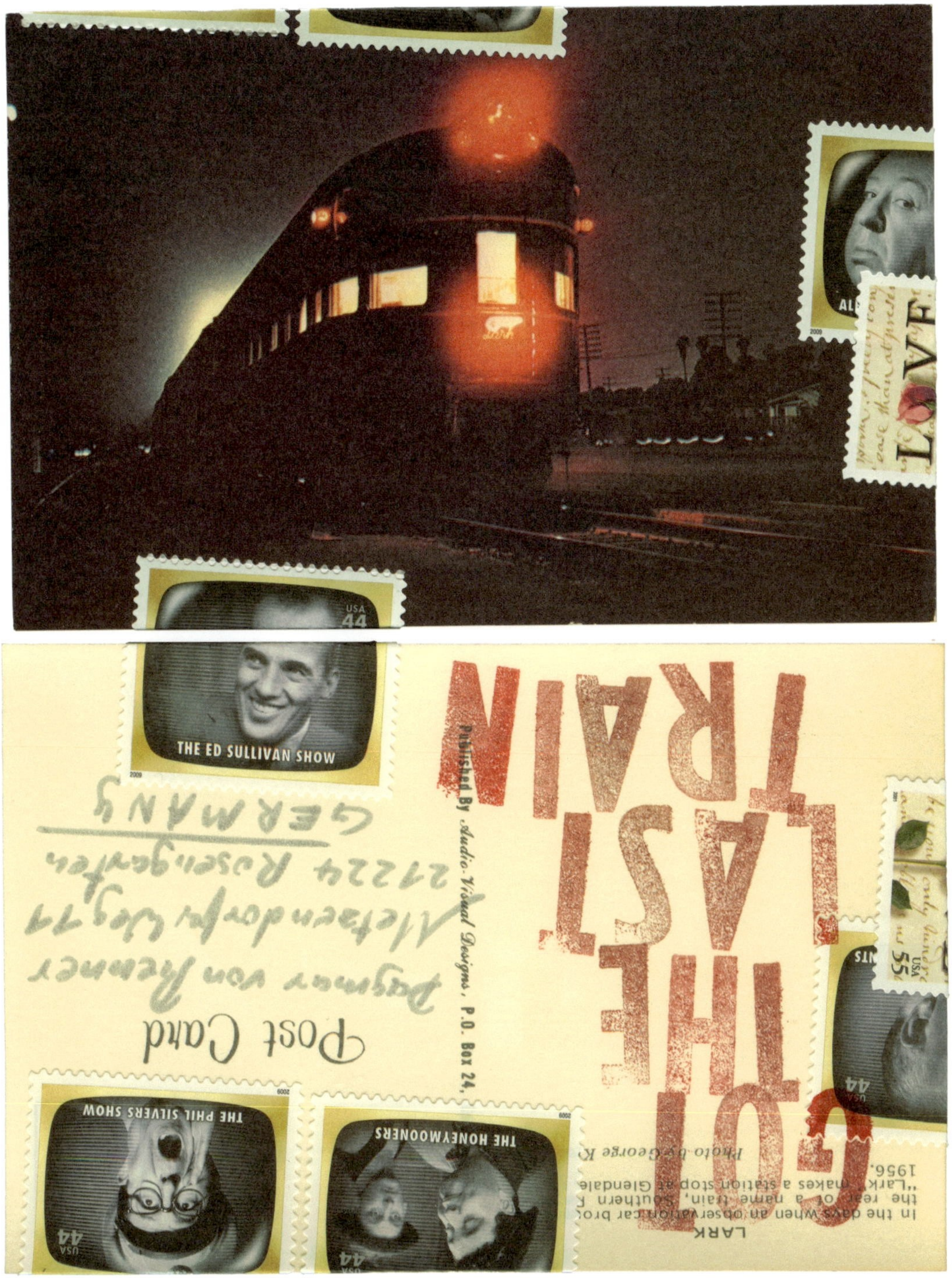

SAN LUIS OBISPO

June, 2011

–

“Got the last train”

I thank all those who sent me on my journeys …

"To you from afar"
for Dagmar, Cecil and Antony

I want to thank all my wonderful supporters that trusted in the fulfilling of this project and so generously helped us realize it and love to travel. Andrea von Senger und Etterlin, Andreas Eckhoff, Angela Larak, Anette Ernst, Annette Meincke-Nagy, Anke Kolberg, Antje Schmidt-Osterweiler, Alexander Kaemmer, Alexander Trattler, Anna Cray, Anna da Costa Henriques, Anna Kranzusch, Anthony Savedra, Arnd Veuskens, Axel Hoppenhaus, Barbara Auer, Barbara Friedrich, Barbara Korn, Beate Rischer, Bernd Singelmann, Bettina Scheffler, Benjamin Lommel, Birgit Klemt, Birgit Rocholl, Botho von Senger und Etterlin, Boris Dolkhani, Carolin Crhak, Caroline Maack, Carsten Behfeld, Calvin Corde, Charles Nicholas Dorr, Christian Struck, Christiane Doemer, Christiane Heldman, Christina Linke, Christine Loerke, Christina Voswinckel, Christof Schmidt, Cornelia Bormann, Conni Kotte, Conny Spross, Cornelia Zimmer-Meyer, Daniel Frericks, Daniel Meyer, Daniele Cima, David Pohle, Darius Ramazani, Dennis Landau, Dietmar Henneka, Dietrich Reimer, Dirk Darmstaedter, Dirk Gross, Duncan Stewart, Elisabeth Ernst, Elisabeth Monereau, Ellen Kleinboelting, Eric Hofstetter, Esin Rager, Esther Riess, Eva Jung, Evelyn Holst-Kusserow, Fatima Mefrouche-Liebke, Florentine Joop, Florian Beisert, Florian Böer, Florian Schüppel, Frank Stöckel, Friederike Voswinckel, Fritz Reuter, Geoffroy Puech, Georgia Menke, Gerald Heinemann, Gesa Brecher, Götz Ulmer, Hamilton Pereira, Hanna Pitzke Gajare, Hannelore Springer, Hans Jürgen Voswinckel, Hans Paul Brauns, Hans-Peter Junker, Heiko Jens Klemme, Heiko Koch, Heino Weber, Henrik Diemann, Ina Kollmorgen, Ingeborg Trampe, J. Konrad Schmidt, James Dubec, Janis Beckedorf, Jens-Peter Bruhn, Jeroen Bours, Jessica Kirsten, Jesta Brouns, Juliane Panny, Joachim Mars, Jochen von Renner, Johann Voswinckel, John Darmstaedter, John Noonan, Juergen Bosse, Julia Bazzini, Julia Brinckman, Julia Waller, Julia Radowitz, Juliane Haidinger, Katharina Daubner, Katharina Müller-Lenz, Kathrin Farwick, Katrin Schaudig, Keith Schwalenberg, Kenneth Bruns, Kerstin Mende, Klaus von Bismarck, Knud Petersen, Knut Post, Lars Jessen, Leila Ivarsson, Madeleine Glinz, Magnus-Matthias Sambo, Manon von Gerkan, Marco Gocht, Marianne Fredrichs, Marie-Delphine Darmstaedter, Marlo Scheder-Bieschin, Martin

Kaeswurm, Martina Leitermann-Krauße, Martina Ziegler, Matthias Bromann, Max von Senger und Etterlin, Melanie West, Michael Sterly, Michael Saul, Mio Al-Hashimy, Monica Zwirner, Moritz Voswinckel, Nadja Vogt, Netty Kinsky, Nicholas Eveleigh, Nika Skok, Ole Grönwoldt, Ole Knudsen, Oliver Moarefi, Olrik Kleiner, Olve Hausen, Wendy Chan, Patrick Palm, Peer-Arne Böttcher, Peter Bernskötter, Peter Strahlendorf, Philip Radowitz, Philipp Rathmer, Phillip Mall, Rainer Saile, Rainer Schacht, Randolph Nolte, Renate Pfab-Viehoff, Richard Voswinckel, Robert Voswinckel, Rolf Kutzera, Ruediger Glatz, Ruth Gorlt, Sabine Hinrichs-Bruhn, Sabine Schmitt, Sacha Rougier, Sally Cheung, Sarah Kattih, Sarah Thomsen, Sebastian Schröder, Silja Koch, Stacy Mueller, Stefan Nimmesgern, Stefan Thoss, Stefanie Ernst, Stefanie Lafrentz, Stefanie Schuster, Stella von Senger und Etterlin, Stephan Ernst, Stephan Röcken, Stephanie Ernst, Silke Lebrecht, Simon Puschmann, Susanna Steinwehe, Susanne Abetti, Susanne Trebitsch, Suse Delius-Küster, Tanya Mayer, Thomas Kampmann, Thomas Lemker, Thorsten Meyer, Tibor v. Jankó, Till Sattler, Timo Voswinckel, Tom Nagy, Tom Todd, Ulrich Schaudig, Ursula Leitzmann, Uta Schwager, Vanessa Lachmann, Victoria Trauttmansdorff, Yves Sucksdorff, Winka Wulff, Zerone …

… special thanks to Anja Rosendahl and Lars Borngräber, who really wanted to make this book happen, but couldn't have anticipated how many stories I have to tell, Marie Grönemeyer for the English translation, Wolfgang Joop for the foreword, and to my now almost 100 year old mother, who passed on the genes of willpower to me.

Author
Ivo von Renner

Idea and design
Rosendahl Berlin, Branddesign Agency

Translation
Marie Grönemeyer

Photo credits: All images Ivo von Renner except:
pp. 28 - 29 Editions MAR, France
p. 63 Photoclub AG, Industriestrasse Ost 10, 4614 Hägendorf, Schweiz
pp. 66 - 699 Air France, 45, rue de Paris F-95747 Roissy CDG Cedex
© Musée Air Francep. 114 Brettger Bildverlag, Witzschdorfer Hauptstraße 94,
09437 Witzschdorf
p. 156 Christian Schiefer, c/o Büro für Fotografiegeschichte Bern
pp. 184 - 201 Paul Stanton, Duckboy Cards

Project management DISTANZ Verlag
Frederik Kugler

Production management
DISTANZ Verlag, Sonja Bahr

Production
optimal media GmbH, Röbel/Müritz

Distribution
Gestalten Berlin
www.gestalten.com
sales@gestalten.com

ISBN 978-3-95476-177-7
Printed in Germany

Published by
DISTANZ Verlag
www.distanz.de

REGLÉ

BASTA

LAS PRIMERAS VACACIONES
DE CECILIA MARIA

AI